AUGUSTINE'S PHILOSOPHY OF MIND

Augustine's Philosophy of Mind

Gerard O'Daly

University of California Press
Berkeley and Los Angeles

First Published in 1987 by
University of California Press
Berkeley and Los Angeles

Library of Congress Catalog card Number: 86-40484

ISBN Number: 0-520-06069-5

Printed in Great Britain

Contents

To Ursula

Preface

Although scholarly research has been lavished on several individual aspects of Augustine's views on the nature and activities of the mind and soul, it will be granted that no substantial monograph has been devoted to a general study of the topic since the pioneering work of Ferraz in the mid-nineteenth century. The main emphasis in the present work is on the analysis and elucidation of Augustine's arguments, particularly his more intricate and obscure ones. Occasional criticism of some of those arguments is thus inevitable, even when due allowance is made for their historical context: but it is my hope that an overall impression emerges of a gifted intelligence applying itself with dexterity to central philosophical problems. The question of Augustine's sources is not a preoccupation of this book, but neither has it been neglected, and if a sharper sense of the influence upon him of Cicero and the Stoics, and a modified view of the supposed Neoplatonic elements in his thought (at least in the topics under discussion), emerge from these pages, so much the better.

The topics dealt with are in the main those which a modern philosopher would recognize as belonging to the philosophy of mind, but animal souls have also been discussed, as well as such traditional problems as the world-soul, transmigration, and soul-vehicles. In Chapter 7 epistemological questions are studied with particular attention to the kinds of psychological activities that they imply. I shall deal with Augustine's ethical theory in a further volume now in preparation.

No apology is offered for the frequent and sometimes lengthy quotations from an author so copious and so incompletely translated as Augustine. All translations of Augustine are my own, as are most of those of other authors quoted (the exceptions are acknowledged), but I have learnt much from F.J. Sheed's version of the *Confessions*, the Loeb Classical Library translation of the *City of God*, and the industrious Victorian renderings in the Edinburgh edition of Marcus Dods. Translations of scriptural passages are based upon the text found in Augustine.

Work was begun on the book in 1980 during tenure of an Alexander von Humboldt Foundation Fellowship at Heidelberg University. I am greatly indebted to the Foundation for the unrivalled opportunity which it gave me to conduct research in congenial and stimulating surroundings, as well as for the renewal of my Fellowship in 1984.

An earlier version of Chapters 2-5 was presented as a *Habilitationsschrift* to the Faculty of Classical and Oriental Studies of Heidelberg University in late 1983: the Faculty conferred the title of *Dr. habilitatus* on me in February 1984. I have benefited greatly from the criticisms of the assessors, but from none more than those of Professor Albrecht Dihle, my Heidelberg host, who also read and commented upon successive versions of much of this work, and who has been the best-informed of interlocutors, and the kindest of friends and counsellors.

I have been privileged to enjoy unrestricted access for a number of years to the excellent specialist library of the Augustinus-Institut at Würzburg, to whose Director, Revd Dr Adolar Zumkeller, I should like to express my thanks.

My debts to individual Augustine scholars, living and dead, are too numerous to record, but I should like to acknowledge invaluable conversations and correspondence with my late teacher, Professor Willy Theiler, at a period when my interest in Augustine was in its beginnings. I have always profited greatly from discussions with another mentor and friend, Professor John O'Meara. My editorial colleagues on the board of the *Augustinus-Lexikon* have been perceptive critics and advisors, and I am, in particular, grateful to Professor Goulven Madec for letting me see an unpublished manuscript of his on Augustine's philosophy.

The University of Lancaster granted me a period of sabbatical leave in 1980, in which the book was started. I owe much to the interest, provocative questioning, and insights of students on my courses on Augustine at Lancaster and at Würzburg University.

It was Professor Hugh Lloyd-Jones who first encouraged me to elaborate my plans for a book on Augustine: his courteous interest and warm encouragement have sustained me during its gestation.

I have great pleasure in dedicating the book to my wife Ursula: she discussed with me, and criticized, each successive part, from planning stage to final realization; she also took on the burden of typing and retyping the manuscript's several versions; and she made the book's completion possible by her sacrifice of leisure, her infectious energy, and her love.

Work on the manuscript of this book was completed early in 1986. I have thus not been able to take into account two new publications: Henry Chadwick's *Augustine* (Oxford 1986) and Ludger Hölscher's *The Reality of the Mind. St Augustine's Philosophical Arguments for the Human Soul as a Spiritual Substance* (London/New York 1986).

I should like to thank Deborah Blake, editor at Duckworth, for her skill and patience in guiding the book towards publication.

Earlier versions of some sections of the book have been published previously: most of Chapter 2 (iv) appeared in a more expansive form in the Festschrift for Heinrich Dörrie; part of Chapter 3 (iv) and the Excursus printed at the end of Chapter 3 are adapted and expanded from a contribution to *Studia Patristica* 16; Chapter 6 is a revision of an article which appeared in a volume of essays in honour of A.H. Armstrong (for full references see the Bibliography). Grateful acknowledgement is here made of permission granted to adapt these publications for the present work.

A version of Chapter 2 (iv) was read at Berne University in 1981; parts of Chapter 3 were presented at an Augustine colloquium in London in 1982; some of Chapter 4 formed a lecture given at Trinity College, Dublin, in 1986;

a version of Chapter 6 was read at the University of Freiburg im Breisgau in 1980; parts of Chapter 7 (iv) were given as papers at Fribourg University in 1981, and at the Ninth International Conference on Patristic Studies held in Oxford in 1983.

February 1987   G.J.P. O'D.

Abbreviations

BA	*Bibliothèque Augustinienne. Oeuvres de Saint Augustin*
CCL	*Corpus Christianorum. Series Latina*
CSEL	*Corpus Scriptorum Ecclesiasticorum Latinorum*
HWP	*Historisches Wörterbuch der Philosophie*
KlP	*Der Kleine Pauly. Lexikon der Antike*
MA	*Miscellanea Agostiniana*, 2 vols., Rome 1930
PAC	*Prosopographie de L'Afrique Chrétienne (303-533)* = *Proposographie Chrétienne du Bas-Empire*, 1 (ed. A. Mandouze), Paris 1982
PL	*Patrologiae cursus completus. Series Latina*, ed. J.-P. Migne
PLRE	*The Prosopography of the Later Roman Empire* (1: A.H.M. Jones/J.R. Martindale/J. Morris. A.D. 260-395, Cambridge 1971; 2: J.R. Martindale, A.D. 395-527, Cambridge 1980)
PLS	*Patrologiae cursus completus. Series Latina. Supplementum*, ed. A. Hamman
RAC	*Reallexikon für Antike und Christentum*
RB	*Revue Bénédictine*
RE	*Paulys Realencyclopädie der classischen Altertumswissenschaft*. Neue Bearbeitung begonnen von G. Wissowa
REAug	*Revue des Etudes Augustiniennes*
RechAug	*Recherches Augustiniennes*
SPM	*Stromata Patristica et Medievalia*
SVF	*Stoicorum Veterum Fragmenta*, ed. H. von Arnim
ThWNT	*Theologisches Wörterbuch zum Neuen Testament*
TRE	*Theologische Realenzyklopädie*
TU	*Texte und Untersuchungen*

CHAPTER ONE

Augustine the Philosopher

There are, according to Augustine in the early work entitled *soliloquia*, two principal (indeed, strictly speaking, only two) subjects of philosophical inquiry, God and the soul (*sol.* 1.7). Knowledge of God is knowledge of man's creator, his 'source (*origo*)'; knowledge of the soul is self-knowledge (*ord.* 2.47). The dichotomy of these two kinds of knowledge is, however, apparent rather than real. For, on the one hand, Augustine is influenced by the Neoplatonic theorem that introspection coincides with contemplation of the One (or highest principle), that, in Plotinus' words, 'knowing itself it (sc. mind) will also know its source' (*Enneads* 6.9.7.33f.), and, conversely, that 'looking towards the Good it will know itself' (5.6.5.17).[1] Moreover, Augustine understands the Biblical doctrine of man's creation in God's image and likeness (Genesis 1:26f.) to imply that through introspection the human mind can attain by analogy to some understanding of God's nature (*civ.* 11.26). Yet the fusion of self-knowledge and vision of the One that Plotinus evokes cannot be accepted by Augustine.[2] For Plotinus, the human mind and soul, though not identifiable with the One, are 'divine' extensions of the hypostases, with which, in a sense, they form a continuity. Augustine, however, insists that there is no such continuity between the 'otherness' of God, who is transcendent and immutable, and the mutability of human nature, even of human reason (*conf.* 7.16). That is why rational understanding of God can, for him, never be more than partial (*conf.* 13.12). The latter is, indeed, only achieved by means of an appropriately directed self-knowledge: God is 'within' us. But the mind must transcend self-knowledge if it is to gain even such incomplete understanding of the divine (*vera rel.* 72; *ser.* 330.3). While there is, therefore, no dichotomy between the quests for self-knowledge and knowledge of God in Augustine's thought, he nevertheless draws an important distinction between understanding the human soul and attempting, through such understanding, to fathom divine substance.

In this connection Pierre Hadot has pointed out a fundamental difference between the expositions of the doctrine of the Trinity in Augustine and that

---

[1] The theme of self-knowledge in Plotinus is discussed in O'Daly (1973) 70-81. Plotinus' concept of mind or intellect (*nous*) is treated by A.H. Armstrong, *The Architecture of the Intelligible Universe in the Philosophy of Plotinus*, Cambridge 1940; T.A. Szlezák, *Platon und Aristoteles in der Nuslehre Plotins*, Basle/Stuttgart 1979; see also Beierwaltes (1967) 11-49.

[2] The similarities and contrasts between Plotinian and Augustinian self-knowledge are well brought out by O'Donovan 60-74.

other fourth-century Christian Platonist Marius Victorinus.[3] The latter undertakes to explain the consubstantiality of the three divine persons of the Trinity through its image in the ternary structure of the human soul, i.e. in its being, life and understanding. Victorinus is primarily concerned with the soul, however, as an ontological reality: it is as an image of divine substance, and hence of the structure of being, that it is investigated. Augustine also identifies ternary schemes in the soul, and these schemes are analogous to the divine Trinity, of which the soul is the image.[4] But in Augustine the schemes (e.g. existence, knowledge, will; mind, knowledge, love; memory, understanding, will) remain psychological: they are not, so to speak, translated into ontological or metaphysical terms:

> Augustine can only think of the Trinity by contemplating it in the mirror of the self.[5]

Such contemplation remains an imperfect and inadequate insight into the nature of the Trinity, for the human self cannot be reduced to the absolute being of God.

Yet it is precisely as a consequence of this inadequacy that Augustine elaborates the most characteristic feature of his philosophy of mind.[6] For, although he shares with philosophers in the Stoic and Platonic traditions the assumptions that reality is ordered and that divine being and the human mind have particular places in that order, it is distinctive of Augustine's thought that he approaches psychological questions through an elucidation of man's perceptive and cognitive *activities*, independently of any *ontological* implications which the latter may have.[7] He is not primarily concerned with the traditional preoccupation of Greek and Roman epistemological speculation, the relation between mind and the structure of reality. As a result, his psychology, in Albrecht Dihle's words,

> seems to be self-sustaining, at least with regard to man's intellectual activity. One need not understand any attached or underlying conception of the order of being to appreciate his ideas about the intellectual life of man. Both the raw material of cognition and the drive towards understanding can be found in the soul without an indispensable point of reference in the outside world.[8]

Augustine's investigation of problems of the soul is none the less conducted in traditional terms and categories. The questions which he asks are

[3] See Hadot (1962).
[4] The best discussions of the Trinitarian analogies in the human soul are Schindler (1965) and Schmaus; see also O'Donovan 75-92; Flasch 326-68.
[5] Hadot (1962) 441.
[6] See Dihle (1982) 123-32.
[7] It is no accident that Augustine's *Confessions* is, among many other things, a masterpiece of empirical psychology, rich in observation and description of infant behaviour, jealousy, anxiety and self-discovery. See Brown 158-81; O'Meara (1954). O'Meara's book remains the best study of Augustine's intellectual development.
[8] Dihle (1982) 125f. On the distinction between ontological and psychological aspects of Augustine's ethical thought see Holte 207-220; O'Donovan 10-36.

recognizable to the student of Greek and Roman philosophy. What is the soul's origin or source? Is soul a material substance? Why are souls embodied? Is God, or necessity, or our will, or a combination of these, responsible for their embodiment? What is the nature of the symbiosis of body and soul, and what are its consequences for the latter? Is soul mortal or immortal? What is its relation to God? What is the soul's destiny after its apparent separation from the body at death? (*beata v.* 1; *ord.* 2.17; *quant. an.* 1) These questions reflect traditional doxological schemes in investigations of problems of the soul (its nature, origin, fate during embodiment, and eschatology): their framework is apparent in writers as different as Tertullian, Iamblichus, Macrobius, and the authors of the Hermetic corpus.[9] Augustine is familiar with the variety of philosophical views held on such matters, as well as on questions of the soul's possible pre-existence and reincarnation (*ser.* 240.4f.; *civ.* 18.41). Psychology is a theme full of problems and difficulties (*beata v.* 5). On some questions Augustine feels that he has reached certainty: soul is a created substance, not a part of divine substance; it is immaterial; it is immortal but not immutable; it is not embodied in consequence of any sins committed in a previous existence. On other questions he remains hesitant and agnostic: he does not know, for example, whether souls are created individually as each new life comes into existence, or created in advance and implanted at the appropriate moment by God, or conceived of our parents' souls, as our bodies are conceived (*ep.* 166.3-10; 190.1-4).[10] In this book, the range of his inquiries into traditional questions concerning the soul can be most readily appreciated by a glance at the subject matter of Chapter 2.

Augustine philosophizes throughout his adult life and evidence of this philosophizing is found in every period of his literary activity, from the dialogues written at Cassiciacum in 386/7 to the last work against the Pelagian Julian of Eclanum, left incomplete at his death in 430.[11] Augustine did not, however, elaborate a philosophical system. This in itself is not unusual in classical antiquity: the same could be said of Plato or Cicero. But these devoted whole works to philosophical topics, and that is seldom the case with Augustine. Some of his early works do concentrate on specific philosophical themes, such as scepticism and certainty (*contra Academicos*), problems of the soul (*de quantitate animae*), or evil, free will and divine foreknowledge (*de libero arbitrio*).[12] But the vast bulk of his writings, even works which are particularly rich in philosophical material (such as *de trinitate*, *de civitate dei*, or *de Genesi ad litteram*), are responses to a variety of personal, theological and church political circumstances. Speculation for its

---

[9] See Festugière, especially 1-26; Flamant 490ff.

[10] See pp. 15-20.

[11] For Augustine's life and times see above all Brown, who also provides chronological tables and references to English translations of Augustine's works. Schindler (1979) provides an excellent survey, with an extensive bibliography.

[12] He planned a systematic treatment of the liberal arts (*retr.* 1.6), of which traces of the works on dialectic, grammar and rhetoric, as well as the complete *de musica*, survive (see Marrou); but no such system is apparent in the purely philosophical works written at the same time (387/90).

own sake, in isolation from such circumstances, is never the driving force impelling Augustine to write, although it often determines the amount of space which he is prepared to devote to analysis of a particular philosophical problem. Thus the investigation of memory in book ten of the *Confessions* arises out of an examination of conscience in a work intended at once to be an *apologia pro vita sua* and an edifying piece of spiritual reading for those who believed themselves called upon to live a quasi-monastic life as 'servants of God'.[13] The discussion of time in the eleventh book of the *Confessions* is, likewise, an exegetical excursus arising out of the difficulty of interpreting the phrase 'In the beginning' of Genesis 1:1. And what is true of the *Confessions* applies to other works as well. Augustine himself intended even so predominantly philosophical a work as *de libero arbitrio* to be a piece of anti-Manichaean polemic.[14] A work with the promising title *de natura et origine animae* proves, upon examination, to be, at least in part, a diatribe against a maverick ex-Donatist, Vincentius Victor; it can also be read as an attack on some varieties of Pelagianism.[15] Augustine appears to have felt freest to speculate in those leisurely works composed over several years – like the *de trinitate* (written between 399 and 422/6) or the *de Genesi ad litteram* (begun in 401, but not finished until about 414) – works which were not begun in response to a pressing, topical need, and whose subject matter offered considerable scope for exploration of issues where doctrinal orthodoxy had not been, or could not be, established.[16]

The nature of his philosophical writing, as it has just been described, has two important consequences for an investigation into aspects of Augustine's thought. In the first place, care is called for in the interpretation of individual texts, especially in their relation to one another. Considerations of context and chronology are important. Continuity of argument and ideas cannot simply be assumed, even in an individual work written over many years. The language of a sermon will differ from that of a work like *de civitate dei*, and so on. The following chapters endeavour to take account of these factors. It has often seemed advisable to expound the immediate context, or devote several pages to an extended discussion of a specific problem in order to elucidate Augustine's analytic method.[17] Longer quotations can convey something of the atmosphere of a particular work. It should, however, be stressed that, at least as regards the themes of this book, a chronological approach reveals no substantial development, still less any fundamental change, of Augustine's views, although individual problems may be clarified or explicated in subsequent discussions of a theme. The main lines of Augustine's approach

[13] The genesis and intended readership of the *Confessions* are brilliantly discussed by Courcelle (1968) 20-40.

[14] *retr.* 1.9.2 and 6.

[15] See the introduction and nn. of *BA* 22.

[16] See *Gn. litt.* 1.18.37-21.41; 2.9.20f.; 2.18.38 for Augustine's attitude to 'open' questions in cosmology. For Galileo's use of these passages in his self-defence see *BA* 48, 134ff.; 176ff.; 210; 578f.

[17] See e.g. pp. 13ff.; 162ff.; 171ff.

to problems of the soul and mind are established by 386.[18]

The last remarks touch upon a second consequence of the particular character of Augustine's philosophical activity, namely, the question of its thematic coherence. Augustine's writings may not construct a system, and he may be described as an occasional philosopher, but it is none the less the case that his thought is governed by fundamental concepts, and that its tendency can be described in general terms.[19] Moreover, he does not draw a radical distinction between the philosophical and theological aspects of his thought.[20] That does not prevent him using the term 'philosopher' to refer to representatives of the Graeco-Roman tradition as opposed to Christianity, or adopting doxological surveys of the history of philosophy, seen as a self-contained process (*civ.* 8.1-12; 18.41). He is, furthermore, aware of a fundamental difference between the philosopher's purely rational method and the Christian's acceptance through belief of the reality and the significance of the key historical events that determine his religion. Nevertheless, Christianity is for him the 'one true philosophy' (*c. Iul.* 4.72),[21] just as the 'true religion' of *de vera religione* is inconceivable without its Platonic components. From his earliest writings onwards he measures Greek and Roman notions of happiness, wisdom and virtue against the authority of Christianity. He appropriates the eudemonistic ethics of ancient philosophy: happiness or 'blessedness (*beatitudo*)' is in principle accessible to all, and it consists in the realization of wisdom (*sapientia*).[22] In his maturity he modifies this thesis in two important respects. The desire for happiness, though universal, and identifiable with the proper activity of the highest faculty in man, the mind, is only fully satisfied in the afterlife; and blessedness is achieved, not in a disembodied mental state, but in the spiritual, resurrected bodily condition of the saints. Blessedness consists in the 'enjoyment of God' (*frui deo*) as an end in itself: this teleological goal should also determine our moral choices, to the extent that all created goods are understood as means to be used (*uti*) to achieve that end.[23] The source of wrongdoing is, therefore, a misdirection of the will, a substitution of means in place of the proper end. No created being or object is lovable for its own sake; creatures are lovable only in subordination to the love of God, which Augustine, adapting the motif of Platonic *erôs* to his own purpose, identifies with the love of truth and

[18] The development of some of his specifically theological doctrines, e.g. on grace and predestination, has no philosophical parallel: see Flasch 172-226.

[19] A particularly perceptive systematic synopsis – focussing on the themes of happiness (*beatitudo*), reason (*ratio*), authority (*auctoritas*) and evil (*malum*) – is provided by R. Lorenz, *Das vierte bis sechste Jahrhundert (Westen)*, in *Die Kirche in ihrer Geschichte* 1, C1, Göttingen 1970, 54-71.

[20] See the remarks of Markus (1967) 344ff.

[21] Cf. *c. Acad.* 3.38; 3.42; *beata v.* 1-5; *ord.* 1.24; 2.16.

[22] Augustine's concept of *beatitudo* is studied against its ancient philosophical background by Beierwaltes (1981). See Holte *passim*. On true philosophy as love of wisdom and the philosopher as 'lover of God' see *civ.* 8.1; 8.8 (ib. 8.10: Paul's warning against false philosophy (Colossians 2:8) is countered by Romans 1:19f. and Acts 17:28). See Markus (1967) 346; G. Madec, 'Verus philosophus est amator dei. S. Ambroise, S. Augustin et la philosophie', *Revue des sciences philosophiques et théologiques* 61 (1977) 549-66.

[23] On *frui-uti* in Augustine see p. 39 n. 95.

wisdom.[24] Knowledge of truth is necessary to the full realization of happiness. The God whose beauty is loved is also enjoyed by means of an intuitive, but none the less rational, vision. Knowledge of the truth is, however, realized by the Christian against the background of belief or faith. For Augustine, the starting-point of knowledge is the authority[25] of divine revelation and teaching in Scripture[26] and church tradition. Belief itself is a form of rational insight, but human reason, by its very nature, desires to attain to the greatest possible understanding of what it believes, and, in so far as the objects of religious belief and knowledge are the same, knowledge may replace belief based upon authority (but, once again, only fully in the afterlife).

It is characteristic of Augustine's thought that the realization of moral perfection is not conceived of in cognitive terms, but in those of will (*amor, caritas, intentio, voluntas*).[27] Will is an intrinsic element of all of the psychological activities discussed in the following chapters of this book. It is an essential motor of sense-perception, memory, imagination and cognition (which is only achieved and applied through the agent's intention). This central role of the will, and its integration into the very act of cognition, are features that distinguish Augustine's philosophy most sharply from its Graeco-Roman predecessors.[28] We have to do here with a direct consequence of that concern with psychological activities for their own sake that was mentioned at the beginning of this chapter. The ternary schemes which Augustine discovers in the human soul are no mere constructs designed to convey an insight, however remote, into the mystery of the divine Trinity. The soul is none other than the coherence of its faculties of memory, understanding and will, whose co-operation is characteristic of all human behaviour. The following chapters explore the implications of this principle for Augustine's concepts of soul and mind.

---

[24] See the fundamental study of J. Burnaby, *Amor Dei. A Study of the Religion of St. Augustine*, London 1938.

[25] See K.-H. Lütcke, '*Auctoritas' bei Augustin. Mit einer Einleitung zur römischen Vorgeschichte des Begriffes* (Tübinger Beiträge zur Altertumswissenschaft, 44), Stuttgart 1968.

[26] For the motif of the Scriptures as the Christian's philosophical books see *civ.* 18.41.

[27] See Dihle (1982) 233f.

[28] See Lorenz (1964); Holte 233-50; 283-94.

CHAPTER TWO

General Theory of the Soul

(i) Terminology: anima, animus *and equivalents*

The terms used by Augustine to refer to the soul, while they do not represent a systematic usage in any sense, are sufficiently consistent to be classifiable. *Anima* can refer to the soul of both animals and men. *Anima*, as well as *animus*, can apply without distinction of meaning to the human soul in general,[1] and in the work *de immortalitate animae* and elsewhere[2] the two terms are employed interchangeably. The mind (*mens, ratio*) is a 'part of the soul' (*pars animi*), namely its best 'part' (*c. Acad.* 1.5), or 'that which is pre-eminent in the soul' (*quod excellit in anima, trin.* 14.26).[3] *Animus* can, however, also mean 'mind',[4] and is not used with reference to the souls of non-rational beings. Augustine can also distinguish between aspects or powers of soul by means of an epithet added to *anima*: thus the *anima rationalis*, the seat of mind and will, is contrasted with the *anima irrationalis*, whose powers of appetite, sense-perception and memory are common to men and animals.[5] Augustine further recognizes the existence of a vegetable soul, even if he usually refers to it as 'life', i.e. non-sentient life, rather than 'soul'.[6]

Sometimes Augustine coins, or, more likely, adopts from their Latin translators, versions of specifically Neoplatonic psychological terms. The 'intellectual soul' (*noera psukhê*) of Plotinus and Porphyry[7] is rendered as *anima intellectualis*;[8] Porphyry's *pneumatikê psukhê*, viz. the irrational soul

---

[1] e.g. *sol.* 1.21; *ep.* 3.4; *div. qu.* 7; *en. Ps.* 145.5; *ser.* 150.5.

[2] e.g. *quant. an.* 22-32; *trin.* 8.9. Cf. Pépin (1964) 53 n. 5 = Pépin (1977) 213 n. 5.

[3] Cf. *civ.* 9.6 (referring to daemons). See Gilson 56 n 1; Pépin (1964) 75 n. 1 = Pépin (1977) 235 n. 1.

[4] e.g. *civ.* 11.3; *trin.* 14.26.

[5] e.g. *div. qu.* 46.2; *imm. an.* 25; *civ.* 5.11; 19.13. For *anima rationalis* see further *mag.* 2; 38; *vera rel.* 44; 82; 110; *ench.* 35f.; *mor.* 1.62; 2.1; 2.59; *Gn. litt. imp.* 16.59; *ser. dom. m.* 1.12; *c. Adim.* 12.1; *div. qu.* 54; *agon.* 9; *c. Sec.* 15; *adn. Iob* 9; *trin.* 3.8; 10.2; 11.6; 15.1; 15.22; *cons. ev.* 1.35; 1.53; 4.15; *Gn. litt.* 6.12.22; 7.9.12; 7.11.17; 10.23.29; 11.32.42; *pecc. mer.* 1.38; 1.67; 2.35f.; *spir. et litt.* 58; 60; *civ.* 7.5; 8.14; 13.24; 19.14; *corrept.* 30; *cont.* 11; *ep.* 137.5; 140.3f.; 140.7. For *anima rationalis* see in particular *Gn. litt.* 7.9.12; 7.11.18; 8.23.44; 10.4.7.

[6] e.g. *civ.* 7.29 ('the merely living *anima*'); cf. *quant. an.* 70. For references to 'life (*vita*)' in this connection see *civ.* 5.11; *doctr. chr.* 1.8. Cf. *Gn. litt. imp.* 5.24.

[7] e.g. Plotinus, *Enneads* 1.1.13.6; Porphyry, *sententiae* 32 (p. 34.10 Lamberz).

[8] *civ.* 10.2; 10.9: there also *anima rationalis*. Cf. *trin.* 15.1.

considered in relation to *pneuma*, as *anima spiritalis* or *spiritalis pars animae.*[9] *Spiritus* itself is often identical in meaning with *anima*, though it can also be equated with *mens*: in the former case it is frequently a translation of the Septuagint's *pneuma* or *pnoê*. Porphyrian influence upon Augustine's use of *spiritus* is not easy to determine.[10]

There is no obvious specific precedent for Augustine's usage: he appears to reflect different aspects of the Latin philosophical tradition.[11] The equation of *anima* with the soul in general, and the description of *mens* as 'part of the soul', are first found in Apuleius, but become thereafter general, so that direct dependence of Augustine upon Apuleius need not be posited.[12] Cicero, always a likely source of Augustine's philosophical language and ideas, translates both *psukhê* and *nous* by *animus*, but *anima*, which is frequently equivalent to *psukhê* in Augustine, is so only exceptionally in Cicero.[13] Calcidius and Macrobius introduce a new stringency into their usage of *animus* (= *nous, mens, intellectus*) and *anima* (= *psukhê*) that reflects the distinctions between the Neoplatonic hypostases, and a similar restricted use of *anima* = *psukhê* is observable in Marius Victorinus.[14] If the 'books of the Platonists' read by Augustine in 386, and indubitably containing Neoplatonic treatises,[15] exercised this sort of care in their distinction between the two terms (something which we cannot verify), then such care is not reflected in Augustine's usage, despite his occasional employment, mentioned above, of Neoplatonic terminology.

(ii) Sources and influences: some preliminary remarks

The concept of soul found in Augustine – an immaterial, dynamic,

[9] *civ.* 10.9; 10.27; 10.32. Deuse 218-30, arguing against earlier interpretations, pleads convincingly for a Porphyrian distinction between *pneuma* and *pneumatikê psukhê*, as well as for the latter's identification with the irrational soul.

[10] *Spiritus* as *mens*: *cat. rud.* 29; *civ.* 13.24; *ep.* 238.15; *Gn. litt.* 7.21.30; 12.7.18; *nat. et or. an.* 2.2; 4.36f.; *trin.* 14.22. For *spiritus* in Augustine see Agaësse/Solignac, *BA* 49,559-66. Verbeke 504 argues against the identification of Porphyry's *pneuma* and Augustine's *spiritus*. Scriptural terminology also influences Augustine's usage of *anima* = 'the whole man', e.g. *civ.* 14.4; *loc. hept.* 3 on Leviticus 15:16; ib. 3 on Leviticus 22:11; *qu. hept.* 1.150; *Io. ev. tr.* 47.12. For scriptural *anima* = 'life' see *loc. hept.* 1 on Genesis 37:22; ib. 5 on Deuteronomy 24:6; ib. 6 on Joshua 20:9; *qu. hept.* 3.86; *ser. dom. m.* 2.50.

[11] For the following see Waszink 201; Flamant 494-8.

[12] Apuleius, *de Platone* 1.13; cf. 1.18. For later usage see Tertullian, *de anima* 10-12.

[13] See Cicero's translation of Plato, *Phaedr.* 245c-e in *de re publica* 6.27f. and *Tusc. disp.* 1.53f. Cicero, however, unlike Augustine, uses *animus* to refer to animal souls, e.g. *Tusc. disp.* 1.80. *Anima* = *psukhê*: *nat. deor.* 1.87. *Anima* in Cicero usually refers to the life-breath: *Tusc. disp.* 1.19; 1.24.

[14] For Calcidius' usage see J.H. Waszink (ed.), *Timaeus a Calcidio translatus commentarioque instructus* (Plato Latinus, 4), London/Leiden 1962, 408f. Macrobius 'corrects' Ciceronian laxity at e.g. *in somn. Scip.* 1.14.3f. For Marius Victorinus see *adversus Arrium* 1.32; 1.61-63. Lucretius' distinction between *animus* and *anima*, corresponding to Epicurus' *logikon meros* and *alogon meros* (sc. *tês psukhês*) respectively, is an early exception of a special kind; and it is a distinction not always kept sufficiently clear by Lucretius (see *rer. nat.* 3.143; 175; 177; 237, and E.J. Kenney *ad loc.*).

[15] See n. 20 below.

inextended and indivisible substance, of its nature good – is Platonic in character and predominantly Neoplatonic in origin.[16] It is worked out in rejection of materialistic theories, from whose tenacity Augustine extricated himself only after considerable speculative exploration of their implications.[17] Both the Manichaean beliefs about the soul, to which he subscribed for many years, and the Stoic/pantheistic views which he held for a time, were corporealist.[18] Yet Augustine's characteristic theory of soul is already fully fledged in the earliest writings of 386-388 (*soliloquia, de immortalitate animae, de quantitate animae*). It is no doubt largely derived from his study of the 'books of the Platonists' in the summer of 386, though contacts with Milanese Christian Neoplatonists and exposure to Ambrose's homiletic exegesis (Augustine was at Milan since 384) will have paved the way, and may have been more influential than is suggested by the highly dramatized account in the *Confessions* of the momentous encounter with the Platonist texts.[19]

The question of what the contents of those texts were – that is, which Neoplatonic writings had been translated into Latin in them – cannot be satisfactorily resolved.[20] Echoes of two of Plotinus' treatises on the soul – 4.2 (*On the Essence of the Soul*) and 4.3 (*On Difficulties about the Soul*) – have been identified, and Augustine may also have known 4.7 (*On the Immortality of the Soul*).[21] But we cannot discount indirect access to Plotinus through Porphyry's commentaries or résumés of his master's writings, or through reported Plotinian views in Porphyry's other works.[22] Among the latter (considered as a source of Porphyry's own distinctive psychology) the *Summikta Zêtêmata* are likely to have been used from 386 on, and the *de regressu animae* is known to Augustine from about 417 at the latest: identification of other Porphyrian sources seems impossible, although Porphyrian elements in Augustine's thought are probable, in so far as much that is Neoplatonic in it

---

[16] The older accounts of Ferraz, Alfaric 451-82, and Nörregaard 183-240 are still valuable. See further Gilson 56-73 and *passim*; Holte 233-271; 295-9. Schneider's Aristotelian interpretation of Augustine's psychology, though unconvincing, has detailed discussions of the vegetative (53-110) and sensitive (111-233) degrees of soul.

[17] See especially *conf.* 7.1-3.

[18] See pp. 21-38.

[19] For Milanese Platonists see Courcelle (1948) 119-29; Courcelle (1968) 153-6; 168-74; 280-6; Solignac, *BA* 14,529-36. For Ambrose and Augustine see Courcelle (1968) 93-138 (but cf. W. Theiler's critical review of the 1st edn. (1950) of Courcelle (1968) in *Gnomon* 25 (1953) 113-22, especially 114-9). Augustine's encounter with the 'books of the Platonists' is described in *conf.* 7.13-27.

[20] Recent scholarly opinion is critically and sceptically surveyed by Hadot (1971) 201-10 (bibliography: 207 n. 30). Cf. Schindler (1979) 660-2. The extreme positions of Theiler (1933) = Theiler (1966) 160-251 (Porphyry, not Plotinus) and Henry (1934), for whom Plotinus' influence is paramount, have been superseded in more recent scholarship by the tendency to see both Plotinian and Porphyrian echoes in Augustine's early writings: see especially Courcelle (1948) 159-76; O'Meara (1954) 131-55.

[21] Plotinus, 4.2.1.47-50 at *imm. an.* 25; 4.2.1.75f. at *quant. an.* 68; 4.3.12.8f. at *civ.* 9.10. Augustine's use of 4.7 is argued by O'Connell (1968) 135-45.

[22] Commentaries, résumés: see Schwyzer (1951) 508f. Reported Plotinian views: Theiler (1933) 2f. = Theiler (1966) 161-3.

is evidently not Plotinian.[23] Specific influence of another Neoplatonist, Iamblichus, is hard to determine: the notion of the twofold 'weight (*pondus*) of the soul' found in *conf.* 13.10 may, however, derive from him.[24]

Of the dialogues which are of most importance for Plato's views on the soul, the *Phaedrus* and *Phaedo* may have been known in part to Augustine through Porphyry: he will not have had access to the Greek originals.[25] Cicero will also have been an intermediary of Platonic texts, as well as of the teachings on the soul of the various Greek philosophical schools and tendencies.[26] Further sources of information will have included Varro, a Platonizing Virgil commentary of (at least) Book Six of the *Aeneid*, and doxographical handbooks.[27] There is, on the other hand, no evidence of Middle Platonic influences (e.g. Apuleius) on Augustine's views concerning the soul.

Specifically Christian influences apart from Ambrose are minimal. Tertullian, with his corporealist views, was to be countered rather than followed.[28] Origen's theories became familiar to Augustine when his own were already long worked out; and Augustine, while approving of some (such as the notion of the soul's medial position), rejected most (e.g. the soul's pre-existence, its embodiment as punishment for previously committed sin, and the theory of its periodic reincarnations).[29] Nor did the Christian

[23] See Dörrie (1959) 152-5; Pépin (1964) = Pépin (1967) 213-67. For *de regressu animae* and Augustine see J.J. O'Meara, *Porphyry's Philosophy from Oracles in Augustine*, Paris 1959, and the critical review by P. Hadot, 'Citations de Porphyre dans Augustin', *REAug* 6 (1960) 205-44, to which O'Meara's *Porphyry's Philosophy from Oracles in Eusebius's Praeparatio evangelica and Augustine's Dialogues of Cassiciacum*, Paris 1969 (= *RechAug* 6, 105-38), is a reply. The fragments of *de regressu animae* in *civ.* are collected in Bidez 27*-44*; cf. ib. 88-97. The title is given in *civ.* 10.29 (written about 417). *sol.* 1.24 need not be an echo of *de regressu*: see *retr.* 1.4.3. The classic (if daringly speculative: see n. 20 above) exposé of the Porphyrian elements in Augustine's thought is Theiler (1933) = Theiler (1966) 160-251; see also E. TeSelle, 'Porphyry and Augustine', *Augustinian Studies* 5 (1974) 113-47.

[24] Iamblichus *ap.* Simplic. *in Cat.* p. 128.32-5 Kalbfleisch, on which see D. O'Brien, '"Pondus meum amor meus" (*Conf.* xiii 9, 10): saint Augustin et Jamblique', *Studia Patristica* 16 = *TU* 129 (1985) 524-7. Theiler (1933) 45 = Theiler (1966) 215 argues for Porphyrian influence here.

[25] Plato quotations in Porphyrian contexts: see Courcelle (1948) 226-9. There is no indication that Augustine knew Apuleius' lost *Phaedo* translation: ib. 158. For the question of Augustine's knowledge of Greek in general see B. Altaner, *Kleine Patristische Schriften*, ed. G. Glockmann (= *TU* 83), Berlin 1967, 129-63; Marrou 27-46; Courcelle (1948) 183-94.

[26] e.g. Plato, *Phaedrus* 245c-e in Cicero, *de re publica* 6.27f. and *Tusc. disp.* 1.53f., or Cicero's *Timaeus* translation. Greek views on the soul are presented in doxological fashion in *Tusc. disp.* 1.18-83; cf. *Hortensius*, fr. 112 Grilli (from *c. Iul.* 4.78) and fr. 115 (from *trin.* 14.26). See Testard 1.205-29; 261-6; Hagendahl 486-553. The doxology on the nature of the soul at *trin.* 10.9 derives from *Tusc. disp.* 1.18-22: see Hagendahl 139f.

[27] Varro: e.g. *civ.* 7.23; cf. Hagendahl 609-17; 620-7. Platonizing Virgil interpretations: *civ.* 13.19; 14.5; 21.3; 21.13; cf. Courcelle (1948) 158; Courcelle (1957); Hagendahl 402-8; Hadot (1971) 215-31 (who considers the possibility that the Virgil commentary might be by Marius Victorinus). See n. 127. Doxographies: Solignac (1958). Doxographical traces can be seen in the schematic lists of problems concerning soul's origin, nature and destiny in *ord.* 2.17 and *quant. an.* 1: see p. 3.

[28] *Gn. litt.* 10.25.41-26.45. Cf. p. 22 n. 68.

[29] The work against the Priscillianists and Origenists (*c. Prisc. et Orig.*) dates from 415; *civ.* 11, which deals with Origen's views (11.23 refers to *de principiis*), was not written before 417. The extent of Augustine's direct knowledge of Origen in *ep.* 82.23 (405) and 143.5 (412) is difficult to

Scriptures themselves provide Augustine with any general concept of the nature of soul, apart from the teachings that it is created, has fallen through sin, and can be redeemed. Scripture presents Augustine with a number of texts referring to *anima* or *spiritus* which require exegetical elucidation:[30] the exegesis put forward by him is, however, Platonic, and firmly rooted in the philosophical tradition. It does not, of course, purport to be any the less Christian for that.

(iii) Soul and life; parts and degrees of soul

For Augustine, 'soul' in its broadest and fundamental sense is the phenomenon of life in things. In this respect he reflects the popular conception of *anima* as the life-breath or life-principle.[31] What is alive is ensouled, what is lifeless is without soul. Reporting Varro's views on the degrees (*gradus*) of soul in nature, he distinguishes between (a) the vegetative soul in trees, bones, nails, hair, etc., (b) the sensitive or perceiving soul in animals, and (c) the highest level of soul, present in man as intelligence (*civ.* 7.23); and he elsewhere indicates that this general, threefold division of souls underlies his more detailed analyses (e.g. *quant. an.* 70 ff.).[32] Awareness that we are alive is awareness that we are, or have, souls, and are not mere bodily entities (*beata v.* 7). It is thus the case that, although we do not perceive soul by means of any of the senses, we are none the less empirically aware that we have a soul, because we are conscious of the fact that we are percipient beings:

> For what is known so closely and so apprehends its own identity as that by which everything else is also apprehended, that is, the soul? (*trin.* 8.9)

By analogy, we infer that life and soul are present in other animals, and this awareness that other bodies are alive and conscious is not peculiar to man: animals also possess it (ib.).[33]

Augustine will employ this equation of soul with life to argue, not merely that it is soul's presence that keeps us alive,[34] but also that soul is itself

---

assess. Origen's influence upon Augustine in general is discussed by Altaner (above n. 25) 224-52; Theiler (1970) 543-63.

[30] e.g. Genesis 2:7; Ecclesiastes 12:7; Wisdom 8:19f. See pp. 15-20 and 31-4.

[31] For a brief survey of early Greek notions of the soul as life-principle see A. Dihle, art. *psukhê,* etc., *ThWNT* 9 (1973) 605-7. Cf. J. Bremmer, *The Early Greek Concept of the Soul*, Princeton, N.J. 1983. See in general R.B. Onians, *The Origins of European Thought about the Body, the Mind, the Soul, the World, Time and Fate*, 2nd edn., Cambridge 1954.

[32] For the Poseidonian background to this see Theiler (1982) 2.262f. The threefold division is ultimately derived from Aristotle's distinction between *threptikê, aisthêtikê,* and *noêtikê* (sc. *psukhê*), frequent in his psychological and biological writings: see e.g. *de generatione animalium* 736a30-b14, where all three types are named.

[33] Elsewhere Augustine asserts that in humans this awareness of the life of the soul is, if not the object of sense-perception, an activity of intelligence or mind: *duab. an.* 2.2; 3.3. For the Stoic concept of self-awareness in Hierocles see Long (1982) 46f.; Pembroke 118f.

[34] See p. 69.

immortal. For if being alive is the defining characteristic of soul, soul cannot admit the contrary of life and cannot therefore cease to live:

> Those (philosophers) who have held its (sc. the soul's) substance to be some kind of life in no way corporeal, since they have found that it is a life that animates and gives life to every living body, have in consequence tried, each as best he could, to prove it immortal, since life cannot lack life (*trin.* 10.9).[35]

Soul (= life) and death are exclusive contraries in the way that light and darkness are (*sol.* 2.23), and if we speak of soul's 'death' it can only be metaphorically (*trin.* 5.5; 14.6; *ser.* 65.4-7; *conf.* 13.30), with reference to its loss of wisdom, or lack of happiness or alienation from God. For this reason, Augustine can only treat the Epicurean thesis that soul disintegrates more quickly than body after death with incomprehending contempt: that the soul 'is dissolved like smoke scattered by the wind' is, he finds, the view 'of Epicurean pigs rather than men' (*ser.* 150.6). At one stage of his philosophical progress this Epicurean lack of belief in the soul's immortality, as well as in a system of posthumous awards and punishments, rather than the school's materialism, was the one factor preventing Augustine from adopting the Epicurean views on the nature of good and evil (*conf.* 6.26). Be that as it may, this theme is more appropriately treated in conjunction with Augustine's other claims for the immortality, if not of all souls, then at least of reason or mind (see Chapter 7 (iii)). For our present purposes it will be sufficient to note that, even if life is indeed the essential characteristic of soul, this does not in itself imply that soul is necessarily immortal, but merely that soul, in so far as it exists, is necessarily alive, unlike bodies, which can be either dead or alive.[36]

Although Augustine discusses general problems of the soul, and particular problems of animal and vegetative souls, as well as such topics as the existence of a world-soul, his main interest is none the less firmly centered upon the human soul (see *quant. an.* 70). He inherits the traditional division of human soul into rational and irrational 'parts': memory, sense-perception and appetition are, for example, irrational powers, whereas mind, understanding and will are rational (*civ.* 5.11). The irrational parts of the soul can be disturbed by emotions and desires (*en. Ps.* 145.5). Augustine knows of the tripartite division of soul in Plato's *Republic*, even if he does not refer to it by name: at *civ.* 14.19 he talks of anger (*ira*) and desire (*libido*), which clearly correspond to the Platonic spirited (*thumoeides*) and desiring (*epithumêtikon*) parts respectively, and of *mens* as a 'third part' (= *logistikon*), a controlling (*imperans*) faculty of soul.[37] The two lower parts of soul can be

---

[35] Cf. *imm. an.* 4; 5; 9; 12; 16. For the unnamed source to which Augustine refers here, and its Platonic (*Phaedo* 105c-e) and, more specifically, Neoplatonic identity see Pépin (1964) 78f. = Pépin (1977) 238f.

[36] A similar point regarding the 'proofs' of soul's immortality in the *Phaedo* is made by D. Gallop, *Plato: Phaedo.* Translated with Notes, Oxford 1975, 88-91.

[37] He may derive his knowledge of the Platonic tripartite division from Cicero, *Tusc. disp.* 1.20, as Hagendahl 141 suggests, even if, verbal resemblances apart (Aug.: '... reason ... as in some kind of citadel'; Cic.: '... reason, in the head as in a citadel'), the two accounts differ. Augustine

perverted, but, under the proper control of mind, they may be put to legitimate use:

> anger ... is allowed for the display of an equitable compulsion, and desire for the duty of propagating offspring.

Augustine will, however, prefer the rational/irrational bipolarity to the Platonic tripartite division, and will, as we shall see, elsewhere regard *ira* and *libido* as affections, as it were, on the same level, rather than gradated powers of a differentiated soul-structure. Thus he often emphasizes the traditional view that it is the function of the rational soul to control the irrational powers (e.g. *en. Ps.* 145.5), and that this controlling power defines soul's proper relation to body. So *quant. an.* 22: soul is

> some kind of substance sharing in reason, fitted to the task of controlling body.

> In its power (is) ... the direction of all the limbs, and it (acts as) a kind of pivot, as it were, in effecting all bodily motions (ib. 23).

But there are also grounds for believing that Augustine finds both the bipartite and the tripartite division of soul less than adequate as a fully comprehensive account of the levels of, and differences between, psychological functions, even if the division schemes may be appropriate as an expression of tensions and oppositions in human behaviour. For Augustine's attempt at such a comprehensive account we must rather turn to the discussion of the *gradus* of soul in *quant. an.* 70ff.

The first and lowest *gradus* or function of soul (I) is found in vegetative and all higher forms of life: it is the life-giving power, the power of growth and organic cohesion, of self-nourishment and the conservation of the appropriate balance and measure peculiar to individual organisms (in this last connection one can also speak of their beauty, *quant. an.* 70). The second function of soul (II) is restricted to animals and men: it comprises the powers of sense-perception, movement, concentration and awareness, appetition and avoidance, the instincts of sex and care for offspring, the ability to dream and to judge, the possession of habitual dispositions and, lastly, of memory (ib. 71). These first two functions correspond to the distinction between vegetative and animal levels of soul, as found by Augustine in Varro (*civ.* 7.23).[38] In his account, however, Augustine proceeds to give a more differentiated analysis of the third, rational level, distinguishing no less than five degrees within it. These latter are several conditions or activities (§78: *actus*; §75: *gradus actionis*) that one can indeed call by the general name of 'rational', but they are clearly understood to be gradated in an ascending hierarchy of value. The first such level (III) amounts to what we may call

---

is not interested in the physical location of the soul-parts, as Cicero is, and the former's vocabulary is more colourful than Cicero's (e.g. 'corrupt parts of the soul ... it (sc. reason) ruling, they being its slaves').

[38] See p. 11.

discursive reason: it is manifest in the memory and skill applied to the various arts and sciences, in aesthetic, social and political behaviour and judgement, in rhetoric, language and speculation (ib. 72). A further level (IV) is characteristically, if not exclusively, ethical: it is concerned with evaluation of the several 'goods', with moral struggle and progress through purification, with belief and authority. At this level the moral subject is in a state of tension and anxiety over unachieved perfection (ib. 73). At the next level (V) this perfection has been achieved, fear is overcome, and the purified soul is confident in its power (ib. 74). The two remaining levels are those of pure intellect. One (VI) is that of the desire to know the highest truths (ib. 75). The other (VII) is their knowledge, or, as Augustine prefers to say, their contemplation or vision, the understanding that God, the highest truth, is the cause and principle of all things. This understanding has ethical as well as religious repercussions: a proper sense of values, and a certitude that specifically Christian truths (Augustine mentions the incarnation of Christ and the resurrection of the body) comprise a new level of knowledge, in which fear of mortality disappears (ib. 76). These two highest levels of pure intellect, that of aspiration (VI) and that of achievement (VII), correspond to the two preceding levels of moral struggle (IV) and success (V), and Augustine also stresses that the moral levels are prerequisites of the success of the intellectual venture (ib. 75).

We have said that Augustine regards the levels of soul as a hierarchical, gradated series: this is clear both from the introductory formulas employed to introduce them, and from the summary concluding remarks (§71: 'ascend, then, to the next stage'; §72: 'raise up your mind, therefore, to the third stage'; §73: 'look up, then, and leap to the fourth stage'; §76: 'the final stage of the soul ... no longer a stage, but a place to stay, arrived at by means of those stages'; §79: 'to those ascending, then, from the lower to the higher'). Although he would clearly wish us to understand that the broad levels of soul are not merely distinguishable but also limited (in descending order: intellectual, ethical, discursively rational, sensible, vegetative), Augustine does not, on the other hand, intend his sevenfold division to be a hard and fast systematic one:

> For the same phenomena can be correctly and accurately divided and given names in countless different ways; but with such an abundance of ways, each employs what he finds suitable to his requirements (§79).

This last factor should make us cautious about seeking too specific a source for the Augustinian scheme, even if it is not implausible that a Neoplatonic hierarchy of degrees (*bathmoi*) is behind it.[39]

[39] O. Schissel von Fleschenberg, *Marinos von Neapolis und die neuplatonischen Tugendgrade* (Texte und Forschungen zur byzantinisch-neugriechischen Philologie, 8), Athens 1928, 81ff., argues that the hierarchy of virtues found in the prooemium to Marinus' *Life of Proclus* and (with variations) elsewhere is adapted by Augustine to his own philosophical needs. Theiler, in a review in *Gnomon* 5 (1929) 315f., suggests that the related hierarchy of Olympiodorus, *in Alc.* 177.3-8 (p.112 Westerink) is a likelier parallel, but not without some adept juggling of both terminology and intent, as Theiler himself later admitted (Theiler (1933) 52 = Theiler (1966) 224). There is,

Much of the detail of the first three levels at least is, however, common ground among philosophers since Aristotle: we cannot exclude the possibility of an Augustinian amalgam of Platonic, Peripatetic and Stoic views, with a strong Ciceronian influence.[40] The distinction between levels four and five – striving for, and achievement of, purification – has, on the other hand, clear Neoplatonic roots:[41] but even so Augustine's scheme does not correspond in its details to the Porphyrian doctrine with which it has been compared, namely the fourfold division of virtue in *sent.* 32. At the same time, the trend of Augustine's argument here has broad affinities with Neoplatonic accounts of conversion and ascent, through the levels of discursive reason and purification, to the intellection of the highest principle – an intellection that can only be achieved if the mind is adequately prepared – morally and intellectually – for the vision. Whereas, however, there is for Porphyry a higher class of virtue than the contemplative virtues (*theôrêtikai aretai*), and it is this class, i.e. the paradeigmatic virtues (*paradeigmatikai aretai*), which achieves this supreme intellection, Augustine will stress that perfection of human vision none the less recognizes the transcendent nature of the truth contemplated: God is superior to the mutable human mind. In other words, Augustine's perfected human intellect is at the level of Porphyrian contemplative virtue.[42]

(iv) The origin of souls

Augustine's discussions of the human soul's origin[43] are chiefly elucidations of the two apparently distinct accounts of man's creation in Genesis 1:26-7

---

in fact, a closer Porphyrian parallel to *quant. an.* 70ff. than those hitherto adduced: *ad Gaurum* 6.2f. (p. 42.17ff. Kalbfleisch) speaks of the following levels of mind and soul: intellect – discursive reason – the irrational part = the desiring part = the opining and imaginative soul – the vegetative soul. (The importance of *ad Gaur.* for Porphyry's psychology has now been shown by Deuse 174ff.) – For *quant. an.* in general see the introduction and notes in Lütcke.

[40] See Cicero, *nat. deor.* 2.33-36 (= Poseidonios F 359 Theiler); *fin.* 5.39f.; *Tusc. disp.* 5.37ff. (there also the idea of virtue as the mind's perfection).

[41] See Plot. *Enn.* 1.2.4; Porph. *sent.* 32 (p. 25.10ff. L.). Schwyzer (1974) 226 notes that, whereas for Plotinus the distinction between imperfect and perfect purificatory virtue is fluid, in Porphyry it is hardened into two distinct classes of virtue. Porphyry's division is, therefore, the closer to Augustine's, even if, for the latter, the distinction is not primarily one between classes of virtues.

[42] Porphyry's paradeigmatic virtues could also be equated with the Ideas in the divine mind, *sent.* 32 (p. 31.8 L.) and Macrobius, *in somn. Scip.* 1.8.10. In this case they would, of course, no longer be human virtues: we could then relate them to Augustine's transcendent, immutable truth. Elsewhere, however, the paradeigmatic virtues (a Porphyrian innovation, as Schwyzer (1974) 226 points out) are equated with hieratic or theurgic virtues, states of enthusiastic union with the divine achieved by ritual means: see A.-J. Festugière, 'L'ordre de lecture des dialogues de Platon aux Ve/VIe siècles', *Museum Helveticum* 26 (1969) 294-6. The seven *gradus* of *quant. an.* 70ff., to the extent that they describe spiritual progress, may be compared with the seven stages of moral and intellectual ascent of *vera rel.* 49 and *doctr. chr.* 2.9-11. Cf. also the seven stages of progress discerned by Augustine in the Beatitudes of the Sermon on the Mount (Matthew 5:3ff.): *ser. dom. m.* 1.10-12; *en. Ps.* 11.7; *ser.* 347.3; *ep.* 171a. 1f.

[43] See O'Daly (1983) for a survey of the most important texts, with full discussion. Cf. F.-J. Thonnard, *BA* 22, 830-3; Agaësse/Solignac, *BA* 48, 695-710; 714-7; *BA* 49, 530-41.

and 2:7.[44] Other souls, animal and vegetable, are created in undeveloped form (*potentialiter*) in the first moment of creation as causal or seminal principles (*rationes*) that mature at the appropriate time (*Gn. litt.* 5.5.14).[45] In the early (388-390) *de Genesi contra Manichaeos* Augustine regards the two Genesis accounts as complementary: they are allegories of every soul's (not merely Adam's) resemblance to God through reason (1.27-8), and of soul's formative and cohesive functions in its symbiosis with body (2.9). Augustine observes that the divine 'inbreathing' (*insufflatio*) of life referred to in Genesis 2:7, if it symbolizes the ensoulment of an already existing body, would be consistent both with soul's pre-existence and with its creation at the moment of the inbreathing (2.10).[46] He is not here concerned to choose between these options: more important to him is the scriptural testimony of the Genesis account that the human soul is created and not, as the Manichees maintain, a part of divine nature (2.11).

In *de libero arbitrio* 3.56-9 Augustine considers four theories of soul's origin. These are:

(a)   the traducianist[47] view:

> One soul is made ... from which the souls of all who are born are derived (*trahuntur*).

(b)   the creationist view:

> They are made singly in everyone at birth.

(c)   embodiment by God of pre-existent souls:

> Souls which are already in existence in some secret place of God's are dispatched to animate and govern the bodies of individuals as these are born.

(d)   voluntary embodiment of pre-existent souls:

> Souls created elsewhere ... come of their own accord to inhabit bodies.

He argues rash affirmation of any one view[48] in the absence of clear Scriptural elucidation: all four possibilities are consistent with divine justice and mercy, human free will, and the inherited consequences of Adam's sin (though (a) would be the clearest solution of the last problem, ib. 3.56).

---

[44] G. May, *Schöpfung aus dem Nichts* (Arbeiten zur Kirchengeschichte, 48), Berlin 1978, 22; 50; 128-30; 178 discusses interpretations of the two accounts in Jewish and early Christian writers; cf. ib. 2 n. 2 for a brief bibliographical survey of modern works on early Christian cosmology.

[45] For the concept of causal or seminal principles in Augustine see Agaësse/Solignac 48, 653-68.

[46] Cf. *civ.* 12.23, where the same two possibilities are suggested and Augustine, once again, does not choose between them.

[47] For traducianist and creationist theories in Christian writers of the third and fourth centuries see J.N.D. Kelly, *Early Christian Doctrines*, 5th edn., London 1977, 174-83; 344-74.

[48] The question of whether Augustine's early writings maintain a belief in the soul's pre-existence (the presupposition of alternatives (c) and (d) of *lib. arb.*) is discussed in Chapter 7 (pp. 199-202), where a negative conclusion is reached. For a bibliography of the opposing views on this question see p. 200 n. 103.

Augustine will subsequently (*ep.* 143 and 166) use these distinctions, but he remains agnostic. (a) loses its force as an explanation of the transmission of original sin, however, when he elaborates his concept of individual responsibility (*ep.* 98.1; 190.5), and a Scriptural text like Ecclesiastes 12:7 ('... and (that) the spirit should *return* (*revertatur*) to God who gave it') seems to be consistent with (a) or (c) until subtle analysis neutralizes its apparent tendency (*ep.* 143.8-10; cf. *ep.* 190.17).[49]

A further theory – that embodiment is a punishment for previously committed sin – is familiar to Augustine both from Cicero's *Hortensius* (*c. Iul.* 4.78; 4.83) and Origen's *de principiis* (*civ.* 11.23). He disapproves of its underlying assumption, that bodies can be evil instruments of punishment in the essentially good creation of the physical world, and he finds it inconsistent with Romans 9:11, clearly not wishing to equate it with the morally neutral alternative (d) of *de libero arbitrio*:

> Nor is any hesitation shown in that sentence of the apostle's about the twins in Rebecca's womb not yet doing any good or evil (*Gn. litt.* 6.9.14).[50]

In the early works – *de Genesi contra Manichaeos* and *de libero arbitrio* – Augustine is only marginally concerned with the problem of the soul's origin. He has other, more immediate preoccupations, to which the problem is incidental. His fullest account of soul's origin is found in *de Genesi ad litteram*, where he argues that Genesis 2:7 is no mere restatement of 1:26-7 (*Gn. litt.* 6.1.1): he proposes and tests the hypothesis that the latter text refers to the creation of a causal principle (*ratio causalis*) of man, a potential realized only in the temporal succession of the creation account (ib. 6.1.2; 6.5.7), i.e. it does not refer to a creation of soul prior to body (ib. 6.7.12). As for the nature of the 'living soul' (*anima viva*) of Genesis 2:7, since it is not divine (ib. 7.2.3-4.6),[51] it is created either (a) 'out of something' or (b) 'out of nothing'. If (a), then the soul's 'matter' must be identified (ib. 7.5.7; 7.6.9). Were it spiritual, it would need to be at least potentially rational and alive, and so enjoy happiness: but embodiment would then be a deterioration (*defluxio*) of soul's condition, i.e. an unacceptable hypothesis (ib. 7.6.9-8.11). To argue that it is irrational or corporeal would be no more acceptable (ib. 7.9.12; 7.12.18-15.21). So (a) must be rejected, even if soul's mutability might suggest that it is formed out of some matter (ib. 7.6.9). Possibility (b) remains, even if it is not what Genesis 2:7 refers to, for that would undermine the hypothetical interpretation of Genesis 1:26-7, as well as suggesting that something new is created by God after the completion of his work referred to in Genesis 2:2 (ib. 7.28.40).

Augustine must therefore accept the causal principle hypothesis adduced

---

[49] R.J. O'Connell, 'The origin of the soul in Saint Augustine's *Letter* 143', *REAug* 28 (1982) 239-52 discusses the context and significance of *ep.* 143 in detail.

[50] Cf. *lib. arb.* 3.34; *ep.* 143.5. For the fall of the soul in Hermetic and Neoplatonic contexts see Festugière 63-96.

[51] Here Augustine directs his argument as much against the Priscillianists as against the Manichees: see Agaësse/Solignac, *BA* 48, 698f.

to explain Genesis 1:26-7. A causal principle created in the primal creation requires a 'container' (*natura, ubi conderetur,* ib. 7.22.32) of its as yet latent force (as e.g. the principle of body may be considered to be latent in its 'matter', earth). Dismissing the options that this container might be God (for soul would not then be a distinct entity), an inactive and so self-contradictory spiritual creation, or the angelic order (which would thus be in some sense the soul's parent), Augustine concludes that the hypothesis fails. Soul itself is created 'out of nothing' in the primal creation, simultaneously with the causal principles of body:

> It should therefore be believed ... that the soul itself was indeed already created, just like the first day was brought into being, and that once created it lay hidden in God's works, until he sowed it at the appropriate time in the body that is formed out of clay, breathing it in, that is, animating (the body) ... (7.24.35; cf. 10.2.3).

As for Genesis 2:7, it refers to the historical creation of the whole man Adam: his soul's embodiment takes the form of alternatives (c) or (d) of *de libero arbitrio.* If alternative (d) holds (which Augustine seems to prefer here), the act of will involved is sub-moral, like the life-instinct (ib. 7.25.36; 7.27.38).[52]

In book ten of *de Genesi ad litteram* Augustine considers the creation of Eve's soul, and hence of those of other humans. Three possibilities are named: (a) an extension to all souls of the hypothesis of ib. 7.24.35, i.e. all are created individually in the primal creation; (b) the traducianist theory; (c) creationism (ib. 10.1.1-3.4). Of these, (c) is the most difficult, for it seems to undermine the completeness of the primal creation, or to revert to the rejected causal principle theory (ib. 10.4.5). The choice between (a) and (b) occupies Augustine until the end of *Gn. litt.* 10.[53] As he finds no clear Scriptural support for either alternative (ib. 10.6.9-9.16; 10.17.31), his discussion remains inconclusive, dismissing only Tertullian's corporealist traducianism (ib. 10.25.41-26.45).

Ep. 166 (written in 415)[54] and 190 (datable to 418) add little new, though the emphasis there is on the question's relevance to Augustine's current preoccupation with original sin and infant guilt: how is the latter to be reconciled with creationism (*ep.* 166.10; 180.2)? Augustine, believing that Jerome (the addressee of *ep.* 166) inclines to the creationist view (in fact,

---

[52] Augustine is determined to avoid what he considers to be the Origenist pitfall of enforced punitive embodiment. Hence his desire to steer clear of alternative (c).

[53] Both here and in *Gn. litt.* 7.24.35 Augustine seems unaware of the Origenist implications of the proto-creationist alternative (a). Origenist views in contemporary Western controversy are reflected in Rufinus, *Apologia ad Anastasium* 6 (*CCL* 20, p. 27). Although Wisdom 8:19f. ('I was allotted a good soul and, although I was better, I came to a befouled body': quoted from *Gn. litt.* 10.7.12) appears to argue for an Origenist version of (a), viz. pre-existence and embodiment in accordance with prior merit or demerit (*Gn. litt.* 10.15.27), it can, upon re-examination, be interpreted in sense (b), ib. 10.17.31.

[54] For *ep.* 166's contemporary relevance see G. Bonner, 'Rufinus of Syria and African Pelagianism', *Augustinian Studies* 1 (1970) 31-47. Its contents are analysed by R.J. O'Connell, 'Augustine's Rejection of the Fall of the Soul', *Augustinian Studies* 4 (1973) 17-29.

Jerome vacillates), was not vouchsafed the latter's answer (*retr.* 2.45).[55]
Mankind's solidarity with Adam and co-responsibility for his sin, which all
men willed through him (*nupt. et conc.* 2.15),[56] might seem to argue for the
conclusion that, just as original sin is propagated by the act of generation (*c.
Iul. imp.* 2.42), so also the soul may be (ib. 4.104; cf. 2.177). But such
traducianism requires the explanation of how souls are actually propagated,
a difficulty that does not make it more plausible (*ep.* 190.15): again,
Augustine stresses lack of Scriptural guidance (*ep.* 190.17-19).[57] He is
resigned to uncertainty (*retr.* 1.1.3: 'I did not know then, nor do I know now')
on an 'inessential question' (*c. ep. Pel.* 3.26) whose solution is not necessary to
man's salvation (*c. Iul.* 5.17). The dogmatic creationism of a Vincentius
Victor[58] is to be opposed for the heterodox consequences which that aberrant
thinker drew from the creationist thesis (such as the belief that the
newly-created soul merits the pollution of original sin, which for its part
derives from the body) rather than because creationism may be in itself
wrong (*nat. et or. an.* 1.33).

Augustine is no less cautious about another related problem, namely,
identification of the moment when animation of the foetus occurs in the
mother's womb: does it (a) coincide with the instant of conception, or does it
(b) occur when the embryo is formed into a human shape, or does it (c)
happen when the embryo first moves itself? Augustine does not opt for any
one of these traditional views (*qu. hept.* 2.80; *div. qu.* 56; *nat. et or. an.* 1.25),[59]
and this despite the fact that the answer given to the question would have
important repercussions on the moral assessment of, for example, the
practice of abortion, a topic which exercised him.[60] Others were less
undecided: Tertullian believed that animation coincides with conception (*de
anima* 25 and 27), although the embryo can only be regarded as a human
being from the time when it attains to its final form (ib. 37.2). But despite his
agnosticism on the question of animation, Augustine is none the less
adamant in his rejection of the Stoic position (which was also that of Roman

[55] For Jerome's views see *adversus Rufinum* 2.8-10; *ep.* 126.1 (*ep.* 165.1 in Augustine's collection, mistakenly attributed to Augustine by Evans 124).

[56] See M.E. Alflatt, 'The Responsibility for Involuntary Sin in Saint Augustine', *RechAug* 10 (1975) 171-86; G. de Broglie, 'Pour une meilleure intelligence du "De Correptione et Gratia"', *Augustinus Magister* 3 (1954) 317-37.

[57] The question of the origin of Christ's soul is raised in *ep.* 190.25, but, although the virgin birth excludes the traducianist hypothesis in his case (cf. *ench.* 34; 41), his exceptional status disqualifies his soul as evidence for any general theory of origins (cf. *Gn. litt.* 10.18.31-21.37). Christ's human soul is none the less fully real (*ser.* 174.2; *Io. ev. tr.* 23.6): Augustine repudiates Apollinarianism's denial of his normal human psychology (*div. qu.* 80; *en. Ps.* 85.4; *conf.* 7.25). On Christ's person and his divine and human natures see W. Geerlings, *Christus Exemplum. Studien zur Christologie und Christusverkündigung Augustins* (Tübinger Theologische Studien, 13), Mainz 1978, 95-145.

[58] See *PAC* 1173f. for bibliographical details of this ex-Donatist Rogatist.

[59] For these and other possibilities in Greek, Roman and Jewish writings see J.H. Waszink, art. Beseelung, *RAC* 2 (1954) 176-83. Still useful is K. Emmel, *Das Fortleben der antiken Lehren von der Beseelung bei den Kirchenvätern*, Borna/Leipzig 1918.

[60] See J.H. Waszink, art. Abtreibung, *RAC* 1 (1950) 55-60, and, for Augustine's views, O. Wermelinger, art. Abortus, *Augustinus-Lexikon* 1, fasc. 1/2, 6-10.

law) that the embryo is a part of the mother's body: it has its own independent life in the womb (*c. Iul.* 6.43ff.).[61]

(v) Self-movement and consciousness

We have seen that, for Augustine, our empirical awareness that we are alive is taken to be an indication that we have a soul. However, he does not confine himself to such basic equations as life = soul. Soul is the principle of movement in bodies, and is itself a self-moving principle. This is, of course, the core of Plato's argument for soul's eternal existence in *Phaedrus* 245cff., a passage that will have been familiar to Augustine in Cicero's versions of it.[62] But Augustine does not offer a formal proof reminiscent of the *Phaedrus* passage. Rather, he argues that the soul's consciousness of its self-movement is its consciousness of its power to will:

> For if we will, another does not will on our account. And that movement of the soul is its own (*div. qu.* 8).

This power of self-motion is, qua potentiality, God given,[63] but clearly understood to be exercised voluntarily in individual actions: although it is not itself extended in space, it causes local bodily motions.

To elucidate his point, Augustine adduces the analogy of the unmoving pivot or axle (*cardo*) which can be a cause of motion of other bodies (ib.; see also *quant. an.* 23). In another text, he gives a more elaborate physical analogy to clarify the notion of non-local movement. In bodily limb movements the joints (*articuli*) function as a type of unmoving hub (*cardo*) between the moving limbs:

limb A   →   joint   →   limb B
(moving)   (unmoved)   (moving)
                    (*Gn. litt.* 8.21.41)

It is argued that if, in the case of bodily movements, an unmoving element is essential, then the incorporeal, inextended soul may be supposed not to move locally, in so far as it, like the joints, is the necessary proximate cause of movements, the hub upon which that which is moved depends (ib. 8.21.41f.). Furthermore, in the case of bodily movements, a moved limb depends immediately for its movement on the proximate unmoved joint, but it is also moved by the adjacent limb, acting, as it were, through the joint (§41: Augustine gives the examples shoulder → upper arm → elbow → hand →

[61] For ancient embryological theories and their influence see E. Lesky, *Die Zeugungs- und Vererbungslehre der Antike und ihr Nachwirken* (Akademie der Wissenschaften und der Literatur in Mainz, Abhandlungen der Geistes- und Sozialwissenschaftlichen Klasse), 1950, 1225-425; E. Lesky/J.H. Waszink, art. Embryologie, *RAC* 4 (1959) 1228-44.

[62] *de re publica* 6.27f.; *Tusc. disp.* 1.53f.

[63] This insistence is, of course, a directly Christian response to the view of the soul as of divine nature, ruling the body as God the universe: cf. the words immediately preceding the *Phaedrus* paraphrase in Cicero, *rep.* 6.26.

finger, and hip → knee → shin → ankle → sole of foot. But what is the initiator of the full sequence of movements? Augustine's answer is, of course, the impulse (*nutus*) or will (*voluntas*) of the soul, which thus becomes a type of unmoved mover within the person (see §21.40: God, temporally and locally unmoved, moves the creation; the soul, unmoved locally but moved temporally, moves its body). We can present the idea as follows:

soul → limb A → joint a → limb B → limb N
(unmoved) moved unmoved moved moved

Thus, what began as an apparent physical example or analogy becomes, in the course of exposition, something more: an explanation of bodily motion in terms of a series of necessarily moved and necessarily unmoved elements, of which the first, unmoved element is the soul.[64]

Furthermore, just as we are consciously aware of possessing this power of self-movement, so too can we infer its presence in other living entities, where there can be no question of our directly perceiving its presence, but only of inferring from its observable effects (*trin.* 8.9):

> For we also recognize the movements of bodies whereby we perceive that others are alive besides ourselves, because of the resemblance to ourselves, since we too, in virtue of being alive, move our bodies in the way that we perceive those bodies to be moved. For when a living body is moved there is no way revealed to our eyes by which to see the soul (*animus*), a thing which the eyes cannot see; but we perceive that there is something within that mass, such as is in ourselves to move in similar fashion our (bodily) mass – and that is life and soul (*anima*).

(vi) Soul's incorporeal, inextended and indivisible nature

The self-moving, inextended cause of bodily motions is not itself a body. Augustine insists that the soul is not a derivative of earth or air, or even of the celestial fiery substance of the heavenly bodies (*Gn. litt.* 7.12.18-19).[65] Nor can he accept that it might be composed of the Aristotelian fifth element, if by the latter is meant a three-dimensional body in space (ib. 7.21.27).[66] Augustine's reasons for not accepting the corporeality of soul in *Gn. litt.* 7 are based on the nature of its activities, and among the latter he does not distinguish clearly between mental and other psychological powers. Thus the mind's ability to abstract itself in thought from its physical surroundings is considered to be a sign of its incorporeality (§14.20). Likewise, the powers of

[64] The analogy with bodily joints on the basis of moving and unmoving parts is found in Aristotle: *de an.* 433b21-5; *de motu animalium* 698a14-b8; 702a22-b11.

[65] Here Augustine unequivocally rejects the quasi-materialistic Hellenistic view of the soul's heavenly origin and substance: cf. Cicero, *rep.* 6.15; Varro, *ling. lat.* 5.59. For the view's probable origin in the exegesis of *Tim.* 41d-e and 42b (on the distribution of souls to 'consort stars') see Festugière 27f.

[66] This text does not mention Aristotle by name. Augustine may get his information from Cicero, *Tusc. disp.* 1.22. Cf. ib. §41 and *Gn. litt.* 7.21.27. The possible influence of the Cicero passages is noted by Hagendahl 141.

perception, volition, and memory are indicators of soul's immaterial nature (§19.25). Finally, the phenomenon of concentration (*intentio*) shows that the mind does not register perceptibles in any physical or mechanistic way: concentration can be so intense that we are unaware of external impressions, or of our bodily motions, which either stop or proceed while our thoughts are 'elsewhere', as when we forget our whereabouts, or walk past our goal unawares, or even stop walking while lost in thought (§20.26).

Augustine will defend his views of the soul's nature against materialist adversaries, such as the ex-Donatist Vincentius Victor. Thus the latter's assertion that, without body, the soul would be a 'an utterly ineffectual, flitting, worthless substance' (*nat. et or. an.* 4.18) provokes from Augustine the remark that, if God be incorporeal, which Vincentius admits, the assertion cannot hold. Furthermore, *aer*, implicitly adduced in Vincentius' phrase as an example of something that is *inane*, is, in fact, corporeal, and so an ineptly chosen instance of supposed incorporeal ineffectiveness. This type of Augustinian argument is polemical rather than analytical, and is not entirely free from sophistry: it reinforces, in rhetorical fashion, Augustine's point of view, rather than providing any proofs in support of it.[67] The same can be said of Augustine's brief dismissal of Tertullian's corporealist psychology (*Gn. litt.* 10.25.41-26.45), or of his anti-Epicurean polemic: the latter is directed as much against the Epicurean concepts of human happiness and the soul's mortality, as against the notion of the corporeality of soul (*ser.* 150.6; 348.3; *en. Ps.* 73.25).[68]

Augustine's most sustained rejection of a corporeal soul is to be found in *de quantitate animae*. The work's title is significant, for it contains the ambiguity which is at the heart of the problem of the soul's nature. As Augustine points out, when we ask 'how great (*quanta*) is the soul?' we may be referring to its supposed physical bulk or strength, or we may be referring to its power, just as the question 'how great was Hercules?' can refer to the hero's height, or to his *potentia* and *virtus* (*quant. an.* 4; cf. §30). The latter reference need not necessarily be to an immaterial power, but it raises the possibility of such a power. If Augustine's interlocutor Evodius[69] has difficulty – like Augustine himself once had (*conf.* 7.1ff.) – in imagining the existence of something non-corporeal (*quant. an.* 4), he can be quickly convinced that, in the case of a virtue like justice, he in fact posits the reality of a non-corporeal entity (ib. §5). What is incorporeal need not be 'nothing' (*nihil*). But to admit that a concept is not three-dimensional is not to agree that soul, too, is incorporeal. Evodius adduces the example of wind: it is invisible, yet real – perhaps soul resembles it (ib. §6).[70] Evodius intends the wind-analogy to be an example of

---

[67] For the Christian Latin background to Augustine's polemic in general see I. Opelt, *Die Polemik in der christlichen lateinischen Literatur von Tertullian bis Augustin* (Bibliothek der klassischen Altertumswissenschaften, N.F., Reihe 2, 63), Heidelberg 1980.

[68] For Augustine's references to Tertullian see Waszink 48*f. For the comparison of soul with smoke in *ser.* 150.6 see Lucretius, *rer. nat.* 3.436; for its dissolution in the air after death, *rer. nat.* 3.456. See further p. 12.

[69] For details of Evodius' career see *PAC* 366-73.

[70] There is no need to see here a reference to the Stoic view of soul, as Lütcke 389 n. 11 does. Evodius' analogy is untechnical.

subtle corporeality; the soul would then be an unseen force, coextensive with its body (ib. §7).

Augustine deals with such notions in much the same way as he does in *Gn. litt.* 7. Analysis of soul's activities and powers is intended to convince us that these are not the activities or powers of a body. Our imagination of remembered objects does not obey the law that corporeal likenesses correspond in size to the bodies in which they are reflected (e.g. the image in the pupil of the eye): we can remember cities, and imagine vast spaces, and must conclude that the remembering, imagining power, and the likenesses, are not corporeal (*quant. an.* 8-9). Furthermore, the mind's ability to think of geometrical figures composed of abstract lines, or of geometrical points, indicates that it can deal with non-corporeal entities, and, on the basis of 'like perceives like', we must conclude that it is itself non-corporeal (ib. §10-22):

> But if bodily objects are seen by bodily eyes through some remarkable affinity between them, the mind (*animus*), with which we perceive those incorporeal things, cannot be bodily or a body (§22).

We may even conclude that it is superior to the geometrical entities which it cognizes. The line, for example, is extended and divisible, even if its one-dimensionality makes it superior (because divisible in only one dimension) to two- or three-dimensional objects (ib. §23). The line has, in other words, an element of corporeality, even if it can be cognized in abstraction by the intelligence. Now intelligence, or mind, has no element of corporeality corresponding to that of the line: it must therefore be superior to the latter (ib.). Nor, suggests Augustine, need this surprise us. For even in the case of the senses, bodily size bears no relation to capability: the smaller eagle's eye sees better than the larger human one. Or – comparing bodily bulk in general – the bee is brighter than the donkey. Why then should rational capability not be consistent with total absence of bodily dimensions?

> The soul can be pictured as something great, believe me – great, but without any bulk (ib. §24).

These arguments convince Evodius of the soul's incorporeality. But problems none the less remain. Evodius articulates two of these, and the subsequent discussion takes them up as evidently serious difficulties which, Augustine assures us, have preoccupied him also (ib. §26). Firstly, why does the soul seem to grow in pace with the body, as when, for example, rational powers develop in growing humans? Secondly, if the soul is extended throughout the entire body, as seems to be the case with sentient beings, how can it lack size?

Augustine's answer to the first question is based upon the distinction between bigger and better. The superiority of the circle to the square is not one of dimension, but of form, of *aequalitas* (ib. §27). Analogously, we may speak of virtue as a kind of symmetry (*aequalitas*) of a life in harmony with reason (*ratio*) and truth (*veritas*).[71] This symmetry is the perfect 'divine' harmony of the soul's affections, and it dominates these, not because it occupies more space, but precisely on account of this perfection of harmony. Progression towards such rational virtue is not therefore progression through physical growth, but rather achievement of greater ethical stability (*constantia*), the soul getting better, not bigger (ib. §28).

Spatial *quantitas* of soul thus seems excluded: but what of its temporal dimension? Evodius seems to be thinking of a non-physical development necessarily occurring over a period of time. Augustine's reply is not very satisfactory. Youthful industry is adduced as an example of the acquisition of mental power in a way that does not depend upon mere physical growth. The further fact that the latter does not occur regularly, or necessarily occur at all, over a given length of time is seen as an argument against the necessity of an extended temporal dimension in the case of mental progress (ib. §29). Thus the time needed to learn, an argument in favour of the temporal dimension, is played down, although it might seem to present the strongest case for the latter's necessity (ib.). For any progression from state A (e.g. ignorance of X) to state B (e.g. knowledge of X) requires at least a temporal medium in which it may be achieved. This is clearly also the case with the development of the corporeal seminal principles (*rationes seminales*) referred to by Augustine as the condition of physical growth: that development cannot be imagined to occur a-temporally. All that Augustine's arguments demonstrate is that growth of soul does not keep pace – even in a temporal sense – with bodily growth, and that the latter is not even temporally uniform. Evodius' original question in §26 may, of course, not have been intended to suggest anything more, but by §29 that question seems to have become submerged in the more general one of temporal necessity. Part of the difficulty throughout the argument is the vagueness of the terms used. In what respect can the soul's 'growth' (*incrementum*) be imagined, in what way can it be considered to become 'more diffused' (*longior*), if not in some physical way? Evodius' problem – that the soul is helped in its progress by the passage of time – is distorted and blurred in Augustine's answer: it will not be surprising to find the problem re-emerging in the next pages of the dialogue. There is, after all, a difference between the necessary temporal medium of progress, and the latter's regular occurrence in a wholly uniform temporal process.

Evodius' next problem is, in effect, a re-formulation of the soul-growth question, this time in relation to the specific acquisition of language (§31). The phenomenon that children, as they grow physically, also learn to talk is contrasted by Augustine with a series of examples and cases that illustrate the view of language as an acquired skill independent of any kind of growth. Once again, Augustine's argument is directed against the idea of any linked stages of physical and psychological development. Physiological and enviromental circumstances may inhibit acquisition of language skills:

---

[71] The evidence of the so-called *telos*-formula of the Stoics is patent. For the development c. Augustine's teleological views see Holte 193-206.

learning language, like learning to walk the tightrope, is a skill derived through observation and imitation, but also (as in the case of learnt foreign languages) through the teaching of one's mentor (§32). Evodius rapidly admits the absurdity of maintaining that the late learner's soul only grows when he begins to learn, or that the soul diminishes in size when it forgets something. Augustine's argument is indeed more effective here than in the preceding section: language learning does not follow any rigid linear pattern that might demonstrate 'soul-growth' (here clearly understood in a physical sense). Augustine can argue that to speak of the soul's growth through knowledge and diminution through forgetfullness is to talk metaphorically (§33), just as we talk metaphorically when we speak of the soul's 'long-suffering' (*longanimitas*) (§30).

Evodius will nevertheless continue to put forward certain problems that seem connected with the necessity of assuming soul-growth. The fact that bodily strength increases with age is one such phenomenon. Evodius argues that strength, like sense-perception, is attributable to the presence of soul, for bodies which are not ensouled lack all strength (§35) He suggests that it follows that increased strength is caused by soul-growth. Once again, Augustine's counter-argument tends to undermine the link between physical growth and proportionately increased strength. Practice, training, habitual exercise, are all factors that facilitate certain corporeal activities, irrespective of the stage of bodily growth reached. The youthful Augustine had more energy for hunting on foot than the sedentary, studious Augustine of later years; the trainers of wrestlers pay more regard to well-proportioned, muscular and mobile physiques than to sheer mass and size – and, in addition to the former, technique and practice count. Smaller, slighter contestants can therefore defeat stouter ones in wrestling and weight-lifting. And the itinerant merchant can outlast the Olympic victor who lacks the practice which the former has acquired on his rounds, even if in other respects he is no match for the athlete. Strength is strength for some specific purpose, acquired by the right type of training of the right sort of physique, rather than, as it were, automatically, by increased bodily stature (§36).

Growth and strength are, of course, related in living creatures, whose weight obeys the physical laws of the natural movements of bodies. But such physical laws are more readily observed in inanimate bodies (§37), whether their movements are initiated by human agency or not. Strength or power (*vires*) in animate beings is, on the other hand, more often exhibited in movements which are originated by an 'impulse' (*nutus*) of the soul (§38) using the sinews as 'engines' (*tormenta*). The sinews are enlivened and made mobile by dryness and warmth, and become weak and slack through cold and moisture: sleep is an instance of the latter condition; insanity – if provoked by lack of sleep, alcoholic consumption, and a high temperature – of the former, a fact which accounts for the often unusual strength of the mentally disturbed (ib.). All three factors – impulse, sinews and weight – go to form what we call 'strength'. Impulse is ultimately effected by the will, so that emotional factors can (as in the case of hope or daring) strengthen or (as with fear) weaken the tendency to movement. Strength is, in other words, a psychosomatic phenomenon, controllable by training and health, but ultimately depending on the effectiveness of the psychical impulse, so that one can almost talk of the soul having its own 'strength' which gives it greater courage or daring (ib.).

Augustine now applies this account of the factors involved in bodily strength to the case of small children. Their impulse – their will – is perfect of its kind, but they lack the developed sinews and weight which would enable them to implement these impulsive tendencies in action. In other words, intention and concentration, as well as movements of appetition or rejection, are present in even the small child:[72] it is not so much they, as the physical means of their expression, that grow as the child gains strength (§39).

Furthermore, if we argue that the soul grows as bodily strength does, then we are forced, absurdly, to conclude that it diminishes with loss of such strength, even when mental powers are simultaneously developing: but the same thing cannot at one and the same time grow and diminish (§40).

Augustine's arguments highlight functions peculiar to soul (willing, reacting emotionally to situations, thinking) in order to indicate that its activities and powers are subject to laws other than those of physical bodies: the interaction of body and soul is not denied – indeed it accounts for the degree to which certain psychical energies are realized in practice – but the strict linking of the observable development of body to a hypothetical development of soul, whether spatially or temporally, is rejected, and from this 'disjunction' arises the notion of a fully developed soul, possessing knowledge (§34), and inhabiting the as yet weak and underdeveloped infant body, needing – as in the case of language – to develop certain skills by acquisitive learning, but, on the other hand, already possessed of impulse and desire (*nutus ... integer*, §39).

The second question asked by Evodius in §26 – how can the soul, being present throughout the entire body, lack size? – is mainly answered by Augustine in the account of sense-perception which now follows (§41-60), and which will be analysed in Chapter 3.[73] The phenomenon of vision in particular – the fact that a bodily organ can receive an impression from an object not contiguous with it – argues for a soul that is not confined to its body, as certain 'most learned men' (§61) have maintained:

> From which it should be obvious to everybody that the soul is not enclosed in any place, since the eye, which is a body, can only be affected by it (sc. the perceived object) if the latter is not where the eye is; and it would never be so affected without the soul.[74]

The commixture (*contemperatio*, §59) of body and soul is clearly to be envisaged in ways other than physical interpenetration: the soul is not diffused like blood throughout the entire body (§61).

---

[72] Augustine establishes this point by empirical observation of infant behaviour in *conf.* 1.8; 1.11.

[73] See especially pp. 85f.

[74] That by the 'most learned men' Porphyry is meant is argued by Pépin (1964) 64f. = Pépin (1977) 224f.

Evodius is still puzzled, however, by the phenomenon of the continued movement of dissected creatures: the lizard's tail still moves when it is separated from the body (§62), and, as this movement seems unaccountable save through presence of soul, it appears to argue for the divisibility – and so spatial extension – of soul as well as body. Augustine's first reply (ib.) to this difficulty is a surprising one, for it offers an explanation purely on the level of the activity of elements. The elements of air and fire, contained in the moist, earthy body because of soul's presence, escape with the departing soul from the wound and tend upwards, in accordance with their natural movements.[75] The bodily movements observed by Evodius are like resultant shock-waves of these escaping elements; they are strongest when the wound is freshest, and diminish as the quantity of air and fire in the body decreases, until finally all movement stops with the total departure of the active elements. This theory, unlike that referred to in doxographical accounts, does not equate the soul with either fire or air, but envisages it escaping from the body along with these, or, as in the case of the lizard-example, from that part of body – the tail – which subsequently dies. Augustine goes on to reject the theory, however, on the basis of another observed natural phenomenon, the continued life and movements of the parts of a dissected centipede. This seems to render the 'escaping elements' theory superfluous, for the wounds caused by the dissection of the centipede do not lead to its death, or to the death of any part of it, unlike the case of the lizard's tail. On the contrary, each divided part assumes its own independent life, 'as if there were two creatures of this kind' (ib.). But this new example does not lead to a new theory. Augustine takes refuge in the observation that, if the explanation of such a phenomenon be obscure, it should not shake one's faith in conclusions already reached about the soul's nature; the phenomenon may not, after all, be explicable to most – or perhaps any – human intelligence. In other words, we should either not investigate it, or, if we do, we should exclude the theory of the soul's divisibility, for it has already been rejected on other grounds. The centipede-example remains an unsolved question,[76] serving only to refute Augustine's first reply to Evodius' lizard-example (an example that presumably attracted Augustine's first reply in so far as the latter does not entail the notion of a divided soul).[77]

[75] For the Stoic theory of the natural movements of lighter and heavier elements, as related to views about the soul, see Cicero, *Tusc. disp.* 1.40.

[76] In talking of the 'centipede'-example I follow scholarly convention: Augustine indeed speaks first of a 'multipede', but then only of a 'worm (*vermiculus*)' (§62-4), and we may more readily imagine the experiment to have been carried out on a worm than on a centipede. For ancient vagueness (at least in non-specialist writings) in such distinctions by name see W. Richter, art. Würmer, *KlP* 5 (1983) 1393-5. – It is unfortunate that, in the sentence devoted to Augustine by R. Specht, art. Leib-Seele-Verhältnis, *HWP* 5 (1980) 189, the second half should be demonstrably false. There is no indication, either in the four passages there adduced, or elsewhere, that Augustine considered the souls of animals to be extended, or specific parts of their souls to be in distinct parts of their bodies. The example of the dissected centipede indicates that, on the contrary, he could not accept such hypotheses.

[77] We cannot penetrate behind the dialogue-trappings of §63 and 64 to the answers given on the occasion of the original centipede-experiment at Cassiciacum (§62). The young men clearly got the kind of answer that Evodius is too advanced to need, along with a promise of treatment of

Augustine now offers an analogy (§66ff.) of the symbiosis of incorporeal soul and body which safeguards the former's indivisibility. The analogy is drawn from language, and is based on the difference between spoken words and their meaning, between sound and sense.[78] The sound of spoken words is clearly formed from material components and it is perceived by a bodily sense, the ear; but the sound is also the bearer of meaning, which in turn corresponds to a concept (*notio*) present in the speaker's mind before the word is enunciated. Just as the word communicates sound from mouth to ear, so to speak, so it communicates meaning from mind to mind. In virtue of its conceptual status the meaning is an immaterial mental phenomenon: the meaning of the word *sol* ('sun') is not physically present to the mind. Analogously, we may say that in the physical body the soul is immaterially present. It inhabits the body as the meaning of a word inhabits its spoken sound. Augustine extends the analogy. The division of the letters of a word deprives the sound of its meaning. The individual letters s,o,l, contain no separate parts of the meaning of the word *sol*: the word, thus divided, is 'dead', its meaning is lost rather than divided. Similarly, we can envisage a division of body which does not presuppose a division so much as a departure of that body's soul (§66):

> But when, with the loss of meaning, the sound in the letters is dispersed, do you consider that anything has happened, other than that the soul has departed because the body has been torn apart, and that a kind of death, so to speak, of the noun has occurred?

Now if the divided word *sol* corresponded to a body which, when divided, was dead, other divided words are parallel to the example of the divided, but still living parts of the centipede. Augustine's example is *Lucifer*, which, if divided into *luci* and *fer*, loses its original meaning, but none the less becomes two words, each with an independent and separate sense (§67). The analogy, though neat, is no solution. Problems remain: what, for example, is the relation of the meaning (= soul) of *Lucifer* to the meanings (= souls) of *luci* and *fer*? If the latter have meanings, they are, so to speak, new ones acquired after the division of the word: does the same apply, by analogy, to the souls of the divided centipedes? All we can say is that *Lucifer* has a meaning, but so have *luci* and *fer*. And we can certainly assert that the meaning of *Lucifer* is not divided into the meanings of *luci* and *fer*. Perhaps Augustine intends no more:

---

such problems, 'if advisable', at some future stage of their studies. Alypius and Augustine speculate – without obviously reaching firm conclusions – on the basis of their knowledge 'concerning the body, corporeal form, place, time, motion', of knowledge, that is, which is classified and clarified by means of the Aristotelian categories (see Lütcke 404 n. 115), and which is described in *ord.* 2.44 as the prerequisite of investigations into the nature of God and the soul. What their speculations consisted of we cannot know: the discussion is not recorded in any of the Cassiciacum dialogues. – For the question of the historicity of the dialogues see, on the one hand, O'Meara (1951) – for the case for a strong fictional element – and, on the other, Voss 197-303 and Madec, *BA* 6, 11-16 (literary casting of real conservations).

[78] Augustine's views on the relations between words and meanings are well discussed by Markus (1957) = Markus (1972) 61-91.

his analogy will suffice to show that physical division does not entail the division of concomitant immaterial entities. The meanings of words are not divisible as are their syllables; a soul is not divisible into parts of the body which it inhabits. The soul should be imagined to animate a body rather than occupy a space, just as the meaning of a word, though not itself extended, 'animates' (i.e. gives sense to) its letters, or their spoken sound (§68). The analogy extends thus far, but no further:

> You shouldn't expect in this instance the sort of very precise discussion which can take place on this subject, with the result that the matter is satisfactorily treated, directly and not by analogies (*similitudines*), which are for the most part misleading (ib.).

Augustine holds out the hope to Evodius that, when he has made further progress in philosophy, he may be able to judge whether

> it may be the case, as some very learned men say, that the soul is in no way divided by itself, but can nevertheless be divided in the body (ib.).

This suggests a view of soul's relation to body's divisibility such as that found in Plotinus or Porphyry, who may be behind the term 'very learned men' here.[79] But Augustine offers us no more than this tantalizing glimpse of his awareness of such Neoplatonic views. Elsewhere he will echo these views; thus soul is said to be totally present in every part of body, a form of presence incompatible with any materially extended presence of soul (*imm. an.* 25). And this total omnipresence is not spatial but 'tensional':

> It is spread throughout the entire body which it animates, not through any local extension, but by a kind of vital tension (*intentio*)(*ep.* 166.4).[80]

The refutation of Vincentius Victor's corporealist view of soul in the later work *nat. et or. an.* uses the example of dream-images to argue against the corporeal nature of soul. Perpetua's dream of herself as a man is only explicable in terms of a 'likeness of a male body' (4.26): it was her *anima*, Augustine asserts (not necessarily representing Vincentius' view: see below), which appeared to her to fight.[81] If the *anima* were corporeal, why, Augustine asks, did it not follow Vincentius' principle that the soul's form is adapted to its body, and keep its female form? Perpetua maintained her female bodily identity as she dreamt, and her soul remained embodied: on Vincentius' principle, her male dream-appearance cannot have direct bodily causes. It can only be accounted for in terms of a non-corporeal likeness in her imagining, dreaming consciousness. The dream-appearance of her dead brother Dinocrates, complete with his face-wound, is a further argument against

---

[79] Plotinus: *Enn.* 4.2.1.71-6, and, more fully, 4.3.19-24: see there esp. 19.6ff. Porphyry: *sent.* 5 (p. 2.10 L.). *Tim.* 35a is, of course, the starting-point of such reflections. Henry (1934) 74f. drew the parallel between *Enn.* 4.2.1.71ff. and *quant. an.* 68.

[80] See pp. 54f.

[81] For the literature on Perpetua's dream and its treatment in Augustine see p. 118 n. 24.

Vincentius' views, which maintained that the corporeal soul withdraws from wounded or amputated parts of the body. On these views, one would expect to dream a soul-appearance that is intact and undamaged, for a vulnerable soul, which would be mortal, cannot be acceptable to Vincentius (ib. 4.27).[82] The appearance of the wounded man is, again, most readily explicable as an appearance of a non-corporeal bodily likeness (ib.), and this latter also serves to explain the variety of such dream-appearances, for the mutilated also appear, for example, whole:

> What else does that fact teach, but that, just as the soul produces a likeness, and not the reality, of the other things which it perceives in dreams, this too is the case with the (sc. Dinocrates') body with which we are dealing? (ib. 4.29)

The notion of a corporeal soul adapted to its body and growing with it is satirized by Augustine at *nat. et or. an.* 4.28. Its withdrawal from a wounded or amputated part encourages the notion of a fully adult soul with a child's hand, if the hand was amputated in childhood – for the soul-part of the amputated limb will cease to develop if deprived of its bodily correspondent part:

> It is not, believe me, the bodily form which makes such souls, but the deformity of error which imagines them (ib.).

It is unlikely that the viewpoint put forward by Vincentius Victor would admit such grotesque consequences. His theory of soul-withdrawal is clearly an attempt to develop a notion of a corporeal, body-moulded soul which is nevertheless invulnerable. He is not concerned with working out the aesthetic implications of amputation, as Augustine chooses mockingly to insinuate. Nor (to return to the dreams of Perpetua) is it clear that Vincentius would have argued for the direct causal link between soul-form and dream appearance; he, or his source, might have had an account of dream-images that involved the imaginative faculty at work on corporeal appearances derived from waking perception. Such an account would have explained both the nature of Dinocrates' appearance and the male appearance of Perpetua herself. Augustine then would have to come to terms with the account's refusal to allow non-corporeal processes, i.e. he would have to combat a corporealist version of dream-images. Elsewhere he argues against such a view of the imagination and its objects:[83] his polemic against Vincentius

---

[82] Perhaps Augustine argues here that Dinocrates' appearance in Perpetua's dream is a soul-appearance because Dinocrates is already dead when the dream occurs, and it was popularly believed that appearances of the dead in dreams were caused by the dead themselves, and so were visionary in character. If, however, that is so, then Augustine's argument is *ad hoc*, for the exclusive purpose of silencing Vincentius: he himself argued against such a view (see below pp. 118f.).

[83] See pp. 95f. below and Chapter 4 *passim*. Cf. also here, §25: the argument is the familiar one that the objects in our dreams or in our imagination cannot be physically present in our minds, given their size, variety and number.

seems, however, to distort, if not actually to falsify, the latter's position.[84] There seems to be no reason, for example, for asserting that it must be Perpetua's *anima* that appears to her to fight in her dream. The claim of 4.26:

> Who would doubt, however, that it had been her soul in that likeness of her body, and not her body ...?

is necessarily the case only if by 'body' the actual bodily presence and literal involvement of Perpetua (A) is meant – but this is absurd. If, however, we maintain that the soul is corporeal, the antithesis breaks down, and while avoiding the absurdity of claiming that Perpetua is actually fighting in her dream, we can none the less assert that she is corporeally involved, in that her corporeal imagination activates corporeal likenesses (B). Thus Augustine cannot force Vincentius to opt between the alternatives of §26:

> Was that likeness of a man a real body, or was it not a body, although it had the appearance of a body?

For 'body' can connote A: but it can also connote B, and so be acceptable to Vincentius without entailing the ridiculous and self-contradictory consequences of A.

(vii) The soul and divine substance

The theory that the human soul is of the same nature and substance as God is familiar to Augustine from Manichaeism, where, as he maintains, the view is held that the good soul in humans is a part of God.[85]

> They say that there are two kinds of soul, the one good in that it is from God in such a way that it is not made by him, either out of any matter, or out of nothing, but that a part of his very substance is said to have gone out from him (*duab. an.* 12.16).

> They suppose that there are two souls in the one body, one from God, which is of its nature identical with him (*vera rel.* 16).

> That good (sc. soul) is formed out of a part of God extraneous (sc. to us) (*retr.* 1.15.1).

Augustine also sees such a view as a consequence of Stoic pantheism, even if it is not actually desired by the Stoics (*civ.* 7.13; 7.23). But with his rejection of Manichaeism, and of the materialist concept of God, Augustine also comes to reject the equation of the divine and human natures. As he develops a notion of God which stresses the latter's necessarily invulnerable, unchangeable, transcendent nature – so that God can neither be the

---

[84] See p. 22 and n. 67.

[85] For Augustine's understanding of the 'two souls' doctrine in Manichaeism see the survey by Decret 1.324-6, who argues, against the prevailing view, that Augustine is not here fundamentally distorting genuine Manichaean doctrine.

Manichaean Light Principle, at constant war with the powers of Darkness, nor the immanent, corporeal Stoic Logos-Deity (*conf.* 7.1-3) – Augustine comes to believe more and more explicitly that between divine creator and human soul a great gulf is fixed. It is therefore precisely because an equation of human and divine natures would render the latter unacceptably mutable that Augustine rejects the equation: his view of the nature of the human soul is, at least in part, a consequence of his view of divine nature. This is clear from the discussion of Genesis 2:7 in *Gn. c. Man.* 2.10-11.[86] Augustine is disturbed by the implications, for God's nature, of an interpretation of this verse in Manichaean terms:

> Our understanding of this passage, therefore, ought not lead us to believe that because it is said, 'He breathed into him the spirit of life, and man was made into a living soul' (Genesis 2:7), that (sc. breath), like a part of God's nature, was changed into man's soul, and we are forced to say that God's nature is mutable. The Manichaeans in particular are logically driven to such an error. For, as arrogance is the mother of all heretics, they dared to assert that the soul is of divine nature. Hence they are plied with arguments by us, who say to them, 'So the divine nature makes mistakes and is unhappy, and is corrupted by the stain of its faults, and commits sins; or again, as you say, contrary natures are alike befouled by pollution'. And (they say) other such things, which it is sinful to believe concerning God's nature (ib. 11).

Human mutability here is understood chiefly in terms of moral ups and downs, which it would be absurd to attribute to a divine nature:

> And the very spirit of man, now erring, now knowledgeable, proclaims that it is changeable: something one may in no way believe concerning God's nature. For there can be no greater indication of arrogance than that the human soul should declare that it is what God is, even as it groans under the enormous weight of its sins and wretchedness (ib.).

Thus Genesis 2:7, a potentially ambiguous text (the inbreathing of the divine breath or life-spirit might seem to make man's 'living soul' part of God's nature), must be interpreted in a way which avoids any equation of divine and human natures: other scriptural texts, as Augustine notes (ib.) are less equivocal. In *Gn. litt.* 7.2.3-3.5 Augustine argues that if there is in humans a clear distinction between *anima* and corporeal *flatus*, and if the former is the cause of the latter but not materially identifiable with it, by analogy God may be said to be distinguishable from the *creatura* that is the formed human soul which he is metaphorically said to 'breathe'. But this subtle explanation will not always have been satisfactory: that Genesis 2:7 could be problematic is clear from *ep.* 205.19 where the possible implication 'divine substance' = 'human soul' is strenuously countered, not because of the wording of the scriptural passage, but, once again, on account of its consequences for divine nature:

---

[86] For Augustine's exegesis of Genesis 2:7 in relation to discussions of the human soul's origin see pp. 15-20, and O'Daly (1983) 185; 187-9.

You also want to know from me whether that divine breath in Adam is the same as his soul. My reply is brief: either it is the same or the soul is made by it. But, even if it is the same, it is created ... for in this inquiry we must above all avoid believing that the soul is not a natural entity created by God, but God's very substance ... or some particle of him, as if that nature or substance, in so far as it is God, could be changeable, as the soul is perceived to be by everybody who is aware that he has a soul.

Here, more naturally than in *Gn. litt.* 7.3.4, the divine breath (*flatus*) is not distinguished from the divine substance, and so it is said to be the cause of the human soul rather than to be identifiable with it.

Vincentius Victor appears to have maintained an interpretation of Genesis 2:7 in which the divine breath somehow becomes the human soul. This interpretation amounted to a form of creationist thesis: the human soul, which Vincentius believed to be corporeal, is not of the same nature as the divine *spiritus* (*nat. et or. an.* 1.4; 1.24; 2.5). Augustine may be distorting Vincentius' view when he summarizes it as follows:

... the soul is not ... made by God in such manner that he created it out of nothing, but is from his own self ... it is a kind of particle of God's natural exhalation ... when he (sc. God) makes the exhalation or breath from himself, he himself remains entire (ib. 3.3).

But Vincentius must have made the last point concerning God's 'undiminished giving', for the example of the inflated paunch (*uter*, §4) is clearly a quoted one: Vincentius will have argued that no loss is suffered by the person whose breath inflates it. Augustine attacks the analogy with breathing: the latter is a necessarily continuous process of inhalation and exhalation, interruption of which at any stage would be fatal (cf. *Gn. litt.* 7.3.4, where the same account of breathing is considered self-evident). By what measure of imagination could God's breathing, even analogously, be compared with this physiological process? Augustine adds that the analogy tends to make God one with the human soul (even if this is not what Vincentius intends) and thus render him 'the material of his own work', §3. The alternative (already denied by Vincentius, *nat. et or. an.* 2.6; 2.9) would be that the air breathed by God is pre-existent, and so created, one must assume, 'from nothing' (*ex nihilo*) – that it is, so to speak, already there like the air which we breathe. In this latter case, use of the paunch-metaphor to refute the *ex nihilo* argument becomes superfluous. Augustine's critique is undoubtedly right inasmuch as it sees in Vincentius' argument the weakness (a) of the unexplained relation of God to his 'breath' (*flatus*) – in what way is it related to his nature? – and (b) of the relation between divine, and so presumably immaterial, breath and the corporeal human soul. But even if problem (b) need not exist as such for Augustine, inasmuch as, for him, the human soul is itself immaterial, he none the less does not resolve (a), as the differing speculations of *Gn. litt.* 7.3.4 and *ep.* 205.19 show.

Be this as it may, Augustine, even when dealing with such intractable problems as the origin of the soul,[87] can nevertheless assert as fundamental principles that the soul is created; that it is immaterial; that it is not of divine substance and possesses, in itself, no 'natural worth' commensurable with God's (*ep.* 190.4). The Manichaean (and Priscillianist) view is dismissed in the later works as absurd (see *ep.* 166.7 and the fuller argument ib. §3) and worthy only of polemical abuse, even if the fundamental reason for rejecting it – the resultant mutability of God – remains the same (see *Gn. litt.* 7.11.17).

(viii) Soul's mutability, form and natural goodness

We have seen that Augustine repeatedly asserts that the human soul is changeable or mutable. In what does this mutability consist? It includes, as has been observed, moral deterioration and progress. Broadly speaking, Augustine can distinguish two kinds (*genera*) of mutability in the soul:

> For indeed the soul can be said to be changed in accordance with the body's affections, or in accordance with its own (*imm. an.* 7).

In the former group the examples given are: ageing, sickness, pain, fatigue, distress and pleasure. In the latter group are included: the affections, such as desire, joy, fear, anger – but also diligence and learning. Thus the soul's changeable nature is affected both by the interaction of bodily and psychological states, as well as by the influence of the former upon the latter, and by specifically psychological conditions, including what we would call mental processes, such as volition or learning. This is consistent with what Augustine says elsewhere:

> Everybody knows, however, that the soul can be changed, not indeed locally, but nevertheless temporally by its emotions (*vera. rel.* 18).

> But what happens to soul in the case of the emotions happens to body with regard to place, for the former is moved by the will, but the body is moved in space (ib. 28).

> They (sc. the philosophers of the soul) discovered that it too is mutable; now willing, now not willing; now knowing, now not knowing; now remembering, now forgetting; now fearing, now daring; now advancing towards wisdom, now declining into folly (*ser.* 241.2).

The soul is mutable, even if it is immaterial, because its existence is durational: in other words, it has a temporal medium within which it can change.

> But that day, by whose name all time, as we have said, is signified, reveals to us that not only the visible but also the invisible creation can experience time. This is made clear to us regarding the soul, which is demonstrably changed in time, both by the great variety of its emotions, and by the very fall through which it

[87] For his (ultimately agnostic) views on this topic see O'Daly (1983).

became wretched, as well as by the restoration whereby it returns to a state of blessedness ... that we might thus realize that not only the visible, but also the invisible creation has to do with time on account of its changeability. For only God, who is before all time, is unchangeable (*Gn. c. Man.* 2.7).

The soul is moved through time, whether by remembering what it has forgotten, or learning what it did not know, or willing what it did not will (*Gn. litt.* 8.20.39).

Conversely, the mutability of soul is an indication that an immaterial entity can have a temporal existence. The soul's immortality cannot therefore be equated with divine immortality, which excludes change of any kind. We can speak of the soul's metaphorical death through sin and alienation from God: indeed, strictly speaking, the soul is not eternal, if by eternity is meant a stable, non-durational existence in a timeless present.

The human soul is immortal in some manner peculiar to itself ... but since it dies through estrangement from the life of God, without however entirely ceasing to live its own natural life, it is found, with good reason, to be mortal and at the same time said to be immortal (*ep.* 166.3).

(Soul is immortal) after some manner of its own (but it can die) ... how does it die? Not by ceasing to be life, but by losing its life (i.e. God), *ser.* 65.4f.

For so great a thing is the soul that it is capable of providing life for the body, even when it is dead (ib. §6).

Everyone without God has a dead soul (ib. §7).[88]

But even if the soul can be said to die metaphorically through sin and loss of God and happiness, it is, if not *per se* eternal, nevertheless *de facto* immortal and sempiternal.

For that which undergoes change in any respect is not properly called eternal. Therefore, in so far as we are changeable, to that extent are we far from eternity (*trin.* 4.24).

For ... the very immortality of the soul is meant in a certain sense, since the soul too has its own death when it lacks a happy life, which should be called the true life of the soul; but it is called immortal because it never ceases to live with some kind of life, even when it is most wretched (*trin.* 14.6).

And that is the difference between the immortal and the eternal, that everything that is eternal is immortal, but not everything immortal is with sufficient accuracy called eternal; for even if something lives for ever, yet undergoes change, it is not properly called eternal, because it is not always in the same state. Yet it could correctly be called immortal, for it lives for ever (*div. qu.* 19).

[88] Cf. *trin.* 4.5; 4.16.

In what way do its changes change the soul? Presumably soul will not be changed in the way that material things are, where X ceases to be X and begins to be Y. Augustine suggests that in such cases the process includes an intermediate stage:

formed Y $\rightarrow$ formless but none the less existent P $\rightarrow$ formed Y.

Here P is like the substrate or formless matter of philosophical speculation (*conf.* 12.6). But soul can never become formless: even in its most corrupt condition, its 'death', it nevertheless lives, and gives life and cohesion to body. To characterize the identity-in-change of soul Augustine has recourse to a technical distinction drawn from Aristotle's *Categories*.[89] In *imm. an.* 7 he distinguishes between *animus* as 'subject' (*subiectum*) and science or art (*ars*) as being 'in the subject' (*in subiecto*). The phrase *in subiecto* is equivalent to Aristotle's *en hupokeimenôi* (*cat.* 2, 1a20ff.), which 'serves to distinguish qualities, quantities, and items in other categories from substances, which exist independently and in their own right',[90] and Augustine's example is taken from Aristotle (1a 25-6: 'For example, the individual knowledge-of-grammer is in a subject, the soul', tr. J.L. Ackrill). What is 'in a subject' cannot exist separately from what it is in (ib.).

> It is clear that not only is an art in the mind of the artist, but also that it is nowhere else but in his mind, and inseparably at that (*imm. an.* 5; cf. §9).

Augustine employs this distinction in the following manner. If S = 'subject' (here: *animus*) and Q = that which is 'in the subject', as a quality (here: *ars*), then, Augustine argues, S cannot change without Q changing. But what constitutes a change of S? There can be changes of Q^1, Q^2 ... Q^n without substantial change of S: Augustine adduces the example of wax, which remains substantially wax, even if changes occur in its colour, shape and texture. This type of change is to be distinguished from a substantial change of S, such that the latter loses its identity and can no longer be called by its former name (ib. §8): thus wax ceases to be wax, and can no longer be called 'wax', if it evaporates under heat. Augustine clearly takes the continuing applicability of an object's name to be a sign of its continuing identity:

> Some change can therefore occur in those things which are in the subject, although the latter itself, the conveyor of identity and the name, is not changed (ib.).

---

[89] Augustine read the *Categories* privately as a young man at Carthage: *conf.* 4.28. He may have read them in a translation by Marius Victorinus: so Courcelle (1948) 156, but Hadot (1977) 188 is sceptical. The use of the *Categories* in the passage under discussion was pointed out by Du Roy 177f.

[90] J.L. Ackrill, *Aristotle's Categories and De Interpretatione*. Translated with notes, Oxford 1963, 74.

Now substantial change of S, and substantial change only, entails change of Q. But qualitative, quantitative change, etc., do not for their part entail substantial change. Now it is precisely qualitative change that Augustine wishes to attribute to soul; what is 'in soul' as in a subject may (but need not necessarily) change: that is to say, soul's affections, its will, or its moral and intellectual condition may alter. These changes do not, however, affect the substantial identity of soul. On the contrary, they presuppose the identity of the subject in separation from which they cannot exist.[91]

The subject or substance soul is the giver of life and form (*species*) to the body. It has its own characteristic form also, and this it has received as a creation of God, or – as the more Platonically coloured language of *imm. an.* 24 would put it – from the sovereign or highest Life or Good or Beauty ('the highest life, which is wisdom and unchanging goodness ... the form which it (sc. the soul) gets from the highest good'; §25: 'More powerful entities, therefore, transmit to weaker ones the form which they have received from the highest beauty, through a kind of natural succession'). The formed soul, in transmitting form, is not diminished in any way, nor does it lose its own form:

> If the soul transmits form to body, that the body may exist to the extent that it does, it by no means deprives itself of form in the process (ib. 24).

These assertions are, in a sense, the answer to what was presented as a problem in *duab. an.* 2-3 concerning the nature and source of the *forma* found in souls and bodies. Just as the soul's immortality is not that of God, so also its form is not that of the highest Good: the soul is, rather, 'like God' (*quant. an.* 3). It is in this sense that Augustine understands the words of Genesis 1:26, that man is made in God's image and likeness. Man, like God, has power over subordinate creation in virtue of his possession of reason (*Gn. c. Man.* 1.27-8), and indeed he has limited creative powers of his own, as when, for example, the human soul forms and enlivens body.

If soul is formed, immortal, godlike, it cannot, in its nature, be bad. Augustine will repeatedly and decisively reject the Manichaean view that there are two kinds of soul, of which one kind, identifiable with the Principle of Darkness, is intrinsically evil.[92] Soul is naturally good, because everything that exists is, to some degree, good, and the very corruptibility of things is an indication that they have a goodness capable of being corrupted:

> And pain itself is evidence of the good which has been taken away and of the good which has been left ... the pain at good lost through punishment is evidence of a good nature (*civ.* 19.13; cf. *conf.* 7.18).

Corruptible goodness is, however, less than pefectly good. Soul, in other words, is a good that is lower than the highest God in virtue of its mutability

---

[91] For the application of this argument to the relation of knowledge to the mind see Chapter 7, pp. 178-89.
[92] See n.85 above.

and potential moral corruptibility, but higher than corporeal goods in virtue of its immateriality and powers:

> The soul ... created by the highest good, is not, however, the highest good, but rather a great good ... living between the highest and the lower goods, that is, between God and the flesh, inferior to God, superior to the flesh (*ser.* 156.6).

> These (sc. more powerful natures) ... which do not have greater capabilities than lesser material masses because of larger bulk, but, without any spatially extended tumidity, are more powerful in virtue of that same form whereby they are also better. In this category is the soul, better and more powerful than the body (*imm. an.* 25).[93]

(ix) Soul's middle state

The situation of the human soul in the hierarchy of being often leads Augustine to talk of its mean or medial position between God and body.

> The rational soul, established in some kind of middle place, has received the law to hold fast to that which is higher, to govern that which is lower (*en. Ps.* 145.5).

> Nor is anything found to be between the highest life, which is wisdom and unchanging goodness, and that which is the lowest recipient of life, that is, the body, apart from the life-giving soul (*imm. an.* 24).

> The rational soul ... has been placed in some kind of middle state, inasmuch as it has the bodily creation beneath it, but its own and the body's creator above it (*ep.* 140.3).

The notion of the medial position of the soul is Middle and Neoplatonic, and is found in Plotinus, Origen and Calcidius.[94] The *medietas* of soul is primarily ontological, between divine and corporeal being, but the human powers of reason and will convey the freedom, and its attendant risks, which allow the soul, in consequence of its moral behaviour, to maintain or sink below its proper level in the hierarchy. Thus Augustine can talk of the soul's *providentia*, which is *voluntarily* exercised in e.g. the quest for knowledge, in social communication, education and culture, and in the search for bodily protection, and which is analogous to the divine *providentia* that is *naturally* operative in the universe, in the formation, growth and decay of man's body, and in the sentient life of man's soul (*Gn. litt.* 8.9.17). Man's medial position means that he can opt to be the means of *providentia* at the level appropriate to him, and over the things within his power. The infant instinctively avoids unpleasantness (*offensiones*) and seeks after pleasure (*voluptas*), and can thus attain to temporal happiness (*ep.* 140.3). But upon reaching the age of reason

[93] On the notion that everything that is is good to a certain degree, and that degrees of being or goodness are degrees of form see Theiler (1933) 11ff. = Theiler (1966) 173ff. For the application of these principles to soul see Theiler (1933) 20ff. = Theiler (1966) 184ff.

[94] See Theiler (1970).

and acquiring the ability to will and choose, the individual may opt either to prefer the goods of the mind ('the goods of the inner and higher nature ... that it may enjoy divinity and eternity', ib.) – equated here with divine substance – or to prefer those of the body ('the goods of the external and lower (sc. nature) ... that it may enjoy the body and time'). The morally right choice is evidently in favour of the former, while making proper use (*bene uti*, ib. §4) of the latter.[95] In this way the soul maintains its level, ethically speaking (*ordinem servare*, ib.), in its choice of preferred goods.[96] Rather than degrading itself and its body through the *perversitas* of preferring bodily to divine goods, it 'turns itself and its body towards the better' (ib.) by its tendance of the latter.

Even its self-centered tendency degrades the soul. For pride (*superbia*), which Augustine often defines as the root of sin, and which he equates with the 'perverse imitation of God' (e.g. *conf.* 2.13-14), is ultimately a desire for self-mastery in an order where one, as a human being, is emphatically not the master.[97] Pride is not to be confused with the soul's just and pious aspiration towards the highest spiritual values:

> The soul, which is a spiritual substance, should be raised up to those things which are high among matters spiritual, not by the exaltation of pride, but by the dutifulness of justice (*trin.* 12.1).

Rather, love of God is preferable to love of self, and, paradoxically, absorption with one's own medial position is tantamount to moral degradation to animal level:

> The less, therefore, it loves what is its own, the more it cleaves to God. But through the desire to put its own power to the test, it falls down to itself as to some middle state by a kind of inherent tendency. And so while it wishes to be as he (sc. God) is, under nobody, it is driven down by way of punishment even from its own middle level to the lowest degree, that is, to those things in which the animals delight (*trin.* 12.16).

The testing of, or experiment with, oneself as the centre of one's own existence (*illud suae medietatis experimentum*) brings about a loss of one's own value or worth, a loss, that is, of what can be achieved and maintained only by preference of the transcendent, divine good:

> So the oppressed soul is thrust out by its own weight, so to speak, from happiness, and through that testing of its own intermediate state comes to learn by its punishment what the difference is between the good it has left behind and

[95] For the concepts *uti-frui* behind this text see Bourke (1979) 29-65; Lorenz (1950/51); O'Donovan; id., '*Usus* and *Fruitio* in Augustine, *De Doctrina Christiana*, I', *Journal of Theological Studies* N.S. 33 (1982) 361-97; G. Pfligersdorffer, 'Zu den Grundlagen des augustinischen Begriffspaares *uti-frui*', *Wiener Studien* N.F. 5 (1971) 195-224.

[96] The concept *ordo* in Augustine's early writings is analysed by Rief.

[97] For pride as the cause of Adam's fall see Dinkler 82-90. For pride in the human condition see the articles of D.J. Macqueen, '*Contemptus Dei*: St. Augustine on the Disorder of Pride in Society and its Remedies', *RechAug* 9 (1973) 227-93; 'Augustine on *Superbia*: The Historical

the evil it has committed (ib).

Once again we must understand such degradation (and any corresponding improvement) as ethical rather than ontological. It is a change in the quality of the subject, soul, which does not affect its substantial nature.

> For just as a sentient nature is better, even when it feels pain, than a stone which can in no way feel pain, so a rational nature, even when it is wretched, is superior to that which is devoid of reason or sensation, and can on that account experience no wretchedness (*civ.* 12.1).

> We must necessarily admit that a weeping human is better than a happy worm (*vera rel.* 77).

> But, among lower and mortal bodies, it (sc. the soul), subsequent to original sin, if it is well ordered, governs its body, not entirely at will, but as the laws of the universe permit. However, such a soul is not on that account lower than a heavenly body, to which even earthly bodies are subject (*lib. arb.* 3.34).

Thus the given ontological medial position of soul cannot be altered, but soul lives in a further dimension – the dimension of values and of moral status consequent upon choice – where its position is changeable and is determined by its actions. Only if its choices are right will its ethical and ontological positions, so to speak, coincide: that is to say, its behaviour and moral standing will reflect its proper place in the scale of being. Augustine sums up this aspect of his psychology and ethics with classic precision in *ep.* 140.4:

> Just as everything created by God, from the rational creation itself to the lowest body, is good, so does the rational soul act well in this connexion, if it preserves right order, and in its discrimination, deliberation and choice subordinates the lesser to the greater, the bodily to the spiritual, the lower to the higher, the temporal to the eternal, that it may avoid precipitating itself and its body into a worse state through neglect of higher things and desire for what is lower – for it is thereby made worse itself – but that it may rather, through a well ordered love (*ordinata caritate*), turn itself and its body to what is better.

(x) Soul's relation to body; the emotions

We have seen that the soul's activities and powers are for Augustine a proof of its immaterial nature. The soul does not grow as the body grows, it is not spatially extended and it is not divisible.[98] On the contrary, it is entirely present in every bodily part. The symbiosis of body and soul may be compared to that of a spoken word and its meaning.[99] It is now time to look at

---

Background and Sources of his Doctrine', *Mélanges de Science Religieuse* 34 (1977) 193-211 and ib. 35 (1978) 78. Cf. *mus.* 6.40; *mor.* 1.20, where *audacia* = *superbia*. On the relation to the Neoplatonic concept of the soul's *tolma* see Theiler (1933) 28-30 = Theiler (1966) 194-6.
  [98] See pp. 23-9.
  [99] See pp. 28f.

Augustine's attempts to formulate, in a definitional sense, the nature of this symbiosis.

In the early treatise *de immortalitate animae* Augustine argues formally that the soul cannot be a condition of the body: mind is not a physical harmony (*harmonia, imm. an.* 2).[100] Body is necessarily mutable, but *ratio* (here meaning 'what is grasped by the mind'), which is either to be equated with, or else is inseparably contained in, the mind, is necessarily immutable. As an example of immutable *ratio* Augustine proffers the necessary truth of arithmetical equations. Now he also understands *ratio* ('reason') in a substantial sense here ('our reason is better than our body', §2), but he wishes to stress the sense of *ratio* being a product of the activity of reasoning (§1: *ratiocinatio*), i.e. truth. Thus arithmetical equations are *ratio immutabilis*, 'an invariable computation', and so *ratio*, 'rational truth'. Now if that which is inseparably contained in the subject cannot change, the subject cannot change.[101] Therefore the *animus* – if *ratio* be inseparably contained in it (and *a fortiori*, if *ratio* be equated with it) – cannot change. What is asserted not to change here is the mind, the faculty which cognizes analytical truths: arguing for its immutability in no way implies that the soul is not mutable in other respects. Neither, of course, does it imply that parts of the soul other than its mind are necessarily immortal. Furthermore, one must observe that this argument does not in itself demonstrate that other parts of the soul are not corporeal harmonies. The last point has to be substantiated from Augustine's account of the other activities of soul, and the way in which these necessarily presuppose an incorporeal substance. At *c. ep. fund.* 17.20, for example, Augustine argues that the phenomenon of memory, which deals in incorporeal images, entails that the soul's intellectual power is an incorporeal capability, inasmuch as it discerns the truth or non-truth of the images. Augustine could also argue for soul's complete incorporeality on the ground that soul is such a unity that, if one part of it is of a certain nature, the others must necessarily share the attributes of that nature: but he does not incline to that argument, presumably because soul's irrational powers cannot be said to share in those of reason.

There is a further, modified version of the harmony argument in *imm. an.* 17, where Augustine maintains that life = soul is not a bodily 'tempering' (*temperatio*). Once again the argument focuses upon cognitive activity and the mind's relation to its objects. Augustine suggests that the whole exercise of withdrawal of attention from sense-activity, of detachment from bodily habit, which leads to sharper intellection of truths, would be nonsensical, indeed impossible, if mind were not a separate substance but a mixture of the four corporeal elements, viz. a quality like colour or shape. He recalls the argument of §2 about the invariable nature of truth and the non-local

---

[100] Behind the notion stands the Pythagorean theory of soul as 'attunement' presented and criticized in *Phaedo* 86aff. There is no indication that Augustine read the *Phaedo* in Apuleius' lost translation (see Courcelle (1948) 158), but the *harmonia* theory will have been familiar to him, if not from a doxographical account, then from Cicero, *Tusc. disp.* 1.19; 24; 41, where it is accredited to Aristoxenus. Another possible source is Plotinus, *Enn.* 4.7.8⁴.2-5.

[101] See pp. 36-7.

relation of mind to its contents. There follow two concise analytical arguments based on the following observations about the possible nature of this relation. Either (A) *intellegibilia* (truths apprehended by the mind) are in the mind or (B) the mind is in them. And either (a) one is in the other as in a subject (i.e. the relation is one between a substance and its quality) or (b) both are substances. Now, if (a), then the mind cannot be in the body as in a subject, as colour and shape are, for either (A) the mind is a substance (for the *intellegibilia* are in it qua subject) or (B) the mind is a quality of the incorporeal *intellegibilia*, and so cannot simultaneously be a quality of body. If (b), then the mind cannot be in the body as in a subject, for it is itself a substance. Therefore mind is not a 'tempering' of body, for 'tempering', like colour, is a bodily quality, and would be in the body qua subject.

This second argument concerning the nature of mind is subject to the same limitations as were noted above in the case of *imm. an.* 2. Augustine, of course, believes that the component parts of bodies form a due proportion (*temperamentum*) and that this is due to the presence of soul. But soul can continue to be present in a body where the proportion is temporarily disturbed and it cannot carry out its controlling function: this is, for example, the case with bodily disorders which lead to the soul's suffering pain or distress. This phenomenon shows that the presence of soul is not to be equated with bodily proportion:

> When it (the soul) is troubled by the experience of bodily distress, it is hurt because its activity, through which it is a controlling presence in body, is hindered by the disturbance of the latter's proportion; and this sense of hurt is called pain (*Gn. litt.* 7.19.25).

Indeed, the very occurrence of pain as an expression of the soul's difficulty in carrying out its ruling function over body merely highlights that controlling function; the soul causes bodily cohesion and harmony rather than being in any sense a product of body:

> For even the very bodily pain in any living being is a great and wondrous power of soul, which holds together with vital force that structure through an indescribable mixture and brings it to some kind of unity in its measure, since not indifferently, but, so to speak, with indignation does it suffer it to be corrupted and destroyed (*Gn. litt.* 3.16.25).

Augustine's talk in this last passage of an 'indescribable mixture' introduces a key term in his attempts to specify the nature of the body-soul relationship. In *ep.* 137.11, defending the doctrine of Christ's incarnation against its pagan critics, he argues that the union of two natures in the single person of Christ is no less incredible and mysterious than the union or 'mixture' – accepted by these pagan critics – of body and soul, two substances, in the single human person:

> In the unity of the person the body uses the soul, so that the human being can exist ... in that person, then, there is a mixture of soul and body ... the listener

should leave to one side the usual behaviour of bodies, where two liquids normally so combine that neither keeps its purity, although even among bodily substances themselves light is mixed with air without adulteration.[102]

We shall discuss the implications of this definition of man, as well as of the term *persona*, below:[103] for the present it will suffice to deal with the concept of the 'mixture' of body and soul here mentioned. It is a concept of a union in which each nature maintains its identity: Augustine offers the analogy of the mixing of air and light, as opposed to that of two liquids where each loses its characteristics in the new mixture.[104] It is to E.L. Fortin's credit that he first drew attention to the influence of the Neoplatonic doctrine of the *asugkhutos henôsis* of soul and body, as formulated by Porphyry, upon this text.[105] Augustine's distinctions are less subtle than Porphyry's: the latter distinguishes between irreversible union (*henôsis* in the strict sense), whereby the specific nature of the unified substances is irrevocably lost, and a mixture (*krasis*) such as that of wine and water, which are separable by means of application of a sponge impregnated with oil.[106] Augustine gives the example of the mixed liquids as one where neither keeps its purity (*integritas*). It is not explicitly said that this mixture is irrevocable; indeed in the case of body and soul *krasis* of subsequently separable substances would seem to be the one possibly acceptable alternative to the theory adopted by Porphyry and Augustine. But Augustine simply fails to draw the Porphyrian distinction between irrevocable and separable mixtures. Moreover, in adopting the 'uncompounded unity' (*unio inconfusa*) concept Augustine follows Porphyry in being aware of its paradoxical nature, but, whereas in Porphyry this kind of union seems to contravene all natural laws, in Augustine it even has an analogy in nature in the mixture of light and air.[107]

This metaphysical mixture[108] of an incorporeal and a corporeal substance is also expressed in a favourite term of Augustine's: *intentio*. The term can mean 'tension' or even 'extension', as well as 'mental concentration', the sense which it will be seen to have in the discussion of awareness and

---

[102] Cf. the terms for 'mixture' (*commixtio, permixtio, mixtio*), ib. See also *ser.* 186.1; *Io. ev. tr.* 19.15.

[103] pp. 54-60.

[104] The analogy is particularly apt if we recall that, for Plotinus, the mixture of light and air is a mixture of an incorporeal entity, light (see *Enn.* 4.5.7), with a corporeal one.

[105] See Fortin, who compares *ep.* 137.11 with Porphyry *ap.* Nemes. *nat. hom.* 3 (p. 127.3ff. Matthaei) and Priscian, *solut. ad. Chosroem*, p. 51.4ff. Bywater. The Porphyrian nature of chs. 2-3 of Nemesius was subsequently elucidated by Dörrie (1959) esp. 39ff. See also Pépin (1964) 55f. = Pépin (1977) 215f.

[106] See Dörrie (1959) 42f.; 45; 47; 54. The Porphyrian distinctions seem to derive from Chrysippus' analysis of different kinds of mixture, *SVF* 2.471-3.

[107] Cf. *Gn. litt.* 3.16.25 ('indescribable mixture') with Porph. *ad Gaur.* 10.5 (p. 47.21f. K.): 'that divine and paradoxical mixture peculiar to animated beings'. For the contravention of natural laws see Dörrie (1959) 173f. Augustine also employs the Porphyrian notion in *trin.* 11, which is roughly contemporaneous with *ep.* 137, to account for the union of *mens, notitia* and *amor* as an image of the Trinity in man: see Pépin (1964) 92-100 = Pépin (1977) 252-60.

[108] On the question whether it derives from the teaching of Ammonius Sakkas, as Nemes. *nat. hom.* 3 (p. 129.9 M.) seems to imply, see now the negative conclusions of Schwyzer (1983) 51-63.

sense-perception in Chapter 3.[109] It is, for example, clearly employed in the sense of 'tension' in *ep.* 166.4:

> Indeed it is spread through the entire body which it animates, not through any local extension, but by a kind of vital tension; for it is simultaneously entirely present throughout all its parts, and is not smaller in the smaller parts or larger in the larger ones, but is in one place more tense and in another more slack, and is totally present, both in all and in the individual parts.

The point of contrast between *intentio* and *diffusio* here is that the latter connotes a physical 'spreading out' of one substance in another, whereas the former is used to express the concept of the soul's omnipresence in every part of the body which it animates. Elsewhere, as, for example, in *mus.* 6.9, *intentio* indicates the volitional power of soul's animating presence to body:

> For I do not believe that this body is animated by the soul, except through the intention of the agent (*nisi intentione facientis*). Nor do I consider that it (sc. soul) is in any way acted upon by it (sc. body), but that it is active from and in the body, as if the latter were by divine providence subject to its dominion.

In other texts, as in *Gn. litt.* 8.21.42, it is almost impossible to separate the 'tensional' and 'intentional' connotations of the term:

> ... the soul is not a corporeal nature and does not fill the body spatially, as water fills a skin or a sponge, but is mixed with the body which it has to vivify in some extraordinary way by its own incorporeal will (*nutu*), by which it also issues commands to the body through some kind of *intentio*, and not through bulk ... that very tendency of its will (*nutus ipse voluntatis*) is not moved locally.

Although the local presence of soul to body is variously expressed by Plotinus and Porphyry, there is no term among those most commonly used in their writings that can be compared with Augustine's use of *intentio* here.[110] In *Timaeus* 34b the Demiurge is said to extend the world soul throughout the universe, and the relaxion of the tension whereby soul animates body is adduced in Peripatetic explanations of the mantic powers of soul in sleep.[111] But perhaps the most striking and plausible forerunner of Augustine's *intentio* concept here is the Stoic doctrine of the tension (*tonos*) of soul, in which both the soul's cohesion and its intellectual powers are included, even if,

---

[109] See pp. 84-7.

[110] The candidates are: *pareinai/parousia, koinônein/koinônia, dedesthai, skhesis, rhopê, diathesis, dunamis, energeia.* See Dörrie (1959) 87-93; 95; 98f. For *skhesis* see also Schwyzer (1983) 79-81. Cf. further Blumenthal 16-19; Smith 1-19. Porphyry, *sent.* 28 (p. 17.6f. L.) speaks of the descended soul's 'extension (*ektasis*)' in body. But the term has here a pejorative connotation lacking in Augustine, and is, further, without the 'intentional' dimension of *intentio*. On the other hand, the latter implication is behind accounts of the soul's wilful descent or 'fall' in Porphyry: see *sent.* 3 (p. 2.2 L.), where it is said of incorporeals that they are not locally present to bodies, but that 'they are present to them whenever they so will, declining towards them in the manner in which they, of their nature, decline'.

[111] See Aelian, *var. hist.* 3.11 and Dörrie (1959) 213.

differently from Augustine, *tonos* does not appear to indicate the volitional energy which results in action.[112]

The presence of soul to the body signified by *intentio* is that of an unmoved substance, if movement is understood to be local (*non locali diffusione, ep.* 166.4). Inextended physically, soul moves, and is moved, temporally. Its lack of physical extension in body does not make it a simple substance. By comparison with body it is, of course, 'more simple' (*trin.* 6.8) inasmuch as it is totally present in every part of body, but the variety and changeability of its qualities and activities show it to be a plurality (*multiplex natura*, ib.). It can be creative or inactive, clear-sighted or reflective, it can experience desire, fear, joy or grief, and all of these activities or conditions are distinguishable; they may be present singly or in combination, and in differing degrees (ib.). The soul is richly variegated.

In the several conditions of the soul just referred to, and in particular in its emotional states, Augustine observes reciprocal influences of body and soul, influences which illustrate and illuminate the latter's nature. We shall find such psychosomatic interaction in the various activities discussed in the following chapters. This is clearly the case with perception, where the precise nature of the roles of soul and body is crucial to the description and definition of our sense-activities.[113] The exercise of our imagination can be so intense that it may affect bodily states;[114] moreover, certain traces of emotions, which remain latent in our bodily disposition, may become the vehicle of demonic dream and thought communication, and this example of reciprocal body-soul influence is analogous to the interplay of anger and bile in our systems.[115] The pathology of our imagination includes physiological as well as psychological factors.[116] Memory of past emotions can be accompanied by feelings, even if these do not necessarily correspond to the emotions actually being remembered.[117]

The reciprocal influence of body and soul allows us to describe their natures and activities in parallel terms. In particular, we may express the less easily understood nature of soul in language drawn from the bodily sphere. This kind of metaphorical elucidation is a favourite with Augustine.[118] Thus knowledge and understanding can be described as the food of the soul (*beata v.* 8), instruction as its medicine, slowness to learn as medical neglect, the soul's life and perception as its growth or ageing, its learning and consent as its provision of food, shelter and care for itself (*Gn. litt.* 8.9.18). The metaphorical death of soul is compared with the real death of body: in the former the soul is abandoned by God to its folly, in the latter the body is abandoned by the soul to its dissolution (*trin.* 4.5). Yet, just as the body will

---

[112] See Dihle (1982) 62.

[113] See pp. 84-7.

[114] See p. 111.

[115] See pp. 122-4.

[116] See pp. 129f.

[117] See p. 146.

[118] See Dinkler 188-90. Similar is the frequent talk of the 'senses of the soul': see e.g. *sol.* 1.12; 1.13; *civ.* 11.3; *nat. et or. an.* 2.3; 4.30; 4.37. For the metaphor of inner senses see p. 90 n. 26.

be resurrected, so can the soul be resuscitated by repentance and faith (ib.; cf. §17).[119] Augustine comments in general terms on this approach in *quant. an.* 30:

> One may observe that many words from the bodily sphere are applied figuratively to the soul ... that one among the virtues which is called greatness of soul is correctly understood with reference, not to any extent, but to a kind of energy, that is, to a capability and power of the soul.

Metaphor ('the adopted transfer of the meaning of a word from its proper object to an object not particularly its own', *c. mend.* 24) should not mislead, but elucidate: it recasts language in the service of comprehension of the realities behind the lingustic signs.

In Augustine's account of the affections we also find analyses of the body-soul relationship.[120] His views on aesthetic perceptions, which are pre-eminently psychosomatic, may be included here: delight at the beauty of bodily movement (such as the actor's dance, *ord.* 2.34) is only possible because soul is conjoined with body and perceives through it. But such perceptions are merely a heightened instance of our emotional lives.[121] Augustine classifies the emotions traditionally as fear (*metus, timor*), desire (*cupiditas*), joy (*laetitia*) and grief (*tristitia*), *trin.* 6.8;[122] following Cicero, he calls them *perturbationes*[123] or, with Apuleius, *passiones* (*civ.* 14.5),[124] or *affectiones* (*conf.* 10.21; ib. §22: *perturbationes*) or *affectus*:

> ... these motions of the soul, which the Greeks call *pathê*, while some of our own writers, such as Cicero, call them perturbations, some affections (*affectiones*

---

[119] For the resuscitation (*renovatio*) of the soul, its passage from sickness to health, and the struggle which this involves, see the unsurpassed pages (which do full justice to Augustine's use of metaphor) of Dinkler 127-59.

[120] For the body-soul relationship in Augustine, see, apart from Dinkler 187-206, Goldbrunner, Schwarz, and Miles *passim*. Augustine's views on the affections are discussed by Thonnard (1952), Thonnard (1953), Duchrow 22-30; see also S. Cuesta, *El Equilibrio Pasional en la Doctrina Estoica y en la de San Agustín*, Madrid 1945, 213-88. On soul and body in Stoicism see Long (1982).

[121] The interplay of body and soul in this passage is well analysed by K. Svoboda, *L'Esthétique de Saint Augustin et ses Sources*, Brno 1933, 25f.

[122] The corresponding verbal forms *metuere/timere, cupire/concupiscere, laetari,* and *contristari/ aegrescere* are found e.g. *imm. an.* 7; *civ.* 14.5; *Io. ev. tr.* 60.3. The terminology is Ciceronian (*Tusc. disp.* 3 and 4 *passim*), but is modified by Augustine, who prefers *cupiditas* to Cicero's *libido* (*Tusc. disp.* 3.24), because the latter term, if it is not qualified (as e.g. in *civ.* 14.15), is used by him to refer to sexual desire (*civ.* 14.16). *Tristitia* is preferred to *dolor* or Cicero's *aegritudo*, because these two terms seem to Augustine to refer primarily to bodily conditions (*civ.* 14.7f.), despite the occurrence of *dolere* in the Virgilian verse (*Aeneid* 6.733) which he quotes more than once (e.g. *civ.* 14.7f.; 21.3) as an enumeration of the four affections. That is presumably also the reason why he prefers *laetitia* to *voluptas* (cf. *imm. an.* 7), even if he knows that *voluptas* is a translation of *hêdonê* (Plato, *Tim.* 69d) in Cicero's *Hortensius* (*c. Iul.* 4.72 = *Hort.* fr. 84 Grilli); cf. Cicero, *de legibus* 1.31; *de senectute* 44.

[123] Cicero, *Tusc. disp.* 3.23f.; 4.11.

[124] Apuleius, *de deo Socratis* 147f. But the negative colouring, especially in Christian usage, of *passio* does not commend it as a suitable term to Augustine: *nupt. et conc.* 2.55.

vel affectus), and some, like him (sc. Apuleius), translating more accurately from the Greek, call passions (*civ.* 9.4).

For a perturbation is that which is called *pathos* in Greek, whence he (sc. Apuleius) chose to call (sc. the daemons) 'passive in soul', because the word *passio*, derived from the word *pathos*, signified a motion of the *animus* contrary to reason (*civ.* 8.17).[125]

These various affections are forms of volition, whether of appetition and consent, or of avoidance and rejection (*civ.* 14.6).[126] In so far as they are manifested in ways which meet with disapproval, they are 'faults of the soul ... rather than of the flesh' (ib. §2). Augustine cannot therefore agree with the Platonists, of whom he asserts that they maintain

that souls are so affected by earthly limbs and dying members ... that from this come their diseases of desires and fears and joys and sorrows (§5).

Indeed, Platonic beliefs in reincarnation presuppose emotions in the disembodied soul, such as the desire to return to a body:

Whence even they themselves admit that the soul is not only affected by the flesh, so that it desires, fears, rejoices and grieves, but that it can also be agitated by these emotions from within itself (ib.).[127]

For this reason Augustine regards the affections as 'the mind's passions' as opposed to 'the body's passions', such as pain, pleasure, and disease (*imm. an.* 7). The very notion of passion = disturbance entails a rational faculty which is disturbed by irrational motions. Animals, lacking reason, do not have affections, although some similarity to affections is discernible in them (*civ.* 8.17; *Gn. c. Man.* 1.31).[128]

Thus Augustine, employing the body-soul parallelism, can say that, just as bodies are contained in space, in a place, so the soul's affection is its 'place' (*locus*: see e.g. *en. Ps.* 6.9): that is, it is the situation, the condition, in which it

---

[125] Cf. *Io. ev. tr.* 46.8. Augustine derives his definition 'motion of the soul contrary to reason' from Cicero, *Tusc. disp.* 3.24 (cf. ib. 3.7; 4.11; 4.47; 4.61): it is, in effect, the Peripatetic view, but is also attributed to the Stoics (*SVF* 3.377-91).

[126] The classification of *civ.* 14.6 corresponds to Cicero, *Tusc. disp.* 4.11. For Augustine's views on our memories of past emotions see Chapter 5, pp. 146-8.

[127] In *civ.* 14.5 Augustine identifies his surprise at this, to him, inescapable conclusion from the Platonic reincarnation beliefs with the question of Aeneas concerning the souls in the underworld: 'What does it mean, such fearful longing of these wretches for the light?' (Virgil, *Aen.* 6.721). Both the frequency with which Augustine refers to *Aen.* 6.724-51 (see especially *civ.* 13.19; 21.3; 21.13) and the way in which Virgil's account is repeatedly equated by him with Platonic beliefs (see *civ.* 13.19, where, after quoting *Aen.* 6.750f., he adds, 'which Virgil is praised for having derived from the teaching of Plato') make it reasonable to suppose that his use of the lines in this context derives from a Platonizing Virgil commentary: see n. 27 above. For further criticism of Platonist views on the emotions see *civ.* 12.14 and 21; *ser.* 240.4; 241.4f.

[128] Augustine's debt to the Stoics here is obvious: it was Chrysippus' belief that animals cannot have affections, since the latter are disturbances of the rational faculty (Cicero, *Tusc. disp.* 4.31 = *SVF* 3.426).

momentarily finds itself. The motif occurs in contexts where spiritual nearness to, or distance from, God is a theme (*mus.* 6.40; *vera rel.* 72). Related to it is the following comparison:

> Our emotions are ... our feet. According to the affection which each individual has, according to the love which each has, he draws near to, or moves away from, God (*en. Ps.* 94.2).[129]

Augustine can therefore adopt the physiological descriptions of the affections given by the Stoics, even if in Stoicism they serve to underline the corporeal conditioning of the soul and their employment by Augustine can, once again, only be figurative:

> Our affections are motions of souls. Joy is the extending of the soul; sadness the contraction of the soul; desire the soul's going forward; fear the soul's flight (*Io. ev. tr.* 46.8).[130]

Thus bodily changes or disturbances, such as paleness, blushing, trembling, can have psychological causes (fear, shame, anger, love), even if they may also be caused by physical factors such as the presence of foodstuffs or liquids in the body (*Gn. litt.* 12.19.41).

The belief in the relative autonomy of the affective life of the soul also underlies the extended discussion of the Stoic views on the philosophical sage and the affections in *civ.* 9.4. Augustine argues syncretistically (explicitly following Cicero, *fin.* 3 and 4) that the Stoic refusal to believe that passions can befall the sage is a verbal quibble: the Platonic and Aristotelian view that the wise man indeed suffers passions, but that his reason controls and minimizes their effect, is in substance the same as the Stoic position.[131] It is no different with the Stoic refusal to speak of external and material 'goods', rather than 'advantages'. Augustine paraphrases at length the anecdote concerning the Stoic philosopher in the sea-storm (taken from Aulus Gellius 19.1), in which the philosopher clearly feels terror but afterwards defends his fear with references to a teaching of Epictetus.[132] This teaching asserts that certain sensations (*animi visa* = *phantasiae*) are beyond the control of reason: they occur spontaneously (e.g. fear and grief). Only reason's consent to these sensations, itself a form of judgement, is within our power. The sage will not

---

[129] Cf. *Io. ev. tr.* 56.4; *conf.* 1.28; *vera rel.* 28. The motif is Neoplatonic: see Plotinus, *Enn.* 1.6.8.21-7. Cf. Theiler (1933) 45; 60 = Theiler (1966) 215; 234.

[130] For these physiological descriptions of the affections see *SVF* 3.463, where *meiôsis* ('diminution') = *contractio* ('contraction'); closer to 'extending' or 'spreading out' (*diffusio*) than the term used there (*eparsis* = 'elation') is *diakhusis* ('relaxation') in *SVF* 1.209, which is related to *hêdonê* (pleasure) in *SVF* 3.400. For *fuga* ('flight') = *ekklisis* ('deflexion') and *progressio* ('going forward') = *orexis* ('yearning after': cf. root meaning of *oregein*, 'to reach out') see *SVF* 3.391. See Pohlenz 1.149; 2.81; 2.224.

[131] More specifically, Augustine here summarizes Cicero, *fin.* 4.56-60. For such Ciceronian résumés in Augustine see Testard 1.261-6.

[132] The Aulus Gellius anecdote is repeated in *qu. hept.* 1.30. Augustine's use of this author is discussed by Hagendahl 673f.

give way to them by such consent, for that would be tantamount to subordinating his judgement to them: rather,

the wise man's (sc. mind), although it undergoes them of necessity, yet retains with unshaken resolve a true and stable judgement regarding those things which it ought rationally either desire or avoid ... and so perhaps the Stoics say that they (sc. emotions) do not affect the wise man, because they never cloud by any error or upset by any blemish the wisdom by which he is actually wise (*civ.* 9.4).

Thus the sage under threat of shipwreck can feel terror, and also believe that it is more 'advantageous' to be saved than drowned, but still remain convinced that his life (i.e. his mere survival) is not a 'good' like justice, and that his rescue or drowning will not affect his moral standing.[133]

Augustine makes this interpretation of Stoic doctrine, which, as was observed, he understands to be in harmony with Platonic and Aristotelian views, his own. Justice must be upheld, even at the cost of forfeiting life or bodily welfare:

Thus the mind in which that resolve is well fixed lets no disturbances prevail in it against reason, even though they strike the lower parts of the soul; on the contrary, it rules over them, and, in not consenting to, but rather resisting them, it exercises the rule of virtue (ib.).

This control by the mind or reason over the 'lower parts' of the soul enables the Christian to apply his emotions rightly; the latter can, if restrained, be 'adapted to the service of justice' (*civ.* 9.5). Because the irrational faculty, no less than reason, is a divinely created part of the human soul (*civ.* 5.11), its affections are both natural and good, if they are kept under the control of reason (*en. Ps.* 145.5) and moderated by it (*Gn. c. Man.* 1.31).[134] That some emotions, such as anger or fear, cannot be controlled without effort is less a matter of natural emotional exuberance than a consequence of original sin (*civ.* 14.19; cf. *civ.* 9.5). The struggle with the emotions is therefore a moral one, almost, one might say, a question of their proper *use*. We should not ask

whether a pious soul is angry, but why it is angry, nor whether it is sad, but what is the reason for its sadness, nor whether it fears, but what it fears (*civ.* 9.5).[135]

And, since the emotions are forms of volition, they are to be considered good or bad according to the tendency of the will in each case:

---

[133] On the so-called *propatheia* doctrine (found in developed form in Seneca: see Pohlenz 2.154) behind the views reported here see Pohlenz 1.307-9.

[134] Other Christian writers of the same period express similar views, e.g. Lactantius, *divinae institutiones* 6.17; Ambrose, *de officiis* 2.19. See A. Solignac, art. Passions et vie spirituelle, *Dictionnaire de Spiritualité* 12 (1983) 345-7.

[135] On the Christian's justifiable anger cf. Tertullian, *de anima* 16.

The morally right will is therefore a good love, and the wrong will is an evil love. Love, then, longing to have what is loved, is desire; and having and enjoying it, is joy; and fleeing what is opposed to it, is fear; and feeling what is opposed to it when this has affected it, is grief. Now these emotions are evil if the love is evil, and good if it is good (*civ.* 14.7).

Good emotions are a foretaste of the blessed life (*civ.* 14.9); evil emotions will be punished, even if they have not resulted in deeds (*civ.* 16.4). Thus one can be angry with sinners and wish for their correction, or be sorry for those in distress and wish to help them, or feel pity and compassion (ib.). Augustine asks whether such emotions in the service of good actions are to be reckoned among the disadvantages of our historical lives. He suggests that they are, and that to speak of angelic anger or sorrow is to speak analogously, in the way that the Scriptures speak of divine anger: angels act like we should or would do under the influence of the emotions in question, and the language of emotional behaviour denotes the consequences of their actions, not the state of any feelings that they may be presumed to have (ib.).

Emotions are felt by the morally good and the morally bad alike: they are an inescapable feature of our psychological condition. Augustine therefore finds the Stoic distinction between 'stable states' (*constantiae*) of the sage (*civ.* 14.8)[136] and emotions superfluous. The Stoics maintained that the sage 'wills' (rather than desires), feels 'gladness' (rather than joy) and 'caution' (rather than fear). There is no stable state correspondiong to distress or pain.[137] Augustine observes that the Scriptures, as well as secular authors, apply the terms denoting stable states and those denoting emotions indiscriminately to good and had alike, and he provides a rich anthology of such usage from Isaiah to Virgil (*civ.* 14.8). His opinion is, he feels, thereby strengthened:

> The good and bad alike desire, fear and rejoice, but the former in a good way, the latter in a bad manner, according as their will is right or wrong (ib.).

As in Book Nine Augustine follows this discussion (here critical of Stoicism) with an application of his conclusions to the right behaviour of the Christian. Christians may fear eternal punishment, desire eternal life, fear to commit sin, feel pain over sins committed, feel gladness at good works, and they may also feel all these emotions on account of others. The emotions felt by Paul and Christ are scrupulously documented. Augustine asks:

> But since these affections, when they are exhibited in an appropriate way, follow right reason, who would dare to assert that they are diseases or evil passions (*civ.* 14.9)?

---

[136] *constantiae* is Cicero's translation (*Tusc. disp.* 4.12f.) of the Stoic term *eupatheiai*, for which see D. Tsekourakis, *Studies in the Terminology of Early Stoic Ethics* (Hermes Einzelschriften, 32), Wiesbaden 1974, 91f.

[137] The *constantiae* are *voluntas, gaudium, cautio*. See further the use of *Tusc. disp.* 4.10-12 in *civ.* 14.5; 14.16; *conf.* 10.22. For the careful summary of *Tusc. disp.* 4.11-14 in *civ.* 14.8 see the juxtaposition of the two texts in Testard 2.60f. Against the Stoics, Augustine identifies a positive form of *tristitia* in e.g. the distress that leads to repentance referred to in 2 Corinthians 7:8-11 (*civ.* 14.8).

Such emotional experiences are, however, a feature of our historical rather than of our future life. We experience these emotions 'because of the weakness of the human condition', unlike Christ, who

> when he wished, submitted to these emotions in his human soul by the grace of his unshaking governance, just as he became man when he so wished (ib.)

But, on the other hand, not to feel them in this life would imply some deficiency in the quality of our lives:

> So long as we bear the weakness of this life, then we are rather living a worse life if we have none of these emotions (ib.).

Such a state, says Augustine, quoting Crantor from Cicero, would be one of mental barbarism (*inmanitas*) and bodily insensitivity (*stupor*).[138] These emotions cannot therefore be faults or morbid passions, if properly exhibited. Augustine will thus criticize the Stoic approval of impassibility (*apatheia* = *inpassibilitas*), not because it would not be a desirable state (it refers, after all, to a mental condition in which no emotions can disturb the reason),[139] but rather because it is unattainable in our present life (ib.).[140] It would be the state of the perfectly good. Yet even they, in their heavenly condition, will feel certain emotions: they will experience love and gladness, though not fear or grief. Augustine concludes that some emotions are not, after all, peculiar to our historical existence: he transposes, as it were, the Stoic distinction between stable states and emotions to a celestial plane. Some emotions are worthier than others. In their paradise state Adam and Eve were not troubled by fear, pain or sadness, any more than they were disturbed by bodily disorders; but they did enjoy love for each other and for God and the gladness ensuing from this:

> Their love for God was undisturbed, and their mutual love was that of spouses living in faithful and pure fellowship, and from this love (sc. arose) a great delight, because it never ceased to have enjoyment of what was loved (*civ.* 14.10).

In heaven, as in Eden, love and joy are the feelings of the blessed, feelings common to the souls of Adam and Eve in their bodies as yet uncorrupted by sin and to all souls of the blessed in their spiritual bodies, for prelapsarian

---

[138] Cicero, *Tusc. disp.* 3.12. The quotation is a good example of Augustine's polemical use of the Academic against the Stoic position. Nor is Cicero cited slavishly: Augustine approves of Crantor more than Cicero does. See further *en. Ps.* 55.6; *Io. ev. tr.* 60.3.

[139] The young Augustine was impressed by the Stoic ideal: *beata v.* 25; *mor.* 1.53f. (where, however, the value of mercy, disputed by the Stoics, is asserted). The rejection of every form of pleasure in Cicero's *Hortensius* (*c. Iul.* 4.72 and 76; 5.33 and 42; cf. *sol.* 1.4) influenced Augustine: see L. Straume-Zimmermann, *Ciceros Hortensius* (Europäische Hochschulschriften, 15/9), Berne/Frankfurt 1976, 181-5.

[140] See also *en. Ps.* 76.14; *Io. ev. tr.* 60.4f. For Augustine's tentative rendering of *apatheia* as *inpassibilitas* cf. Jerome, *ep.* 133.3. Further criticism of the Stoic ideal is found in *civ.* 9.14; 19.4. Augustine, therefore, does not approve the one teaching (the *apatheia* thesis) commended by his

and resurrected bodies are comparable (*civ.* 14.10). Augustine does not, however, seem to be saying that the body is a necessary condition of our feeling the emotions of love or gladness. If that were the case, he would have to maintain that in the period between their death and bodily resurrection the blessed feel no joy, and the damned no distress: in fact, the contrary is implied in *civ.* 21.3.[141]

Even if impassibility were the desired state in this life,[142] the fact that it is unattainable does not entail that those emotions that are peculiar to our historical existence are without benefit to our moral condition. Fear and pain can be salutary means to choosing the good:

> If it (sc. impassibility) is a condition in which no fear terrifies nor pain causes distress, it should be avoided in this life, if we would live rightly, that is, in accordance with God (*civ.* 14.9).[143]

It is in this sense that Augustine understands the Platonic account of the tripartite soul, in which, though the subordinate spirited and appetitive elements are 'vicious parts', they can nevertheless, if restrained and directed by reason, be put to legitimate use:

> anger in the enforcement of just restraint, lust for the duty of propagating offspring (*civ.* 14.19).

Control here implies struggle and coercion in the service of the 'law of wisdom' (*sapientiae lege*, ib.). Because both use and misuse of the emotions are alike subject to the will, the behavioural sequence is emotion (e.g. anger) →

---

principal source of philosophical views on the emotions, books three and four of Cicero's *Tusculan Disputations*. Augustine's stance is consistent with his bipartition of the human soul into rational and irrational faculties (see pp. 12f.).

[141] Quoted p. 53. Cf. *Gn. litt.* 12.32.60-34.67.

[142] Augustine avoids the naïve equation of *inpassibilitas* with insensitivity. By analogy, bodily health can be defined as 'feeling nothing (sc. adverse)', *ser.* 277.5, but is clearly not to be reduced to a state of insensitivity: 'not so not to feel as a stone, a tree, a corpse lacks feeling, but rather to live in the body and feel nothing of its burden, this is to be healthy' (ib. §6). In fact, bodily health is a balance (*temperamentum, concordia*) of hot/cold, dry/wet (ib. §4). Far from being an inert condition, it is a constant process of deficiency (*defectio*) and renewal (*refectio*). To return to the affections: the citizen of the heavenly city enjoys the good emotions of love and gladness in an unperturbed way, and is free of fear and pain, whereas the citizen of the impious city 'is shaken by these evil emotions as by diseases and disturbances' (*civ.* 14.9).

[143] Augustine distinguishes (*civ.* 14.9) between two senses of 'fear': (a) the ordinary language usage, meaning 'being frightened by an evil that can happen'; (b) the fear referred to in Psalm 18:10 ('the pure fear of the lord endures for ever'). (b) is the fear 'holding fast in the good that cannot be lost'. It is an aspect of love (*caritas*), and, as the Psalmist indicates (Augustine inevitably interprets the verse eschatologically), it lasts eternally. It is not, like (a), a 'care arising from weakness', but rather the 'tranquillity of love'. But can this be called fear? Augustine speculates that the 'fear' of Psalm 18:10 may be like the 'endurance' of Psalm 9:19 ('the endurance of the poor will never perish') when both are understood eschatologically. What these verses may then mean is that the goals or states to which fear and endurance lead are permanent. In *civ.* 9.5 Augustine explained the attribution of emotions to God and the angels by saying that such language denoted the type of state or action which would be the consequence of such emotions in humans: here he suggests that the human feelings of fear and endurance may

will (consent to emotion) → action (angry words; hitting somebody), ib.[144] Augustine recognizes one exception to this rule: sexual desire activates the sex-organs directly, with or without consent. The will is, as it were, bypassed. He observes that this phenomenon corresponds to the fact that the other bodily organs can be activated by the will, with or without emotional stimulus (one can talk or move the hand without feeling angry), whereas the sex-organs require the emotion in order to be stirred. Yet not merely do they dispense with the consent of the will, but they cannot be aroused at will. Indeed, desire often fires the mind, but the sex-organs are not responsive (*civ.* 14.16). Our sexual mechanism serves as a warning not to understand the interaction of feeling, mind and body too simplistically.[145]

Augustine, in order to avoid postulating torpor (*stupor*) as the condition of the perfectly happy mind or soul, admits the emotions of love and gladness even to the disembodied soul. Similarly, the soul can itself experience pain. As an example Augustine adduces the counterpart of the joy of the blessed – the suffering of the damned:

> The soul itself, by whose presence the body lives and is ruled, can suffer pain and yet not die. Here then something is found which, although it can feel pain, is immortal. And this capacity, which we know is now in the souls of all, will also be hereafter in the bodies of the damned. Moreover, if we consider the matter more carefully, the pain that is called bodily belongs rather to the soul. For it is the soul, not the body, which is pained, even when the cause of its pain arises in the body, when the soul feels pain in that place where the body is hurt … the soul, then, feels pain with the body in that part where something succeeds in causing it pain; it also feels pain alone, although in the body, when it is distressed by some cause which is actually invisible, while the body is unimpaired. Even when not in the body it is pained: for without doubt that rich man was suffering in hell when he said, 'I am tortured in this flame' (Luke 16:24) (*civ.* 21.3).

Behind the distinctly Christian belief of these lines lies a conviction regarding what was a *quaestio disputata* of the Platonic tradition: namely, the belief in the immortality, not merely of reason, but of the irrational part of the soul.[146] Whether Augustine subscribes to this theory out of philosophical conviction,

---

be said to be exhibited in paradise inasmuch as that state realizes the rewarding consequences of such feelings, if the latter were properly exercised by the individual during his or her life.

[144] For the will as the motor of impulses see *quant. an.* 38. In *ep.* 7.7 Augustine observes that emotions like joy or anger can affect the body before our reflective processes form images of possible responses to the emotions in question. Our facial expression and complexion are affected, as it were, spontaneously by feelings before we react to them at the mental level (*cogitatio*).

[145] On desire (*libido, concupiscentia*) in Augustine see Bonner. Augustine's subtle remarks here have generally been overlooked by those theologians who write on his views of sexuality: an exception is Dinkler 115-16.

[146] For the problems involved in interpreting Plato's views see Robinson 50-4; 111-18; 125-7; T.A. Szlezák, 'Unsterblichkeit und Trichotomie der Seele im zehnten Buch der Politeia', *Phronesis* 21 (1976) 31-58 (for the arguments of *Republic* 10). On the fate of Plato's views in the hands of later Platonists see Merlan 23-9.

or rather because it suits his eschatological picture of the bliss of the saved and the sufferings of the damned, is a moot point.

(xi) Soul and the definition of man

On a number of occasions Augustine discusses the question of a definition of man. We shall look first at his adoption of a traditional school definition: 'man is a rational mortal living being' (e.g. *ord.* 2.31).[147] Augustine is aware of its traditional nature ('that ... definition of man himself by ancient philosophers', ib.) and its roots in the logical distinctions of *genus* and *differentiae*:

> Here the genus, called 'living being', having been established, we observe that two differentiae are added ... by one term he (sc. man) is separated from the animals, because he is said to be rational, by the other from divine beings, because he is said to be mortal (ib.).

Behind this passage lies the following stemma:

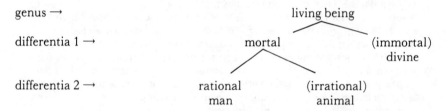

Augustine adopts here the Platonic system of division (*tomê, diairesis*): his example corresponds to that adduced in the Middle Platonic handbook of Albinus, the *Didaskalikos*, where it is described as an exercise in the division of a genus into species, p. 156.29 H. The following stemma can be constructed from ib. p. 157.5ff:

Although the order of the *differentiae* (*diaphorai*) is inverted in Augustine, the same principle is at work in both passages, and Albinus' definition of man is reached in the same way, by addition of the particular *differentiae* to the genus (p. 157.8-9). We need not, however, assume that a specific source or

---

[147] The definition is common in Augustine: *dial.* 9.63f.; *mag.* 24; *quant. an.* 47, etc.

connection links Albinus and Augustine: we have to do here with a tradition of scholastic logic, exemplified also by Philo, Maximus of Tyre and Seneca.[148] Augustine can, however, Christianize this school definition by indicating that it expresses man's proper place in the created order:

> Man is a kind of mean, but between the animals and the angels, the animal being an irrational and mortal living being, the angel a rational and immortal one, while man, inferior to the angels but superior to the animals, having mortality in common with the animals and reason in common with the angels, is a rational and mortal living being (*civ.* 9.13).

At *trin.* 15.11 Augustine follows the definition, which he describes there as traditional, with another: 'Man is a rational substance composed of body and soul'.[149] By focussing upon the dichotomy body-soul this definition at once raises the question of their relation and relative importance in any attempt to define man. Man is not merely considered here as a particular type of living being – not divine, because mortal, not bestial, because rational – but rather as a phenomenon *sui generis*, whose complex structure calls for a more precise delineation. This second definition also raises the question of those powers of the soul, such as intellection, which seem to indicate that it is immortal.[150]

That man is composed of body and soul and nothing more is commonplace in Augustine. In this description soul includes the mind or reason, which is not considered to be a separate part or faculty of man, distinct from soul. 'Soul' (*anima*) may or may not connote 'mind' (*mens*), but it always in fact comprises mind when we talk of man:

> We find nothing in man beyond flesh and soul: this is the whole man, spirit and flesh (*en. Ps.* 145.5).

> There is nothing in man that pertains to his substance and nature apart from body and soul (*ser.* 150.5).

> We are, he (sc. Cornelius Celsus, quoted approvingly) said, composed of two parts, of soul and body (*sol.* 1.21).

> What do we consist of? Body and soul (*ep.* 3.4).

> Who ... would doubt that there is nothing better in man than that part of soul, whose rule it is appropriate that the rest of what is in man should obey? Now this ... can be called mind or reason (*c. Acad.* 1.5).

---

[148] For the tradition of the division see Theiler (1930) 3ff. In pseudo-Apuleius, *peri hermêneias* 6 (pp. 181-3 Thomas) the definition is used, as in *quant. an.* 47, to exemplify the testing of the truth of propositions by logical conversion or transposition of their terms.

[149] See also *trin.* 7.7.

[150] See pp. 59f.

The word 'soul' is sometimes so used that it is taken to include mind, as when we say that man consists of soul and body (*div. qu.* 7).

Thus in *trin.* 15.11, after the two definitions of man have been given, Augustine adds:

> If, again, we leave the body aside and think of the soul on its own, the mind is some part of it, like its hand or eye or face, but these are not to be thought of as if they were bodies. It is not then the soul, but that which is superior in the soul, that is called mind.

If the mind is, metaphorically speaking, the 'head' or 'eye' of the soul, it is as much a part of soul as the head or eye are parts of the body.[151]

Now, if mind is a part of soul, its presence as the highest power of an incorporeal entity raises a question that is not posed by the 'neutral' definition of *ord.* 2.31 and elsewhere. If man is composed of body and soul, and if the latter is the 'better', 'ruling', 'higher' part, may not man be defined primarily, if not exclusively, in terms of this higher part? Greek philosophical definitions of man of this kind appear to originate in the pseudo-Platonic *First Alcibiades* 128e-130c. There, having argued that man uses his various bodily parts (i.e. hands) in the exercise of the crafts, just as he uses instruments, and that therefore 'man' is identifiable with the principle using the body, it is proposed that soul is this 'using' and so 'ruling' faculty (129d-130c). One can therefore conclude that, of the three possible definitions of man – 'soul or body or the composite of both' (130a) – if the latter two be dismissed, inasmuch as they are not ruling principles, it follows that 'the soul is man' (130c). A rider can be added to the effect that this soul = man uses the body as an instrument. Augustine knows the traditional question and the alternatives from Varro, who favoured the composite (*civ.* 19.3).[152] The question is not raised by Varro in a purely definitional context, but as part of an attempt to define ethical goals by deciding which form of life is to be approved: the active (body), the leisured (soul), or the combination (composite) of these two. This was also the preoccupation of Varro's forerunners, the Old Academy and Antiochus of Ascalon (*civ.* 19.3). Indeed, the discussion about the definition of man in the *First Alcibiades* was a prelude to the theory of 'self-knowledge' as the prerequisite of ethical discourse.[153] Augustine is in line with this tradition: his references to the question of a definition of man often occur in contexts where the highest good, or happiness, are under discussion.[154] Thus the mention of the school-definition

---

[151] For the definition of man in terms of body and soul, and for the pre-eminence of mind (*mens*) in the latter, see Cicero, *fin.* 5.34.

[152] See also the earlier *mor.* 1.6: is man body or soul? Even if neither be called 'man', says Augustine, 'it can none the less be the case that one of these be considered and called man' (i.e. as part of the composite). Or 'man' can be a composite of both. For the examples given for each of the three possibilities see also *civ.* 19.3. In *mor.* 1.6 Augustine postpones the difficult choice: the later *civ.* 13.24 provides the answer.

[153] See O'Daly (1973) 7-19.

[154] See, apart from *civ.* 19.3, ib. 8.8 and *c. Acad.* 1.5; 3.27.

of man in *ord.* 2.31 becomes the occasion for a typically Augustinian ethical-metaphysical expansion, in which the Neoplatonic themes of procession, fall and conversion are introduced: the two *differentiae* serve as admonitions

> by which, as I believe, man was to be reminded to what he should return and from what he should flee. For as the advance of the soul to things mortal is a fall, so its return should be to reason.

The order of discussion therefore is: (A) What is the good for man = the condition of man's happiness? (B) What is the definition of 'man'? (C) Given the explicit definition of 'man' (answer to B), one may proceed to answer A. Even if Augustine will disagree with the definition of the highest good given by the philosophical tradition of which Varro is a part, he will none the less accept Varro's definition of man as the composite of body and soul:

> Not the whole man, but the better part of man, is the soul; nor is the whole man the body, but it is the lower part of man; but when each is joined to the other, that is called man (*civ.* 13.24).

But Augustine is also influenced by the tradition deriving from the *First Alcibiades*, which defines man as a soul using a body:

> Man therefore, as it seems to one man, is a rational soul using a mortal and earthly body (*mor.* 1.52).

He will not, however, go so far as to assert that 'the soul is man'. Thus he can say: 'What is man? A rational soul with a body' (*Io. ev. tr.* 19.15). But previously he has made the crucial qualification:

> The soul with a body does not make two persons, but one man (*ib.*).

We might say that Augustine understands the definition of the *First Alcibiades* in the light of the Varronian alternative. Man is indeed the composite of body and soul, but if we consider man in terms of his dominant part[155] man is his soul, with the body as a possession or tool of the soul, or – in a close echo of the language of the *Alcibiades* – his soul rules his body:

> It (sc. the soul) seems to me to be a certain substance sharing in reason, fitted for rule over the body (*quant. an.* 22).

Augustine's references to the definition of man as *persona* do not add anything to the conclusions already reached. His employment of the term *persona* with definitional force is mostly derived from assertions of the unity of Christ's *persona*, despite his two natures, divine and human. The term refers

---

[155] For this definitional possibility see Aristotle, *Eth. Nic.* 1168b35; 1178a2ff.; Plotinus, *Enn.* 3.4.3.22. Rist 86ff. and 255 n. 12 provides a discussion and further examples.

to man in contexts where this dogma, or problems regarding the persons of the Trinity, are under discussion. Thus in *Io. ev. tr.* 19.15 and at *ep.* 137.11[156] the context is Christological, whereas in *trin.* 7.7-11 it is Trinitarian. Where there is a Christological discussion, the term *persona* naturally serves to stress the unity of the composite of body and soul in man, without, however, disregarding the dominant function of soul:

> In the person, then, there is a mixture of soul and body ... in the unity of the person the soul uses the body, that man may be (*ep.* 137.11).

In Trinitarian contexts Augustine can employ *persona*, with some qualms (e.g. *trin.* 7.7),[157] as a translation of *hupostasis*: the term is applicable as referring generally to humans as well, but it does not denote anything that *homo* does not denote. In the spare and often largely traditional definitions of *persona* = *homo* we do not therefore find any trace of a concept of 'the person' or 'personality' or 'self' such as might make Augustine a forerunner of later speculation of this kind in the European tradition.[158] That is not to say that Augustine could not occasionally equate *persona* with *ego*, in the sense of the human self, as distinct from the person's emotional or mental powers or activities:

> Through all these three (sc. memory, understanding, love) I remember, I understand, I love, who am neither memory nor understanding nor love, but rather I possess these. These, then, can be asserted by one person, who possesses these three, but is not these three (*trin.* 15.42).[159]

Nor can it be denied that there is a wealth of observational detail about the individual's feelings and psychological motivations, amounting in effect to a description of personality, in a work like the *Confessions*: but that is not the same as an articulated concept of 'personality'.

Augustine explicitly rejects trichotomic definitions of man: he was familiar with them, and from different sources. One such source is referred to cryptically at *beata. v.* 7:

> Therefore ... you do not doubt that these two – body and soul – exist, but you are uncertain if there is anything else which completes man and makes him perfect ... What this might be we will investigate elsewhere if we can.

Pépin is undoubtedly right to identify the unnamed third element in man as *mens*.[160] A trichotomic view is found in Apollinarian accounts of the natures of

---

[156] See pp. 42f..

[157] See Schindler (1965) 166f.

[158] Flasch 361 rightly observes that, for Augustine, the word *persona* is equivalent to 'human substance'. The metaphysical problems of the mind's self-knowledge and its relation to the (equally metaphysical) concept of the person constitute a different topic which cannot be discussed here: see Lloyd; Henry (1960).

[159] See also *ord.* 2.50, discussed below pp. 59f.

[160] Pépin (1964) 75f. = Pépin (1977) 235f. See also Goldbrunner 29.

Christ, in whom the mind is said to be divine, and the soul and body human.[161] Augustine was familiar with such views as early as 384-386 (*conf.* 7.25; *agon.* 21). Whether other, secular philosophical influences worked upon him, or were familiar to him, we cannot tell. It is at least possible that Pépin's theory of Porphyrian influence may be correct.[162]

In *nat. et or. an.* 4.19 the text of 1 Thessalonians 5:23, which refers to spirit, soul and body in man, is adduced as the inspiration for Vincentius Victor's trichotomic view of man as *spiritus-anima-corpus*. According to this view the 'inner man' is the soul (*anima*), a 'congealing substance' of the divine breath (*flatus*), corporeal and enclosed in the body, and also 'like its own body and similar to its appearance'. Spirit, on the other hand, is the 'particular understanding' and 'inmost intellect' of the soul (ib. 4.20). Augustine observes that man is thus constituted of three elements, exterior, inner and inmost (ib.). His answer to this interesting speculation is disappointingly narrow: he focuses polemically upon the materialistic theory characteristic of Vincentius, a feature of which is that each inner element in turn is moulded by its enclosing body. How, asks Augustine, can one decide which one of these elements will be renewed according to God's image (Colossians 3:10)? How can a body receive God's image, while simultaneously being moulded by another body? (The assumption here is that *spiritus* or *anima*, rather than the external *corpus*, are renewed in the divine image.) The analogy of the coin (which is probably Augustine's rather than Vincentius') with its twofold stamp (*caput et navia*, 'heads or tails', ib.), only exposes the absurdity of Vincentius' views, Augustine feels: for, if applied to them, it suggests that different parts of the same corporeal soul are stamped in divine and human likenesses.

Augustine goes on to offer an explanation of 1 Thess. 5:23 and similar Biblical passages which is consistent with the dichotomic view discussed above (*nat. et or. an.* 4.36). *Spiritus* is a specifically named (*proprie/distincte dici/nominari*) faculty of the *anima*, viz. the rational faculty:

> That by means of which we reason, comprehend, understand ... is not the entire soul (*universa anima*), but some part of it (ib.).

In Greek philosophy, as Pépin's discussion of *beata v.* 7 reminds us,[163] a trichotomic view of man is found above all in Aristotle, where, in *de anima* (especially 3.4-7), *nous* is clearly distinguished from *psukhê* and *sôma* (cf. also *gen. animal.* 2.3,736b27). The pure activity of intellect, unlike ordinary everyday thinking, is, for Aristotle, not dependent on psychophysical processes. Such an intellect is literally separable from body, and can be called 'divine' even when it is found in humans (it is, of course, also the self-thinking intellect of the God of the *Metaphysics*).[164] Without necessarily

---

[161] See E. Mühlenberg, art. Apollinaris, *TRE* 3 (1978) 362-71.

[162] Pépin (1964) 70-6 = Pépin (1977) 230-6. See also Dörrie (1959) 41, who does not, however, attribute Nemesius, *nat. hom.* 3 (p. 125.12ff. M.), to Porphyry.

[163] Pépin (1964) 72f. = Pépin (1977) 232f.

[164] See J.L. Ackrill, *Aristotle the Philosopher*, Oxford 1981, 62f.

being influenced by these Aristotelian notions in any direct way,[165] Augustine can pinpoint the problem to which the concept of pure thought leads when we try to reconcile it with the empirical definition of man as a rational, mortal animal (*ord.* 2.50). The invariable nature of arithmetical proportions (1:2; 2:4) is, Augustine says, 'immortal' (*immortalis ratio*). Now either I, who comprehend or compute such proportions, am likewise 'immortal reason', in which case (a) my so-called 'mortal' aspect is not really 'mine', or (b) *anima* is not to be equated with *ratio*, and I none the less use *ratio*. In the first (a) of these alternatives *ratio* is considered a part of soul, or an activity of soul: now if I am somehow 'immortal reason' I cannot be defined as a 'mortal animal'. The two terms, rational and mortal, are contradictory, and so the latter cannot be part of my definition.[166] What does Augustine mean by the second (b) alternative? Clearly this: I can transcend my everyday, mortal self by pure intellection, and so 'become' immortal:

> If I am actually better through my reason, I should fly from the worse to the better, from the mortal to the immortal (ib.).

This intellection must, we have to assume, become 'mine'. Now we cannot use this passage to demonstrate that Augustine dallies with a trichotomic view of man (he immediately afterwards postpones the discussion), or that the *ratio* of the second alternative is like Aristotle's *nous*. But the problem raised by both thinkers is essentially the same. As we have seen, Augustine elsewhere adopts the first alternative, but in so doing he undermines the strict accuracy of the definition of man as mortal and rational: for that which is best in man is not mortal. This best part, the soul, has both rational and irrational powers, and the former guarantee its immortality. Even the latter, though not necessarily immortal, are so in fact.[167]

(xii) Soul: unity or plurality?

Augustine appears to refer to the problem of the number of souls on only one occasion, in *quant. an.* 69. In so doing, he is clearly influenced by Neoplatonic treatments of this topic. Plotinus had devoted a treatise (4.9) to the question whether all souls are a unity, and Porphyry dealt with the matter in his writings.[168] Augustine enumerates three possibilities, each of them likewise considered by the Neoplatonists, but he does not clearly opt for any of them.

(a) 'If I shall say that soul is one, you will be disturbed': presumably this possibility would be disturbing inasmuch as it would undermine the status of the soul as the principle of individuation *par excellence*, and fly in the face of the

---

[165] See Pépin's speculations about the possible indirect influence of Aristotle through Porphyry, or Apollinarian views, or both: Pépin (1964) 73-6 = Pépin (1977) 233-6.

[166] Of course the definition can be, and is, understood to be applicable to my historical or temporal existence, which ends with my death. This is clearly how Augustine understands it in *civ.* 9.13: see p. 55. The ambiguity of *mortalitas*, as indeed that of *immortalis*, is a stumbling-block here and elsewhere.

[167] See pp. 46-54.

[168] See Pépin (1964) 89f. = Pépin (1977) 249f.

evidence of different intellectual capabilities and moral achievements. It is evident that, as Augustine says, one person's soul is happy, another's wretched, but S (on this hypothesis, the identical soul in both persons) cannot simultaneously be both P and -P. Plotinus had faced the same difficulty, and argued that identity of feeling would require corporeal identity (though, as he points out, even in the one body feelings in one part are not necessarily registered in other parts). The goodness and badness of the same soul in different individuals is, however, as acceptable to Plotinus as states of rest or movement of the same entity in different individuals (4.9.1-2). He feels that he must defend the unity of soul against common-sense objections because so much depends upon it: the unity and sympathy of the universe and the individuals within it (§3). For Augustine, on the contrary, human sympathy, whether expressed in friendship or in the harmony of an individual's behaviour, depends, not upon unity of soul, but rather upon similarity between souls and consistency (*constantia*) within the soul (*Gn. litt. imp.* 16.59). It may be, however, that Augustine is not merely thinking of the common-sense objections when he expects Evodius to be disturbed by the unity thesis. For that thesis is also uncannily like Manichaean assertions that the individual good soul is part of the universal Light Principle. It was certainly Porphyry's understanding that the Manichees believed

> that there is one single soul of all, divided into small parts and cut up among ... bodies (Porph. *ap.* Nemes. 2, p. 110.8-10 M.),

and, although there seems to be no need to assume that this Porphyrian passage, rather than others or any of the Plotinian passages dealing with the theme, is Augustine's source, it is interesting to speculate whether Augustine, prompted by Porphyry or not, may not be reacting to the Manichaean belief here.[169]

(b) 'If I shall assert that it is at once one and many, you will laugh': this formulation, that soul is one and many, is typical of Plotinus (it is the 'answer' of *Enn.* 4.9.2, for example), and it was also adapted by Porphyry (*ap.* Nemes. 2, p. 112.8-9 M.; *sent.* 37, p. 42.14-15 L.). Plotinus draws an analogy between the one/many nature of an immaterial entity and the relation of the constituents of a science to the whole: the constituent parts derive from the whole which is potentially present in them, and their unity is the prerequisite of scientific systems (4.9.5).[170] Although Augustine will also argue for the unity of science (e.g. *ord.* 2.44), he does not appear to have taken over the idea of its one/many nature. At the same time, he implicitly regards the individual soul as a unity with several distinct powers which can be exercised singly or in combination. In other words, we might expect him to argue, as Plotinus does in *Enn.* 4.9.3, for an underlying unity of the soul which can be active in so many distinct ways, behaving both rationally and irrationally, as well as functioning at vegetative level. And, granted such unity-in-

---

[169] For Porphyry's understanding of the Manichaean view see Dörrie (1959) 142-7. For Porphyry's possible influence on Augustine see Pépin (previous note).

[170] See W. Theiler in Harder/Beutler/Theiler 6.123f.

multiplicity within the individual soul, we might expect him to be tempted to explore the possibility of a similar relationship between souls. Why does he not then explore the one/many thesis here? Its acceptability may be compromised by the absence in his thought of the principle underlying the Neoplatonic theory, that individual souls are manifestations of the hypostasis Soul. But it is just as likely that the reason for his hesitation is pedagogical rather than philosophical. Evodius, in the role of learner in the dialogue, cannot be expected to understand the point, much less examine it critically. For similar pedagogical reasons Augustine will not wish to go into the other Neoplatonic thesis of the indivisible soul's divisibility 'in the body' at *quant. an.* 68.[171]

(c) 'If, however, I am to say that they (sc. souls) are a mere plurality, I shall laugh at myself': Augustine appears to come closest to outright rejection here. Why? Presumably to speak of a mere plurality of souls would be to attribute to soul what is characteristic of body. Augustine is, moreover, enough of a Platonist not to be unattracted by the thesis of some kind of unity of soul. He may not explicitly subscribe to this thesis, but it gives expression to his belief in the kinship and generic relationship of all souls. On the scale of being which extends from God to matter, souls are more akin to the unity of God than to the plurality of matter. Nor should we forget that Augustine has just argued for soul's indivisibility. He was, of course, speaking of the individual soul, but the problem applies to all souls. If soul is to be divided (if, that is, souls are to be plural) there has to be a dividing factor. Your soul and mine are separate in so far as we have distinct corporeal identities: remove these, even conceptually, and what keeps our soul-substances apart? It is not so much that Augustine feels that disembodied souls must necessarily merge into an undifferentiated unity; it is rather that he cannot easily identify a continuing cause of their separateness. Quantitative division of disembodied soul is problematic, as the older Evodius himself points out in *ep.* 158.5.[172]

We may conclude that Augustine is likely to favour possibility (b) as the one most consistent with his general views on the nature of the soul, and that the dramatic fiction of *quant. an.* (which may, of course, be corroborated by Evodius' genuine lack of experience in advanced psychological problems) would not allow him to defend it explicitly with any degree of success.[173]

(xiii) World-soul

Owing as he does much of the detail of his views on soul to Platonic and Neoplatonic sources Augustine might well be expected to subscribe to the theory – elaborated in the *Timaeus* and a standard part of subsequent

[171] See p. 29.
[172] See pp. 76f.
[173] The aporetic nature of *quant. an.* is stressed by Voss 251-60.

Platonic teaching – of a world-soul.[174] He knows the theory and can evoke the belief underlying it, that the universe is a living, intelligent, ordered, harmonious organism:

> You (sc. Platonists) say that this world is a living being (*animal*), that is, the heavens, earth, seas, all the huge bodies that exist, and the vast elements everywhere; all this, and the entire body that is composed of all these elements, is, you say, a great living being, that is, it has its own soul, but without possessing bodily senses, for there is nothing outside it to be perceived. Yet it has a mind, and it cleaves to God. And that same soul of the universe is called Jupiter or Hecate, that is, it is like a universal soul ruling the world and making it a kind of single living being (*ser.* 241.7).

> This world is a living being, as Plato and many other philosophers believed (*retr.* 1.11.4).

In his earliest writings he appears to allow for the possibility of a world soul:

> Body therefore remains alive through soul, and exists in so far as it is animated, whether generally, like the universe, or individually, like each individual living being within the universe (*imm. an.* 24).

> Reason is a motion of the mind (*mentis motio*) with the power of distinguishing and connecting what is learnt: only the very rarest of human beings is capable of using it as a guide to the knowledge of God or of that soul which is either in us or everywhere (*ord.* 2.30).

The reference to world-soul is less obvious in *mus.* 6.44, but Augustine's comment on the passage in *retr.* 1.11.4 makes it likely that he meant cosmic soul there also. Similarly, *vera rel.* 18 contains a cryptic reference to cosmic soul, as *retr.* 1.13.2 reveals.

But the most significant and intriguing attempt of the earlier Augustine to integrate belief in the world-soul into his Christian and Biblical understanding of the cosmos is to be found in *Gn. litt. imp.* 4.17, where, discussing Gen. 1:2 'And the spirit of God moved over the water', Augustine offers the interpretations that the words refer to the Holy Spirit or the element of air, as well as the suggestion

> that we should understand the spirit of God as the living creature by which this whole visible universe and all things bodily are held together and moved.

This interpretation is not mentioned in the exegesis of the same verse in the other Genesis commentaries (cf. *Gn. c. Man.* 1.8-9; *Gn. litt.* 1.7.13) or in *conf.* 13.6ff.[175] It is found, however, again in the pseudo-Augustinian *ser.* 157.3.[176]

---

[174] For the world-soul in Greek philosophy see above all Moreau. For Augustine's discussions of the topic, see Bourke (1954); O'Connell (1968) 122-4; Teske. Plato's views are analysed by O. Velásquez, *Anima Mundi. El alma del mundo en Platón*, Santiago (Chile) 1982.

[175] See Pelland 22-6, 37-9, 68-72.

[176] This is pointed out by Bourke (1954) 437f.

Why did Augustine not continue to maintain or develop it, at least as a possibility? One reason appears to have been the lack of Scriptural backing for such a notion. Thus, in *retr.* 1.11.4 Augustine argues that the concept of a world-soul is neither rationally certain,

> nor have I seen that it can be held with conviction on the authority of the sacred scriptures.

The words of *retr.* 1.13.2 are similar in their purport:

> By 'soul' here I meant the entire incorporeal creation, not speaking in the manner of the scriptures, which, when they are not using the word metaphorically, probably intend 'soul' to be understood as none other than that in virtue of which there is life in mortal animals, among whom men, inasmuch as they are mortal, are included.

We shall investigate other reasons presently: but it should be emphasized that the reticence of the *retractationes* is one of suspended judgement rather than explicit rejection of the world-soul thesis. Augustine may comment on his remarks at *imm. an.* 24 that 'it was rashly expressed' (*retr.* 1.5.3), but he can now so judge them

> not because I am demonstrating that it is false that the universe is a living being, but because I perceive that this is not a true fact (*retr.* 1.11.4).

This is precisely the view expressed in *cons. ev.* 1.35:

> But whether this entire bodily mass called the universe has some soul or quasi-soul of its own, that is, a rational life by which it is ruled, like each and every living being – that is a vast and abstruse subject; and this view should not be affirmed except when it has been ascertained to be true, nor repudiated except when it has been found to be false.

The question of the world-soul is thus considered to be an open one, like that of the soul's origin, and Augustine can be equally dismissive of its relevance to human happiness or wisdom:

> But what does this matter to man, even though it should always remain unknown to him, since no soul is actually made wise or happy by any other soul, but rather by that highest and unchangeable divine wisdom alone (ib.)?[177]

When Augustine criticizes theories of a world-soul he objects to particular consequences of these theories rather than to the positing of the existence of a world-soul as such. Thus he criticizes the Stoic notion of a world-soul, as known to him from Varro,[178] on the grounds that it seems to make the universe the body of the God whose soul permeates it,

---

[177] For similar remarks on the question of the origin of souls see O'Daly (1983) 191.
[178] See Cardauns 1.96f.; 2.226f.

so that ... nothing at all would remain that was not a part of God. And if that is so, who would not perceive what enormous ungodliness and impiety would ensue, so that whatever one tramples, he tramples a part of God, and if any living creature is killed, a part of God is slaughtered (*civ.* 4.12)?

Thus God would be physically susceptible to suffering, his transcendence would be denied, and he would be reduced to the status of a soul, albeit a dominant one, among others, whereas he is the creator of all souls (*civ.* 4.31; 7.5-6). Against this view Augustine subscribes to the notion of the earth

full indeed ... of its own living beings, but, for all that, a great body among the elements, and the lowest part of the universe (*civ.* 7.23).

On account both of their fecundity and their rationality men would be more obviously divine than the universe, Augustine argues. The divine-human distinction breaks down in Varro's Stoic pantheism, despite his assertion of its reality; to maintain that stones and earth are, as it were, the bones and nails of God, in so far as they are living but not permeated by sensibility, is to be compelled to attribute intelligence to them (and, by analogy, to the bones and nails of men) if they are to be divine. This seems to Augustine to lead to an absurdity: it is tantamount to claiming that there is more intelligence in a stone than in a human being (ib.). Augustine leaves open the question of the nature of the cohesive power that makes of earth and stones what they are. Given Varro's division of the degrees of soul they would only be permeated *per analogiam* by the lowest, non-sensible degree (ib.).[179]

The various elements of this critique – its objections to the deification of the universe, and to the immanent and spatially extended presence of the divine in it, as well as to the undermining of the divine-human distinction – are also features of Augustine's anti-Manichaean polemic.[180] Augustine does not explicitly relate the concept of the warring good and evil principles of Manichaeism to the world-soul theory, and his opposition to the Manichaean doctrine is rather to be found in his analysis of volition, his account of personal identity and moral growth, and his conviction that all souls are naturally good. Only his objection to the lack of distinction between the divine and human natures in Manichaeism raises specific points about pantheistic implications whose affinity to world-soul theories is unmistakable. But it is not without significance that Augustine can use this theory of the soul to counteract the Manichaean concept of God. In *c. ep. fund.* 19.21-21.23 he argues that the human soul's lack of spatial extension, as manifested in its perceptive powers, as well as in the activities of memory and imagination and the power of judgement, is an *a fortiori* argument for the transcendent, inextended, non-corporeal nature of God. A proper understanding of the nature of soul will, in other words, effectively undermine any equation of God with an immanent, materialistic cosmic principle. This conclusion is not merely the product of Augustine's

[179] For the Stoic background to Varro's views see Long (1982), especially 36-49.
[180] Augustine's critique of Manichaeism is surveyed by Alfaric 279-320.

disinterested reasoning: he himself appears at one time to have subscribed to a concept of God that closely resembled the Stoic one which he knew from Varro. During the period immediately before his Milanese encounter with Neoplatonism his notion of the divine substance could be described as follows:

> ... that though I did not think of you (sc. God) in the shape of a human body, I was none the less compelled to think of you as some corporeal substance spread through all space, whether infused in the universe or also diffused beyond it through infinite space, and furthermore yourself incorruptible and inviolable and immutable ... since whatever I deprived of such space seemed to me to have no being (*conf.* 7.1).

God would thus be extended: there would, as Augustine mockingly remarks, be more of God in an elephant than in a sparrow (ib. §2). The only clear difference between this notion of God and the Stoic one is the concept of the infinite extension of the divinity, which is unlimited and unconfined by any other body,

> so that the earth should hold you, and the sky, and all things should hold you, and that all should be bounded in you, but you be nowhere enclosed (ib. §2).

It would seem that the notion is not unaffected by Manichaeism, or at least that it grows out of Augustine's critical preoccupation with Manichaean views about God: in *conf.* 7.3 he clearly relates the concept of God of ib. §1 to debates with the Manichees about the possible corruptibility and vulnerability of the divine principle. There he recalls that Nebridius argued that the cosmic war of good and evil seems to be either unnecessary, if God be invulnerable and invincible, or unworthy of God, if his nature can be harmed. We should probably understand the concept of God in *conf.* 7.1 then as a transitional theory: Augustine's later, developed doctrine will attempt to reconcile God's transcendence with his non-corporeal immanence in nature, especially in human nature.[181]

Augustine found a fully-fledged theory of world-soul in Plotinus and Porphyry, and he refers to this in a number of passages of *de civitate dei*. He is aware that for Plotinus the notion of world-soul is maintained alongside a belief in a transcendent divine principle, distinct from soul, and that this principle is soul's 'creator':

> Plotinus, elucidating Plato's meaning, repeatedly and emphatically asserts that not even the soul which they believe to be the soul of the world enjoys its happiness from any other source than ours, that is, from the light which is distinct from it and by which it is created, and by whose intelligible

---

[181] For possible Stoic and Neoplatonic influences on Augustine's later view see Courcelle (1968) 393-404.

illumination it shines intelligibly (*et quo intellegibiliter inluminante intellegibiliter lucet*), *civ*. 10.2.[182]

This clearly refers to the doctrine of the hypostases, but Augustine does not here explicitly identify more than one hypostasis higher than the *anima intellectualis*. The world-soul in the Neoplatonists, as Augustine indicates, is that of *Timaeus* 30ff., as interpreted in later Platonic exegesis:

> But his (sc. Porphyry's) view should rather have been corrected, especially as you (sc. Platonists) hold such incredible views in common with him about the soul of this visible world and massive material mass. For, following Plato, you hold that the world is a living being, and the happiest of living beings, and you want it to be everlasting also (*civ*. 10.29).

Rather than scrutinizing this theory, however, Augustine employs it as an eristic weapon with which to expose contradictions in Neoplatonic beliefs. Thus the ensouled, eternal, blessed heavenly bodies of Platonism are contrasted with Platonic refusals to countenance the incarnation of Christ (ib.). And the same Platonic belief about the heavens is, Augustine argues, inconsistent with the Porphyrian injunction to escape from the body,[183] and with Porphyry's rejection of Christ's incarnation on the principle of this injunction:

> As ... you say that among the heavenly bodies are the undying bodies of those immortally happy, why do you maintain that, in order to be happy, we must flee every kind of body, thereby giving the impression of fleeing the Christian faith in an ostensibly rational way ... (ib.)?[184]

The same attitude is observable in Augustine's Eastertide sermons on the resurrection of the body:

> You (sc. Porphyry) who say that all body must be avoided, kill the universe! You are saying that I should escape from my flesh: let your Jupiter[185] escape from sky and earth (*ser*. 241.7)!

In fact, Augustine argues, Plato's own position in the *Timaeus* makes nonsense of the Porphyrian injunction. The Demiurge endows the heavenly bodies with *animae intellectuales*, they are gods, the universe is eternal, and the immortality of these divine *animae* is explicitly guaranteed by the Demiurge's

---

[182] Scholarly opinion on Augustine's source for this Plotinian doctrine differs: Theiler (1933) 2 = Theiler (1966) 162 suggests that the theme of the source of the world-soul's happiness is Porphyrian rather than Plotinian, and sees Porphyry as the mediator of Plotinus' views; Henry (1934) 129f. adduces parallels from *Enn*. 5.1.10 and 5.6.4 for much of the passage's phrasing.

[183] For this theme in Porphyry's *de regressu animae* see Bidez 88-97, 39*; Smith 20-39.

[184] In *civ*. 10.30 the words 'God gave (a) Soul to the world' refer, not to the world-soul, but to the creation of individual souls, as the context (transmigration, soul's conversion to God) makes clear.

[185] Cf. ib.: 'the soul of the universe is called Jupiter ...'.

will and design (*ser.* 241.8, quoting *Tim.* 41b).[186] Augustine can conclude that, for Plato:

> See, God frees from anxiety the gods made by him: he gives them the unconcern of immortality, he frees them from the worry of having to leave their spherical bodies. Is every body really to be fled (ib.)?

Augustine understands Platonic cosmogony to consist in the creation of a hierarchy of deities. The highest God (*deus summus*) creates the subordinate great God (*magnus deus*), that is, the ensouled universe (*mundus*) and it in turn has precedence over the deities within the universe (*civ.* 13.17). The universe possesses a rational or intelligent soul:

> And this same (sc. universe) they suppose to be a living being, with, as they assert, a rational or intellectual soul enclosed in the huge mass of its body ... for this soul Plato believes to be diffused and extended by musical harmony from the innermost middle of the earth ... throughout all its parts to the heights and extremities of the heavens (ib.).

In the living, everlasting universe this soul enjoys 'the perfect bliss of wisdom' (*perfectam sapientiae felicitatem*, ib.). Much as Augustine would like to see in this model a parallel to the life of the ensouled, resurrected human body, he refrains from pronouncing on its truth with reference to the universe:

> Whether this view of Plato's about the stars is true, is another matter. For we cannot concede to him out of hand that these luminous spheres or globes, which shine with their corporeal light upon the earth by day or by night, are animated by their own individual souls, and that these are intellectual and blessed (*civ.* 13.16).

Thus in *de civitate dei*, written over several years after 412, Augustine maintains the same agnostic view evidenced in the earlier *de consensu evangelistarum* and reaffirmed at the end of his career in the *retractationes*.[187] In *cons. ev.* there is a reference to a Platonic allegory, explicitly said to be of recent (i.e. Middle or Neoplatonic) date, where 'Kronos' is etymologically explained as *koros* and *nous*, fullness of intellect or mind, and the equivalent Latin divine name *Saturnus* is derived in a parallel explanation from a bizarre Graeco-Roman hybridization of *satur* and *nous*.[188] According to this allegory Jupiter (Zeus), son of Saturn (Kronos), is the world-soul emanating from (*profluentem*) the supreme mind (*cons. ev.* 1.35). The fullest Neoplatonic elaboration of this allegorical/etymological *topos* is found in a number of

[186] Cf. *civ.* 13.16, where the same passage is said to be taken from Cicero's Latin translation of *Tim.* (= Cicero *Tim.* 40, which is, in fact, loosely quoted by Augustine).

[187] For the chronology of *cons. ev.* and *civ.* see Zarb 50f.; 62f.

[188] For the approximate age of the allegory see *cons. ev.* 1.35: 'More recent Platonic philosophers ... who lived in what was already the Christian era'. Augustine further refers to a 'new explanation', unknown to Varro and Cicero (ib.). In fact, Cicero's etymological explanation of *Saturnus* is different: 'Saturn is so called because he is sated with years' (*nat. deor.* 2.64, cf. ib. 3.62).

passages of Plotinus (the etymology of 'Kronos' derives ultimately from Plato, *Cratylus* 396b).[189] Augustine does not refer to the Ouranos (= Plotinian One) part of this allegory, just as he does not intimate in *civ.* 10.2 that, for Plotinus, there are two hypostases higher than soul (although he is aware of the three hypostases doctrine, referring in *civ.* 10.23 to *Enn.* 5.1 by name). There is no compelling reason to believe that Augustine knew the allegory from Plotinus, even if *Enn.* 5.1, where it is twice evoked (5.1.4.9-10; 5.1.7.33-35), was probably available to him in translation.[190] We know that the allegory was employed in varying forms in Middle Platonic *Timaeus* exegesis, including that of Atticus' pupil Harpocration of Argos in the late second century.[191] Augustine's explanation of *Saturnus* may even require us to presuppose a Latin version of the allegory – or at least a version showing familiarity with Latin – upon which he draws.[192] Whatever Augustine's source, it is precisely this sort of polytheistic allegory that will have made aspects of Neoplatonic metaphysics, including the notion of the world-soul, appear potentially alien to his Christian philosophy. But Augustine may also be ill-disposed towards acceptance of the world-soul theory because in both Plotinus and Porphyry it is inextricably related to a strong version of the doctrine of the unity of all souls.[193] Augustine cannot accept the full implications of such a doctrine. He would clearly have preferred the later Neoplatonic hierarchy of a plurality of stratified soul-kinds, in which souls remain in the order to which they belong. That hierarchy could (and did) accommodate the world-soul, but the latter's existence is not a necessary condition of its acceptability.[194]

We might therefore expect Augustine to be less hesitant than he is on the question of the world-soul. Why does he vacillate? He accepts the general principle that bodies receive their existence and form, and continue to subsist as organized entities, because of the presence in them of soul (*imm. an.* 24; *quant. an.* 70; *mus.* 6.44: cf. *retr.* 1.11.4). If that is so, then the great body of the universe might seem to require a soul. That is why Augustine hesitates to dismiss the world-soul theory. That is also the reason why he can temper the agnosticism of *retr.* 1.11.4 with an alternative theory, which, while not making it necessary to call the universe a living being (*animal*), does account for its cohesion. This theory is that such cohesion is due to angelic agency:

[189] The Plotinus passages are collected and discussed in Hadot (1981).

[190] See Henry (1934) 126-33.

[191] See Proclus, *in Tim.* 1.304 Diehl. On Harpocration see Dillon 258-62.

[192] To speculate: a Latin writer, conveying the sense of the 'Kronos' = *koros* + *nous* etymological allegory, might well have been struck by the parallel *koros/satur* and glossed his translation or paraphrase from the Greek accordingly. Marius Victorinus, translating Plotinus, could well have done so. Or – to speculate further – Porphyry, presumably familiar with Latin after years spent in Italy, might well comment on the parallel in a Greek treatment of the allegory.

[193] See Dörrie (1959) 128f.; 154; 170; 193, for the Porphyrian theory's 'strong version'. For the possibility that some milder version of the unity theory might have appealed to Augustine see pp. 60-2.

[194] Such a stratified arrangement of souls is found e.g. in Iamblichus: see Wallis 118-20; Dörrie (1959) 128f.

There is nevertheless a spiritual and living power present, even if the universe is not a living being. This power in the holy angels for the embellishment and management of the universe serves God, and is quite properly believed in by those who do not fully comprehend it (*retr.* 1.11.4).

Now the angels, Augustine observes, are never called *animae* in Scripture: they are 'spirits' (*spiritus*). It was such angelic spirits, he adds, that he meant by the 'rational and intellectual numbers (*numeri*) of blessed and holy souls' in *mus.* 6.58, even if he wrongly called them *animae* there.[195] It would be a mistake to see in this alternative theory a substitute for the world-soul view in all its aspects. For one thing, angelic spirits are not immanent in the universe, as is the world-soul. Moreover, they are a plurality, whereas world-soul is one. But Augustine can none the less contemplate the possibility that some functions of the cosmic soul – such as the ordering and cohesion of the universe – may be due to the agency of this rational creation, a creation of whose Scriptural pedigree he was in no doubt, even if he could give a strong Platonic colouring to its details. The cosmic soul could boast no such pedigree.[196]

(xiv) Reincarnation and transmigration

Both Manichaeism and Pythagorean and Platonic elements in the philosophical tradition will have introduced Augustine to theories of the reincarnation of the human soul and its transmigration into animal bodies. His rejection of such theories is, broadly speaking, consistent. We may distinguish between reincarnation as a natural process, and reincarnation as punishment for sin. In the former case, in which all souls can be reincarnated, Augustine's attack is based on his understanding of the inalienable happiness (*beatitudo*) of the good souls in paradise, a happiness which the proponents of reincarnation admit:

> For how can that be real happiness of whose everlastingness one can never be sure, when the soul is either completely ignorant of the truth regarding its future wretchedness, or in its happiness is utterly miserable through terror at the prospect (*civ.* 12.14)?

For Plato[197] is said to claim that the souls of the good 'fly to the heavens' (*ser.* 241.4), but after a lengthy period, in which they have come to forget the

---

[195] Cf. *Gn. litt.* 8.24.45-25.47. On the role of the angels in creation see *Gn. litt.* 4.32.49. For this theme in *Gn. litt.* see Agaësse/Solignac, *BA* 48, 645-53. For Augustine's use of *spiritus* with reference to angels see Schumacher 36-44. For his angelology in general see the literature referred to below p. 124 n. 36.

[196] Teske's attempt to demonstrate that Augustine believed at least implicitly in the existence of the world-soul as late as the time of writing of the *Confessions* is ingeniously argued, but is too dependent on special pleading to be convincing. See further p. 154 n. 11.

[197] Plato is not here explicitly named, but see §6. The view is explicitly associated with Plato at *civ.* 13.19: *Phaedrus* 248-9 is meant. But Augustine's account is a gross simplification of Plato's views there (see Hackforth 78-91 for these), and he seems unaware of the different views of Plato

miseries of earthly life, they wish to return to bodies. The following passage is more explicit:

> They (sc. the good) go to the upper reaches of the heavens, rest there among the stars and lights visible to us, or in some secret and hidden heavenly place, forget all their previous misfortunes, and are once again filled with a keen delight to return to bodies, and come back to endure these (*ser.* 240.4).

Augustine finds it difficult to account for this wish for re-embodiment if we do not grant to souls, as a necessary prerequisite, memories of their previous embodiment (*ser.* 241.4). And these memories must include recollections of life's miseries, for to argue that the souls of the blessed are ignorant of future suffering is to ascribe to them in their blessedness less knowledge of this life than we who are embodied. It is to make them 'mistakenly ... blessed ... not because of their eternity, but on account of a lie' (ib.§5). Thus, quoting Virgil, *Aen.* 6.719-721, Augustine can impute to Aeneas in the underworld ('what does it mean, such fearful longing of these wretches for the light?', 721) his own incredulity that the souls of the fortunate should desire to regain the light of day (ib.).[198] In this respect, Augustine can only approve Porphyry's modification[199] of Plato's and Plotinus' alleged views:

> He (sc. Porphyry) was of the opinion that the souls of wise man are so completely freed from bodily bonds that, fleeing every kind of body, they are preserved for ever in their blessedness at their Father's side ... he maintained that they (sc. the souls) would live for ever, not only without earthly bodies, but without any bodies whatsoever (*civ.* 13.19; cf. §30).

But what of the second aspect of the theories of reincarnation, namely as punishment for previously committed wrongs? Plato had maintained that the rest of mankind apart from the true philosophers would be re-embodied after a very short period of time in appropriate human or animal form:

> those, however, who have led a life of folly return very soon to bodies, whether human or bestial, in accordance with their deserts (*civ.* 13.19).[200]

In this view human life is a place of punishment and the body is 'like a prison of the soul' (*ser.* 240.4). Augustine's critique of reincarnation as punishment is chiefly based on this concept of the body.[201] He argues that such a view

---

on the same subject in the *Timaeus*, as well as in the *Meno*, *Phaedo* and *Republic* (see Robinson 86-9). We must assume an indirect knowledge of *Phaedr.*, probably Porphyry's critique of Plato's views. For Plato quotations embedded in Porphyrian contexts in Augustine and Claudianus Mamertus see Courcelle (1948) 226-9.

[198] See n. 127 above for Augustine's use of *Aen.* in this connection.

[199] For the significance of Porphyry's views see Smith 56-68.

[200] See Robinson 128-31 on Plato's differing views about punishment for wrongdoing.

[201] For a history of the motif, derived from *Phaedo* 62b and 82e, in Latin literature from Cicero to Boethius see Courcelle (1965). Cicero (*Tusc. disp.* 1.74; *rep.* 6.13; *amicit.* 14; *pro Scauro* 4) is a likely source for Augustine; he may also have read a version of *Phaed.* 62b and 82e in Porphyry's *de regressu animae* (cf. n. 25 above). See also *c. Acad.* 1.9.

contradicts other views of Plato's. For if the lesser gods of *Tim*. 41a-d and 69c are the makers of man's bodies (*civ*. 12.25; 12.27) then these gods, far from being our benevolent, paternal creators, are

> none other than the artisans of our fetters or prisons, and are not our makers, but our gaolers, and the ones who lock us away in dreadful penitentiaries, and bind us in the weightiest of chains (*civ*. 12.27).

Moreover, Plato himself maintains that animate beings, mortal and immortal, are a necessary condition of the world's goodness and beauty (*Tim*. 30d; 92c):

> How can the same Plato assert that the world could not have been of such surpassing beauty and goodness if it were not filled with every kind (that is, both mortal and immortal) of living being (*civ*. 12.27)?

Finally, it is claimed that the Platonic Demiurge held in his intellect the forms of the universe and all its animate beings, and might even be assumed to be their most appropriate creator:

> And if God, as Plato constantly reminds us, held in his eternal intelligence the forms not only of the entire universe but also of all living beings, how can it be that he did not create them all himself (ib.)?[202]

If that is so, then creation cannot but be good. But if the body is a good it can hardly function as the vehicle of punishment for sin. Punitive reincarnation is thus disallowed: for the same reason Augustine will also reject all theories of original embodiment as punishment for sin committed in a pre-bodily condition.

Augustine does not therefore need to become embroiled in one particular Platonist controversy over metempsychosis, the question whether human souls can be punitively embodied in animals.[203] Neither does he spend much time arguing the untenability, for a Christian, of transmigration, despite such Scriptural texts as Ps. 48:13 ('he is made equal to the animals and has become like them') and the pro-transmigration theses of Origen. He approves what he understands to be Porphyry's modification of the views of Plato and Plotinus, viz. the limitation of metensomatosis of human souls to human bodies:

> However ... Porphyry is to a great extent (*ex magna parte*) correct in this belief, in that he at least held the view that human souls can only be precipitated into

---

[202] These lines are less an account of what Plato says than of what Middle Platonists (followed elsewhere by Augustine: see p. 97 n. 40) maintain, viz. that the Ideas are thoughts of God.

[203] For an account of the controversy in the Platonism of the Imperial period see Dörrie (1957) = Dörrie (1976) 420-40 (but cf. the following note).

human beings, and did not hesitate at all to do away with prisons of the bestial kind (*civ.* 10.30).[204]

The phrase *ex magna parte* might seem at first sight surprising, given Augustine's fundamental rejection of reincarnation. To appreciate its significance we must elucidate the assumptions and concerns behind it. This elucidation can only succeed if we appreciate that there are two very different forms of transmigration critique in Augustine. One kind is polemical, pouring ridicule on the notion that humans might return in animal form and so be confronted with surviving human relatives. This form of ridicule is stock anti-Pythagorean polemic, and Augustine can use it against the Manichees: could killing animals not be homicide, if not parricide? (*c. Adim.* 12.1-2) Elsewhere he can oppose Manichaean views in a more fundamental and serious way. Their thesis would expose the divine nature qua soul to mutability and unworthy incarnation in grass or worms (*Gn. litt.* 7.11.17).

Polemic of the kind just noted lies behind Augustine's speculation that the reason for Porphyry's reported rejection of metempsychosis was that

> he was evidently ashamed to believe in it, for fear that a mother, returning as a mule, might carry her son on her back (*civ.* 10.30).[205]

For this reason Augustine can adopt the view, also ascribed to Porphyry, that talk of metempsychosis is figurative rather than literal: what occurs is moral, rather than physical transformation, and it occurs, Augustine adds – himself possibly modifying Porphyry – in this life:

> Through a kind of moral perversity and depravity people become like animals and so in a certain manner are changed into animals (*Gn. litt.* 7.10.15).[206]

Thus apparent recollection of having been in an animal body may be due to demonic influence: the parallel of dream-suggestions is cited (*Gn. litt.* 7.11.16). Such recollections, particularly as adduced by the Pythagoreans in

[204] For Origen's view on transmigration see *de principiis passim* and the nn. in H. Görgemanns/H. Karpp (edd.), *Origenes. Vier Bücher von den Prinzipien* (Texte zur Forschung, 24), Darmstadt 1976 (references: 877f.). Courcelle (1968) 374 n. 1 argues that it is Origen at whom the remarks of *Gn. litt.* 7.9.13 are directed. Augustine's attitudes to transmigration are discussed by Agaësse/Solignac, *BA* 48, 706-10. As for Porphyry's views, Deuse 129-67 has convincingly demonstrated that Augustine, and the indirect tradition in general, misrepresent them: the soul's primary choice (to which the indirect tradition does not refer) can indeed opt for human or animal existence. It is only the secondary choice that is limited in the sense described by Augustine.

[205] On the motif of shame determining Porphyry's view see the passages in Augustine assembled by Courcelle (1968) 436 n. 1.

[206] Dörrie (1957) 423-6 = Dörrie (1976) 429-31 argues that the view is to be attributed to Porphyry, referring to Aeneas of Gaza, *Theophrastos* 12.21f. Colonna and Stobaeus 1.447 Wachsmuth. But Deuse 162-4 has advanced plausible grounds for attributing the Aeneas passage's contents entirely to Iamblichus. In Aeneas we also find the motif of shame leading to a critique of the transmigration theory (12.13-14 C.). But the notion of moral, as opposed to physical, metempsychosis is older, as Courcelle (1968) 373 n. 1 points out: it is already found in Cicero, *off.* 3.82.

support of their views, are 'untrue memories' (*trin.* 12.24). Augustine argues from the viewpoint of common sense that recollection of previous incarnations, whether animal or human, ought to be relatively common, like our recollection of dreams, if we have, in fact, undergone such successive embodiments (ib.).

Augustine therefore criticizes the transmigration theory by pouring scorn upon its implications, and he explains apparent memories of previous embodiments by reference to the imagination, to dream and hallucinatory experiences which may caused by some malevolent supernatural agency. But a second kind of critique has been mentioned above. It is more basic and more serious. An underlying concern behind Platonic controversies over transmigration was: can the rational capability of the human soul become so completely inefficacious that it is, so to speak, submerged in the soul of an irrational animal?[207] For if one accepts the Platonic principle that reason is not an accidental property of the human soul but belongs to its essence, it would seem to follow that a human soul cannot become an irrational soul of the animal kind without destruction of its substance. This consideration led Iamblichus, for one, to deny the possibility of human transmigration into animal bodies.[208] Now Augustine does not appear to have explicitly and expressly adopted this argument, nor need he have done so: we have seen that his objections to all forms of reincarnation are fundamental. But there is some indication that he was aware of the argument. In *Gn. litt.* 7.10.15, where, as we have seen, he puts forward his idea of moral 'transmigration', he argues that what has led to the belief in physical transmigration was an alleged 'similarity in behaviour' (*morum similitudo*)[209] between certain men and certain types of animal, so that misers become ants, rapacious men become kites, fierce and haughty man become lions, and voluptuaries become pigs. But, Augustine suggests, this similarity of behaviour or character is, upon closer examination, patently false. A pig will never be more a man than a pig; tame lions are more readily comparable with dogs or sheep than with humans. Even animal behaviour which deviates from the norm is always more like animal than human behaviour. This factor is sufficient to discount the hypothesis of human souls causing certain types of apparently anthropomorphic animal behaviour:

> Since, then, animals do not desist from animal behaviour, and those who become in some minor way different to the rest are none the less more like their own species than like humankind, and resemble people far less than animals, these souls (sc. of animals) will never be human, if they assume characteristics which are more like (sc. animal ones), *Gn. litt.* 7.10.15.

Likeness of character or behaviour between men and animals is therefore only analogical. But we can apply the metaphors of animal courage, timidity, etc. to human behaviour, and vice versa.

---

[207] This point is well brought out by Dörrie (1957) 414; 433f. = Dörrie (1976) 420; 438f.

[208] Similarities and differences between Iamblichus and his Neoplatonic predecessors, especially Porphyry, on the question of transmigration are clearly observed by Deuse 129-67; 205f.; 212.

[209] Cf. Cicero *Tim.* 45: 'And it (sc. the morally bad soul) should be transferred to the animal and bestial forms most similar in character (*moribus simillimas*) to it' (after Plato *Tim.* 42c).

Now the argument that animal behaviour is always intrinsically animal and human behaviour always intrinsically human supports the tenet that animal and human natures are not interchangeable, but are substantially what they are. The impossibility of human nature becoming animal nature is an inevitable consequence of such an argument. This argument is at once broader and less stringent than the argument that the rational human soul cannot become an irrational animal soul. The latter argument is under-pinned by the concept of the inalienable nature of reason, a concept with which Augustine was familiar. For the claim that the relation between mind and rational knowledge is substantial rather than accidental is the basis of his demonstration of the soul's (mind's) immortality in *sol.* 2.22; 2.24 and *imm. an.* 8-9, etc. Why did he not re-employ that argument in contexts such as *Gn. litt.* 7.10.15? The reason must surely be that, as has been suggested above, the transmigration controversy of later Platonism does not really concern him, since he rejects all such theories. Unlike Iamblichus, for whom the very identity of the human soul is at stake if Plato's transmigration views are to be adopted literally, Augustine is not obliged to defend his substantially similar concept of mind or soul on this particular front. But Augustine can nevertheless appreciate what he believed Porphyry to be opposing: that is why he can be generous to his stand on the transmigration issue and, as we have seen, claim that the Neoplatonic philosopher is 'to a great extent' (*ex magna parte*) correct against Plato.[210] He is correct on the, for Augustine, irrelevant issue, but in order to safeguard the vital principle that reason is of the essence of the human soul. So when Augustine deals with a supporting reason for transmigration in *Gn. litt.* 7.10.15 he can confine himself to countering it on its own terms by means of the argument about the self-contained nature of human and animal behaviour. That argument is sufficient to his immediate purpose, for it undermines the specific transmigration theory under discussion.

(xv) The soul-vehicle

In an early letter to the sharp-witted Nebridius Augustine reminds his correspondent of their frequent, eager and excited discussions about the possible existence of a soul-vehicle:

> You must remember what was frequently discussed by us in conversation and disturbed us, keen and agitated as we were, namely, the question of a kind of permanent (so to speak) body or quasi-body of the soul, which, as you recall, is also called a vehicle (*vehiculum*) by some (*ep.* 13.2).[211]

---

[210] See p. 72.

[211] A brief but illuminating survey of soul-vehicle theories is given by Dodds (1963) 313-21. For the theory in Neoplatonism see also Verbeke 351-85. For Augustine cf. Alfaric 468 n. 2; 497 n. 3. The Manichaean form of the theory does not appear to have influenced Augustine or his correspondents: for it see A. Henrichs/L. Koenen, 'Der Kölner Mani-Kodex (P. Colon. inv. nr. 4780) *peri tês gennês tou sômatos autou.* Edition der Seiten 1-72: *Zeitschrift für Papyrologie und*

It is its intermediate status, neither as material as the body nor as immaterial as the soul, which causes him difficulty in this letter. How can we be aware of the existence of something that is neither intelligible nor perceptible? Even if we do not so much perceive bodies directly as cognize 'many things ... relating to body' (§3: Augustine is thinking of the immaterial nature of the images that we perceive), and so, in a sense, perceive something intelligible, our senses must nevertheless convey information about bodies to our understanding:

> Nobody can know whether that body exists unless a sense has reported something about it (§4).

In other words, what is intelligible to our perceptions is necessarily a consequence of sensation. Now our senses have not registered the existence of the *vehiculum*: it has therefore never been perceived. Augustine suggests that it might conceivably be perceived by a being with sharper senses than ours (§3). In the circumstances, however, he recommends abandonment of the unmanageable 'little question' (§2). We note that he understands the hypothesis of the *vehiculum* to be an attempt to account for a medium for soul's local movement –

> It is evident beyond doubt that if it (sc. the vehicle) is moved in space, it is not an object of intellection (§2).

> It is conceived as some kind ... of body upon which soul depends to move from place to place (§3).

– presumably when it is not otherwise embodied (see Evodius, *ep*. 158.6).

In *ep*. 158.5 Evodius poses certain questions about the soul after it has quitted its earthly body. Is it none the less still embodied? If not, then its substance must be merged with that of other souls, for it lacks the apparently necessary, distinguishing or individualizing body.[212] The localization of the rich man and Lazarus, in the flames and in Abraham's bosom respectively, seems to imply corporeal existence of some kind (Luke 16:22ff.).[213] Or is it possible that the one soul-substance, though undifferentiated in its essence, is none the less differently affected in different respects, now rejoicing, now in pain, on the analogy of the various faculties of memory, will and intellect incorporeally coexisting and fulfilling their several functions without infringing upon each other? If this view of the 'one substance assembled out of many souls' is not acceptable, then what is there to prevent the soul having

---

Epigraphik 19 (1975) 17; 72-4. The vehicle *metaphor* is applied to the relation of soul to body by Augustine, *ser. Denis* 2.4, where the soul is the 'charioteer', echoing Plato, *Phaedrus* 246a-b. The voice is described as the 'vehicle' of the inner, unspoken word in contexts where it serves as an analogy for Christ's incarnation (Christ = Word; flesh = vehicle): *ser.* 288.4; *ser. Denis* 2.2; cf. *ser.* 119.7; 120.2; 300.5.

[212] Evodius may betray Porphyrian influence here: see p. 69. and n. 193 above.

[213] Augustine interprets the same Scriptural passage in *civ.* 21.3 as indicating that the disembodied soul can feel emotions: see pp. 53f.

another body after it has left this fleshly one, so that it continuously animates a body of some kind and can, because of this embodiment, move locally to whatever place it must go (§6)? Such embodiment would not necessarily be inconsistent with subsequent resurrection of the fleshly body, and we could even speculate that the body thus posthumously possessed is related to the element of fire, whose warmth departs from the corpse at death – alone of all the elements to do so (ib.). The soul embodied in its vehicle would be active ('it makes use of a lively mental concentration', §7); one should not imagine it in a state of lethargy, for that would be a sign of an 'annihilated ... soul' (ib.). It might even be possible that such a vehicle has the senses of sight and hearing, if no others (§8). Evodius speculates on whether such a hypothesis might not also account for appearances of the dead to the living (§8-10), and whether we might not conclude that God alone is always without a body, and that soul can never be without one (§11).

There is no comparable account of the soul-vehicle in the writings of Augustine and his correspondents. We may assume that Evodius gives full expression to the hypothesis as it was known to Augustine's circle, although the well-informed and philosophically talented Nebridius might have had further details to add.[214] Augustine's reply to Evodius in *ep.* 159 does not take up the question of the vehicle directly, confining itself to an explanation of imaginative vision by means of incorporeal images (§2; §4): in such exercises of the imagination the soul is its own world, without need of contemporaneous corporeal faculties. If he is silent on the matter here, Augustine is elsewhere openly agnostic about it. In *Gn. litt.* 8.5.9 he refers to the theory that souls, once departed the earthly body, 'are contained bodily in visible places', recalling, like Evodius in *ep.* 158.5, the case of the rich man and Lazarus. But he finds the problem a 'deep ... question and one needing much discussion', on which no firm conclusion can be reached: 'it is better to remain in doubt concerning arcane matters than to quarrel over what is uncertain'. In *Gn. litt.* 12.32.60 Augustine is inclined to the view that the soul does not have a pre-resurrection body after death. Punishments in the afterlife are spiritual rather than corporeal (§61-62). We should not think of souls as being in a place after death, if by 'place' is meant physical space. Perhaps they have some form of incorporeal bodily appearance (*corporis similitudo*), just as dreamers have of their own bodies, so that they may be said to subsist without bodies in a non-corporeal medium (§62).

It would seem plausible that Augustine learnt of the astral body from Porphyry, just as he learnt of theurgy and the *pneumatikê psukhê* from him. But the evidence does not allow us to assert this with confidence.[215] Missing from Augustine's (or Evodius') references are such typical Porphyrian characteristics of the *pneuma* as its adherence qua aetherial substance to the soul in the heavens (*ouranos*), its progressive 'darkening' and 'thickening' in the course of its descent through the air, so that it becomes moist, its role of

[214] See p. 78.
[215] Theiler (1933) 38 = Theiler (1966) 206 and Dodds (1963) 318 n. 5 are too confident.

substrate to the lower soul, and its function as an organ of perception.[216] We might not expect to find the first two notions in Augustine, given his disinclination to believe in the soul's pre-existence. But it is striking that the other two characteristics do not appear either, and that, in general, speculation about the *vehiculum* seems confined to its role as a posthumous body for the soul, without any discernible function in this life (though we cannot be certain what lies behind the phrase 'a kind of permanent body' in *ep.* 13.2). Moreover, the two characteristics of the vehicle mentioned in our texts – its possible fiery nature and its function as a medium of the soul's local movement outside the fleshly body – do not point unequivocally to Porphyry. The fiery body is found (alongside an airy alternative) in Plotinus, *Enn.* 4.3.9.5 and 3.5.6.37 (of daemons), but not in Porphyry (not that this makes Plotinus the source of Evodius' tentative remarks); the 'carrier' function of the vehicle, which is, of course, the reason for its designation as *okhêma* or *vehiculum*, is common to most accounts, being ultimately derived from the Platonic boat and chariot metaphors which gave the Neoplatonists the authority for their theory, even if its substance is not to be found there.[217] Either Augustine has greatly simplified and streamlined the vehicle theory, or his references to it derive from another source than the assumed Neoplatonic one, and respond to other problems.[218]

It might be that the motive behind the discussions of the vehicle theory in Augustine's circle is the belief that it is natural for the soul to be embodied. Augustine refers to this belief in a passage dealing with the resurrection of the body, which may be accounted for

> either through some other less evident cause, or because it (sc. the soul) has an inherent natural longing (*appetitus*) to control a body (*Gn. litt.* 12.35.68).

Soul can only achieve perfect vision of the unchangeable substance of God when this appetite is stilled by the provision of a spiritual, resurrected body totally under its control:

> It is somehow hindered by the appetite from proceeding with all its attention to that highest heaven, so long as there is no body at hand, through whose management that appetite is assuaged (ib.).[219]

---

[216] See Porphyry *sent.* 29 and *antr. nymph.* 10f. See the remarks of Dodds (1963) 318 and Smith 152-8; Deuse 218-29.

[217] See Dodds (1963) 315.

[218] Augustine has less qualms about assigning a bodily vehicle to God (*ser.* 7.4), or to angels and demons, to facilitate their interventions in human affairs: *divin. daem.* 9; *Gn. litt.* 8.25.47. See Pépin (1964) 56f. = Pépin (1977) 34f. Verbeke 504 points out that there can be no link between the *pneuma* of Porphyry and Augustine's *spiritus*: for the latter's relation to Porphyry's *pneumatikê psukhê* see, however, Agaësse/Solignac, *BA* 49, 564-6. Cf. Deuse 218-30 and n. 9 above.

[219] For the doctrine of the resurrection body (treatment of which is beyond the scope of this book) see Miles 99-125; H.-I. Marrou (with A.-M. La Bonnardière), 'Le dogme de la résurrection des corps et la théologie des valeurs humaines selon l'enseignement de saint Augustin', *REAug* 12 (1966) 111-36 = H.-I. Marrou, *Patristique et Humanisme. Mélanges* (Patristica Sorbonensia, 9) Paris 1976, 429-55. On possible influences of Porphyry's views on

Given this perspective, the vehicle, far from being what it was for the Neoplatonists, a psychical envelope to be shed when the heavenly sphere was transcended and the irrational soul dissolved, might rather have become for Augustine the foreshadowing of the resurrected body, the necessary and even desirable substrate of the soul between physical death and the final resurrection. But Augustine cannot be sure about the vehicle, and he maintains that it is not necessary to posit a bodily substrate in order that psychological functions may occur.

---

pneuma and *pneumatikê psukhê* upon Augustine's account of the resurrection body see G. Watson, 'St. Augustine, the Platonists and the Resurrection Body: Augustine's use of a Fragment from Porphyry', *Irish Theological Quarterly* 50 (1983/4) 222-32 (cf. n. 218 above).

CHAPTER THREE

Sense-perception

In his discussion of sense-perception Augustine shares the preoccupations of philosophers in the Graeco-Roman tradition, and the problems which he identifies remain in many cases those of the modern philosophy of mind. He recognizes that external objects somehow affect our sense-organs, and cause certain physiological changes to occur in our bodies. At the same time, he is convinced that perception is a psychological activity, over and above physical and physiological processes. But how are the activity and the processes related? And what epistemological claims can we make for our perceptions of the external world? These are the chief questions which Augustine's account of sense-perception attempts to answer.[1]

(i) The physiological mechanism of sense-perception

It will be appropriate to begin with a brief examination of Augustine's account of the physical and physiological aspects of sensation, even if, as we shall see, this raises questions which can only be answered in the subsequent discussion of the psychological processes involved in sense-perception. Augustine was concerned to adopt a satisfactory explanation of the means whereby the sense-organs receive impressions, and of how and where we co-ordinate and correlate such impressions. Like Plotinus, he was able to take over the discovery and theoretical exploitation of the nervous system and its functions, as elaborated by the Alexandrian physicians Herophilus and Erasistratus, and subsequently by Galen.[2] Thus Augustine accepted that it is the sensory nerves which transmit stimuli, and that they transmit these to the brain, to which they are attached and where they originate. Fine, pipe-like passages (*tenues fistulae*) lead from the central part of the brain to the outer surface of the body and the various sense-organs: in the case of touch,

---

[1] The clearest account of Augustine's theory of sense-perception is still that of Kälin 8-40. See also Bubacz (1981) 93-132; Gannon; Gilson 73-87; Markus (1967) 374-9. Miles 9-39; Nash 39-59; Thonnard (1958). None of these accounts, however, takes the physiological basis of Augustine's theory into consideration. A general survey is provided by R.F. Newbold, 'Perception and Sensory Awareness among Latin Writers in Late Antiquity', *Classica et Mediaevalia* 33 (1981/2) 169-90.

[2] For Plotinus' use of the discovery of the nervous system in his theory of sense-perception see Blumenthal (1971) 75. For an account of the discovery and its historical significance see Solmsen. The interaction of scientific and philosophical speculation in the medical schools from Erasistratus to Galen (particularly in relation to the doctrine of the *pneuma*) is brilliantly described by Verbeke 175-220.

especially fine channels (*tenuissimi ... rivuli*) run through the cervical and spinal marrow to all parts of the body (*Gn. litt.* 7.13.20). This, says Augustine, is what the physicians not merely assert, but also claim to demonstrate (ib.).[3] Less technically, he can talk of 'roads', 'streets' or 'paths' leading from sense-organ to brain (*iter, via sentiendi: Gn. litt.* 12.20.42). The sense-organs can be described as the body's doors (*fores corporis*, ib.). In his sermons, Augustine popularizes the image of the city or the house in accounts of sense-perception: the sense-organ, for example, the eye, is a window, through which the indwelling mind may, or may not, look at the external world (*en. Ps.* 41.7; *ser.* 126.3).[4] Augustine is precise concerning which part of the brain is the source and terminus of sensation: it is the foremost of the three ventricles in the cerebrum. The other two function as the seat of memory and the source of the motor nerves (*Gn. litt.* 7.18.24). Memory is the indispensable link between sensory stimulus and the subsequent voluntary movement (*spontaneus motus*) of bodily actions. If the ventricles are damaged or defective, sensation or memory or movement, or all three, will be frustrated (ib.), just as individual senses may be incapable of functioning through a defect of the sense-organ, as is the case, for example, with blindness (*Gn. litt.* 12.20.42).

We may therefore say that the basis of Augustine's theory of sense-perception is physiological in character: it reflects long-established, but none the less advanced scientific opinion.[5] At the same time, however, his account derives from a long philosophical tradition. This should not surprise us, for philosophers and physicians addressed themselves to the same questions, and, if the philosophical schools had sometimes defended alternative, older physiological theories against the new discoveries of Herophilus and Erasistratus, the latter had decked out their empirical observations with speculative assertions that had a long philosophical pedigree. The cardinal example of such speculative survivals in the new physiological theories is the persistent belief that the nerves contain soul *pneuma* as a means of communication between the brain and the senses and limbs. The notion occurs in Augustine:

> And the air which is infused into the nerves is obedient to the will in moving the limbs, but is not itself the will (*Gn. litt.* 7.19.25).[6]

[3] With *fistulae* cf. Strato fr. 108 Wehrli: 'like a breath in a reed'. This source (Tertullian, *an.* 14) will have been known to Augustine.

[4] Cf. Cicero, *Tusc. disp.* 1.46f.: the soul perceives, the senses are its 'windows, as it were'. There are passages from the soul to the individual sense-organs (= 'openings'), and the soul is the co-ordinator and index of information given through the five senses as 'messengers'. See Theiler (1982) 2.248; 251; 344.

[5] Here as elsewhere Augustine may have got his knowledge of medical theory from his friend Helvius Vindicianus (*PLRE* 1.967): see *conf.* 4.5; 7.8. Vindicianus was the master of Theodorus Priscianus and author of several medical treatises, of which one, the *Gynaecia* (for its surviving epitomes see Theodorus Priscianus, *Euporista*, ed. V. Rose, Leipzig 1894, pp. 426ff.), appears to be echoed in *nat. et or. an.* 4.2-6: see Agaësse/Solignac, *BA* 48, 711f. – For Augustine's medical knowledge in general see Agaësse/Solignac, *BA* 48, 710-14; Bardy.

[6] For this pneumatic intermediary in Augustine see Verbeke 505-7.

This *pneuma* belief also appears in the account of sense-perception, in the course of a comparison made between the elements and the senses. Augustine suggests that the soul, as agent of sensation, activates the force of sentience through a fine corporeal medium (*per subtilius corpus*). This medium is fiery, but it does not extend to the senses in its original, mobile fiery form. It is, however, somehow present as light in sight, as pure air in hearing, as the vaporous air of the atmosphere in smell, as moisture in taste, and as earth in touch (*Gn. litt.* 3.4.6-7). A different, but not necessarily contradictory, version is given ib. 12.16.32: the element of light, which is present in sight in unadulterated form, is mixed with the other elements in each of the remaining senses. Augustine's reference there to the light of the heavenly bodies shows that he may be thinking of the fiery star-substance when he talks of the light element in the senses: but he can hardly wish to *identify* the light in human sight with fiery ether.[7]

The ear, for example, as an animated sense-organ, contains 'something like air' (*mus.* 6.11): when this is moved or activated, such activation is caused by the immanent vital force of soul encountering bodily stimuli:

> Furthermore, it (sc. the soul) moves, in my opinion, something luminous in the eyes, something airy – exceptionally clear and mobile – in the ears, something dark in the nostrils, something moist in the mouth, something earthy and muddy, so to speak, in touch (ib. §10).

In the case of sight, Augustine resorts to the theory of rays (*radii*) emanating from the pupil of the eye to impinge upon objects (*trin.* 9.3; *ser.* 277.10), so that seeing becomes a kind of visual touching, just as hearing is, so to speak, aural touching.[8] The ray travels at great speed, thus accounting for instantaneous perceptions of distant objects (*ep.* 137.8). It 'bursts out' (*erumpit*) of the eyes and ranges abroad in vision (*quant. an.* 43): 'to have opened the eye is to have arrived' (*ser.* 277.10) at the seen object, no matter how far distant the latter is. In fact, seeing presupposes a space, not too great but none the less existent, between eye and object (*ser.* 277.14). Just as the eyes cannot see themselves (*trin.* 9.3), so can they not see a body directly superimposed upon their surface. This seems at first to create a difficulty, inasmuch as it appears to run counter to the principle that bodies are physically contiguous with that which they feel (*quant. an.* 43). But the ray theory counters precisely this difficulty. It is not so much the eyes as their sight (*visus*) that senses something when we see: Augustine adopts the Stoic metaphor of the rod (*virga*) as an illustration of the quasi-tactile extension of

---

[7] There may be a trace of the soul-vehicle theory here: see pp. 75-9.

[8] The systematic correspondence between the elements and the senses originates in the Old Academy: see Baltes. The ray theory of vision is common to all philosophical schools (with the exception of the Epicureans) since Plato *Timaeus* 45b-d, 67c-68a (and it is already found in Democritus B 9 DK), as well as to scientific optic theory (Euclid, Ptolemy): see Dihle (1983) 85-7. Plato's account differs (with that of Democritus?) from the others, including Augustine's, in that it envisages, at least in the case of colours, counter-rays emanating from bodies to meet the optic rays (*Tim.* 67c).

sight beyond the eye to the seen object (*quant. an.* 43).[9] Sight is where it sees, and at the same time the eye, which is not self-perceiving, can only sense something where it is not.

For Augustine, the senses are, in general, not reflexive (*lib. arb.* 2.9). Their activity, in so far as it is not one of communication with the central controlling organ, the brain, is directed towards their objects. Here Augustine distinguishes between those objects which can be perceived by one sense only – like colour, sound, smell, taste, and texture – and those which can be perceived by more than one sense – like shape, which may be both seen and felt (*lib. arb.* 2.8). The distinction corresponds to the Aristotelian one between the special and the common sensibles (*de anima* 418a9-19). In general, perception of objects is perception of entities in the external world available to different percipients. We can, however, distinguish between the objects of sight and hearing, and those of the other senses. The former can be perceived in their entirety and simultaneously by different percipients. In the case of touch, different percipients can only perceive the same part of the same object at different times. But different percipients can only taste or smell different parts of the same object, and when we do so we absorb and transform the objects of perception, which is not the case with the objects of the other three senses (*lib. arb.* 2.15-19; *ep.* 137.7). Smell in *lib. arb.* 2.19 is considered to be the infusion of air particles through the nostrils. In *ep.* 137.6 Augustine none the less finds the contrast posited there between perception of things external (in sight and hearing) and the contactual sensing (*apud se ipsos sentiunt*) of the other senses problematic precisely in the case of smell.

Sensation can be considered a form of motion or change. If this description is to hold, this would seem to render necessary either something which moves or changes or somewhere in which change or movement, however it be understood, can occur. Now Augustine can describe sensory motion as one which runs counter to the motion set up in the body by the sensory stimulus: sentience is the product of the interaction of two movements. Thus, the reason why we do not feel certain actions upon our bodies, as when hair or nails are cut, is that these bodily substances are relatively impervious, due to the fact that they contain less air than other more rarefied parts of the body, so that they do not allow the essential sensory counter-motion to occur:

> Since, therefore, sensation itself is a motion of the body counter to that motion which has occurred in it, don't you think that the reason why we do not feel anything when bones, nails and hair are cut is not because these parts of us are utterly lacking in life (for otherwise they would not be preserved or nourished or grow, or indeed display their vigour by reproducing themselves), but because they are not sufficiently permeated by the spaciousness of air, that is to say, an active element, to allow the soul to effect a motion as rapid as the counter-motion which occurs when it is said to 'feel' (*mus.* 6.15)?

That these movements are ones of qualitative change, and not mere locomotion, seems to emerge from an assertion of Augustine's in the same

[9] Cf. *SVF* 2.864f.; 867.

context: when the body is affected by a certain change, the percipient's activity of heightened concentration (*attentiores actiones*) induces sense-perception (*mus.* 6.10).

But *what* changes when this sensory motion occures? Augustine says that the motion is *caused* by the soul (ib.), but what does *it* move, itself or another part of the percipient? It surely cannot be the sense-organs themselves that are moved. In the description of hearing and seeing discussed above we have seen that it is 'something in' the sense-organs that is activated when we sense, the 'something' which, in each of the senses, corresponds to one of the elements of the material world. We saw that this 'something' is related to the soul *pneuma* theory of Greek philosophical and physiological tradition. We must surely assume that it is this same substance that is set in motion – that changes – in the counter-motion described in the text under discussion. That it is a corporeal substance is indicated by the fact that it requires an airy medium (witness the counter-example of hair and nails) in which to function. This requirement would be met by the pneumatic content of the nervous system. Even if the nerves and their contents are communicators of sensations to the central organ, the brain, these sensations are not considered to be transmitted from one bodily part to another by any non-sentient intermediary. Rather the percipient subject, the soul, is itself somehow present throughout the body: it perceives as an entirety in individual bodily parts (*tota sentit in singulis, c. ep. fund.* 16.20). It can do so in more than one bodily part simultaneously (ib.; *imm. an.* 25).[10] How a non-corporeal and inextended entity like soul can be present in such a way to body has been examined elsewhere.[11]

Clearly, then, the sensory nerves themselves are, for Augustine, fully sentient, in that the perceiving subject is entirely present in them, and not merely in a central receptive organ with which they communicate in a non-sentient way. That this is so is evident from Augustine's explanation of the consequences of physical defects or damage in the brain, sensory nerves or sense organs.[12]

(ii) Intentio: *the active nature of sense-perception*

If, for Augustine, sensation has a physiological mechanism, sense-perception is none the less a psychological process. There is in fact interaction of body and soul in sense-perception, and the terms which come closest to expressing this interaction are *intentio* and *(con)temperatio*. *Intentio* refers primarily to mental concentration (*cogitationis intentio*) which, if particularly intense, can even distract us from normal perception, interfere with the functioning of memory, and interrupt bodily activities already started (*Gn. litt.* 7.20.26). This mental *intentio*, if excessive, as in instances of disease or demoniacal possession, can lead to hallucinations, in which images of previously

---

[10] For the Plotinian and the Porphyrian background of the concept of the soul's omnipresence see Pépin (1964) 86-9 = Pépin (1977) 246-9.

[11] See pp. 21-31.

[12] See pp. 129-30.

perceived corporeal objects become indistinguishable from normally perceived images of corporeal objects currently within the percipient's range of perception (*Gn. litt.* 12.12.25). In its normal state, however, *intentio* remains firmly related to actual sense-perception (ib.). It has its physical source in the brain (*Gn. litt.* 12.20.42), and its path to the various sense-organs can be blocked. The senses are its implements (*vasa*, ib. §43), and it is in virtue of its concentration that they actually sense:

> ... that which keeps the sense of sight on the object seen, as long as it is seen, namely the attention of the mind (*trin.* 11.2).[13]

The sense-organs, often described as the corporeal instruments of perception (*mus.* 6.10; *trin.* 11.2), are finely tempered or attuned for the activity of dealing with corporeal affections:

> This sense ... is an instrument of the body moved by the soul in such a tempered manner that it (sc. soul) can more readily use it to activate and concentrate on the body's affections (*mus.* 6.10).

More explicitly, Augustine can speak of a proper tempering by mixture (*contemperatio*) of body and soul which makes vision of external objects possible where the perceiving organ is not physically contiguous (*quant. an.* 59). Presumably he means by this that vision is not explicable either in terms of a purely physical process, or in mere psychological terms. The visual ray is the necessary physical counterpart of mental concentration.

Intentio is an *activity*: Augustine will give particular emphasis to the active nature of perception.[14] We have seen that he can describe sensation as a counter-motion to that of the sensory stimulus. While it is true to say that we are moved by what we perceive (*Gn. litt.* 9.14.25), and also that the body effects something in the soul when a bodily affection is sensed (*mus.* 6.7), this is not to be understood as a case of the body qua craftsman (*fabricator*) acting upon the soul as material (*materia*, ib. 6.8). On the contrary, just as embodiment is the active concentration of soul power –

> I hold that this body is only animated by the soul through the agent's concentration (*intentione facientis*), ib. 6.9

---

[13] Pohlenz 2.220 is probably right to see in the term *intentio* an echo, however dematerialized, of the Stoic concept of *tonos*, particularly as applied to vision, in which the light rays emitted from the *hêgemonikon* create 'tension' in the *pneuma*-stream and lead to the formation of the *phantasia* (*SVF* 2.863-72). The Stoic terms *sunentasis, tasis, tonikê kinêsis* (2.864), *enteinein* (2.866) are in fact translated as *intentio* in Latin versions of the theory, e.g. 2.863 and 871. For a discussion of the texts, and the Stoic ray theory in general, see Ingenkamp, who remarks (245) upon its application by Augustine.

[14] Augustinian scholars should stop talking as if an active theory of sense-perception was an innovation of Plotinus, to whom Augustine is therefore inevitably indebted: so Nash 43, followed by Miles 11. More judicious was Gannon 175-80. Only the Epicureans held a passive theory of perception, even if Aristotle and the Stoics (and, to some extent, Plato) identified both passive and active elements in the process (see n. 8 above).

– in which the soul exercises lordly authority over the subject body (ib.), so perception is an activity exercised upon the sensory stimulus rather than a passive reception of the latter (ib. §10). The awareness of such activity or motion in the soul is precisely the Augustinian definition of perception.

> Soul is aware of (*non latere*) its motions, or activities, or workings, when it perceives (ib. §11).[15]

In the prolonged discussion of this definition in *de quantitate animae* Augustine is concerned to maintain, on the one hand, the common-sense view that something happens to the body in perception, that it is affected by stimuli:

> I hold perception to be the soul's awareness of that which the body experiences (*non latere animam quod patitur corpus*) (*quant. an.* 41.)

At the same time he argues from the example of sight, with its details of the visual ray and the rod, for the active role of perception. This active aspect is to be understood also in the revised definition of sensation offered in the treatise:

> I see now that the definition should be as follows: perception is something directly undergone by the body of which the soul is aware (*passio corporis per se ipsam non latens animam*) (§48).

The first definition was found to be too wide, in so far as it can include perceptions other than those directly transmitted by the senses (such as inferences and conjectures based on our experiences, ib. 45-6). Augustine may wish to distinguish here between sensation (*passio corporis*) and perception (*non latens animam*), but it is probably truer to say that he is rather thinking of the external source of most sensory stimuli when he speaks of the *passio corporis*, and including under awareness (*non latere*) all forms of sensation and perception.

Now our sensations can be pleasurable or painful. They are not merely motions of the soul's concentration and awareness, they are also the indispensable motors of appetition or rejection. Perception is not always dispassionate. A few remarks must suffice to indicate how Augustine can apply the notions of *intentio* and counter-motion to descriptions of feelings.[16] Our emotive reaction to sensations is the activity of a natural power of perceptive judgement (*mus.* 6.5), but this judgement is not an exercise of the reason. Even the delight (*delectatio*) which, for example, we feel for poetry is not in itself rational evaluation (*mus.* 6.23). Yet when we delight in sensory rhythms it is their 'balance (*parilitas*) and symmetrically measured intervals' (*mus.* 6.26), i.e. a rational substructure, that we admire. There is, of course, a

---

[15] *non latere* here and in *quant. an.* 41 may be derived from Plotinus, *Enn.* 4.4.19.25 (*mê lathein*). See Lütcke 398. However, the Stoic concept of *sunaisthêsis* is also likely to have been influential: for it see Dihle (1982) 52, Pohlenz 1.113f.; 2.65 and – for its influence in later Greek philosophy – Schwyzer (1960), esp. 361-8, and Warren 90-2 (for Plotinus).

[16] See pp. 88f. below, and (for the affections in general) pp. 46-54.

proper and improper delight in physical beauty (though this is not the place to discuss that distinction): but common to both is the affinity of the percipient's adaptable affections with qualities of the objects delighted in. This affinity, whether morally right or wrong, causes the pleasure (*voluptas*) we feel in a beauty that is compatible with our own inner order (cf. *mus.* 6.34-58). Just as there is a ratio of form to form in perception,[17] so also there is compatibility of order with order in pleasurable sensation.

And as with pleasure, so with pain. When sensory stimuli effect disturbance and resistance in the percipient, the concentration of perception is indeed there, but now it is accompanied by discomfort, even pain (*labor, dolor*):

> It (sc. the soul) becomes more concentrated because of the trouble which it has in functioning; this trouble is called 'perceiving', since soul is aware of it on account of its concentration (*attentio*), and this (sc. perception) is called 'pain' or 'distress' (*mus.* 6.9).

We might say that the sensation of pain is an excessive case of the sensory counter-motion which, as was observed above, is characteristic of sense-experience.

(iii) Perception and memory

Sense-perception is a process occurring in time. This process is, like time and space themselves, infinitely divisible.[18] But our perceptions also have the durational continuity of their spatio-temporal context. Divided and analysed into the 'before' and 'after' of a continuum, perception reveals its dependence on memory. To hear even the shortest syllable, memory is needed, for the beginning of the syllable does not coincide temporally with its end, and it cannot therefore be perceived simultaneously in its entirety. The mental concentration (*intentio*) or movement (*motus in animo*) must persist over a time-span for even the briefest perception. It is the same with sight: we cannot perceive an extended body, even the smallest perceptible extended body, simultaneously in its entirety (*mus.* 6.21).

Here Augustine seems to be saying something like the following: the awareness implicit in any perceptive process is guaranteed by the instantaneous operation of memory. An infinite series of memory-impressions is stored in the mind in the course of any perception. This series is not merely necessary for the recollection of such perceptions at some later time: it is essential to the very process of perception itself.

> For when something is seen by the eyes, an image of it is immediately (*continuo*) formed in the mind (*spiritus*) (*Gn. litt.* 12.11.22).

> Therefore, although we first see an object which we had not previously seen, and from that moment its image, by means of which we can recollect it when it

[17] See p. 96.   [18] See pp. 154-6.

is not there, begins to be in our mind (*spiritus*), it is not the object which produces that same image of it in the mind, but the mind itself which produces it in itself with singular rapidity ... as soon as it (sc. the object) has been seen by the eyes, its image is formed in the percipient's mind before an instant of time has elapsed (ib. 12.16.33).

What we perceive is formed, articulated.[19] In *de musica*, Augustine explores the implications of his theory in numerical terms.[20] His use of number there is immediately influenced by the metrical example (iambic verse) discussed: he is dealing with the perception and appreciation of musical measure or rhythm (*numerus*). But the numerical descriptions can be applied to all perception. The 'sounding numbers' (*sonantes numeri*) are in the sound heard (the object perceived); the 'reacting numbers' (*occursores numeri*) are in the percipient's sense (*mus.* 6.2-3). The use of the term 'reacting' reminds us yet again that Augustine, in the same work, describes sensation in terms of a sensory counter-motion to the sensory stimulus (*mus.* 6.15). These reacting numbers (we can compare them with the 'forms' of *trin.* 11.3 and 11.16, induced in the sense by the form of the perceived object = sounding number[21]) are perceived and grasped by the mind through the intermediacy of memory (or, in the terminology of *mus.* 6, through the 'remembered numbers', *recordabiles numeri*). Memory submits to our judgement (or *iudiciales numeri*) the 'fresh traces of their fleeting course' (*mus.* 6.22). This is merely the expression in numerical terms of the indispensable role of memory in our awareness of sensations.

(iv) Perception and judgement; internal sense

The objects of sense-perception, in so far as they are perceived, are discriminated: the concentration involved in perceiving (the *intentio sentiendi*) is a judging activity:

> Thus we discern (*diiudicamus*) colours by the eyes, sounds by the ears, smells by the nose, flavours by taste, warmth by touch (*ser.* 43.4).

In the case of colours, for example, we do not merely sense them with the eyes, we distinguish, categorize, whether or not we explicitly label the colours 'red', 'green' or 'yellow'. To illustrate this point, Augustine has resort to a light metaphor. He distinguishes between the corporeal light seen by the eyes, and another sentient light – a live light – which can discriminate what is referred to the soul's or mind's judgement by the body. This latter light is 'in the soul', even if it employs bodily means to perceive: it is in fact a constitutive power (*potentia*) of soul, the power of perception, which, though

---

[19] pp. 95f.
[20] The sources and full ramifications of Augustine's numerology, especially in *de musica*, require further research. See Du Roy 282-97 (284 n. 1: bibliography); Marrou 251-62; 292-8.
[21] See p. 96.

always present, may be thwarted in its activity by defective or missing bodily instruments (*Gn. litt. imp.* 5.24). We are dealing here not so much with the subtle material light-element in sight discussed above, as with an analogous non-corporeal, embodied, metaphorical 'light', the soul-force present in perception:

> A sentient life, capable of discerning what is referred by the body to the soul's judgement (ib.).

This 'light' is to be distinguished in turn from the 'light' of reason or intelligence: the 'light' of perception is also possessed by animals:

> ... the incorporeal (sc. light), such as is in the soul, to which the assessment of what is to be avoided or sought is entrusted by the bodily senses, and which the souls of animals also possess (ib. 5.20).[22]

In the corresponding numerical language of *de musica*, the 'sounding numbers' are judged in the 'reacting numbers' (i.e. the sensibilia are judged in the percipient's sense) with the aid of memory (*mus.* 6.22).

It might seem at first sight as if the ability to judge sensibilia must be a rational activity only, and so peculiar to man among the animals, despite Augustine's attribution of perceptive 'light' to them in *Gn. litt. imp.* 5.20. Now it is the case that all living beings are affected by sensibilia, and it is indeed characteristic of man that he can voluntarily assent (*consentire*), or not assent, to them, in a discriminating way that is totally different from the instinctive reaction of other animals. Here 'assent' is not so much cognitive as action-directed: it is the necessary prelude to movements of appetition or rejection following upon perception (*Gn. litt.* 9.14.25). There is a close connection between such assent, and the activity of the will displayed in emotional behaviour:

> For what is desire or joy but an exercise of the will in accord with those things that we wish, and what is fear or grief but an exercise of the will in discord with those things that we do not wish (*civ.* 14.6)?[23]

Augustine has adapted the Stoic notion of man's ability to withhold or grant assent (*sugkatathesis*) as the distinguishing characteristic of man from beast, changing the former's intellectualist aspect into a voluntary power.[24] But, just as for the Stoics it is correct to assert that animals also exercise assent, so for Augustine there is a sub-rational 'judgement' of sensations common to animals and men, and to be distinguished from the rational and voluntary

---

[22] The distinction of three kinds of light may be a reaction to the undifferentiated corporeal Light-Principle of Manichaeism. In §5.24 Manichaean attribution of sentience and intelligence to plants is rebuked in passing. – For the Neoplatonic background of the concept of transcendental light see *conf.* 7.16: the concept is discussed in Beierwaltes (1961). Plato, *Tim.* 45b distinguishes between two kinds of light: see Cornford 152.

[23] See pp. 46-54.

[24] See Pohlenz 1.457f.

assent (or rejection) just described. This ability to judge sensations Augustine calls the 'internal sense' (*sensus interior*), and his most explicit account of it is given in *lib. arb.* 2.8-13. But before we turn to that account it must be pointed out that the term *sensus interior* is also used by Augustine to describe the rational, discerning faculty, peculiar to man, described above.[25] We have here to do with the metaphor of the 'senses of the soul' (*animae sensus*), of which Augustine is fond.[26] Augustine argues that

> there is a certain inner sense to which everything is referred by the five well-known senses (*lib. arb.* 2.8).

It is common to animals and men. In animals it is observable in their ability to avoid or seek what they have perceived. It controls the senses, and is not knowledge but the necessary medium whereby the data of sensation lead to knowledge. Augustine stresses the distinctions between sensation, internal sense and knowledge, with relevant examples. We know, he argues, the proper objects of the individual senses, e.g. colour in the case of sight, sound in the case of hearing. An animal lacks such discernment, which is made by the reason. On the other hand we are conscious of our sensations, and this consciousness cannot be a perception made by the senses themselves: Augustine takes it as self-evident that the senses are not reflexive. He asserts that awareness of the activity or non-activity of the senses is a perception of the internal sense, and he argues for this viewpoint by demonstrating that animals must also possess this awareness – in other words, that it is not a rational awareness.[27] For, he says, such awareness is a necessary precondition of movement in animals:

> An animal could in no way open its eye and move it to look at what it desired to see unless when the eye was closed or not so moved, it perceived that it did not see it (sc. the object, ib. 2.10).

The awareness is the impulse (*appetitus*) which causes the movement, in this case the activation of the animal's sense of sight. Similarly, because it arrests the impulse which led to the sensation, the animal indicates that it is aware that it sees. Augustine adds that the internal sense is superior to the five senses because it controls and judges them (ib. 2.12). He speculates briefly whether internal sense perceives itself, as opposed to perceiving the senses and sensations, but concludes that this, though likely, cannot be clearly proved (ib. 2.10).

In this account Augustine is dealing with some aspects of the so-called

---

[25] See *civ.* 11.27; *en. Ps.* 148.3; *nat. et or. an.* 4.30; 4.37; *qu. hept.* 2.114; *retr.* 1.1.2.

[26] See *nat. et or. an.* 2.3; *sol.* 1.12. Possible Ambrosian influences on Augustine's language in this connection are listed by Gannon 173; 175. Despite Platonic parallels (e.g. *Republic* 533d2), the ultimate source of the metaphor in Augustine is, however, Biblical: for examples of the metaphorical use of sight in New Testament texts see *ThWNT* 5.378, 22ff. A key influence upon Augustine is Ephesians 1:18, quoted e.g. *in nat. et or. an.* 2.3.

[27] Augustine appears to echo here Stoic views about the pre-rational source of ethical concepts: see Pohlenz 1.57; 2.34; Pembroke.

koinê aisthêsis or *sensus communis*.[28] He does not employ the latter phrase in *de libero arbitrio*, but it is implicit in his statements that internal sense 'superintends all the senses together *(omnibus communiter praesidet)*' and that 'some senses have objects in common *(communia)*', e.g. the shape of a body is commonly perceptible by sight and touch *(lib. arb.* 2.8).

As is well known, the concept of common sense has, above all, Aristotelian, but also less clearly definable Stoic antecedents. Moreover, it underlies several Plotinian texts whose closeness to Augustine's views is remarkable.[29] But despite this pedigree its appearance in Augustine is brief. It does not occur in his other discussions of sense-perception, although he refers to it in passing in *conf.* 7.23, where he speaks of

> the soul's inner power *(interior vis)*, to which the bodily senses communicate external things,

and which animals also possess. There is a further reference in *conf.* 1.31,

> I kept guard by means of the internal sense over the soundness of my sense-perceptions,

which must refer to the internal sense's power of judging the perceptions of the senses.[30] But if the concept disappears, its functions do not: they are carried out by the power of concentration *(intentio, attentio)*.[31] This psychological power, as we have seen, effects perception, as well as engaging in other activities, such as avoidance or appetition, association of impressions, and habitual memory *(quant. an.* 71). Augustine stresses that the sense-organs are bodily instruments which can be activated by the soul's *attentio (mus.* 6.10). Such passages indicate that, for Augustine, the sensitive soul's powers include those of internal sense, and that the notion of concentration in particular is a new formulation of the concept of the internal sense's reflexive power. Augustine specifically asserts that the sensitive powers of *quant. an.* 71 are common to animals and men.

In his later writings Augustine does not fundamentally change his views on the nature of this aspect of sense-perception. In *de trinitate* he stresses the importance of *intentio* and of memory in perceiving the data of sensation. Animals share this ability to perceive and retain images in the memory *(trin.* 11 *passim*; 12.2). In *de Genesi ad litteram* he speaks of 'spiritual sight *(visio spiritalis)*' in terms corresponding exactly to those describing internal sense: the *spiritus*, as distinct from the *mens (Gn. litt.* 12.9.20), includes the irrational, and spiritual sight is, therefore, also a capacity in animals which controls the sense-activities and recognizes their data *(Gn. litt.* 12.11.22).

---

[28] For the concept in Greek philosophy see Beare 250-336. Augustine will, of course, use the term *sensus communis* for 'natural common sense', e.g. *beata v.* 6; *mend.* 5.

[29] There is a discussion of these antecedents in the Excursus, pp. 102-5. See further the discussions by Madec 566-7, Mondolfo and Wolfson; cf. O'Daly (1985,2).

[30] For speculation on the background of this passage see n. 53 below.

[31] Discussed, pp. 84-6.

It is therefore not correct to suggest, as one modern discussion does, that the concept of internal sense is not found in Augustine's other accounts of sense-perception because 'he may have come to believe that he did not need this notion.'[32] The power of perceptual synthesis and consciousness is adequately described in other terms.

(v) Perception, error and image; our knowledge of the external world

When we perceive, we are aware of something in, or deriving from, the external world. Our sensory mechanism and perceptible objects, each existing independently of the other, come into some kind of contact (*trin.* 11.2: the sense is a 'bodily instrument' whereby the embodied soul senses. It exists in the percipient prior to acts of sensation. Ib. 11.3: 'We cannot ... assert that the visible object generates the sense.'). What is the nature of this contact, and what is perceived, when we have sensations and perceive? This is the central, and at the same time most complex, question in Augustine's account of sense-perception. At one extreme, he can give rhetorical expression to the doctrine of sensible flux, which is constantly in motion and whose lack of stability makes it, in strict logic, 'non-being':

> We agree fully, I believe, that everything with which the bodily sense comes into contact cannot remain in the same condition for even an instant of time, but passes away, disappears, and has no present, or, to put it in plain Latin, is not (*non esse*) (*ep.* 2).

If the perceptible object is constantly changing it cannot be perceived, for perception implies the acquisition of some kind of knowledge about the perceived object, and knowledge is excluded in virtue of the mutability of the physical world:

> For that which is grasped through knowledge (*scientia*) is perceived; but what constantly changes cannot be grasped (*div. qu.* 9)

But if knowledge is excluded, then so is truth: we should not expect the 'purity' (*sinceritas*) of truth from the senses (ib.). Can we then know nothing about 'how things are' in the physical environment in which we find ourselves? Augustine's common sense revolts against the strict Heraclitean (in the sense of Plato, *Theaetetus* 152c-153d) stance implied in the passage just quoted. When he wishes to contrast the true intelligible universe with the sensible universe, he can indeed assert that the former is 'true' (*verus*), whereas the latter 'seems true' (*verisimilis*) and made in the former's image, and that we can have knowledge (*scientia*) of the former and only opinion (*opinio*) of the latter (*c. Acad.* 3.37). It is precisely the claim to be a definition of the *verum* that he criticizes in Zeno's definition of what is perceptible, arguing that it is impossible to find in the sense-world an object fulfilling the requirements of the definition.[33] There are no characteristics of our sense-perceptions, Augustine feels, which enable us infallibly to distinguish between false and true (ib. 3.39). There is no sensible object without the possibility of there being something 'resembling what is false (*simile falso*)' that cannot satisfactorily be distinguished from the genuine object, perceived 'as it is' (*div. qu.* 9).

In the discussion of *error* in *c. Acad.* 1 Augustine offers a definition that, although not specifically applied there to sense-perception, will appear in *c. Acad.* 3 in connection with perception: error is 'the approbation as true of what is false' (*c. Acad.* 1.11).[34] In *c.Acad.* 3.24 Augustine makes the point that in all perceptive acts something 'appears to be', whether it is in fact or only apparently the case: error occurs only if we rashly judge this appearance to be what it is not – if, for example, we judge an illusory world to be real. Augustine apparently approves of the Epicurean view of the infallibility of the senses and the impressions which they convey: all sense-contents are 'true'. Even recognized optical illusions are true, and have some cause independent of the percipient. Of course, sensations are 'true' in this respect only in a trivial sense. In fact, Augustine's Epicurean assents to no more than the sensation:

Do not assent to more than that you are persuaded that it appears thus, and there is no deception (ib. 3.26).

And this sensation appears to be of secondary qualities only, and to be relational: taste in itself (supposing it to exist), as opposed to somebody's sensation of taste, cannot be determined. Yet, Augustine adds, we can talk of knowing (*scire*) such sense-contents: although he suggests that we should rather be talking of belief (*opinio*) than of knowledge in such contexts. This discussion is inconclusive. Fundamental questions remain unanswered: how, if at all, can I distinguish between real and illusory appearances? Does not the Epicurean viewpoint make all sense-contents equally 'true'? Augustine's other early discussion of the problem, in *sol.*, does not resolve these difficulties. He argues there that awareness that X is false does not entail being deceived (*falli*) by X, if perceiving X, we withhold assent to its truth (*sol.* 2.3). Indeed, recognizing X for what it is, namely, 'something that is other than it appears to be', is one way of avoiding error (ib.). We appear to make such recognitions, or at least to presuppose their validity, as when we distinguish between real experiences and dreams. We also recognize the 'falsity' of certain real objects or occurrences, such as mirror-images, representational works of art, and literary fictions (*sol.* 2.11). In other words, 'false' seems to presuppose 'true', just as 'falsity' presupposes 'reality'. So,

[33] Cf. *c. Acad.* 2.11; 3.18; 3.21. Augustine derives his formulations of Zeno's definition from Cicero, *Acad. prior.* 18; 113: see Reid *ad loc.* J.M. Rist, *Stoic Philosophy*, Cambridge 1969, 133-51, discusses the various Greek and Latin formulations of the definition, with particular attention to Cicero.
[34] A full discussion of the connotations of *error* and *falsum* in the early writings of Augustine is given in O'Daly (1981,2). Its conclusions are summarized here.

just as 'falsity' does not entail 'non-existence', error is not tantamount to blank ignorance: error is being deceived with regard to the truth or reality of X, it is a failure to assess X properly, taking X for real or true because it has 'some likeness to truth' (*sol.* 2.10). Error, like 'false', presupposes a criterion of truth and falsehood.

Augustine's discussion in *soliloquia* establishes greater clarity than the *contra Academicos* account does concerning the concepts of error and falsehood. It argues for the necessary existence of truth, if these concepts are to have any meaning. But it does not solve the problem that *contra Academicos* raised. To say that perception X is false may presuppose a concept of truth, but does not entail that there are *perceptions* (as opposed to e.g. ideas) that are true. And even granting that there are such perceptions, what enables us to say, of particular sense-impressions, that they are 'true', and to say of others that they merely display some potentially deceptive likeness to the truth?

Against such discussions we may place those which adopt a position of scientific realism, and make claims for our ability to know the external world.[35] This is precisely the point of the distinction drawn between *sapientia* and *scientia* in *de trinitate*. If *sapientia* is the knowledge of eternal and immutable truths, *scientia* is the knowledge of temporal, changeable realities, a knowledge necessary for the conduct of our active lives (*trin.* 12.16f.). In its relation to action, *scientia* is close to appetition, but it is its cognitive aspect which makes it an essential prerequisite of the practical virtues:

> Appetition, however, borders on the reasoning of knowledge, seeing that what is called the knowledge of action reasons about the very bodily objects that are perceived by the bodily sense (*trin.* 12.17).

> Indeed, without knowledge the virtues themselves, by which one lives rightly, cannot be possessed (ib. 12.21).

Even if we often mistakenly perceive things to be other than they actually are, Academic scepticism and universal doubt are unjustified (*trin.* 15.21; *civ.* 19.18). For optical illusions deceive by a sort of 'resemblance to truth', which in itself seems to imply our possession of a standard of what is, in the sensible world, 'true' (*trin.* 15.21). Augustine piously observes that it is through the senses that we know the heavens and earth of the universe created by God. We accept the truth of what we have come to learn in this fashion, and we also accept as true the testimony of others on matters geographical and historical:

> We must confess that not only our own senses, but those of others also, have made great additions to our knowledge (ib.).

Of such knowledge we can indeed say that it is *scientia*, and this is itself both an indication and a guarantee of the necessary role of the mind in sense-perception:

[35] For scientific realism in the Stoics and Antiochus of Ascalon see Dillon 64-9.

What is perceived through the body cannot be retained in knowledge if the mind does not attentively take in such information (*ep.* 147.38).

Augustine can actually attempt to turn the tables on Academic scepticism resulting from optical illusions, by arguing that, given the appropriate conditions, such illusions are, in fact, 'right': if the oar in the water did *not* appear bent, we would trust our senses even less:

> Is, therefore, what they say regarding the oar in the water true? Of course it is true. For, given that the cause of its appearing so is present, if the oar submerged in water should appear straight, I should have greater reason to accuse my eyes of a false report. For they would not have seen what should have been seen, given the existence of such causes (*c. Acad.* 3.26).

Although Augustine, as we have seen, can reject Zeno's definition of *kataléptiké phantasia* as a criterion of truth in the strictly intelligible sense in which the term is understood in *contra Academicos*, he will none the less, like the Stoics, speak of the *evidentia* of true sense-perceptions in his critique of scepticism.[36] This *evidentia* is compatible with the recognition that the senses sometimes do deceive.[37] One condition of such *evidentia* would be the comprehensive nature of our perception of the several parts or aspects of an object:

> For it is one thing to see, it is another to grasp the totality through seeing ... that totality is grasped through seeing, which is so seen that no part of it escapes the percipient's awareness, or whose extremities can be comprised in the perception (*ep.* 147.21).

In other words, the object's proximity, visibility, etc. would have to be adequate. Another condition would be the normal functioning of the percipient's faculties. On the whole, however, Augustine assumes, rather than demonstrating, that most, if not all, sense-perceptions convey genuine and reliable information about the external world. The reasons for that assumption may throw light on why it is held, and may further elucidate what precisely we know when we perceive. Augustine repeatedly stresses that sense-perception is perception of images of bodies (*imagines corporum*), and not of the bodies themselves, and that these images are not, and cannot be, themselves corporeal. That we do not directly take in the bodies which we perceive is obvious: even in the case of taste and smell a distinction is to be drawn between the absorption of physical quantities and awareness of their characteristics or qualities (sweet, sour, pungent, slimy, etc.). But it would be perfectly defensible to maintain this, and at the same time to argue, with Epicurus and the Stoics, that the images we perceive are none the less corporeal. Augustine does not adopt this course. Like Aristotle, he argues

[36] Cf. *civ.* 19.18. For *evidentia* as a translation of the Stoic *enargeia* see Cicero, *Acad. prior.* 17 and Reid's n. *ad loc.*

[37] Cf. *ep.* 118.19 for a report on Epicurean, Stoic and Platonic views on sense-perception and truth-claims.

that perception is the ability to receive forms without matter.[38] He does so on the grounds that corporeal likenesses correspond in size to the bodies in which they are reflected. The image in the pupil of the eye is a case in point. Were the soul corporeal, the likenesses it receives and stores would be commensurate with its size (which would presumably correspond in turn to the size of its body). But this is not the case, for we can imagine huge spaces and distances formerly perceived (*quant. an.* 8-9). The nature of such images must be something other than corporeal. What their nature is remains problematic, however. It is uncannily *like* bodies (*nat. et or. an.* 4.25), and in calling it 'spiritual matter' (ib.) Augustine is not saying very much about it, merely expressing the difficulty of categorizing it.

When we perceive, we perceive the likenesses of the objects perceived. Augustine can also call these likenesses 'forms' (*formae*, e.g. *civ.* 11.27). He will further distinguish two forms, the form of the perceived object, and the form induced in the sense. Yet this distinction is conceptual rather than really discerned: the two forms are so united in any perceptive act that actual discernment of their duality is impossible. In *trin.* 11.3, an analogy is drawn with wax upon which a seal has been impressed. After the seal-ring is removed we can indeed observe that there is both the form of the seal and the form impressed upon the wax. But we can also infer, without being able to observe, that the two forms are there while the stamp is actually being impressed. Our very perceptive processess, Augustine feels, confirm the hypothesis of such a duality: when we have been looking at brightly lit or coloured objects, and close our eyes, or cease to look, we continue to have gradually fainter visual impressions of the lights or colours: these must be the forms induced in the sense in perceptions by the forms of the objects perceived (*trin.* 11.4). We can therefore speak of the senses being formed by objects (ib. 11.2), in that forms are thus induced in them. Indeed, Augustine can actually extend the series, and speak of no less than four forms (*species*) in the process leading from sensation to thought: the two already identified, a third produced in the memory, and a fourth in the mind, each form deriving from the preceding one (*trin.* 11.16), but not passively caused by it (*Gn. litt.* 12.16.33). This process indicates that, for Augustine, perception is the perception of like by like. There is an affinity between the percipient's reason and the articulated form of the object. Ultimately, it is this affinity which makes perception both possible and reliable. If, says Augustine, we can apply the term 'rational' to sense-impressions, it is on account of the 'traces of reason in the senses' which perceive proportion and measure (*dimensio, modulatio*) in objects (*ord.* 2.32-3). Objects are perceptible because they are formed.[39]

Furthermore, objects are formed, for the Platonist Augustine, by the Forms, or Reasons, or Ideas, to which they owe their existence (in a sense not excluding the creative activity of God). The Ideas are in the mind of God, and are the 'chief causes' of (at least) all neutral entities: the latter participate in

[38] Aristotle, *de an.* 424a17ff.
[39] See Lorenz (1955/6) 50-4; and, for our knowledge of perceptibles in general, ib. 214-16; Lorenz (1964) 47-9.

these exemplars or numbers or laws.[40] Because our minds have access to
these Ideas, which transcend them in their immutable perfection, we can, in
the last resort, identify and evaluate the genuineness of sense-perceptions.
For the Ideas can function as standards (*regulae*) whereby we may distinguish
between the truth and falsity of the images with which we deal in all
perceptive and imaginative processess.[41] Since for Augustine all perception
depends upon the instantaneous and continuous transfer to the memory of
the images of things perceived we can apply what he says in *trin.* 9.10 about
the judgement involved in distinguishing between genuine memories and
products of our imagination to that involved in assessing the genuineness of
sense-perceptions:

> Hence, even in the cases of images (*phantasiae*) of corporeal objects taken in
> through the bodily senses and in some manner poured into the memory, which
> are also the sources of the false image (*phantasma*) in our conceptions of what
> has not actually been seen, whether these latter are different from the reality or
> by chance just as it is – even here, whenever we approve or reject anything
> rightly, it is clearly demonstrated that we approve or reject in our own minds
> by reference to quite different rules (*regulae*) which unchangeably transcend our
> minds. For when I recall the walls of Carthage, which I have seen, and when I
> imagine those of Alexandria, which I have not seen, and among forms equally
> imagined prefer some to others, my predilection is rationally founded. The
> judgement of the truth is strong and clear from on high, and rests firmly upon
> absolutely indestructible and independent rules; and if it is obscured by the
> cloudy sky (so to speak) of corporeal images, it is not, however, overwhelmed
> and confused by it.

Distinguishing between remembered Carthage and imagined Alexandria is a
rational act, and is somehow referable to the criterion of the ideas qua
standards. Augustine distinguishes elsewhere between the animal activity of
perceiving and storing images in the memory, and the specifically human
activities – deliberate and cognitive – of memorizing, recalling and imagining
(without confounding products of the imagination with true recollections):

> The animals can also perceive external corporeal objects through their bodily
> senses and recall them, once they have been fixed in the memory, and strive
> after the advantageous among them, and avoid the disagreeable. But to note
> these things; and to retain them not only as naturally grasped perceptions but
> also as something assiduously entrusted to memory; and, just when they are
> slipping into forgetfulness, to engrave them afresh by recollection and thought,
> so that, just as thought is formed from that which the memory contains, so also
> that which is in the memory is secured by thought; further, to combine
> imagined objects of sight by taking what is remembered from this source and
> that, and, as it were, sewing it together; to investigate in what way among
> objects of this kind that which resembles the truth may be distinguished from

---

[40] See pp. 191-5. For the Middle Platonic background of *div. qu.* 46 see Solignac (1954).
[41] For Forms or Ideas as *regulae* cf. *vera rel.* 58. That *regulae* = Ideas in *trin.* 9.10 is clear from the
account there of their unchangeable, transcendent truth; cf. §9; 11. see Plotinus, *Enn.*
5.3.4.15-18.

the truth, and this not among spiritual things but among the corporeal objects
themselves – this and the like, although they are activities dealing with objects
of sense-perception and with what the mind has derived thence via the bodily
senses, are not, however, devoid of reason, and are not common to men and
animals (*trin.* 12.2).

Animals are capable of building up a stock of empirical experience which will
influence their instinctive behaviour: they can remember, recognize,
anticipate. But they can neither memorize nor imagine, much less compare
imagined with genuinely remembered images. The knowledge which we have
of sense-perceptions, viz. that they are true or not, is, and can only be,
rational: such knowledge cannot be possessed by animals. Yet animals
undoubtedly do have some kind of awareness akin to knowledge: as Evodius
points out in *quant. an.* 50, even if they are not rational beings, they
nevertheless 'know' certain things, and he adduces the example of Odysseus'
dog (cf. §54) recognizing its master:

> For neither can I assert that animals use reason nor can I deny them
> knowledge. For I believe that the dog who is said to have recognized his master
> after twenty years knew him, not to mention countless other cases.

Augustine argues that this awareness in animals is sub-cognitive: it is a
particularly acute power of perception, which, together with appetite and
habit, enables the animal to single out instinctively what gives it pleasure
(and, implicitly, avoid what causes it pain). The acuteness of animal
perception is a consequence of the greater attachment of animal souls to their
bodies; they depend exclusively upon the latter's senses for their
self-preservation and propagation:

> What then do you think that this is, if not some power of perception rather than
> of knowledge? For many animals surpass us in their perceptive power ... God
> has, however, made us superior to them in mind, reason, and knowledge. But
> the aforementioned faculty of perception can, together with habit, whose power
> is great, discern what gives pleasure to such souls; and all the more readily, as
> the soul of animals is more attached to their body, whose senses are used by it
> with a view to sustenance and the pleasure which derives from that same body
> (*quant. an.* 54).[42]

We might say that the relation between body and soul in animals is a
teleological function of their particular form of existence and that hence
animal perceptions have, for them, the force and effectiveness which
knowledge has for us. Their perceptions are an 'imitation knowledge':

---

[42] The same point regarding the superiority of individual animal senses is eloquently made in
ser. 277.5. The motif is Epicurean: see Lucretius, *rer. nat.* 5.222-34. The idea that animals possess
by nature what men acquire only through cultural effort is current in fifth-century Greek
(Sophistic and other) speculation: see Plato *Protag.* 320c ff. For the contrary argument see
Panaetius *ap.* Cic. *nat. deor.* 2.145f.

> Wherefore consider whether you are now convinced that animals do not possess knowledge, and all that, as it were, image of knowledge which impresses us is a perceptive power (*quant. an.* 56).

> There is nevertheless in the senses of irrational animals, if not any kind of knowledge, then at any rate some semblance of knowledge (*civ.* 11.27).

This 'knowledge' includes, as we have seen, the awareness of the activity or non-activity of the senses which animals enjoy in virtue of internal sense.[43] It can, however, hardly be claimed that animals are, for example, aware of being deceived, though they may, of course, be deceived. A kitten may take a runner bean to be something threatening, like a snake. Increased familiarity with the bean will dispel the sense of menace: the animal becomes conditioned to a reaction of approval or indifference. And so with other objects, whether deception is initially (or permanently) involved, or not. The reaction of the animal is never a judgement in any reflective, articulated sense: still less can an animal adjudge a sense-perception to be illusory rather than real.

To return to man. It is the same rational faculty, the same mind, which has cognition of the Ideas and evaluates sense-perceptions, as well as planning action based upon these:

> But that faculty of ours which is occupied with the activity of dealing with corporeal and temporal things in a way that rules out our having it in common with the animals, is indeed rational, but it is fashioned, so to speak, out of that rational substance of our mind whereby we cleave to intelligible and unchangeable truth, and it is allotted the task of handling and managing lower things ... Our mind, with which we refer to celestial and inner truth, gets no help adequate to human nature for dealing with corporeal things ... from those parts of the soul which we have in common with the animals. And so a certain power of our reason, not separated so as to divide its unity, but diverted, so to speak, to give help by association, is assigned the duty of its appropriate task ... The one mental nature embraces ... our intellect and activity, or planning and performance, or reason and rational desire (*trin.* 12.3).[44]

When the mind errs in its evaluation of perceptions it does so through deficient application of its intelligence to the phenomena in question: it succumbs to a false opinion regarding them:

> The mind is, however, deceived by the likenesses of things, not through any defect in the latter, but because of a faulty opinion, when, lacking in

---

[43] See pp. 89f.

[44] When Augustine speaks of the 'higher reason' judging corporeal objects in accordance with incorporeal and eternal principles (*trin.* 12.2) he cannot be referring to a particular higher form of reason or rational activity. He is rather contrasting the evaluative role of reason in judging sense-perceptions with its roles in memorizing, imagining, etc., as previously discussed. On the other hand, cognition of the Ideas in the strict sense demands an exercise of the mind that few attain to: see *trin.* 12.23.

understanding, it assents to that which resembles something rather than to the thing which it resembles (*Gn. litt.* 12.25.52).

The mind is, therefore, fallible, even if it has access to the Ideas. The latter enable the mind to distinguish genuine from false sense-impressions, but they do not guarantee the correctness of the distinction in each and every case. That correctness can only be achieved by assembling the evidence of all the relevant senses (so that – to take a Stoic example – the wax pomegranates which look like real ones to the sense of sight will prove to be imitations when tasted) and by the use of our intelligence (not further specified, but Augustine is surely thinking of the use of our reason in testing a perception, as when e.g. we observe a steady fall of white particles through a study-window, and initially mistake them for snow, until we reflect that it is late May, that there is a cherry-tree in blossom in the garden, and that its petals are likely to be scattered by the wind which is blowing, and resemble snow falling). Augustine makes this point succinctly, in general terms, in *Gn. litt.* 12.25.52:

> Whence in all perceptions both the testimony of the other senses, and especially that of the mind itself and reason, is adduced, that the truth appropriate to this class of things may be found, to the extent that it can be found.

The last words make it clear that, strictly speaking, sense-perceptions do not fulfil the requirements for knowledge or, in themselves, lead to the intellection of truths. Elsewhere, Augustine makes the distinction explicit between strict and habitually loose talk about knowledge, while at the same time defending the usage of *scire* with reference to perceptions and beliefs:

> When, in fact, we speak strictly (*proprie ... loquimur*), we only call that knowledge which we grasp by firm mental understanding. But when we use language more adapted to convention ... we should not hesitate to say that we know both what we perceive with our bodily senses and what we believe on the testimony of reliable witnesses, provided only that we understand the difference between the former and the latter (*retr.* 1.14.3).[45]

But Augustine is far too much of a realist not to admit that we are, in fact, able to establish working distinctions between those perceptions which represent the physical world as it is and those which are illusory and deceptive. In this, despite features of his account of perception that differ fundamentally from that of the Stoics, he is a child of Stoic dogmatism. The truth-claims which can be made for our cognition of Ideas, or for the knowledge that we exist (*civ.* 11.26; *trin.* 10.14), cannot be made for perceptions, but in the last resort Augustine will evaluate the information derived from the latter in a way that, even when compared with his Platonist reservations, strikes one as more positive than the Platonist tradition, strictly speaking, would allow. Even if the Ideas are the guarantors of the correctness

---

[45] See the similar remarks regarding 'knowledge' of perceptibles in *mus.* 6.32.

of our perceptions, knowledge of the Ideas does not generate empirical scientific knowledge. Augustine can even come close to asserting the autonomy of the empirical sciences in *trin.* 4.21. There he argues that knowledge of 'sublime and unchangeable substance' does not ensure knowledge of 'the changes in mutable things' or of 'the linked succession of historic periods'. Those who

> argue in the most truthful manner and persuade us by most certain proofs that all temporal things are made in accordance with eternal ideas cannot thereby determine the facts of zoology or history, which they have not investigated through that unchangeable wisdom, but through the history of places and periods of time; and they have taken on trust what others have written down.

If we apply this argument to sense-perception, we may conclude that the best metaphysician is more likely than the best ornithologist to mistake one variety of finch for another. That *rara avis* the true metaphysician (*trin.* 12.23) has actualized his knowledge of the Ideas, but the latter nevertheless function in an inexplicit though effective manner in the non-metaphysical activities of judging and evaluating perceptions. *How* they function Augustine does not fully explain: he gives no direct answer to the question of what kind the standard (*regula*) provided by the Ideas is.[46] We can scarcely be assumed to recognize a physical object as e.g. a tree solely because we have a mental concept, an Idea, of tree. Still less can we presume to recognize an optical illusion of a tree for what it is because of the Idea. Yet it is precisely in the evaluation of perceptions that the Idea is said to play its role. How does the Idea help us? We have already seen that *Gn. litt.* 12.25.52 suggested that evaluation was achieved with the assistance of more general powers of reflection and applied intelligence, along with experience and the assembling of information from the various senses. But all this is not enough. When we assert that 'X is a true perception', as opposed to an illusion, or that 'X and Y are two distinct objects', really there and not imagined, we do so with reference to criteria of truth and number, which, as Augustine will often argue, are not derived from sense-experience. In other words, we refer to the Idea as criterion.

But we judge of corporeal things by the rule of dimensions and forms,

> of whose unchanging permanence the mind is certain (*trin.* 12.2).

> The judgement of truth is strong and clear from on high, and rests firmly upon absolutely indestructible and independent rules (*trin.* 9.10).

But this reference to the Idea does not appear to presuppose explicit cognition of the Idea in a strict epistemic sense. Divine illumination, in the

---

[46] The question is not answered satisfactorily by Platonists: see Blumenthal (1971) 105f. (Plotinus); Blumenthal (1982) 8f. (Proclus). Discussions of Augustine's theories of sense-perception and knowledge avoid the problem: Nash 67; 109 shows some awareness of it, but can suggest no solution. See also Lorenz (1955/6) 50-4; 214-16.

sense of such cognition, is not the precursor of good perceptual judgement, or, as we have seen, even of good empirical science. But the *implications* of illumination are also those of sound perception. That is to say, the presence of God to the human mind, a presence that does not compromise divine transcendence or imply any contact as of equals between the divine and human minds, enables the mind to perform all its appropriate functions. In virtue of this presence the mind has access to a criterion of truth which enables us to say of a sense-perception that it is 'true'. For to predicate 'true' of a perception is to assert – even if one is not fully aware of this – that it participates in the Idea of truth and can therefore be so qualified (*sol.* 1.27). Asserting that sense-experiences are true is thus similar to asserting that things are beautiful (*trin.* 9.11) or good (*trin.* 8.4): in all cases we do so with reference, conscious or otherwise, to the transcendent criterion, the Idea.

Excursus: Internal sense; antecedents and influences

The question whether the senses are reflexive is raised in Plato's *Charmides* (167c-d), and answered in the negative.[47] But it is to Aristotle that we must turn for the most extensive discussion of *sensus communis* prior to Augustine's (*de anima* 418a7-25; 424b22-427a16).[48] Aristotle examines the perception of the common sensibles (like shape), the perception that we perceive, and our ability to distinguish between the objects of different senses. His isolation of the functions of common sense is thus remarkably similar to Augustine's, even if his conclusions are radically different. For Aristotle, there is no sixth sense, but sense is a faculty which has generic and specific functions. Hence the common sensibles are perceived by this faculty, which also discriminates between the objects of the different senses. Further, the senses are reflexive, for, Aristotle argues, the assumption of a subsidiary sense is both superfluous and involves an infinite regress. And quite apart from these differences, a direct influence of Aristotle upon Augustine seems, in any case, to be out of the question. Augustine knew the *Categories* (*conf.* 4.28-9), surely in Latin translation,[49] but cannot have had access either to *de anima* or other Aristotelian texts, such as the *parva naturalia*, which deal with problems of perception.

It is no more easy to pinpoint any Stoic influence upon Augustine's account of internal sense. The Stoic *hêgemonikon* recognizes, co-ordinates and judges sense-impressions and here as elsewhere in the account Augustine gives of sense-perception – such, as we have seen, as in the notions of concentration and assent – he will not have been unaffected by Stoic discussions of the topic.[50] According to one doxographical account, the Stoics identify *koinê*

---

[47] See Schwyzer (1960) 360f. For the following see O'Daly (1985,2).

[48] The best analysis is still that of Hicks 422-52. Cf. C. Osborne, 'Aristotle, *De anima* 3.2: How do we perceive that we see and hear?', *Classical Quarterly* 33 (1983) 401-11.

[49] See Chapter 2 n. 89.

[50] For the co-ordinating and judging role of the *hêgemonikon* in sense-perception see *SVF* 2.879; 2.885. Augustine's adoption of Stoic notions of judgement and assent is discussed by J. Rohmer, 'L'intentionnalité des sensations chez Saint Augustin', *Augustinus Magister* 1 (1954) 491-8.

aisthêsis with an 'internal touching' (*entos haphê*) which is also the vehicle of self-consciousness.[51] If we knew more about this latter we might be able to discern specific influence upon Augustine of the Stoic notion of *sensus communis*.[52] Finally, self-awareness is an element in the concept of *oikeiôsis*: in Cicero's account of the latter in *fin.* 3.16 it is observed that even the appetites of young animals seek what is pleasurable and avoid what is painful, and Cicero adds:

> It could not, however, happen that they would strive after anything, unless they had self-awareness (*sensus … sui*) and for that reason loved themselves.

The Stoic *oikeiôsis* doctrine influenced Augustine's concept of self-love:[53] it is not impossible that the aspect just referred to lies behind his view of the nature of internal sense.

It is often argued (not always convincingly) that Augustine's account of sense-perception is influenced by Neoplatonism.[54] A number of passages might seem to indicate that this influence may be behind his account of internal sense. Plotinus, in his discussions of the faculties of the sensitive soul, refers to common sense (*Enn.* 1.1.9.12). He does not define it, but he presumably understands it to be a generic faculty of perception.[55] In 4.3.26.1-9 he says that perception is called common because it is a 'common activity' of body and soul, but he may not intend us to take this as a definition of common sense. Some light is thrown on his views of sensation at 4.3.23, where he describes a single sensitive soul of which the specific senses are powers (cf. 4.3.3.12-16), and at 4.7.6, where he argues that various sensations in the perceptions of a single object must somehow be unified and co-ordinated by an incorporeal perceptive faculty. At 4.8.8.10 Plotinus speaks of a 'power of internal perception' whereby we become conscious of desire. The phrase is reminiscent of Augustine's internal sense. And the purpose of both Plotinus' and Augustine's talk of internal perception is the same, namely, to distinguish between sensation and affections on the one hand, and perception of these on the other. Plotinus is rightly credited with a clearer differentiation between sensation and perception than earlier philosophers.[56] At 1.1.7.5-14, for example, he distinguishes between

[51] Diels, *Doxographi Graeci* 395.16-19 = *SVF* 2.852.

[52] Cicero, *Acad. post.* 40 (= *SVF* 1.55) does not refer to the *sensus communis*, as *SVF* 4 (Indices), p. 9, col. 1, implies. For the anacoluthon in that passage see Reid's n. *ad loc.* and Madvig 798. The references to *tactus interior* (Cic. *Acad. prior.* 20 = test. 213b Mannebach) and *tactus intimus* (ib. §76 = test. 213c M.) in Cyrenaic accounts of the affections of pleasure and pain as the sole criteria of truth do not appear to have any connection with the Stoic *entos haphê*.

[53] See Holte 233-40; O'Donovan 48-56. In *conf.* 1.31 (see above p. 91) Hadot (1968) 2.292 n. 1 finds an echo of the *oikeiôsis* doctrine, but in the Platonically transmuted form which he attributes to Porphyry (ib. 285-93).

[54] See Gilson 76 n. 1; Nash 39-59. Miles 9-22 offers a more differentiated comparsion between Plotinus and Augustine, which owes much to Buckenmeyer's discussion of the body-soul relationship in Augustine's early writings.

[55] See Blumenthal (1971) 79; Harder/Beutler/Theiler 5.446. Of a quite different order are the interpretations of *koinê aisthêsis* in the later Neoplatonic commentators: see Blumenthal (1981).

[56] Blumenthal (1971) 67-79; Dodds *ap.* Schwyzer (1960) 385.

sensation, directed outside, and the conscious perception, by the impassively contemplating soul, of the impressions produced by sensation. Augustine distinguishes equally clearly between internal sense and the non-reflexive senses. And there is a further parallel between the two philosophers' accounts. At 1.6.3.1-5 Plotinus speaks of the 'judgement' which the sensitive faculty exercises in perception. He is referring to a type of perceptual (and fallible), as opposed to rational, identification, similar to the 'judgement' of the senses by the internal sense in Augustine.[57] Unlike Augustine, Plotinus rarely discusses the sensitive faculty of animals. However, he does assert that animals, like us, have consciousness (1.1.11.11). Presumably, like human consciousness, this can be awareness of bodily processes (cf. 5.3.2.4).[58] Finally, Porphyry, in his account of perception in the *sententiae* (which follows Plotinus closely), twice asserts that sensation is non-reflexive.[59] Plotinus does not discuss the problem of whether the senses are reflexive. But his account of sense-perception would imply that he must conclude that awareness of sense-activity can only be a form of consciousness of the sensitive faculty.[60]

The likelihood of Neoplatonic influence on Augustine's account of internal sense is increased by the following consideration. A close parallel to the passage in *de libero arbitrio* is in *conf.* 7, where, describing the ascent of the self through the degrees of being, Augustine says:

> And so by stages I passed from bodies to the soul which perceives through the body and thence to soul's inner power, to which the bodily sense reports external things, and which stage the animals are able to reach (*conf.* 7.23).

The context of this passage and that of the *de libero arbitrio* text are as relevant as their specific content. In both cases Augustine is describing a hierarchy of degrees extending from bodies to reason and culminating in God, who transcends human reason. His immediate purpose in each case is different. In the *Confessions* he is evoking an experience or experiment: in *de libero arbitrio* he is elaborating a philosophical argument. But this difference should not obscure the common background of the two passages. In the former it is Neoplatonic: Augustine himself makes this clear (*conf.* 7.13; 7.16; 7.26). The latter account must also derive from Augustine's reading of the 'books of the Platonists' (*conf.* 7.13), although it cannot be proved that the specific texts referred to above are the direct source of Augustine's views.[61]

Why is the concept of internal sense so attractive to Augustine in *de libero arbitrio*? He may wish to describe the mechanism of sense-perception in this particular way because of his preoccupation in that work with the analogy between (a) the hierarchy body-soul-mind and (b) perception and knowledge and their objects (2.13; 2.15-20). In (b) a middle term

---

[57] Blumenthal (1971) 105f.

[58] For consciousness in Plotinus see Schwyzer (1960) 363-77 and Warren 90-2.

[59] Porphyry, *sent.* 41 (p. 52.16-18 L.) and 44 (p. 57.3f. L.).

[60] A. Graeser, *Plotinus and the Stoics. A Preliminary Study* (Philosophia Antiqua, 22), Leiden 1972, 136.

[61] The controversy over the contents of the Neoplatonic readings of Augustine is not resolved, and is unlikely ever to be so. See Chapter 2 n. 20 above.

corresponding to soul in (a) is missing. By adducing the traditional concept of internal sense Augustine can complete the analogy of two corresponding hierarchies on three levels:

mind	knowledge
soul	internal sense
body	sense-perception

But in his other writings he does not need this correspondence. The functions of internal sense can be described in terms more suited to his general account of perception.[62]

---

[62] See pp. 90f.

CHAPTER FOUR

Imagination

Sense-perception is perception of incorporeal images of the objects perceived. These images are stored in the memory, and when we call something to mind it is an image that we recollect. Remembering is, for Augustine, a form of imagining. Imagination can be merely *reproductive* of the images in the memory, but Augustine can also talk of the *creative* exercise of the imagination. A discussion of his views on the role of imagination has not only to deal with this distinction, but also with the attendant problems of accounting for dreams, hallucinations, visions and prophecy, and the apparent activity or passivity, insight or fallibility, variously exhibited by the mind in these processes.[1]

(i) Terminology: phantasia *and* phantasma

When Augustine wishes to distinguish between what we have called reproductive and creative representations of the imagination he often resorts to the Greek terms *phantasia* and *phantasma* (e.g. *mus.* 6.32; *trin.* 8.9; 9.10). The use of this terminology in contrasting senses appears to be of Stoic origin,[2] even if Augustine's demarcation of *phantasia* from *phantasma* does not correspond to the Stoic distinction between *phantasia* as the making of an impression or alteration (*tupôsis, alloiôsis*) in the mind by the perceived object, and *phantasma* as the product of an 'empty attraction (*diakenos helkusmos, SVF* 2.54f)' or 'appearance of thinking (*dokêsis dianoias, SVF* 2.55)' without any direct external cause: into this latter category the Stoics appear to insert at least some dream-images, as well as the hallucinations of the insane.[3] It has

---

[1] There is no satisfactory account of Augustine's views on imagination. The older studies of Ferraz 195-239 and Nourrisson 1.159-64 are now outdated, but they showed an awareness of the philosophical problems which has since been lost. See also (with particular reference to dreams) Dulaey, especially 93-107; Agaësse/Solignac, *BA* 49, 568-75; Markus (1981); Amat; J.P. Mackey (ed.), *Religious Imagination*, Edinburgh 1986 (with contributions by G. Watson on ancient and early Christian views, and by J. Dillon on Plotinus).

[2] Pépin (1964) 102 = Pépin (1977) 262.

[3] Not all dreams and trances can be called *phantasmata* by the Stoics in this sense: those which are prophetic have a direct divine cause and cannot be described as 'empty' or 'deceptive'. For Peripatetic, Stoic and other testimonies about divinatory dreams see Del Corno 75-97 and 156-96 (nn.). It is precisely the Stoic belief in significant dreams that the Academic sceptics of Cic. *Acad. prior.* 47 criticize; cf. ib. §34. One may question whether the testimony of *SVF* 2.55 (Diog. Laert. 7.50) is reliable. Or is there an implicit distinction, such as that between 'true' and 'false' dreams in Cic. *div.* 1.60 (see n. 18 below), in the description of some dreams as deceptive?

been suggested that Porphyry may have adapted the Stoic distinction and influenced Augustine here, but for Porphyry, in the passages cited in support of this suggestion, *phantasia* is rather the faculty which forms images of external objects, while the images themselves are given the name *tupos* (*sent.* 16, p. 8.3 Lamberz; ib. 29, p. 18.10f; ib. 43, p. 55.5-10). Nor is there adequate evidence for a Porphyrian contrast of *phantasma* with *phantasia* along the lines employed by Augustine.[4] In fact, Augustine's usage of *phantasia* seems to betray no real awareness of its ambiguity (i.e. that it can refer to mental faculties or processes as well as to their products): he uses it predominantly (an exception is *sol.* 2.35) in the sense of 'image' or 'impression'.[5] Is he influenced by the fact that Cicero, in his discussion of *kataléptikai phantasiai* in *Acad. post.* 40 and *Acad. prior.* 18, translates *phantasia* as 'percept' (*visum*)?[6] Surprisingly, it is Augustine's close friend and correspondent Nebridius who appears to use *phantasia* in the sense of a mental power or faculty (*ep.* 6.2; cf. *ep.* 8: 'in their *phantasia*' = 'in their imagination (*phantastico*)'): though the fact is perhaps the less surprising if we recall the technicality of Nebridius' philosophical interest in such problems as the possible demonic cause of dreams (*ep.* 8) and the question of the soul's vehicle (*ep.* 13.2), interests which bear out Augustine's description of him as

an ardent searcher after the happy life and the shrewdest of investigators of the most difficult questions (*conf.* 6.17).

We can only conclude that Augustine either adopted a scholastic or doxographical distinction unknown to us, or that he himself adapted the Stoic distinction, referred to above, between *phantasia* and *phantasma* to his own technical purposes.

(ii) Creative imagination; imagination and the disciplines; imagination's effect on bodily states

The reproductive exercises of imagination will clearly be dependent on memory, in so far as that kind of imagination involves a conscious reactivation of images or *phantasiae* stored in the memory (*mus.* 6.32). But

---

It is, of course, possible that the Stoics called dreams 'deceptive' for the plain reason that they induce apparent perceptions of what is not 'out there'.

[4] For the suggested Porphyrian influence upon Augustine see Pépin (n. 2 above). But the text of *sent.* 16 (p. 8.1-5 L.) is too corrupt to establish the sense of *phantasma* suggested by Pépin: 'image qui suit la pensée indépendamment de la sensation'. In Porph. *ad Gaur.* 6.1 (p. 42.7-9 Kalbfleisch) Porphyry appears to use *phantasia* and *phantasma* interchangeably. Dulaey 93-6 is too easily convinced of the rightness of Pépin's views.

[5] By the time he came to write *civ.* 9.4 he knew from his reading of Aulus Gellius (19.1 = test. 397a Hagendahl) that the Stoics gave the name *phantasiae* to mental impressions which impinge upon our awareness without our being able to prevent their impact. The rhetor Augustine will not have been unaware of the value attributed by his profession to the vivid presentation of impressions. Cf. Quintilian, *inst. or.* 6.2.29; 11.3.62. See R. Godel, 'Similitudines rerum (S. Augustin, Conf. X 8, 14)', *Museum Helveticum* 19 (1962) 190-3.

[6] Cf. *c. Acad.* 3.18; 3.21; *ep.* 7.1.

Augustine insists no less strongly on the dependence of creative imagination on memory:

> For I imagine my father, whom I have seen often, in one manner, and my grandfather, whom I have never seen, in another manner. The first of these two is a *phantasia*, the other a *phantasma*. I find the former in the memory, the latter in that movement of the mind which is derived from those that memory possesses (ib.).

Difficult as it is to explain the origin of such a process, it cannot plausibly be held to occur without in some way originating in images of perceived objects:

> I consider, therefore, that if I had never seen human bodies, I could in no way picture them in a perceptible appearance by thinking (ib.).

When Augustine asserts that we 'form *phantasmata* from the memory' (ib.) he is expressing a fundamental conviction that not even the most extreme form of hallucination, or the most absurd dream, can shake.

In *mus.* 6.32 Augustine seems to suggest that the production of *phantasmata* is analogous to the formation of images of perceived objects. Just as the latter process can be accounted for in terms of sensory motion and counter-motion, and its product – the perceived image – can be considered to be itself a motion, in so far as it is a consciously registered mental change, so also can we envisage such mental changes (*motus animi*) reacting upon one another under the influence of *intentio*, and generating in turn 'images of images':

> When these motions rush against one another, and rage as if blown by the contrary and contending blasts of concentration, they give rise to successive new motions ... like images of images, which are by convention called *phantasmata* (ib.).

Despite the vivid storm metaphor adopted here, the reference to concentration (*intentio*) indicates that this imaginative process can be willed and subject to our control, even if it is not always so. Thus a favourite explanation given by Augustine of the imaginative process is that it is one of contracting and expanding the images of that which we have perceived, or of combining and separating their data:

> Whence, therefore, does it follow that we imagine what we have not seen? Surely it is because the soul must bring with it wherever it goes an inborn power of lessening and increasing ... The imagining soul can, therefore, generate that with which it has never come in contact as a totality through any sense by adding to ... and subtracting from what perception has conveyed to it: it had indeed come into contact with the parts of that (sc. which it imagines) in several different objects (*ep.* 7.6).[7]

---

[7] Cf. *ep.* 9.5; 162.5; *c. ep. fund.* 18.20; *vera rel.* 18; *trin.* 11.8; *conf.* 10.12.

We may say that in this creative exercise of the imagination the will, if not the caprice of our fancy,[8] is sovereign.

The distinction between will and fancy is significant, for Augustine distinguishes between the various types of creative imagination in respect of their relation to reality. We can imagine objects with which we are unfamiliar, but of whose existence there can be no doubt. Augustine's standard example here is imagining Alexandria, which he has never seen, in contrast to Carthage, which he knows. There can be no question of one's picture of Alexandria corresponding specifically to the reality, even if elements of that picture may be derived from, for example, a description one has heard or read, or a depiction one has seen: the overall picture is none the less 'as we imagine it'.[9]

The status of imagined Alexandria is thus that of an object, similar objects (i.e. cities) to which we have perceived, and of which we have received verbal or pictorial descriptions. It corresponds to the more personal example given by Augustine in *ep.* 7.6, of imagining the sea, which, as a boy brought up in the inland plateau of Numidia, he had never seen, by looking at the water in a cup. Augustine distinguishes such an imagined object from others – no less real – which we cannot imagine because of the lack of any antecedent related perceptual experience: for example, the taste of strawberries or cherries, to those who have never tasted them, or – for those who are born blind – light or colour (ib.). In these instances an element necessary to imagining them in some way even remotely related to how they actually are, is missing. To the North African who has never been to Alexandria his picture of that place is none the less 'like' it in so far as he pictures a city, a harbour, great buildings, etc. But to the blind, whatever the associations which the word 'colour' conveys to them, these associations cannot, except by coincidence, correspond in any way to 'real' colours.

Now when I imagine Alexandria I do so deliberately: as Augustine would say, I exercise my *intentio* and my will. Intentional imagination can also be exercised upon non-existent objects, or upon objects whose existence is unknown to us. In such cases, the process of modification of images of perceived objects is particularly obvious. We can imagine a black swan, or a four-footed bird, by combining images of objects really perceived (*trin.* 11.17).[10] Thus

> It (sc. the mind) often imagines things to be of such a kind as either it knows they are not or does not know that they are ... because it has the power ... to

[8] See *pro arbitrio* in *trin.* 11.8; *Gn. litt.* 12.23.49.

[9] Cf. *trin.* 8.9; 9.10; *Gn. litt.* 12.6.15; 12.23.49; *c. Faust.* 20.7. The use of Alexandria as an example may be due to Porphyrian influence, as Pépin (1964) 102f. = Pépin (1977) 262f. has observed: but it is not to the imaginative power of soul that Porph. *ap.* Nemes. *de nat. hom.* 3 (p. 136.6-11 M.) refers, but rather to the notion that the soul is not contained in any place, e.g. in Rome or Alexandria; and the supposed example of pre-Porphyrian school practice adduced by Pépin (1977) xxxviii from Seneca, *ep.* 102.21 refers also to the lack of specific localization of the mind (*humanus animus*) e.g. in Ephesus or Alexandria, both chosen as examples of particularly large places.

[10] Note that here Augustine uses the term *phantasia* for such imaginary representations.

imagine, not only what is forgotten, but also what has not been perceived or experienced, by increasing, diminishing, changing or connecting at will what has not escaped (sc. its memory) (*trin.* 11.8).

Broadly speaking, this category corresponds to the second class of images distinguished by Augustine in *ep.* 7.4 ('the (sc. kind) impressed ... by objects of thought') although this class can also include such images as the 'Alexandria' discussed above (the first class is that of images 'impressed by sense-objects'). Augustine names, as additional members of the second class, images of historical or fictional figures, or of mythical places, such as the geography of Classical or Manichaean world-pictures, or of hypothetical cosmic models. The figures of fiction or myth can be those imagined by the reader or listener, but can also be those embodied by the poet or artist in his artistic representation (ib.). Elsewhere, Augustine can refer in similar terms to the Manichaean figments of the imagination, calling them *phantasia*, as when the divine kingdom is identified with the light of the sun in their cosmology (*c. Faust.* 8.2).[11]

In *ep.* 7.4 Augustine distinguishes a further class of images, the kind 'impressed by represented objects'. In this class he includes real but necessarily imagined natural objects, such as a representation of the entire universe, as well as the objects of certain sciences or branches of theoretical knowledge (*disciplinae*), such as geometrical figures, musical rhythms, and metrical patterns. He asserts that these latter are objectively existing phenomena, and not subjective figments, but they can generate illusory images (ib.). This would seem easier to grasp in the case of imagined natural objects, for our representation of the universe is likely to be false, or at least not entirely correct. But Augustine clearly wants us also to think of imagination as related to geometrical or metrical pursuits. Even in logic, he adds, classification and syllogistic conclusions may produce false results (ib.). We must assume that he is thinking either of formally invalid arguments or conclusions, or of formally valid ones where the inferences of the premises are false (he may, of course, have both kinds in mind).

In this connection it is important to bear in mind the distinction Augustine himself draws in *sol.* 2.34 between the purely mental concept we have of a geometrical figure and the imagined form of the latter. The former is an intellectual judgement, and it can include such pure mathematical notions as, for example, that of the inextended point where plane touches sphere, or that of the infinite number of radii in a circle (§35). Imagination cannot picture such notions, though it *can* picture squares, circles, spheres, etc., and certain of their characteristics. In talking of geometrical figures in *ep.* 7.4, then, Augustine is referring to these as we imagine them, not as we know them qua mathematical 'forms'. In the disciplines, the imagination works on a highly complex and abstracted level – whether in geometry, metrics or logic

---

[11] Manichaean figments of the imagination can also be called *phantasmata*: *c. Faust.* 14.11; 15.5; 15.6, etc. At *c. Fel.* 2.3 'solid truth' is contrasted with 'empty *phantasma*'. When it is a question of deceitful, empty illusions, there is little to choose between *phantasia* and *phantasma* in Augustine's usage.

– but these are not activities of pure reason. The rules and principles of these sciences are not themselves derived from sense-perception, nor are they dependent upon images *(conf.* 10.16-19), but their implementation is inextricably involved with images, and this can both distort the material upon which they work, and generate illusory images.[12]

The same *intentio animi* which is exercised in sense-perception can also be observed, as we have seen, in the workings of the imagination. Normally this power of the will is active in the recollection to our minds of stored images in the memory (cf. *trin.* 11.6): during such a process sense-perception continues. It can, however, happen that we become so fully absorbed with the stored images that our attention is totally diverted from normal sense-perception, and the memory-images are so vivid that we take them for those of external objects actually being perceived at that very instant. There is usually an emotional element, whether desire or fear, at work on such occasions *(trin.* 11.7). The imaginative activity can be so intense that it can affect our bodily condition: we cry out; a man can so imagine copulation with a woman that he has an orgasm (ib.). Augustine clearly wants to distinguish between such states and analogous conditions in dreams or ecstasy, hallucination or possession, and the ground for the distinction is precisely that the former are willed and the latter involuntary (ib.).

In general, the susceptibility of animal bodies to such influences varies, and depends upon the constitution of the bodies. Augustine's example of extreme susceptibility to perceptions is the chameleon *(trin.* 11.5), but even the unborn young of other animals can be affected by the pregnant mother's imagination, especially when that imagination is so strong that it is tantamount to desire. In illustration, Augustine refers to Jacob's coloured flocks (Genesis 30:41) as an example of this principle:

> The offspring for the most part betray the desires of the mothers, the things these have looked on with special pleasure. For the more tender and, so to speak, the more malleable the seminal principles are, the more effectively and susceptively do they adapt to the mother's will *(intentio)* and the *phantasma* formed in the latter by the object eagerly looked at *(trin.* 11.5).

There is a fuller account of the process in *trin.* 3.15, which stresses the 'sympathetic mixture *(compassio commixtionis)*' of body and soul, the 'rule of formation' of psychosomatic interaction, that makes the process possible. The theory is advanced by Porphyry in explanation of the old and popular belief about such influences upon embryos: Augustine may well owe it, as well as references to the influence of imagination upon such bodily processes as blushing or growing pale, to that source.[13]

---

[12] Behind the distinction of *sol.* 2.34 lies the Platonic understanding of the intermediate status (between *intellegibilia* and *sensibilia*) of geometrical entities. For the distinction between mental and sensible-imaginative origins of geometrical figures see Porph. *ap.* Procl. *in Eucl.* p. 56.23-25 Friedlein, noted by Theiler (1933) 38 = Theiler (1966) 206.

[13] For influences upon embryos see Porph. *ad Gaur.* 5.4 (p. 41.21-26 K.): the parallel with Augustine was pointed out by Theiler (1933) 38 = Theiler (1966) 207. For imagination's influence upon other bodily processes see *Gn. litt.* 12.19.41 and Porph. *ap.* Procl. *in Tim.* 1.395.24.

(iii) The nature of images

We have seen in the discussion of sense-perception that Augustine insists upon the non-corporeal nature of the images of the objects of our perceptions, even if he has difficulties categorizing this nature.[14] In *ep.* 162.4 he addresses himself, somewhat exceptionally, to an aspect of the latter problem. The question is, how are the images formed in, and present to, the mind? Augustine considers two main possibilities. Either one substance (the image) is superimposed upon the other (the mind): Augustine adduces the example of letters written in ink upon parchment. Or the mind is somehow qualified by the images: here the example of a seal impressed upon wax is given. The wax is the *subiectum* thus qualified, and corresponds to the mind. Augustine does not exclude the possibility that both processes could occur at different times and under different circumstances, but neither does he assert that he favours the one or the other, or indeed that either of the possibilities adduced appeals to him. The problem is partly one of explaining the presence in an immaterial substance of a likeness clearly derived from a corporeal object, partly also one of accounting for the continued separateness of the likenesses in the mind, for these maintain the identity which can be recalled in specific acts of recollection. It is difficult to explain

> through what causes and how they come into existence, their natural constitution or their substratum (ib.).

But Augustine does not seem to get beyond registering the problem.

Given the difficulties posed by Augustine's account of the generation of images, it is not surprising to find a view put forward which would obviate many of them, a view which Augustine none the less cannot accept. In *ep.* 6.2 Nebridius suggests that the imagination (*phantasia*) might contain its images (a priori, so to speak) just as the mind contains its ideas, so that the imaginative faculty (*phantasticus animus*) would be activated in an admonitory way by the senses to contemplate its contents, rather than taking in any images from sense-perception. This theory would incidentally also explain why the imagination can picture what the senses are not, at that moment, perceiving, or do not, in general, perceive (ib.). In his reply Augustine discounts this theory. His answer (*ep.* 7.3) is puzzling. He does not refer to the most obvious objection: that the nature of our stock of images is so personal that they would seem to derive by necessity from our individual experiences. Rather, he argues that, on Nebridius' hypothesis, since the mind is better off independently ('before') imagining corporeal objects than depending upon our error-prone senses for its images, by analogy dreamers and the insane would be better off than those awake and sane, for the former also imagine things 'prior to' sense-perception. The argument is puzzling because it appears pointless. For there seems prima facie to be no analogy between the freely imagining mind envisaged by Nebridius, and the activities of dreaming or hallucination. In the former case, we have to assume a process

[14] See pp. 95f.

that is totally independent of sense-perception, except in so far as perception acts as an activating admonition: in the latter case, we would normally presuppose that the images present to the mind of those thus afflicted are, or at least could be, distortions and conglomerations of previously registered perceptions. And to speak of them as *prior to* sense-perceptions is misleading, unless 'prior to' is to be understood as a way of saying 'independently of': they are indeed prior to some, but later than others.[15]

Be this as it may, the argument put forward by Augustine here none the less reasserts unequivocally the dependence of the mind upon sense-experience for the generation of its images (*ep.* 7.3-5). This is so, even if Augustine appears to admit that there can be emotive 'motions of the mind', which may affect the body, independent of such images (ib. §7). The incorporeal nature of the images should not tempt us into doubting that they are derived from perceptive experience, difficult as it may be to give an account of such derivation.

(iv) Image, name and word

Augustine is aware of the connection between perceived object, image, and name.

> Almost all images are called by the names of those things of which they are images (*div. qu. Simpl.* 2.3.2).

We call the painting of a human being by the name 'human being', and paintings of known individuals by their individual names. If we see a known person in a dream, we say 'I saw Augustine', meaning thereby that we saw his image. The name thus stands for both the perceived object and its image.

Augustine uses the term *verbum* in a similar way, in relation to *phantasia* and *phantasma*, in *trin.* 8.9. My image of Carthage, really perceived, and my image of Alexandria, imagined by me, both function as internal 'words' corresponding to the spoken words 'Carthage' and Alexandria', when I think of either Carthage or Alexandria, and these internal words are in our minds as objects of thought, whether or not we actually speak the words. The internal word is expressed, with all its specific associations for us as individuals, in the spoken word:

> And indeed, when I wish to say 'Carthage' I search within myself in order to speak (sc. it), and I find within myself an image (*phantasma*) of Carthage. But I have received that through the body, that is, through a corporeal sense, since I have been in that city and have seen and perceived it, and retained it in my memory, so that I might find within myself a word referring to it whenever I might wish to mention it. For its word is the image of it in my memory, not this sound of two syllables when Carthage is named or even when the name itself is

[15] In *ep.* 7.3 the analogy appears, oddly, to depend on (a) 'the soul was ... in a better ... condition *before* it was involved with these deceptive senses', and (b) dreamers and the insane are 'affected by these ... images, by which they were affected *prior to* these most unreliable messengers, the senses'.

thought of in silence from time to time, but that which I perceive in my mind when I express that disyllable vocally, or before I express it. So also when I wish to say 'Alexandria', which I have never seen, an image (*phantasma*) of it is present to me ... I formed an image of it in my mind as best I could, and this is its word present to me when I wish to mention it, before I express the five syllables vocally (*trin*. 8.9).

Augustine does not make it absolutely clear here whether the images are stored as internal words, or whether they only 'become' (i.e. function as) words when my attention is focussed on them. The latter seems more likely in view of his repeated emphasis upon the intentional nature ('... when I *wish* to say ... whenever I might *wish* to mention ...') of the process in question: our stored images only acquire the significance of 'words' when we deliberately think them. This interpretation is corroborated by *trin*. 15.22, quoted below.

> The activity of sense-perception is the formation of likenesses: When we learn of bodies through the bodily sense, a likeness of them, which is a memory image (*phantasia memoriae*), arises in our mind (*trin*. 9.16).

The process 'learn of' → 'likeness' = 'image' corresponds to the counter process 'image' → 'word', in *trin*. 8.9. More specifically, Augustine readily envisages the formation and storage of facts in the memory as the storage of *word-potentials* in a non-linguistic and non-sounding way in the mind. Because we, in a sense, *know* what we have perceived, our knowledge (*scientia*) produces (brings forth) both word and image when we consciously think that which we know:

> Therefore, all these things ... which the human mind has perceived and knows ... through the bodily senses, it retains, stored in the treasury of memory. From them a true word is born when we express what we know, but a word that is prior to all sound, and to all thought of a sound. For then the word is most like the thing known, from which its image also is born, since the vision of thought arises from the vision of knowledge ... (*trin*. 15.22).[16]

The word thus functions as the actualization of the memory's latent contents in acts of deliberate thinking: it is at once articulated, formed and significant, a vehicle of communicable meaning.[17]

(v) Involuntary imaginings; dreams

Hitherto we have been considering the exercise of the imagination, whether reproductive or creative, in forms which may broadly be described as

---

[16] For the development of the metaphor and its implications cf. ib. §19-25.

[17] Cf. *trin*. 15.40; ib. §25: the *potentially* formable knowledge can also be called 'word', even if Augustine is not terribly enthusiastic about its designation as such. – To relate the foregoing remarks to Augustine's complex semantic and linguistic theory is beyond the scope of this work. See Darrell Jackson = Markus (1972) 92-147; Duchrow 101-48; Markus (1957) = Markus (1972) 61-91; Ruef; Schindler (1965) *passim* (esp. for *trin*.); Mayer; Watson.

voluntary or deliberate, through the agency of *voluntas* or *intentio*. We must
now turn to those imaginative processes which seem to be involuntary, and,
in certain cases, caused by some inexplicable or hypothesized external force.
Augustine refers in *Gn. litt.* 12.23.49 to apparently spontaneous imaginative
occurrences, where,

> from whatever quarter, and without our causing or willing it, divers forms of
> corporeal likenesses course through our minds.

This observable phenomenon clearly defies explanation: that is to say, we
cannot offer a hypothetical explanation of it. Augustine clearly wishes to
distinguish it from, on the one hand, fanciful imaginative flights which are
somehow within our power, and, on the other, dream or hallucinatory states.
Nor does he wish to attribute so normal an occurrence as, for example,
day-dreaming to any disturbance of our faculties of perception or
imagination. Yet the closest correspondence to such a phenomenon is, in
fact, found in dreaming, and although Augustine does not draw the parallel,
it would appear to be implicit in his account of dream activity.

Augustine distinguishes between dreams with, and dreams without,
significance (*Gn. litt.* 12.23.49). He appears to mean by this that some dreams
have a prophetic meaning, whereas others do not. This emerges from the
distinction between 'true' and 'false' dreams in *Gn. litt.* 12.18.39, where,
although the false dreams are not more clearly defined, the true dreams are
further divided into clearly and symbolically prophetic ones. We may assume
that the false ones have no *prophetic* significance:

> For ... these (sc. dream visions) are also sometimes false, sometimes, however,
> they are true; sometimes they are disturbed, sometimes calm; moreover, the
> true ones are sometimes quite similar to future events, or are clearly
> communicated; at other times they are announced in obscure signs and in, so to
> speak, figurative expressions.[18]

The false dreams are not, however, incoherent or necessarily illogical: in fact,
they are the normal dreams of our experience. To account for them,
Augustine simply has to refer to the activation of perceived likenesses:
dreaming is a form of imagining. The activated images may be those deriving
from the day's preoccupations – here Augustine shares the commonly held

---

[18] The distinction 'disturbed ... calm' as Dulaey 90f. plausibly argues, seems to correspond to
'false ... true', and would appear to be even more clearly indepted to Cicero, *div.* 1.60-1 than she
suggests: there, in the presentation of a paraphrase of Plato, *resp.* 571c-572b, Cicero
distinguishes between 'true dreams' experienced when we are in a moderate state of repletion,
and in control of our emotions, when the rational part of soul is in control, and we have dreams
that are 'calm and veracious' – and the 'disturbed and confused' dreams of those whose
appetitive or spirited parts of soul are in dominance. – For the subdivision of clear prophetic
dreams into 'quite similar to future events' and 'clearly communicated' cf. the parallels with
Macrobius and Calcidius drawn by Dulaey 91f., and her speculation on the possible Porphyrian
background of the classification.

ancient view of the source of our dream-impressions.[19] Thus, Favonius Eulogius continues to be preoccupied with the obscure passage in Cicero's rhetorical works that he is preparing for the next day's teaching, and dreams that Augustine explains it to him (*cura mort.* 13). Similarly, bodily needs or desires can determine the nature of our dreams. There is a parallelism between dream and waking behaviour, and between dream and waking aspirations:

> For not only when they are awake do people occupy themselves in thought with their concerns, in the form of likenesses of bodies, but they also often dream in their sleep of what they desire; for they conduct their affairs with thoroughgoing avidity and, if it so happens that they have gone to sleep hungry and thirsty, they hanker greedily after banquets and drinking bouts (*Gn. litt.* 12.30.58).[20]

Nor need such aspirations be merely ones of physical need or desire: in his dreams the good man will, like Solomon, ask to be granted wisdom (*Gn. litt.* 12.15.31). Augustine can take the parallelism of waking and dream states to its fullest extreme. The mind's activity can continue unimpaired in sleep and its reasoning has the same validity in dreams, even if certain attendant features, such as places, persons, words used, are images only:

> And if it (sc. the mind) thinks anything, it is equally true whether one is asleep or awake (*imm. an.* 23).[21]

Indeed, there is, in many cases, a mixture of awareness that one is dreaming, and unrealized acquiescence in the illusions of dreams. Thus, one can be aware that one is perceiving the images that normally deceive one into believing that one is seeing real bodies: Augustine can recall dreaming an attempt to persuade a friend that both were dreaming and so perceiving only dream-images, but at the same time he remarks that the very attempt at persuasion betrays the illusory aspect even of so self-conscious a dream. For he talked with his interlocutor, not as if the latter were a dream-image among others, but as if he were really present (*Gn. litt.* 12.2.3).

For Augustine, this parallelism cannot fully extend to the moral dimension of human behaviour, for responsibility in dreams cannot be admitted: our will is not sovereign. Thus, even if our dream and hallucinatory life is illusory, it is so in a sense which falls short of any sinfulness (even if the illusion or error is due to the contamination of human nature by original sin, *ench.* 20-1). We appear to consent in dreams to actions which would be abhorrent to us, or to moral sense in general, were they to occur in waking states. In deciding that such consent is not responsible, and therefore not morally reprehensible, Augustine is guided by his explanation of the

[19] See Dulaey 98f., with examples from several authors. Cf. Cic. *div.* 1.45; 2.128; 2.140 (and Pease's nn. *ad loc.*).
[20] See the frequent allusions to dreams of finding treasure, e.g. *en. Ps.* 72.26; 75.9; 131.8.
[21] For Porphyrian influence upon Augustine here see Pépin (1964) 80-2 = Pépin (1977) 240-2.

mechanism of imagination in dreams. In our waking state, we can only discourse about e.g. sexual matters by somehow representing to ourselves, and thinking about, that which we discuss: this thinking about sexual matters need not be morally wrong. The mental image thus produced can re-emerge spontaneously in a dream, when we take it for real, so that it activates our sexual desire. Augustine asserts that this is no occasion of sin: the voluntary element is absent, and this is the reason for the moral 'neutrality' of such dreams (*Gn. litt.* 12.15.31). For the deception of our imaginations effectively undermines our ability to judge: lack of discernment precludes guilt as well as merit.

At the same time, Augustine is not unaffected by the belief, common in antiquity among philosophers, that our dreams somehow reflect our moral character. We may not be able to control our fantasy in dreams, but the morally better among us will be capable of dreaming laudable desires. The example of Solomon's desire for wisdom has already been mentioned; Augustine can also recall resisting temptation in dreams (*conf.* 10.41), and can feel anxiety about the persistence of sexual desire in one who, like himself, is committed to chastity (ib.). Such dreams are indicators at once of lack of personal perfection, and, in general, of lack of human perfection (*conf.* 10.42). There is an obscure and unanalysed connection, it would appear, between the sort of images we dream about, and our everyday moral selves. Strictly speaking, our dream-thoughts carry no moral weight; but their nature is a symptom of our personal and universal condition. Augustine can thus include nightmares and disturbing hallucinations among the morbid symptoms of man's fallen state as a 'son of Adam':

> Finally, sleep itself, which has the special name of 'rest' – who can express in words how restless it often is because of what we see in dreams, and with what great terrors (which, even if they are of unreal things, are so displayed and somehow represented that we cannot distinguish them from reality) it disturbs the unhappy soul and senses? Even when they are awake people are wretchedly afflicted by such hallucinations under the influence of disease and drugs. Sometimes malicious demons deceive even healthy people with such apparitions, using various kinds of trickery, so that, even if they cannot by these means bring them under their power, they none the less delude their senses through no other desire than to make them believe in the falsehood in whatever way they can (*civ.* 22.22).[22]

It will be clear from the foregoing pages that the creative, as well as the reproductive imagination is at work in dreams; indeed, one should perhaps accord more influence to the former. In what looks like an attempt to define dreaming, Augustine stresses this creative aspect:

> It (sc. soul) withdraws for a certain period of time from the senses, and, refreshing their motions as if through a kind of rest, it occupies itself with the

---

[22] See the remarks of Brown 394-7 on the nightmare vision of the human condition in the writings of the elderly Augustine.

many varied crowds of images of objects taken in through the senses: and all
this is sleep and dreaming (*quant. an.* 71).[23]

This creative ability can account for the more bizarre dreams. Perpetua,
while retaining her female bodily identity, dreamt that she was a man:
Augustine finds that the only explanation consistent with this phenomenon is
the imagining, in her non-corporeal soul, of a non-corporeal bodily likeness
(*nat. et or. an.* 4.26). It is, he believes, Perpetua's *soul* which appears to her to
fight as a warrior (ib.).[24] Augustine faces a further phenomenon in the case of
John the monk, who prophesied that he would appear to a woman in a dream
(*cura mort.* 21). Did he appear personally, 'his soul in the likeness of his body',
as we appear to ourselves in dreams? By this, Augustine seems to be thinking
of a conscious presence of John in the other's dream, analogous to our
awareness of our own persons in our dreams, or analogous to Perpetua's
awareness of her own presence, albeit in masculine form, in her dream. If this
explanation is to hold in John's case then it is not accounted for by any
natural process, but is a gift of God, beyond human agency:

> Through a wondrous grace ... not naturally; and by divine gift, not by any
> capability of his own (ib.).

If, on the other hand, John's appearance is not conscious, but through some
external, e.g. angelic agency, then we are also in the realm of the more than
merely human: moreover, we have not accounted for John's forecast of his
appearance, which was presumably due to some prophetic gift. Augustine
does not offer a view on the relative plausibility of the two explanations: but
John's case clearly points to the borderline between accountable exercises of
human imagination and possible external influences of a supernatural kind.

One such commonly accepted external influence in antiquity was in
dreams where the dead appear. In dealing with this phenomenon, Augustine
is determined to counter supernaturalism wherever possible: he is intent
upon limiting the latter to those cases where no normal psychological
explanation seems adequate. In the case of appearances of the dead, he
points out that these are like appearances of living persons in dreams. The
latter appear, but are not normally consciously present to those to whom
they appear; in fact, neither their soul nor their body, but rather a likeness, is
seen. Why can we not assert the same of dreams involving the dead? How
these happen Augustine cannot say (*cura mort.* 12f.), but he points out that
the hallucinatory visions of the insane or temporarily unbalanced, as well as
those in comatose conditions, give rise to images of the dead as well as the
living. There seems no reason to give a privileged account of the former (ib.
14f.). Throughout this discussion, Augustine stresses that the living persons
so imagined have not consciously caused their appearance in any way: he
appears to Favonius Eulogius, but is not aware of so doing (§13). In so far as

[23] Cf. *ep.* 162.5. Dulaey 76 compares Cic. *div.* 2.139-40.
[24] For the dream-visions of Perpetua see F.-J. Thonnard, *BA* 22, 817-9 (with bibliography);
Robert; Amat 118-30.

Augustine speaks at all of causal factors these appear to be angelic (§12). The humans dreamt about are not actively involved. Just as he draws parallels between dreaming and waking states, so Augustine seems to insist upon analogies between images of living and dead persons in dreams. The belief in the soul's survival does not make active appearances of the dead plausible, any more than the fact of physical existence does in the case of the living who appear in the dreams of others.

The example of John the monk's appearance in a dream is a case where Augustine would be inclined to call the dream 'significant' or 'true'.[25] In this instance, the significance is corroborated by the prophecy of John that he would appear in the dream. John, however, is, as we have seen, considered incapable by his own unaided effort of effecting his appearance in another's dream: only a supernatural cause, whether divine or angelic, can account for such a phenomenon. From this and other points of view, what Augustine has to say about significant dreams has much in common with what he has to say about prophetic inspiration, and it will be best to deal with these phenomena together.

However, before we do so, there remains one unusual type of phantasm to be discussed. Augustine believes that it is possible to dream what others experience as a normal perception, in which the dreamer appears to be physically present to the others: dream and vision are, in such cases, contemporaneous. Thus a philosopher dreams that he appears to deal with Platonic problems in conversation with another man who experiences his presence as if it were real (*civ.* 18.18). To account for this Augustine posits the existence of a 'phantom (*phantasticum*)' of the person, which, though not corporeal, can take on corporeal appearances in locations other than that of the person's body, often when the latter is in a comatose state. This hypothesis is also offered as an explanation of apparent metamorphoses of men into animals, where the human consciousness of those metamorphosed seems to be in the animal body, as was the case with the hero of Apuleius' *Golden Ass*, or the drugged victims of notorious Italian landladies,[26] or the father of Praestantius, who claimed to have become for a time a pack-horse in the service of the Roman army (*civ.* 18.18). Here the faculty of imagination appears to be conceived of as a soul-power with extra-territorial possibilities while normal sense activity is in abeyance. However, the bodies in which the phantom appears are not real: we must therefore assume that there is a necessary hallucinatory element in the percipient's experience of such appearances, even if he is not aware of the presence of another's phantom in the illusory bodily form. Augustine cannot explain how these phantom appearances occur, but he points out that demons could bring about such occurrences inasmuch as they do not involve the creation of any new reality: one would thus have the bizarre phenomenon of a real phantom in an unreal

---

[25] See p. 115.
[26] Cf. N. Moine, 'Augustin et Apulée sur la magie des femmes d'auberge', *Latomus* 34 (1975) 350-61.

body, seeming to carry real burdens, all through demonic agency (or through some inscrutable divine intervention in the natural order) (ib.)[27]

(vi) Prophetic vision

Augustine makes it clear that prophetic inspiration, whether through dreams or other psychological means, involves the exercise of our imagination. Distinguishing between the several types of vision found in scriptural accounts (*c. Adim.* 28), he pinpoints the differences between physical, perceptual visions (giving the examples of Moses and the burning bush, and the transfiguration of Christ) and imaginative visions, where images of corporeal objects, with figurative significance, are shown to us in a state of possession (an example given is Peter's vision at Joppa of the vessel let down from heaven, Acts 11:5-6). The significance need not be communicated with the vision, and in any case it requires intellectual activity (*mentis intuitus*) for its elucidation: the *spiritus* which imagines does not interpret, a Daniel is needed to explain the writing on Balthasar's wall, or the significance of Nabuchodonosor's dream (ib.).[28]

The imagination is at work in both Peter's vision and Nabuchodonosor's dream. In both cases what happens does so

> through a mental representation (*per informationem spiritus*) ... in which images of objects are manifested (*div. qu. Simpl.* 2.1.1),

as Augustine describes it in a text which further systematizes the various kinds of revelatory vision. The 'mental representation' can (as the examples given in *c. Adim.* 28 show) be effected either through dreams, or through a revelation in ecstasy

> ... when there is an estrangement (*alienatio*) of the mind from the bodily senses, so that the human spirit is taken over by the divine spirit and can freely contemplate and grasp images (ib.).[29]

Again, Augustine insists upon the necessary role, itself also part of the prophetic gift (and so no normal exercise of human reason, even if it be the same human reason which knows truth and wisdom), of the interpretative understanding of images thus induced (*div. qu. Simpl.* 2.1.1; *c. Adim.* 28). Such understanding may be that of the person having the vision, or of another, and may be either simultaneous with, or subsequent to, it. An individual may also be an unconscious prophetic medium: the example is given of the high-priest Caiaphas, whose assertion, concerning Christ, that it be fitting

---

[27] See Dodds (1973) 174f. on such reciprocal phantasms. The term 'phantom' (*phantasticum*) here most likely refers to popular beliefs about such phenomena.

[28] There is a useful analysis of this and other Augustine texts on the theme of revelation in Wieland: see especially his account of what he calls the 'epistemological basis' of revelation theory in Augustine (39-106).

[29] For a discussion of the implications of this text see Wieland 107-47. *Alienatio* is discussed by Evans 48-53. For the term cf. *ekstasis* in Acts 11:5.

that one should die on behalf of the people (John 11:50), was intended by him to have a completely different significance from that prophetically assigned to it by the evangelist.[30]

Even if divine agency, direct or indirect, is posited in the case just described, this cannot be an adequate account of the *mechanism* of such imaginative behaviour. Augustine is aware of this. Thus, while he will use emotive and colourful language to evoke the passive state of our perceptive faculty in such experiences, he will also seek to integrate them into his other accounts of imagination.[31] Two texts in particular, one early, one late, stand out as attempts to speculate on the problem. In *ep.* 8, Nebridius poses certain questions on the ways in which 'higher powers' can send us dreams. He distinguishes three possibilities:

(a) Do they set our minds in motion through their thoughts, so that we can also picture (*imaginemur*) them (sc. the dreams) through thinking?
(b) Or do they present and reveal the (sc. dreams) themselves to us in their own bodies?
(c) Or are they (sc. the dreams) formed in their imagination, and so presented and revealed to us?

(a) appears to envisage some form of direct communication between minds. Nebridius does not elucidate it further, but in so far as it is distinguished from the other two, it appears to exclude corporeal or imaginative intermediaries between what the higher powers think and what we dream: *imaginemur* is here used, not in the technical sense of exercising *phantasia* by actualizing images latent in the memory, but in the sense of mental picturing of the induced dream-sequence. It leads to a particular aspect of Augustine's reply, as we shall see.

(b) assumes that higher powers are, if only temporarily, embodied for the purpose of dream communication. And it conceives of the latter as a type of perceiving. We take in the images intended to form our significant dreams by a type of internal perceiving, not to be confused with inner sensing, for unlike the latter, this perceiving presupposes the existence of internal *bodily* senses capable of perceiving the corporeal images presented to them while our ordinary senses are inactive in sleep. Nebridius does not offer any further details, or any judgement on the plausibility of this remarkable suggestion, with its implications that our five senses are, as it were, doubled by a corresponding set of five internal physical senses.

(c) posits a transferal of images from imagination to imagination. But, Nebridius asks, if imagination is capable of such delivery and reaction, why cannot we similarly affect one another in our dreams?

[30] Cf. also *Gn. litt.* 12.22.45, and – for two cases of unconscious prediction – ib. 12.22.46-7. That they are not products of chance but of unconscious 'possession' is clear from ib. 22.48.
[31] The terms most frequently occurring are: *adsumi, rapi, extasis, alienatio, alienari*: see *c. Adim.* 28.2; *div. qu. Simpl.* 2.1.1; *Gn. litt.* 12.13.27; 12.13.28; 12.21.44; 12.23.49.

> But if, on the other hand, they (sc. the higher powers) are assisted towards such things (i.e. the images), not by their bodies, but they form them in their imagination and so they reach our imaginations and a perception, consisting in a dream, occurs, why, I ask you, can I not with my imagination force yours to produce those dreams which I myself have first formed in mine (ib.)?

That we might be expected to be capable of so doing is, Nebridius argues, plausible, when we consider how our bodies appear to affect our souls in dreams. We are thirsty or hungry, and dream that we eat or drink,

> and many such things, which are communicated by the imagination from the body to the soul in a kind of partnership, as it were.

These dreams, mediated through the imagination, are the result of communication between a corporeal and a non-corporeal entity. One might argue that, *a fortiori*, two non-corporeal entities (viz. your imagination and mine) might communicate. That this is not so puzzles Nebridius, and makes his acceptance of possibility (c) problematic.

Augustine's reply in *ep*. 9 is, as he says, intended only as the start of an investigation whose complexities disturb him (§2). He nevertheless offers a fully-fledged theory to account for the phenomenon (§3). Every emotion or 'movement' of the soul (*motus animi*) has some effect upon the body. Our senses, however, register only the bigger movements, such as anger, sadness or joy. Yet higher powers,[32] with their more subtle senses,[33] are capable of registering the finer traces (*vestigia*) of such movements; they can even register thoughts of ours that leave no trace upon our bodies, for their senses are acute enough to 'pick up' thoughts.[34] Now the traces that do affect our bodies, even if we are unconscious of them, remain latent in the body as a sort of disposition (*habitus*) that can be activated by a demonic will, and so become the medium of dream and thought communication.

The implications of this account are important. Firstly, it contains an indirect reply to possibility (a) of *ep*. 8. For Augustine asserts that thoughts can indeed be communicated from demons to us, but only through corporeal means, i.e. through the bodily traces just described, and, we must assume (see *divin. daem.* 9, quoted below), through the images resultant upon them. In the second place, Augustine takes up and adapts Nebridius' observation concerning the effect of body upon soul in dreams. In fact, this influence of

[32] Augustine (*ep*. 9.3) distinguishes, in a tradition deriving from *Epinomis* 984d-985a, between the etherial body of good demons, and the aerial body of evil ones. See Courcelle (1948) 166 n. 8 for the likely Porphyrian source of Augustine's concept of aerial demons in *c. Acad.* 1.20 and *divin. daem.* 7f. See further Pépin (1964) 54f. = Pépin (1977) 32f.

[33] Note how Augustine accepts the embodiment of the powers, as in possibility (c) of *ep*. 8.

[34] Some such 'reading' of human thoughts by demonic senses seems to underlie the explanation given of the extrasensory perceptions (especially mind-reading) of the Carthaginian diviner Albicerius (*c. Acad.* 1.17-23). The line of Virgil in the questioner's mind is picked up by the subtle demonic sense in some inexplicable way (§20), and this demonic power (disparagingly dubbed an *abiectissima animula* ('utterly contemptible little soul') by Augustine's high-minded friend Flaccianus) communicates the verse to the receptive Albicerius (§21). See Dodds (1973) 175f.

body and soul upon one another is reciprocal. In the case of anger, a psychological state, bile is built up in the body, and this bile, in turn, makes renewed outbursts of anger increasingly possible:

> So, what soul has, through its own motion, formed in the body will be capable of moving it in turn (*ep.* 9.4).

Augustine wishes to draw an analogy between the unconscious build up of bile in our system and the presence of corporeal traces of other emotions upon which demonic influences could be exerted. The analogy, as indeed the whole theory put forward, depends on the type of close psychological and physiological interaction observed by Nebridius. Thirdly, the account given by Augustine, while it accepts the thesis of communication between demonic and human minds, does so in a way which does not call for any abnormal functioning of the imagination, for the latter works exactly as in the everyday manner, receiving and forming images from corporeal sources, and the demonic imagination does not communicate directly with us, but only via the traces, already present in our bodies, upon which it acts: thus the difficulties noted by Nebridius in possibility (c) are obviated. Fourthly, the account renders the hypothesis of abnormal corporeal sensing – as mooted in possibility (b) – unnecessary. For there is no direct perceiving by us of anything corporeal in such visions: on the contrary, it is our minds, which even in sleep are active, that register the images of corporeal traces. All that seems unusual about this explanation is that the actual appropriation of the images occurs in sleep or in vision, whereas in normal dreaming we, as it were, work upon images already present, which have been perceived in a waking state. Augustine will return to this point.

In *divin. daem.* Augustine insists upon the subtle senses of demons, which allow them to pick up and transmit to us advance signs of future events:

> Such is the nature of demons, that with the sense of their aerial body they easily excel the sense of earthly bodies ... they foretell or report much that is known (sc. by them) in advance (§7).

> They foretell future events, which they know in advance through natural signs which cannot reach human senses (§9).[35]

He repeats there the point made in *ep.* 9, that it is through corporeal and

---

[35] Cf. *Gn. litt.* 12.17.36 for the prophetic power of a medium (*phreneticus*) to predict somebody's death. For the demonic ability to move at great speed, cf. *divin. daem.* 7 and – an example of its efficacy in reporting distant events almost simultaneously – *Gn. litt.* 12.17.35. Augustine's speculation that this last case may have been a *phreneticus* suggests an alternative to possession, i.e. something like telepathy (Dodds (1973) 174). Is this also the case with the example of §17.36, where possession would also, at first sight, seem an explanation? Augustine appears to wish to demythologize certain visions, and compare them with 'normal' prophetic dreams (cf. §18.39): of course, this still leaves the mechanism of prophecy unaccounted for, even if possession, in the popular sense, is not adduced.

imaginary intermediaries that demons communicate with man in dreams and visions:

> They persuade, however, in extraordinary and unseen ways, entering human bodies by means of their own corporeal fineness, without the humans feeling this, and mingling with their thoughts, whether they be awake or asleep, through certain representations of the imagination (§9).

Later texts of Augustine's appear to suggest a modification of these views, in so far as they allow the possibility of bypassing the intermediaries. A text which is tentative and questioning, rather than assertive, is *ep.* 162.5. Angelic appearances are not necessarily corporeal; in Matthew 1:20 the angel appears in a dream, when the eyes are not actively seeing. Augustine will not accept (ib. 3) that there can be internal corporeal senses, any more than Nebridius is enthusiastic about the notion in *ep.* 8. Can it be that the angels appear in some non-corporeal bodily likeness, analogous to the way in which we appear to ourselves in our own dreams? How this could occur is not discussed.[36]

Augustine has similar difficulties with angelic voices: once again, he can only proffer a human analogy. Since the angelic voice is not external but internal (here he draws support from Zechariah 1:9, 'And the angel who spoke *in me* said to me'), Augustine can compare it with our mentally going over e.g. a song, using internal 'words': the angel would be the 'speaker' of such inner words.

What characterizes both these suggestions is not merely Augustine's determination to explain such phenomena in credible terms, but also his willingness to investigate how normal human activities can accommodate such invasions of our psychical identity. But if, from the human point of view, the receptive mechanism is explained, the problems of communication with the superhuman power, and its access to our psyche, remain.

It would be unwise to read too much into the sparse remarks of *ench.* 59. All that Augustine says there is that it is through some 'spiritual power' that angels induce visions in minds. Yet what he adds about angelic voices is intriguing: as in *ep.* 162.5 he assumes that they are *within* the recipient, and that this can be so because the angels themselves are *within the recipient's mind*:

> Who can explain ... (sc. with what) spiritual power ... they can say something, not externally to the ear, but within, to the human soul, being themselves, moreover, actually ensconced there (*ench.* 59).

---

[36] Even when angelic appearances seem corporeal, and can be apparently touched by humans, as when Abraham washes angelic feet (Genesis 18:4), or Jacob wrestles with an angel (Genesis 32:24), the problems are not lessened, merely different: how account for such embodiment? (*ep.* 162.5; *ench.* 59) Augustine seems readier to accept corporeal appearances of malevolent demons, or their influence upon our imaginations (*trin.* 4.14), presumably because of the tradition of aerial bodies in demonology (etherial bodies are not automatically assigned to angels, see above n. 32). On the question of bodily appearances of angels and demons see Augustine's continued uncertainty at *nat. et or. an.* 4.35. For Augustine's angelology see, besides Pelz: Lechner; Lohse; Pépin (1965) = Pépin (1977) 29-37.

This possibility of a direct presence of the angelic power in us will form one of the alternatives broached in Augustine's most detailed late account of the problem in *Gn. litt.* 12.

In that account we may distinguish three possibilities of accounting for spiritual visions induced by a superhuman power.

> (i)   Does something occur in the body, so that its (sc. soul's) concentration (*intentio*) is, so to speak, slackened (*relaxetur*) and springs forward to reach to where it may perceive in itself likenesses full of meaning, which were already there but not seen, just as we have much that we do not always consider in our memory as well?
>
> (ii)   Or are they (sc. the likenesses), not previously being there, formed in it (sc. soul)?
>
> (iii)   Or are they in some spirit, where it (sc. the soul), breaking out and freeing itself, sees them (*Gn. litt.* 12.13.27)?

In (i) Augustine envisages a *corporeal* influence upon us, which turns the soul's *intentio* upon images latent in it, images present either in the memory, or in some analogous fashion: the *intentio* is relieved (*relaxetur*) of its normal body-directed activities (cf. ib.: 'bodily impediments are removed and, so to speak, eased (*relaxantur*)'). The problem with this explanation is that it raises the question of why the mind was unable, of its own accord, to focus upon and understand these latent images. Augustine is clearly not satisfied with either the explanation or the attempt to base it on the mind's liberation from bodily impediments by a spirit, for such liberation is also a normal feature of the ordinary thinking activities of mind and even of *intentio*. Perhaps the external influence is as much responsible for the mind's understanding, as for its perceiving, the vision? But again, in that case, it is not different from the ordinary illumination of the intelligence, even if it influences an extraordinary application of intelligence, viz. the prophetic understanding. Augustine is clearly not happy with this account: we may note, however, that it is like accounts in earlier texts in so far as it specifically stresses the *corporeal medium* which is primarily influenced in order that *intentio* may function upon the desired objects.

(ii) considers the hypothesis that the vision is formed initially and directly in the human mind.[37] Nothing more is said of this hypothesis, but it clearly presupposes direct demonic/angelic access to our minds, in the way, noted above, in which it is envisaged in *ench.* 59.

In (iii) a similar direct access is hypothesized.[38] The terms 'break out, free oneself (*erumpere, emergere*)', like 'spring forward (*emicare*)' in (i), stress the active role of the mind's *intentio*. No matter how powerful the external influence, the human mind must none the less somehow take in, even if it

---

[37] See Dulaey 124. Cf. *Gn. litt.* 12.22.48: '... whether they are formed there in the first place ...'. The term *formare* may be anticipated in *div. qu. Simpl.* 2.1 (*informare, informatio*).

[38] Cf. *Gn. litt.* 12.22.48: '... or, already formed, are introduced and perceived through some kind of affinity'.

does not fully – or at all – understand, the vision. This third view necessitates a direct communication of already formed thoughts and images:

> ... so that the angels should thus show (*ostendant*) men their thoughts and the likenesses of bodily objects, which they form in advance in their spirit through their knowledge of the future (*Gn. litt.* 12.22.48).

The contents of such communication are called 'manifestations (*ostensiones*)', ib. 12.20.42. How does this communication occur? The term *coniunctio*, employed in §22.48, is used by Cicero to translate the Stoic *sumpatheia* (*div.* 2.124).[39] The term may imply, for Augustine, no more than some 'affinity' between angelic and human minds (cf. *div.* 2.119, of prophetic dreams: 'through an affinity (*coniunctione*) with other minds'). But there are indications that he may mean more. In *Gn. litt.* 12.30.58, on the same topic, he can talk of communication occurring 'by a joining (*iunctio*) and mixing (*conmixtio*)', where the terms used are clearly not intended to be mutually exclusive alternatives. At ib. 12.12.26 *conmixtio* is also adduced in passing as an explanation of ecstatic vision (*extasis*). Even more explicit is §13.28 (on malevolent demons):

> Some kind of hidden mixture (*mistura*) of that same spirit occurs, so that it is as if (sc. the spirits) of tormenter and sufferer are one.[40]

These passages seem to be sufficient evidence for Augustine's acceptance, as a hypothesis, of some kind of mingling or conjoining of human and superhuman spirits: that the notion is familiar to him is clear from his quotation of Fonteius of Carthage's vivid account of the invasion, by a malevolent demon, of human senses and the mind (*div. qu.* 12; *retr.* 1.26). Notions of possession by, and exorcism of, spirits were in any case both widespread and popular in late Roman society.[41]

There is no reason why the term *commixtio* need not be applied to possibility (ii) also, but Augustine (e.g. *Gn. litt.* 12.22.48; 12.30.58) seems to wish to distinguish *informare* from *miscere*. And we can see why, if we consider that in (ii) the images formed, albeit by external agency, are none the less formed as ours in our minds, whereas in (iii) such images are, as it were, imposed ready-made upon our minds: the mind's role is, initially at any rate, passive. But these are nuances: the terms 'deprived of reason (*alienari*)', 'snatched away (*rapi, assumi*)' can be used of all three possibilities mooted, for all are forms of possession by a more powerful mind.

Despite the fact that Augustine devotes relatively greater attention to possibility (iii), he remains agnostic (§30.58). We could say that his own objections are severest in regard to (i), and that he excludes this hypothesis in §30.58 and the latter part of *Gn. litt.* 12 generally. Significantly, his hypotheses in that work hark back to those of Nebridius in *ep.* 8. Hypothesis

[39] Cf. *div.* 2.34 and Pease *ad loc.*
[40] Cf. *trin.* 11.7; *div. qu. Simpl.* 2.1.3.
[41] See K. Thraede, art. Exorzismus, *RAC* 7 (1966) 44-117; Amat 185-95.

(ii) corresponds to Nebridius' (a); hypothesis (iii) to his (c). There is no strict correspondence to hypothesis (b). Equally interesting is the fact that Augustine now entertains what in *ep.* 9 he was above all intent upon avoiding: direct communication, bypassing corporeal means. He is none the less interested enough in the psychology of possession to report a case where visionary experiences and acute physical suffering go hand in hand, *Gn. litt.* 12.17.37-8. But he is severest on the one hypothesis – (i) – which contains an element of corporeal pre-conditioning. This shift has been acutely observed by Dulaey, but how conscious an acceptance of Neoplatonic, and, in particular, Porphyrian hypotheses it amounts to, and whether, as she argues, the Porphyrian views are now more acceptable to Augustine because he has detached them from the notion of the psychical vehicle (*okhêma, pneuma*), remain questionable.[42]

(vii) Anticipation

In the summary account of the dealings of *spiritus* with likenesses of corporeal objects given in *Gn. litt.* 12.23.40 Augustine remarks that these latter are formed

> when, on the point of performing some bodily action, we map out (*disponimus*) the details of that future action and anticipate (*antecedimus*) them all in our thought; or when in the very course of the action, whether it be a question of words or deeds, the likenesses of all the bodily motions are anticipated (*praeveniuntur*) internally, in the spirit, as a necessary prelude to their occurring: for no syllable, no matter how short, would sound in its proper place if it had not been anticipated (*prospecta*).

We may compare *conf.* 11.23-4: we think over beforehand (*praemeditari*) our future actions; strictly speaking, only their 'causes or signs' are present to our minds, as, for example, the dawn is a sign of the sunrise, and enables us to predict that the sun is about to rise, a prediction which is in turn dependent on our ability to imagine the sun rising (ib.). But the ability to imagine the sunrise and to recognize that the dawn is its *signum* is in turn dependent on our having experienced the phenomenon before:

> But it makes a very great difference whether future events are conjectured on the basis of experience of things past (*trin.* 4.22).

There the examples of doctors and farmers predicting on the basis of experience are given. Likewise, so we must assume, having the *causa* of future X present to our minds is the empirical inference that, given C, X will, in the normal course of events, follow. Our anticipation of a future event, or even of our future actions, is therefore the anticipation of what is likely to, or what we intend to, happen: it may be frustrated by other unforeseen factors. To give

---

[42] Dulaey 126f. Although the author is well aware of the speculative nature of her Porphyrian reconstructions and their influence upon Augustine, there is a danger that her speculations may be accepted as a new orthodoxy: see Wieland 58-64.

Augustine's extreme example: the sun may, upon divine intervention, stand still (*conf.* 11.30).

This anticipation is called *expectatio* by Augustine (*conf.* 11.26). In the *Confessions* account he also refers to the second aspect of the *Gn. litt.* passage quoted above, the phenomenon, not of prediction or of anticipation before a sequence of action, but of the anticipation of the individual stages of an action during its course; and he also uses the same example, of reciting a verbal sequence (*conf.* 11.36-8). Here again anticipation is dependent on experience (§38), though the experience can simply amount to knowledge of words and rhythms in general (§36). As Augustine says elsewhere, it is a form of anticipation, or imagination, that is founded on memory rather than prophetic foresight:

> This may be tested in the case of words or songs, whose sequence we are reciting from memory; for unless we foresaw in thought what came next we could not in any way express it. And yet it is not foresight (*providentia*) but memory that teaches us, that we may foresee it (*trin.* 15.13).

And it works through the creative manipulation of images:

> From the same abundance I can myself join to past experiences various new likenesses of things either experienced or believed on the strength of things experienced; and from these I can, furthermore, think about future actions and events and hopes – all as if they were present. 'I shall do this and that,' I say to myself in the huge recesses of my mind, filled with so great a quantity of images of so many things: and this or that follows (*conf.* 10.14).

Meijering, in an otherwise good discussion, tries too hard to distinguish the 'images' of past perceptions, caused by past events, from the 'causes or signs' of future events anticipated by the mind. As he himself goes on to observe, the 'causes' here referred to are not the efficient causes of future events.[43] They are rather the recognized, because empirically observed (or imagined, because empirically known), antecedent (and occasionally causal) factors in natural sequences of events. The dawn is not a cause of the sunrise, but it is an antecedent factor normally preceding sunrises; the experienced sailor recognizes certain weather signs as advance warnings of bad weather, even if they do not cause the storm, and so on. In fact, the term 'signs' is equivalent to 'causes' in *conf.* 11.24, though occasionally 'causes' will indeed be the more appropriate term. Predictions of the kind in question are expressions of strongly-held beliefs, backed up by empirically observed sequences of events: they are not accounts of efficient causality, still less formulations of necessary truths. That Augustine envisages them occurring through imaginative activity is clear from the passage in *conf.* 10 quoted above. The application of this theory to our anticipations (as opposed to our predictions) of our own actions is easy: we only 'foresee' these because we can form images of what we intend or expect from the raw imaginative content of our experience and

---

[43] Meijering 69-71.

beliefs, that is, from memory. What is important is that such anticipation is not merely *possible*, but also that it is *necessary* for the carrying out of any deliberate action: action is the effort, not necessarily always successful, to translate into practice what we must have already imaged to ourselves, and we can only act deliberately on the basis of experience. But because our imagination can be creative, action can be adventurous.

(viii) Distortions of the imaginative faculty

Augustine was fascinated by what we may call the pathology of imagination. He understands this quite literally, as a morbid state of our physiological or psychological faculties. Thus it may be because of excessive mental concentration, as well as through disease, that we take mental images to be indicators that the objects imagined are actually present to our perception, and this hallucination can even be accompanied by normal perceptions, so that we perceive X to be present and simultaneously imagine that Y is also actually there (*Gn. litt.* 12.12.25). Such a hallucinatory state, if it takes a more serious form, can lead to a coma in which normal perceptive activity stops (*Gn. litt.* 12.19.41).

Augustine understands such states as ones of physical disruption. If the link between brain and sense-organ (i.e. the sensory nervous system) is disturbed or blocked, concentration (*intentio*), a cerebral activity necessarily transmitted by the nervous system to the sense-organs, cannot function normally. But this activity will nevertheless necessarily occur, and it generates images in a wholly introverted way, taking these for the proper objects of perception:

> If the path of concentration from the brain, through which perceptive activity is directed, be without feeling or disturbed or blocked, the soul itself cannot by its own motion break off this task, and as it is not, or not fully, allowed to perceive corporeal objects through the body or direct the force of its concentration towards them, produces in the spirit likenesses of corporeal things ... these are mere images (*Gn. litt.* 12.20.42).

This disturbance or blockage can also be in the brain itself (ib. §20.43; cf. 7.18.24). Such is the vividness with which the mind can generate images, however, that we may speak not merely of an inability to discern appearance from reality, but also, on occasions, of a degree of awareness different from what is normal. Augustine draws a parallel with conscious dreaming (i.e. dreaming of which we are aware that it is dreaming), when we none the less take the dream-images for reality (§20.43): that is to say, though at one level we are aware that our imaginings are not real perceptions, at another level we are nevertheless deceived by their vividness. Dreaming is, in general, a state similar to the hallucinatory condition, for in both cases the normal activity of concentration is diverted from its sense-perceptive role (ib. §21.44).

Augustine finds it important to distinguish the actual place of the blockage, i.e. whether it is in the sense-organ or in the brain or in the links from brain to sense-organ (§20.43). If it is in the sense-organ, perception is indeed blocked, but concentration is not so diverted that hallucinations necessarily ensue: the blind or deaf are not in a perpetual state of illusion (ib.). In the case of blindness, the concentration is thought of as extending as far as the sense-organ, but of course no further, and conveying to the blind, not any perception, but the consciousness that they are awake (§20.42), or, more basically, conveying conscious awareness of their physical existence (§20.43). For, since the blind also dream, their concentration is directed in sleep, in entirely normal fashion, upon dream-images, but they can, in their waking state, clearly distinguish between such illusory 'seeing' and the state of being awake. They can further, like those who are not blind but simply close their eyes, distinguish between corporeal likenesses and real bodies, and do not take the former for the latter: presumably the one difference being that the seeing think, 'This likeness is not equivalent to the real bodies which I have perceived', whereas the blind think, 'This is only a likeness; although I have never perceived a real body, I know this is not one'. (The assumption in my example is that the blind in question have been so from birth; in other cases, the difference between blind and not-blind would, in this respect, disappear.) To sum up: we can only speak of an abnormal functioning of the imagination, in the case of those whose sense-organs are defective, in a very limited sense of the term indeed. Abnormality is rather to be sought where there is damage or disturbance, temporary or permanent, to the brain or sensory nervous system.

CHAPTER FIVE

Memory

In the preceding chapters frequent reference has been made to the function of memory as the indispensable factor, both in our perceptions of spatio-temporal continua,[1] and in the reproductive and creative exercises of our imagination.[2] It is now time to look more clearly at what Augustine says about the formation of memory-images, the processes of remembering and recollecting and the role of the will in these processes, the relationship between memory-image and previously perceived object, and the phenomenon of forgetting, with its attendant implications for our identity as conscious subjects. This chapter will confine itself to Augustine's treatment of memory in the empirical sense, and will not therefore deal with such characteristically Augustinian notions as our 'memory of God' (*memoria dei*) – the presence of God to our minds – or our recollection of the objects of rational knowledge.[3] It will, however, prove necessary to take account of the mental processes of understanding and discrimination when analysing empirical memory.[4]

(i) The formation of memory-images

Between our recollection of a past event or a previously perceived object, and the event or object themselves, the memory-image plays an essential intermediary role. The mind which can recall spatial distances and so, as it were, see them again in the memory, can do so, Augustine argues, only if their images are contained or held in the memory (*quant. an.* 8), and these contents can only be of a non-corporeal kind, for corporeal images correspond in size to the bodies in which they are reflected, and this is evidently not the case with e.g. the mind's memory of immense spaces previously perceived (ib. §9).[5] What is true of the likenesses which we perceive is also true of those which are stored in our memory. Indeed the latter derive from the former:

---

[1] See pp. 87f.

[2] See pp. 106-8.

[3] For these subjects see pp. 199ff.; 211f.

[4] There are accounts of Augustine's theory of memory by Gilson 134-40, 289-93; Markus (1967) 370-3; Mourant; Söhngen; A. Solignac, *BA* 14, 557-67. Augustine's views may be compared with Cicero, *Tusc. disp.* 1.57ff., whose arguments for the complexity and subtlety of memory may have influenced him.

[5] Cf. pp. 95f.

> For from the form (*species*) of the body which is seen arises that which comes
> into existence in the percipient's sense, and from this, that which comes into
> existence in the memory (*trin.* 11.16).

Incorporeal sense-impression leads to incorporeal memory-image (*c. ep. fund.*
16.20). Even in animals memory is not just a physiological faculty (*Gn. litt.*
7.21.29). It is rather the second function or *gradus* of soul, along with
perception, concentration, judgement, dreaming, motions of appetency or
rejection, and so is common to men and animals (*quant. an.* 71). The habitual
life of animals (e.g. their ability to return to nests or lairs) is dependent upon
memory (*conf.* 10.26). Besides, not merely in their quality, but also in their
quantity and kind, do memories depend upon and correspond to perceptions
(*trin.* 11.13). Images can, but need not, maintain their individual distinction
in the memory, though the manner in which they are formed, and how
precisely they derive from sense-impressions, cannot be ascertained (*conf.*
10.13).

Two things are, however, certain. In the first place, memory-images are
continuously being formed while our perceptive processes are taking place,
and actually enable such processes to occur.[6] Moreover, memory, like
expectation, is an essential prerequisite of any conscious action, if the
moments of that action are to cohere:

> Besides, in such a process, expectation is necessary for its completion, and
> memory for its comprehension, to the extent that this is possible ... nor can the
> end of a bodily movement be anticipated without memory. For how could one
> anticipate the end, if one forgets that there has been a beginning, or even that
> there has been a movement at all (*imm. an.* 3)?

In the second place, memory-images are not formed spontaneously, as a
type of necessary by-product of our sense-impressions. Their formation is
rather a willed one; failure to commit sense-impressions to memory is not a
failure of perception, but is due to distraction of the will from its task:

> Furthermore, as the will directs the sense to the body, so it directs the memory
> to the sense, and the eye of thought to the memory. But the same faculty which
> harmonizes and joins these, also disjoins and separates them, that is, the will ...
> So the will acts through a bodily movement to prevent the bodily sense from
> being joined to sensible things ... the will averts the memory from the sense
> when, intent on something else, it does not allow what is present to cling to it
> (*trin.* 11.15).

Augustine argues this point with practical examples. If we do not concentrate
on what another is saying we appear not to have heard him: in fact, we have
sensed the sounds of his words, but our failure to concentrate the 'will's
purpose (*nutus voluntatis*)' prevents us retaining them. Or we can read a page
without 'taking it in'. Our eyes have indeed sensed the letters, but these – still
less their meaning – have not been committed to memory. Or one can walk

[6] See pp. 87f.

while one's thoughts are elsewhere: one sees where one is walking, but, in a sense, does not know this, and cannot later recall what one has seen. In deliberate actions, concentration (*intentio*) is the necessary link between memory and expectation:

> And expectation is of future things, but memory is of things past. The concentrated will to act, however, is in the present, and through the latter the future turns into the past (*imm. an.* 3).

This concentration is envisaged as a will, not necessarily acted upon, to act on bodies (ib. 4): the will is likewise seen as the necessary link between sense-impressions and the formation of the memory-image. Augustine is, furthermore, clear about the physiological seat of memory: it is the central ventricle in the cerebrum (*Gn. litt.* 7.18.24). Physiologically, therefore, memory is directly linked with sensation and the initiation of bodily actions (the other two ventricles being the terminus and source of the sensory and motor nerves respectively), although Augustine is careful to stress that the cerebral ventricle is the servant (*ministerium*) of memory rather than memory itself (ib. 19.25). On the metaphorical level, Augustine's favourite physiologically-inspired description of memory is that it is the 'stomach' (*venter*) of the mind (*conf.* 10.21; *trin.* 12.23) – a description which at once suggests its great powers of absorption and its ability to digest and reuse its images in knowledge, skills and action. Yet the metaphor is not, as we shall see, without its limitations as an evocation of the powers of recollection.

(ii) The process of remembering; memory, understanding and will

What happens when we remember or recollect past experiences? In answering this question Augustine applies once again the analogy with sense-perception. Acts of recollection are like acts of perception. Just as our senses are, so to speak, formed by external, visible, sensible objects, so too the mind's vision is formed by the memory-image and can recall previously perceived objects (*trin.* 11.6). Our will directs our senses to external objects, which we then perceive; in like manner, the will directs the mind towards the memory's contents, and recollection occurs. The form (*species*) actualized in recollection and the memory-image appear to us as one: their distinction is purely conceptual (ib.).

This description is tantamount to saying that recollecting is perceiving memory-images; in other words, that it is primarily concerned with actualizing memory-*traces*. It is, remarks Augustine, not the objects of our past perceptions themselves, but rather the images derived from them, that we speak of when we talk about past perceptions (*mag.* 39). What prompts our will to actualize such memory-traces? Augustine argues that the 'movement' (which can have physical as well as mental components) set up by sense-perception persists in us. The power of association (whether in consequence of similar experiences or of thought is not clear) reactivates this movement, and recollection occurs, often with some mental and volitional effort:

> But the movement of the mind which is not spent returns to our thought when something similar happens, and this is what is meant by recollection. This is the case when we go through (sc. musical) rhythms – which we have already gone through once – whether in thought only, or with movements of our limbs (*mus.* 6.22).

We can recall that we once met a person if, having failed to recognize him immediately, he tells us where, when and how we met: this information can act as so many indicators (*signa*) whereby we may recall the meeting (*trin.* 14.17). If we do so, then our forgetting of the meeting has not been total, for some memory-trace has survived and has been activated:

> But if you do remember (sc. him), you certainly return to your own memory and find in it what had not been entirely erased by forgetting (ib.).

Just as it is possible not to entrust to memory what one senses, so too can our memories fade into total forgetfulness. A constant unconscious process of attrition occurs:

> From the very moment in which it cleaves to the memory, it begins to pass away ... but this diminution is not perceived (*mus.* 6.6).

Any forgetting which falls short of complete oblivion can, however, be converted into recollection. Thus, if we have forgotten X, but can still recognize that Y and Z are not X, forgetting has not been total: this is quite a different case from our failure to remember infant experiences about which we know only because others have told us about them (*sol.* 2.34; *conf.* 1.12). Sometimes forgetting seems only partial, as when we see X and recall that we know it from some unremembered time, place or condition (*sol.* 2.34). Or, seeing a person's face, we try to recall his name: we may reject Y and Z as false names of the person, while not yet recalling the correct name X. Eventually recognizing X to be the right name shows that it has not been entirely forgotten (*conf.* 10.28), but even the lesser achievement of rejecting Y and Z, while not yet remembering X, is an indication of a less than complete forgetting of X, inasmuch as it includes the negative ability of dismissing the wrong names.

We cannot recollect without willing to do so, and conversely there can be no will to recollect unless that which we wish to recall is either totally or partly in the memory. By the mere fact of wishing to recall X, we recognize that X is somehow present to us. If I wish to recall yesterday's dinner menu, I may recall that I ate dinner yesterday, or that there was a yesterday and that it had a dinner time, as well as that the verb 'to dine' has a meaning. These recollections (whichever of them, singly or in combination, actually applies to my situation) bring about the will to recall more fully that which is already admitted to be in the memory (*trin.* 11.12). We cannot will to recall what we have totally forgotten.

The ability to remember, which Augustine also calls the formation of the mind's 'eye' (*acies animi, trin.* 11.6), or its direction, by the will, is not merely confined to recollection of specific memory-images.[7] It is present in mental activities in a much more fundamental manner. Our imaginations can vary and multiply the recollections derived from our perceptions (*trin.* 11.13), and it is not difficult to see memory's role in such an exercise of the imagination; but memory is also present in less obvious cases of recollection, such as, for example, taking in what others tell us, but we have not ourselves perceived. Doing this would be impossible were it not for the fact that we have certain memories – viz. of the meanings of the words that others use, or of the forms or images of the bodies to which their words correspond:

> For I do not think what was hidden in my memory, but what I hear when something is told me. I do not mean the speaker's actual words ... but I am thinking of those forms (*species*) of material things, which the speaker indicates by words and sounds, and which I certainly think of, not by remembering, but by hearing, them. But if we consider the matter more carefully, the bounds (*modus*) of the memory are not overstepped even then. For I could not even understand the speaker if I did not remember in a general way the individual things of which he spoke, even if I was on that occasion hearing them combined for the first time (*trin.* 11.14).

The ability to form a concept of anything corporeal, such as might be described to us by a witness to what we have ourselves not seen, depends on having had a perception which, when activated by the memory, endows the concept with meaning:

> The bounds of thought (*cogitandi modus*) are in the memory (ib.).

Memory is in the 'mind's eye' formed or directed in a certain way. When Augustine speculates on the connection between memory, understanding and will he sees them as aspects of a single substance, the mind (*mens*):

> For memory, inasmuch as it is called life and mind and substance, is so called with reference to its own being; but it is called memory relative to something (*trin.* 10.18).

The category of relation is appropriate. Just as understanding is understanding of something and will is will to effect something, so too memory is memory of something: the terms, and the activities to which they refer, cannot be understood in an absolute sense, as can 'substance' or 'life' or even 'mind'.[8]

It is surely in this relative sense that we must understand a remarkable passage in *conf.* 10.26:

---

[7] Augustine can describe in metaphorical terms the relation between memory-image ('parent') and form recollected actively by the 'eye of the mind' ('offspring'), while adding the corrective that the 'eye of the mind' itself exists as a power or potentiality prior to its formation by its 'parent' the memory-image (*trin.* 11.11).

[8] This characteristically Augustinian approach to psychological activities has been explored in Chapter 1, pp. 2ff.

> Great is the power of memory, something awe-inspiring ... a deep and endless multiplicity; and this thing is my mind, and this thing am I myself.

It would be easy to read into these words an assertion of the identity of the memory with the mind and even the self.[9] But that is hardly what Augustine means, even if he is inclined to the view that our remembered experiences form the basis of our historical identity:

> And so this age (sc. infancy) ... in which I do not remember having lived ... I am not happy to count it as part of my life lived in these times ... And what has that of which I can recall no trace got to do with me now? (*conf.* 1.12).

In this respect, Augustine remarks, his infancy is no more 'his' than the period prior to his birth.

We might apply Frege's distinction between sense (*Sinn*) and reference (*Bedeutung*) here, and say that, for Augustine, 'mind' and 'memory' have the same reference but different senses. Memory is indeed the mind, but engaged in certain pursuits, directed in a certain way and in relation to certain objects. The assertion that memory is the mind is supported by the evidence of linguistic idioms for remembering (*in animo habere*) and forgetting (*non esse in animo, elapsum esse animo*), though Augustine goes on to assert that it is more appropriately called the 'mind's stomach' (*venter animi, conf.* 10.21). It is perhaps true, then, to say that whatever is in the memory is in the mind, for our memory-images are mental pictures (*conf.* 10.26), but that is not the same as saying that 'mind' and 'memory' are identical. We shall, however, see that Augustine is genuinely puzzled by the implications, for our identity, of loss of memory.

One can think of the individual's memory-images as a kind of depository (*thesauri, conf.* 10.12) of empirical knowledge. This knowledge is not, however, amassed indiscriminately. If sense-perception is a rational process,[10] then so must the formation and ordering of memory-images be. The knowledge thus acquired is the *scientia* of which Augustine writes in *trin.* 12 and 13:

> The knowledge of those temporal and mutable things, necessary for the performance of this life's actions (*trin.* 12.17).

Such knowledge is necessary for the exercise of virtue (ib. §21) as well as for the performance of sub-ethical actions.[11] The development of such knowledge can only be fully explained against the background of the inherent rational structure of our minds, i.e. by an analysis of Augustine's theory of a priori knowledge.[12] However, one aspect of the topic can be treated here, namely

[9] The modern reader influenced by the work of Proust and Joyce is particularly prone to make the equation memory = self here. See the epigraph to Martin Walser's novel *Das Einhorn* (Frankfurt 1966); '*Ich bin mein Erinnern.* Augustin,' and his use of texts and themes from *conf.* 10 throughout the book.

[10] See p. 96.

[11] See pp. 94f.

[12] See pp. 178ff.

the acquisition, with memory's aid, of the scientific knowledge of the disciplines.[13]

It is clear to Augustine that this latter is not derived from sense-experience. We possess direct cognitive awareness of its objects; they are not known through images, as are the objects of perceptively derived knowledge (*conf.* 10.16-19). This direct awareness can only be possible if the objects are in our minds, or memories, in a latent state, needing to be actualized, ordered and vivified, so that learning them is

> ... by thinking to bring those things, as it were, together which the memory contained, but scattered and in disarray, and by directing the mind to them to ensure that they are placed within reach in that very memory where they were formerly lying hidden, scattered about and ignored, and that they now come easily to us because of the habitual application (sc. of our minds to them) (*conf.* 10.18).

These objects or principles are unchangeable: they are the *rationes* underlying all bodily objects and movements or changes (*trin.* 12.23). When we, as embodied historical beings, have actual knowledge of them, the experience is rare, difficult for the mind to grasp, and transitory:

> To attain to these with the mind's eye is given to few; and when they are attained, to the extent that they can be, he who has done so does not himself remain in them, but the eye of his mind is, so to speak, rebuffed and repulsed, and so the transitory thought of something that is not transitory comes into being (ib.).

But it is precisely the training in acquisition of this actual knowledge which the cumulative skills of the sciences, with memory's aid, can mediate. The richer our memory is with such skills, the more we can order and assimilate the corporeal conglomerates, the principles of which are contained in the sciences:

> Nevertheless, this transitory thought is entrusted to the memory through the disciplines by which the mind is instructed, so that the mind which is compelled to pass from there may be able to return there (ib.).

We are clearly meant to understand that, even if they are not derived from sense-perception, the principles may none the less be grasped via their temporal particulars, as the underlying atemporal structures of these:

> Or if the rhythm of any well-crafted and musical sound that lasts an interval of time were to be apprehended in a timeless state, in some hidden, deep silence, it

---

[13] Lorenz (1955/6), especially 30-50; 229-42, analyses the concept of scientific knowledge and related themes in Augustine. The fundamental work on the role of the liberal arts in Augustine's life and thought is Marrou's classic study; cf. I. Hadot, *Arts libéraux et philosophie dans la pensée antique*, Paris 1984.

could at least be thought of as long as the song could be heard (ib.).[14]

When the disciplines are thus developed by the memory, the ability to retain and work on such knowledge is increased. This account is the full and explicit exposé of the role of memory that is elsewhere referred to only briefly and in passing (e.g. *trin.* 14.8). It is particularly significant that Augustine stresses that the knowledge of these principles is realized gradually, and in the course of perceptive experience, although one should also understand that its insights, once grasped, are firmly possessed, provided, that is, memory can work, in ruminatory fashion, on the hastily 'swallowed' principles:

> Yet what the mind's sight, even though it was transient, seized from there and, so to speak, gulping it down into its stomach, stored it thus in the memory – on this it will be able to ruminate somehow through recollection, and transfer what it has so learned into knowledge (*trin.* 12.23).

(iii) Memory-image and past perception

We have seen that Augustine believes that our sense-perceptions convey reliable information about the external world, and that through them we gain a kind of knowledge.[15] Now if recollection is analogous to perception it might be reasonable to assume that recollection also conveys trustworthy reports about sensible things once perceived. However, Augustine is reluctant to assert this. The analogy between perception and recollection is primarily an analogy between two processes or types of mental activity, rather than between the objects of these activities. After all, the sensible external object is not of the same kind as the incorporeal memory-image, despite their similar functions in the two processes in question. And this is precisely what worries Augustine. The worry is not necessarily caused by the phenomenon of images: in sense-perception we also perceive images of the things perceived. But in perception the external object is actually there, present to the percipient, and, simultaneously, to other percipients, actual or potential. This last fact may not affect the nature of our perceptive act, but it certainly helps to assure that it is verifiable; we are not necessarily the sole witness of the things which we perceive. This is not the case with the objects of recollection. What we remember relates in some way to what we have perceived, but, even in the optimum case of our being able to compare our memory-image with that of another percipient of the same things at the same time, both of us are referring to images, not of present things, but of things absent. The relation between image and object is problematic, even if one confines one's worries to the possible distortion caused by the passage of time between original perception and recollection: divergent reports by witnesses

---

[14] Cf. *conf.* 10.19: 'I have also perceived with all my bodily senses the numbers which we count; but those *by* which we count are different; nor are they images of the former, and so they really exist.'

[15] pp. 92-102.

of the same past occurrence only confirm this concern. A modern philosopher might, of course, have similar problems with the relation between present objects and sense-impressions of them: how can one verify the supposition that the latter are impressions of the former? As we have seen in Chapter 3, Augustine does not have this problem – successful perception is for him an immediate form of knowledge.

The difficulty under discussion is faced by Augustine in a passage in *de magistro*. There he writes that we have a power of discernment of physical objects in the external world (§38), so that:

> When we are questioned about them we answer if what we perceive is at hand, as when we are asked, while looking at the new moon, how or where it is (§39).

But past perceptions are a different matter:

> But when a question is asked, not about those things which we are at that moment perceiving, but about things which we have perceived in the past, and we speak then, not of the things themselves, but of the images impressed by them and committed to the memory, I do not know at all how we can call them 'true', when we are looking at what is false, unless it is because we say that we do not see and perceive, but rather have seen and have perceived, them. Thus we carry those images in the recesses of the memory as kinds of proofs of previously perceived things. Contemplating these in the mind, we tell the truth (*non mentimur*) with a clear conscience when we speak; for these proofs are ours (ib.).

Augustine adds that these images are proofs (*documenta*) only for the percipient: the listener who has no access to personal images of the same things can only believe our words and accept them, as it were, on trust.

When Augustine calls the memory-images 'false' he clearly means no more than that they are not actually the things which they represent. He does not appear to be commenting on the mutability of sensibilia. Now it is obvious that the originally perceived objects are not there as we perceived them when we are recollecting them, or attempting to do so. Recollecting is not a direct awareness of the past. But Augustine, in making this valid point, appears to cut the lifeline between memory-image and perceived object. He will grant that the former has evidential character – but, as we have seen, adds that it has so, strictly speaking, only for the percipient: such a 'proof' would, in principle, allow of any measure of distortion of the original impression. Augustine can only assert that if we give our attention to these 'proofs' we may rest assured that we 'do not lie' (*non mentimur*) when we make assertions concerning them. 'Not lying' here does not mean that we cannot be mistaken or deceived about the things themselves, but merely that our memory-impressions are correct qua impressions. If we are honest we can report them accurately. Whether they are a true representation of the formerly perceived objects is another matter, and this is precisely the point at issue if our impressions are to have any validity as memory claims.

Gareth B. Matthews has characterized this argument of Augustine's as follows:

Augustine seems to be saying that whenever we are asked about familiar, but absent, sensible things we respond by changing the subject, that is, by talking of our memory images instead.[16]

Matthews believes that Augustine's analysis takes this direction because he restricts the problem to one of specifying the mental mechanism of recollection, and overlooks the no less important but different problem of how one makes a response count as an answer to a question about sensible things. The former question is indeed answerable in terms of images, lack of direct access, and so forth. The latter question – in effect, one about the verifiability of memory-statements – cannot be dealt with in terms of internal images alone. Now Augustine begins to deal with this second question when he posits the presence of another percipient (B) of the same things, who can compare the speaker's (A's) impressions with his:

> For he who hears them (sc. the proofs), if he has been present and perceived them (i.e. the things themselves), also recollects through the images which he has taken away with him (§39).

Augustine must be referring to the sensible things here, though his language is imprecise. But even this point does not get us beyond a comparison of two sets of images, and Augustine does not apply it to the question of verifiability, being concerned rather in the passage to argue that such recollection is not a form of learning by B from A's words, for, in the case of perception, learning consists of no more and no less than the acquisition of the immediate perceptual impression itself.

Thus far, Matthews' critique of the *de magistro* passage seems justified. We cannot really read the latter otherwise. In an answer to Matthews, Bruce S. Bubacz broadens the scope of the problem and introduces other texts and analyses. Bubacz argues that, given the notion that memory is essential to any type of knowledge claim,

> for Augustine, knowledge claims about material objects are essentially inner. They take as objects images.[17]

Moreover, Augustine's account of the functional relations between words (inner and outer) and images stresses the meaningful nature of talk about absent material objects. I find myself in broad agreement with Bubacz's modified acceptance of Matthews' critique; but I cannot follow two further assertions of his: that Augustine's advocacy of the utility of memory claims – especially in anticipatory planning of future actions (cf. *conf.* 10.14)[18] – makes him an implicit pragmatist; and that the question of the confirmation or

---

[16] Matthews 168. Madec 138 n.82 is sceptical about the pertinence of this criticism, but does not go into details.

[17] Bubacz (1975) 189. The views put forward in this article are reprinted with some insignificant minor modifications in Bubacz (1981) 61-92.

[18] The passage is quoted, p. 128.

disconfirmation of memory claims is irrelevant for Augustine in the *de magistro* passage.

The texts adduced by Bubacz, and other relevant ones, must now be examined. As has been observed in the discussion of sense-perception, what we perceive is an articulated form or image, a rational structure with affinities to our minds.[19] When Augustine wishes to stress this rational aspect of perception, he will employ the terms *forma* and *species* (where he elsewhere would use *imago* and *phantasia*) for the object of our perceptions. These mental data are stored in our memory as a form of knowledge (*trin.* 15.19f.). When we wish to reactivate this knowledge (for it need not remain actual, but can become latent, and so require recollection) by directing our thought (*cogitatio*) upon it, we generate an inner 'word' (*verbum*): our *phantasia* becomes an actualized memory-image, itself articulated and significant.[20] Bubacz is thus right to say that 'the image in memory and the inner-word are co-extensive',[21] but he does not bring out the essential role of the desire or will to remember in the production of the inner-word, and the essential function of the latter in *all* acts of remembering: it is not, as he would claim, because we *communicate* memories that we utilize inner-words; we need the inner-word to realize private memories as well. Inner-words are thus not so much the necessary preludes or 'cues' (so Bubacz) to the generation of outer words, as the mental recovery and articulation of memories that need never be expressed in language. The inner-word serves initially as the means whereby we communicate our memory-image to our consciously thinking selves, in purely introspective manner. These memory-images are word-potentials.

The linguistic metaphor and analogy here employed by Augustine can be clarified by his remarks in *de dialectica*[22] on the mental understanding and retention of the meaning of words:

But whatever is perceived of a word, not by the ears, but by the mind, and is held fast within the mind itself, is called a 'meaning (*dicibile*)' (*dial.* 5.50-2).

The *dicibile* is a thought, which, like the inner word, exists in the mind prior to its expression in language (ib. 5.74): it too is a word-potential, capable of being expressed.[23] The distinction 'ears-mind' in the perception of a word is appropriately compared by H. Ruef with Stoic accounts of the difference between sensation and *katalêptikê phantasia*: Ruef further compares the *dicibile*

---

[19] See p. 96.

[20] See pp. 113f.

[21] Bubacz (1975) 191.

[22] References to passages in *dial.* are to chapter and line of the text printed in *PL* 32.1409-20; the text used is J. Pinborg's, in the critical edition of B. Darrell Jackson/J. Pinborg, Dordrecht/Boston 1975.

[23] The *dicibile* is most plausibly identified with the Stoic *lekton*, as it was by Thomas Stanley in the seventeenth century (see *dial.* Pinborg p. 126): so Barwick 12. For the *lekton* is also that which 'may be expressed' (*SVF* 2.167), it subsists in, or 'in accordance with', the *logikê phantasia* (*SVF* 2.187), and as an 'incorporeal' (*asômaton*) (*SVF* 2.132; 166; 170; 331) it is not to be confused with the bodily, expressed sound of the spoken word. Nuchelmans' critique of the *lekton* = *dicibile* equation (116f.), which Ruef 109 adopts, does not, therefore, appear convincing.

with the Stoic *logikê phantasia*, an impression expressible in words.[24]

We note the difference between a *dicibile* and the image of a perceived object (e.g. Carthage) qua *phantasia*. The latter is, as it were, stored in the memory *pre-verbally*: it becomes a 'word' when the thought directed upon it is formed by it (*cogitatio formata*). The *dicibile*, on the other hand, is always present to the mind (though presumably the presence can be latent) in a *verbal* manner: *its* potentiality is its expressibility in spoken language. We may express the difference thus:

image → inner word, in the mind (*in corde*) → expressed word
meaning → expression (*dictio*), *dial.* 5.52-4 = expressed word

Furthermore, the *dicibile* may have a generic semantic function. For, even if it is the mental counterpart of a specific sense-perception, the understood meaning of a word may enable us, not merely to identify the specific object once perceived, but also to identify similarly named objects, in so far as the named object is not unique:

What I have called the *dicibile* is a word, yet it does not indicate a word, but rather what is understood in a word and retained in the mind (*dial.* 5.60-2).

The *dicibile* corresponding to the word 'city', for example, has a generic potentiality qua meaning that is not possessed by the *dicibile* corresponding to the word 'Carthage'. The *phantasia* or memory-image which we have of Carthage is actualized as a 'word' when I think of the word 'Carthage', with all its associations for me as a percipient. If, on the other hand, I think of the word 'city', the actualized 'word' may include my memory-image of Carthage, but can include more, and, most important of all, can enable me, not merely to recall or recognize known objects, but to identify new objects of the same kind (e.g. 'This – Alexandria – is a city'). Ruef aptly remarks upon the similarity between the *dicibile* and the Epicurean notion of *prolêpsis* or preconception.[25] Both are mental concepts ultimately derived from sense-perceptions; both enable us to judge our experiences, and to classify or express them in language.[26]

Identifying, understanding, naming, recalling and recognizing are inextricably linked. Only the perceived 'recognized thing' (*res nota*) can be expressed as the 'formed thought' (*cogitatio formata*) or 'word' (*verbum*); and only that percept can be said to be understood or known, to be the content of knowledge (*scientia*), which is not merely sensed but also verbally identified (i.e. its name functions as a sign whereby the percept is both stored in the memory and subsequently recollected). Taking in the meanings of words, and taking in the forms of objects, are not therefore for Augustine merely analogous or parallel mental activities. That is not to say that a perception

[24] Ruef 108. For Ruef's questionable identification of the *dicibile* with *logikê phantasia* see the preceding note.

[25] Ruef 187 n. 203a.

[26] For the Epicurean notion of *prolêpsis* see Long (1974) 23.

must necessarily be accompanied by an overt linguistic naming of the object perceived. What Augustine wishes to say is, that normally perceptions are indeed accompanied by their overt verbal signs or by an expectation of these, i.e. we either say or think 'This is a cat' or ask – in the case of unrecognized objects – 'What is this?' In the latter case, we expect to be given or discover a name for the object. And the role of words in such normal perceptions has its cognitive parallels in perceptions where overt naming does not, or cannot (e.g. because of physiological hindrances), occur. On the other hand, Augustine feels that he can best elucidate the mechanism of (1) perceiving, (2) storing, (3) recalling, by the illustration from language: (1) mental grasping of a word's meaning; (2) storage of the latter as *dicibile*; (3) expression as *dictio*. To make the recalling of Carthage understandable, Augustine has recourse to the analogy with language: recalling my memory-image of Carthage is like actualizing the semantic content of an understood, stored word; it is like bringing to mind, through the activity of introspective thought, the meaning of a word. When I recall Carthage, I generate an inner-word; similarly, when I utter the word 'Carthage' I (in so far as the word is known to, and understood by, me) express in language what is expressible in my thought. The analogy may be presented diagrammatically.[27]

We might say, therefore, that the analogy with language stresses the coherence and objectivity of our recollected perceptions, for Augustine is not to be saddled with problems of private languages or doubts about the general communicability of meaning through the medium of language. In this respect I can only agree with Bubacz: the notion of the inner-word points towards the meaningful nature of memory-claims. The passages from *de dialectica* – not used by Bubacz – support, and in certain respects clarify, this notion of Augustine's. Bubacz is also right to insist that Augustine's recognition of the complexity of knowledge claims leads him to the belief that memory is essential to all such claims. An a priori functioning of memory is the prerequisite for the simplest perception and the most complex mental activity alike.

Against this undoubted general tendency of Augustine's views, we may have to set the *de magistro* passage discussed above[28] in a context where it is the puzzling exception rather than an indication of the rule. We have seen that, even if he does not develop the implications of the point, Augustine does adduce percipient B, whose memory-images would allow comparison with A's otherwise private memories. To object that B can only offer images for comparison with further images, and that the verifiability of all these images remains problematic, is to make a valid analytic point, but it may also distort the purport of Augustine's remarks in *de magistro*. For these remarks are primarily directed, not against the tenets of knowledge and verifiability as such, but towards a sharper definition of the epistemic function of learning in its relation to sense-perceptions. In this connection, we should neither

---

[27] See p. 144. The diagrammatic presentation of the analogy was inspired by Ruef 83-5, who employs similar diagrams to illustrate other arguments in *dial*.

[28] pp. 139ff.

(i) perceiving and recalling

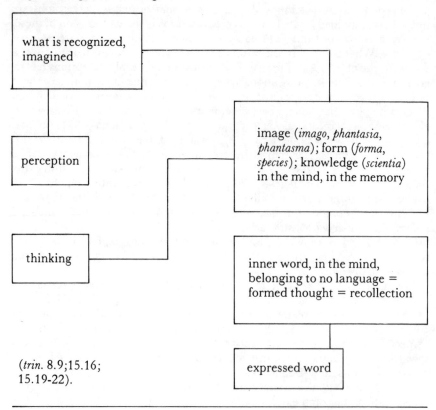

(*trin.* 8.9; 15.16;
15.19-22).

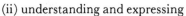

(ii) understanding and expressing

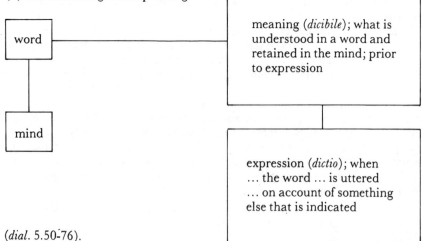

(*dial.* 5.50-76).

underestimate the value, for Augustine, of believing as a form of acquisition of knowledge,[29] nor should we see in the introduction of the metaphor of the *documentum* a reduction of our memory-images to mere private claims without any verifiable relationship to perceived reality. They are, after all, 'proofs' liable to examination, and so to verification or rejection, whether through the introduction of other witnesses, or on grounds, we might add, of inherent plausibility, in so far as they may or may not represent claims worthy of credence.[30] To this extent, Bubacz cannot be right to assert that the question of the confirmation of such memory-claims is irrelevant for Augustine in *de magistro*: granted, the confirmation of such claims is indeed problematic and complex, but the context suggests that it is *ex hypothesi* possible. The *documentum* can be tested, and, moreover, it must be verifiable if the basis of Augustine's epistemology is not to be disturbed. Ultimately, however, the introduction of credibility or belief as a factor favouring the reliability of memories does not solve the difficulty of validating the resemblances between memory-images and past experiences: Augustine's worry in *de magistro* may betray more insight into the problem of verifying memory-images than either Matthews or Bubacz have given him credit for, even if it is a worry that his theory of communication and understanding would tend to dispel.

What of Bubacz's other argument, that

> the suggestion that memory claims (and other knowledge claims) are important in the degree to which they have utility ... makes Augustine seem a pragmatist,

albeit an unconscious one?[31] It may be best not to waste words on what is likely, in the end, to be no more than a terminological quibble. For by the same token, Bubacz might well call Aristotle's teleology pragmatist, and there can be no doubt that, for Aristotle as for Augustine, animal faculties (such as perception) are powers which make practical activity and reaction, and ultimately survival, possible.[32] Yet herein lies the crucial difference between a teleological and a pragmatist view of utility. From the teleological viewpoint, the purposive aspect of natural phenomena is to be accounted for in terms of definable goods: it is both practicable and right that we should, for example, have memories that function in the way they do. The mere utility of memory is not an indicator of its importance, as a pragmatist might maintain; rather its utility is in itself an indicator of the order and purposefulness of nature. Now it is clear that there are elements of pragmatism in a teleological viewpoint; but that is not to say that the one theory is reducible to the other, still less that Augustine's view of memory's

---

[29] See M. Löhrer, *Der Glaubensbegriff des hl. Augustinus in seinen ersten Schriften bis zu den Confessiones*, Einsiedeln/Zürich/Köln 1955.

[30] The term 'verification' is used here in the sense in which Augustine would accept it, not in the stringent analytic sense.

[31] Bubacz (1975) 192.

[32] See the remarks of J.L. Ackrill, *Aristotle the Philosopher*, Oxford 1981, 63-5.

utility has anything like the implications for a view of truth or value which pragmatism, as the term is generally understood, would have.

(iv) Memory and emotion; forgetting

We can remember past feelings or emotional states, such as joy, sadness, fear or desire:

> There (sc. in the memory) too I meet myself and recall myself – what I have done, when and where, and in what emotional state I was when I did it (*conf.* 10.14).

But we do not necessarily relive the emotion remembered: often, indeed, we remember one emotion to the accompaniment of another, as when we sadly remember past joy (*conf.* 10.21). Augustine is aware that this type of memory is not immediately explicable in the ways in which memories of perceived corporeal objects, or numbers, or scientific knowledge, are. For what is remembered is lacking precisely in the quality – a particular emotional colouring – which gave the original experience its character. Yet somehow the same or similar recollective processes must be in operation in this as in other memory-acts. Augustine puts forward his celebrated metaphor of memory as the mind's 'stomach' (*venter*), taking in, but transforming, different emotions, so that they remain, but lose their individual 'taste' (*conf.* 10.21). But his attempt to extend the metaphor by comparing remembering with the regurgitation of food by ruminants is not successful; for these experience the taste of the food thus regurgitated, and something similar does not necessarily occur in the case of recalled emotions (*conf.* 10.22). Yet despite the difficulty of accounting for such processes, Augustine is convinced that the 'ideas of the emotions themselves' (*rerum ipsarum notiones*, ib.) are in our memory if we can recall them, whether these ideas have been committed to memory by the mind or retained by the memory in some other way.[33] And he assumes that these ideas are necessarily present to the memory in the form of images: they are not physically present (§22), and there is no other plausible hypothetical account available. Despite the problems involved, therefore, in making their retention similar to that of e.g. images of perceived corporeal objects, Augustine feels obliged to accommodate his image-storage theory to the phenomenon of remembered emotions.

This particular phenomenon leads Augustine to define more accurately the implications of X 'being in the memory'. Naming X and recognizing what the word means, or refers to, is an indication that we remember X (*conf.*

---

[33] We should not misunderstand the significance of 'ideas' (*notiones*) as applied to memories of feelings. Augustine adopts the term because he wishes to emphasize that my memory of e.g. 'joy' is not merely the recollection of the sound of the word, but also the recollection of its meaning: presumably we cannot know the meaning of an emotional term unless we have experienced the emotion (§22).

10.23). We have already met the analogy from language[34] in Augustine's account of recollecting: here Augustine seems to be saying that knowing the meaning of a word is remembering what that word refers to. By this token, I can remember memory, for I can name 'memory' and recognize what the word refers to (§23), just as I can experientially remember remembering, and remember remembering that I remembered (§20), certain facts which I know. The self-conscious nature of memory is unproblematic for Augustine: he is only uncertain as to whether this self-consciousness is achieved by means of a self-presence of memory to itself in its own right, or by means of an image (§23). In §24 the former seems to be preferred.

But if our memory of memory is clearly established, our memory of 'forgetting' (*oblivio*) is not.[35] Applying the criterion of *conf.* 10.23, Augustine is obliged to accept that recognizing the meaning of 'forgetting' is tantamount to remembering it (§24). Here again, as in the case of remembered emotions, the nature of the presence to the mind of what is recalled is puzzling. For, since forgetting is the absence of memory (*privatio memoriae*), how can it be present to the memory?

> So it is present, in order that we may not forget that which we do forget, when it is present (ib.).

On these grounds it seems necessary to argue that at least recalled forgetting is not present in its own right: should we rather assert that its image is what is present? But even this is not without difficulties. For in order that an image be impressed upon the memory, the original of that image must be, or have been, present to the percipient: this is clear from the example of our every-day sense-perceptions. But if we are to envisage forgetting as at some time present to the mind in order that memory might capture its image, we cannot readily account for its image impressing itself upon the memory when by definition its presence should obliterate even previously stored memory-images:

> If, therefore, forgetting is retained in the memory by means of an image, not in itself, it must most certainly have been present itself, in order that its image might be grasped. But when it was present, how did it inscribe its image on the memory, since forgetting, by its presence, obliterates even what it finds already recorded? (§25).

Augustine's answer to this dilemma is based on his analysis of the phenomenon of losing things (§27). We can lose an object, but still retain a memory of it, the memory which is effective when, for example, we find and recognize what has been lost. This memory is present to us as an image, and by means of the image we recognize what we have been looking for. The

---

[34] pp. 141-4.

[35] I translate *oblivio* by 'forgetting' rather than 'forgetfulness', since Augustine's argument deals with instances of loss of memory rather than a stable mental condition or tendency, such as is implied by 'forgetfulness'.

object was, therefore, lost to sight, but not to the memory. Augustine goes on to apply the example of loss to the phenomenon of forgetting. Forgetting is the loss of memory of something. When we try to remember what we have forgotten, we search our memories for it. We recognize it when it comes back to us, and this indicates (as the criterion of §23 maintained) that it is in the memory, so not totally forgotten – as when, for example, we see or think of a person whom we know, but cannot recall his name. Rejecting the wrong names and recalling the right one imply that what has been apparently forgotten has not been entirely so (§28).[36]

Now if we do not entirely forget what we remember having forgotten, an experience of forgetting that is considerably less drastic than total oblivion is possible and even common. When we remember forgetting, therefore, we need only recall such instances of partial forgetting, searching and rediscovering, where 'forgetting' was not tantamount to total obliteration from the mind, but was rather temporary failure to actualize what was latent in the memory. Knowledge of loss implies awareness of possession. Forgetting is indeed absence of memory, but not necessarily its total absence.

The style of *Confessions* makes the train of thought leading from the *aporia* of 10.25 to the suggested solution of 10.28 implicit and associative rather than direct and argued. But there can be no doubt that in positing an instance of forgetting that is less than total, and so implies the latent presence of what is forgotten to the mind, Augustine attempts to solve the problem posed by this tenet that, if we recognize the meaning of the term 'forgetting', we remember forgetting.

(v) Memory and identity

We have seen that Augustine maintains that our remembered experiences go to make up the fabric of our personal identity as historical individuals.[37] Basic to this notion of identity is the assumption of self-knowledge or self-awareness: our identity is the identity of which we ourselves are conscious. The fluctuating nature of this awareness poses a problem for Augustine: is our identity not affected by its ebb and flow? Thus, reflecting on the power of memory as a 'deep and endless multiplicity' leads Augustine to assert:

> What am I, then, my God? What nature am I? A changing, many-sided and completely unmeasurable life (*conf.* 10.26).

The range and mutability of the emotions provoke similar thoughts:

> Man himself is a great deep, Lord. You have his very hairs numbered and they are not made less in your sight: and yet his hairs are more easily numbered than his feelings and the movements of his heart (*conf.* 4.22).

[36] See p. 134.
[37] pp. 135f.

In what sense, therefore, can we be said to have stable natures? In one text, Augustine addresses himself to the particular problem of the implications, for our identity, of unsuspected powers of memory, as well as the related implications of forgetting what we had known. We know that we are living, remembering, thinking and willing beings, but we are unaware of the capabilities of our memories, intelligences or wills. Augustine cites the case of his boyhood friend Simplicius, whose phenomenal memory enabled him, when questioned, to recite passages of Virgil or Cicero from any given place in the works chosen by his questioners. Before his memory had been put to this practical test, Simplicius was unaware that he possessed such powers (*nat. et or. an.* 4.9). Augustine sees this new awareness as a gain in self-knowledge that brings with it the question: why did Simplicius not know this about himself beforehand, given that he was the same person then?

> So, as far as his memory is concerned, his mind got to know itself then, and, no matter when it got to know itself, it could only do so by trial and experiment; and before he put it to the test, he was beyond doubt the same person: why, then, did he not know himself? (ib.).

Augustine addresses himself to the case of forgetting what one once knew: does the difference in our state (ignorance in place of former knowledge) indicate some change of identity?

> Did *we* not exist when we thought that? For we are not what we were, when we cannot think it (ib. 4.10).

If there is change of identity, then this would seem to imply that parts of ourselves can be added to, or subtracted from, us, and, as it were, located in separate places, so that we are obliged, paradoxically, to seek ourselves outside ourselves:

> Why is it, then, that we are somehow withdrawn from and denied to ourselves and likewise somehow revealed and restored to ourselves, as if we were other persons and were elsewhere, when we seek and do not find what we have deposited in our memory, and as if we ourselves could not reach ourselves when we have, as it were, been deposited elsewhere, and could then reach (sc. ourselves) when we find (sc. our memory contents)? For where do we search, if not in ourselves? And what do we search, except ourselves, as if we were not in ourselves, and have withdrawn somewhere from ourselves? (ib.).

Augustine recoils from this image of a scattered and fragmented identity, but does not offer any explanation that would account for the phenomenon while saving the integrity of our natures:[38] the latter remain a mystery to us, and we cannot really be said fully to know ourselves:

---

[38] The reference to 'our nature ... not as it was, but as it now is' in the next passage suggests, however, that he is thinking of original sin as an explanation.

> Do you not mark and shudder at such great depth? And what is this, other than our nature, and not as it was, but as it now is? See, it is more investigated than comprehended. I have often believed that I would understand a problem laid before me, if I should consider it there and then: I considered it without success. Often I had no such belief and yet I succeeded. My powers and my understanding are by no means known to me (ib.).

Nevertheless, our partial self-knowledge is greater than our insight into the minds and wills of others, or our knowledge of percepts:

> For who could rightly say that he had known somebody, except to the limited extent that he was able to know his life and will ...? In that respect we ... know ourselves more surely than we know others, because our conscience and will are known to us. We see the latter clearly and yet it is not any bodily likeness that we see thereby (ib. 4.30).

Augustine evidently wishes to keep this question of self-knowledge in an experiential sense distinct from the notion of the mind's self-reflexion, a Neoplatonic doctrine to which he subscribes (cf. e.g. *trin.* 10.5-16).[39] He relates the two only inasmuch as he maintains that experiential self-knowledge may be an aberrancy or accretion: thus the mind which has turned away from God to itself tends to confuse its nature with the corporeal images with which it has occupied itself. This accretion must be rejected and purged if the true self-knowledge of our mind's nature is to be realized:

> When, therefore, it is commanded to know itself, it should not search for itself as if withdrawn from itself, but it should withdraw what it has added to itself (*trin.* 10.11).

It is precisely the conglomerate of wishes, desires, fears and memories which go to form our historical identity that Augustine finds puzzling. This puzzlement reads to us like the first step towards an understanding of the complexities of personality, such as modern psychoanalysis has attempted to achieve. We therefore almost tangibly sense the absence of its complement: the recognition of the unconscious, which is a part of ourselves, even if not actually known by us. We have seen that Augustine is familiar with the notion of latent memories that can be actualized: he does not, however, appear to have done more than merely suspect the existence of layers of our identity beyond our conscious awareness. And yet he might well have applied the theory of latent memories to that of identity: for, just as what we have forgotten may still be in our memory and so, in a sense, ours, so what is ours (i.e. part of our psychological make-up), even if we are not at the time aware of it, is a part of our identity at that time also.

That our memory continues to be a part of our identity even in the afterlife is maintained by Augustine in *trin.* 14.4-5. We shall, he asserts, retain in the memory the contents of our temporal religious faith; however, vision of the

---

[39] For the notion of self-reflexion in Plotinus see O'Daly (1973) 70-81; W. Theiler in Harder/Beutler/Theiler 6.161f.

truth will have superseded this faith, and the latter will be recalled as something belonging to the past, just like other memories of our previous life:

> Although we recall this past mortal life, and bring it back to our memory that we once believed what we did not see, this faith will be classed with what is past and done with, not with what is present and lasting for ever (*trin.* 14.4).

This faith (and presumably also the other recollected experiences) leave an imaginative trace (*imaginarium vestigium*) in the memory, capable of being recalled (§5). Recalling (at least some – Augustine does not specify) experiences of our former lives in the afterlife is an act of reproductive imagination, rather like recalling past events of our lives here and now. Augustine does not explicitly state that such posthumous memory is an essential characteristic of our surviving selves, but he clearly accepts that it is a legitimate postulate, and he is not troubled as, for example, Plotinus was, by the problems of whether the disembodied soul has memories, and, if so, of what kind and duration these are.[40]

[40] For Plotinus' views see O'Daly (1976) 462ff.

CHAPTER SIX

The Measurement of Time

Augustine's most sustained discussion of time, in book eleven of the *Confessions*, is without doubt one of the subtlest attempts to analyse the phenomenon in antiquity.[1] It can fitly be compared in importance with Aristotle's account in *Physics* 4.10-14,[2] and with that of Plotinus in *Enneads* 3.7 (*On Eternity and Time*),[3] and it shares with these accounts a vigorous sense of philosophical urgency concerning the problems of time. Furthermore, perhaps uniquely among ancient Platonists, Augustine does not attempt to understand time with reference to its supposed *paradeigma* or model, eternity. Elsewhere, indeed, he will refer to time as a 'trace (*vestigium*)' or 'copy (*imitatio*)' of eternity,[4] but in *conf.* 11 it is rather the total contrast between God's transcendence of time and man's anguished experience of dispersion and fragmentation in time that he wishes to emphasize. It is against such a background of radical disjunction between the created and temporal, on the one hand, and the unity and eternity of the divine, on the other, that the details of Augustine's account must be read. Plotinus' approach is quite different. For him, understanding the model, eternity, of which time is the image, elucidates the nature of time itself. Plotinus does not exclude the possibility that one might begin with an understanding of time and advance from it through recollection (*anamnêsis*) to contemplation of eternity, but he clearly prefers, and adopts, the former approach (3.7.1.18-24). By contrast, Augustine will neither proceed from model to image, nor from image to model. Despite the goodness of creation there is, he believes, a great gulf fixed between the creator and the universe. Whatever he may hold in principle, Augustine does not behave very Platonically in practice in *conf.* 11. His method is, rather, empirical: he considers time as a fact of everyday experience, as a practical problem. This has liberating consequences. The relative speculative freedom of Augustine's discussion has made it appear

---

[1] Meijering provides a detailed running commentary; see also A. Solignac, *BA* 14, 584-91; Flasch 263-86; Sorabji 29-32; 165-8; J.P. Schobinger, 'Augustins Begründung der "inneren Zeit"', *Schweizer Monatshefte* 46 (1966) 179-92 For Augustine's views on time in general see Guitton *passim*. An earlier version of this chapter appeared as O'Daly (1981,1).

[2] See P.F. Conen, *Die Zeittheorie des Aristoteles* (Zetemata, 35), Munich 1964; Sorabji 7-16; 46-51; 72-8; 89-94; E. Hussey, *Aristotle's Physics: Books III and IV.* Translated with notes, Oxford 1983.

[3] Beierwaltes (1967) is the fundamental commentary; see also Guitton *passim*.

[4] *Gn. litt. imp.* 13.38; *en. Ps.* 9.17; *mus.* 6.29.

to some modern philosophers (one thinks in particular of Wittgenstein[5]) a suitable example of one kind of discourse (for Wittgenstein a flawed kind) about time: as a result, a substantial critical literature has grown up around the text.[6]

The purpose of the present chapter, however, is not to look at the modern reception of Augustine's views, but rather to analyse those views, and establish what Augustine is saying and doing. For, surprisingly, there is no general consensus among historians of philosophy about this. Nor is it clear what particular earlier discussions of time were known to, and influenced, Augustine. His account has frequently been compared with the Aristotelian and Plotinian treatments of the subject, as well as with Greek Christian texts.[7] In this chapter I suggest some parallels with Stoic views, where these seem appropriate. I do not wish to argue that Augustine is using a Stoic *source*, although Stoic influences on his thought are both frequent and always inherently probable, and he is likely to have been familiar with Stoically influenced doxologies on the topic.[8] My purpose is rather to put Augustine's discussion into sharper focus by comparison with an important antecedent usually neglected in historical accounts of that discussion.

Augustine suggests at the beginning of his exposition that he is inquiring into the nature of time itself:

> What more familiar and better known concept do we call to mind, when we speak, than time ... what, then, is time? (*conf.* 11.17)[9]

He does not, however, give an answer to this question, or, as I have argued elsewhere,[10] a definition of time in the course of his investigation. His famous description of time as a *distentio animi* cannot be a definition, but is, rather, a metaphor which evokes whatever accompanies or follows upon the cognitive act of measuring time. It is a colourful and highly novel metaphor, to be translated not so much by the term 'extension' as by 'tension' or 'distraction

---

[5] L. Wittgenstein, *Philosophische Untersuchungen (Philosophical Investigations)*, Oxford 1968, 42f.; Flasch 284-6; Sorabji 14 n. 9.

[6] See e.g. R. Suter, 'Augustine on Time with some Criticisms from Wittgenstein', *Revue Internationale de Philosophie* 16 (1962) 387-94; C.W.K. Mundle, 'Augustine's Pervasive Error concerning Time', *Philosophy* 41 (1966) 165-8; J. McEvoy, 'St. Augustine's Account of Time and Wittgenstein's Criticisms', *Review of Metaphysics* 38 (1984) 547-77.

[7] See especially the writings of J.F. Callahan: *Four Views of Time in Ancient Philosophy*, Cambridge, Mass. 1948; 'Basil of Caesarea: A New Source for St. Augustine's Theory of Time', *Harvard Studies in Classical Philology* 63 (1958) 437-54; 'Gregory of Nyssa and the Psychological View of Time', *Atti del XII Congresso Internazionale di Filosofia*, vol. 11, Florence 1960, 59-66; *Augustine and the Greek Philosophers*, Villanova, Pa. 1967, 74-93. Cf. Beierwaltes (1967) *passim*, and the literature referred to in n. 1 above.

[8] See especially G. Verbeke, 'Augustine et le stoïcisme', *RechAug* 1 (1958) 67-89; J. Pinborg, 'Das Sprachdenken der Stoa und Augustins Dialektik', *Classica et Mediaevalia* 23 (1962) 148-77; R.J. O'Connell, '*De libero arbitrio* 1: Stoicism Revisited', *Augustinian Studies* 1 (1970) 40-68; Pépin (1976) 72-98; Ruef. The best discussion of Stoic views of time is in V. Goldschmidt, *Le système stoïcien et l'idée de temps*, 3rd edn., Paris 1977, 30-45; see also S. Sambursky, *Physics of the Stoics*, London 1959, 98-108; J.M. Rist, *Stoic Philosophy*, Cambridge 1969, 273-88.

[9] Cf. Plotinus, *Enn.* 3.7.1.4ff., and Beierwaltes (1967) 147f.

[10] O'Daly (1977); cf. Lacey.

causing anxiety'.[11] The term *distentio* leaves untouched the question of *how* we cognitively measure time, even if it graphically depicts the psychological side-effects of such a process.

In fact, Augustine's initial question ('what, then, is time?') is modified and re-formulated from the start. He notes that we speak of long and short time-periods: we presume to estimate and compare time-spans (§18). The problem, therefore, is, how can we *measure* time? How can a period of time have length? How do we know its length?

This modified formulation is not without subtlety. Far from evading the issue of a definition, Augustine appears to be admitting, at least indirectly, that time may not be explicitly definable. Just as one may, for example, be unable to define 'length', but can give a perfectly adequate account of how we measure and compare different lengths, so, too, it may be perfectly feasible to analyse how we measure time-spans without defining time. A reading of Augustine's discussion that concentrates on the problem of measurement rather that on that of definition is more likely to elucidate his intention. It may be helpful to set out the main points of his argument and discuss these stage by stage.

(A) Both Augustine and the Stoics assume that time is an infinitely divisible continuum.[12] Augustine's language in §20 seems momentarily to suggest the alternative possibility of a minimal point of time that is indivisible, a 'time-atom':

> If we can conceive of any part of time which could not in turn be divided into even the smallest instantaneous parts, that alone should be called 'present'.[13]

But he immediately undermines this possibility by remarking that there cannot be such an atomic point of time:

> For if it is extended it is divisible into past and future: but the present has no length.

An indivisible minimum time is, however, necessarily extended, and so cannot constitute a present. Later in the discussion, Augustine is more explicit. Passing time, he says, is extended over a certain measurable period, but at any given instant it has no actual measurable extent (§34). Elsewhere Augustine unequivocally asserts that time, like space, is infinitely divisible.[14]

---

[11] It should not, therefore, be compared with the Stoic definition of time as 'extension of movement (*kinêseôs diastêma*)', *SVF* 1.93; 2.509f., or with Plotinus, *Enn.* 3.7.11.41, which, speaking of time and the world-soul, says that 'the spreading out (*diastasis*) of life involves time' (transl. A.H. Armstrong). Beierwaltes (1967) 207f.; 265-7 discusses these and related terms. J.F. Callahan's attempt (art. cit. above n. 7) to demonstrate that Basil, *adversus Eunomium* 1.21 is a source of Augustine's *distentio* is unconvincing. Teske 84-9 argues that Augustine means by *distentio animi* a distension of the world-soul, and that his account is, therefore, Plotinian: but it seems evident that in *conf.* 11 Augustine is talking of the individual human soul.

[12] For the Stoics see Diels, *Doxographi Graeci* 461.29-31.

[13] For time-atoms in Greek philosophy (Diodorus Cronus, Epicurus) see Sorabji 19-21; 365-83.

[14] e.g. *mus.* 6.21; *vera rel.* 80.

(B) Augustine draws an erroneous conclusion from (A), inasmuch as he asserts that only the present 'is' (in the sense of 'exists now'), despite its being extensionless and so having no duration (§22-6). This error is at two different levels.

(1) We may question the implicit hypostatizing of the 'present', even in the limited sense of 'exists now'. Augustine seems here to share a misconception common to most ancient and many modern accounts of time. Time is conceived of as a flow or sequence of events.[15] Plutarch, criticizing the Stoics, puts it thus:

> The conception of time for them, then, is like clutching water, which falls away and slips through one's grasp the tighter one squeezes it (*comm. not.* 1082A).[16]

Now if one thinks of events as a flow or sequence one gives them a history – a past, a present, and a future. But events do not exist, whereas things – stable or changing – do. To talk of the existence of persons or things makes sense; to speak of the existence of parts of time does not.[17] Epicurus, alone among ancient philosophers, may have seen this.[18] Augustine's problem is traditional. The apparent non-existence of past and future is a paradox in Aristotle (*phys.* 4.10).[19] The problem is exacerbated by reflection on possible implications of the meanings and tenses of the verb 'to be': Augustine, however, shows no awareness that tensed utterances – like the words 'past, present, future' – may be token-reflexive, that is, they may be utterances which can only be defined in terms of each other, whether covertly or explicitly.[20] As we shall see below, Augustine may be partly aware that tensed utterances behave in this way, even if he cannot follow up the consequences or implications of such an observation.

(2) But even within the terms of ancient philosophical discourse Augustine is at fault. For his conclusion about the present suggests that 'now' is a point or part of time, albeit durationless, and he fails to see that the division of an extended entity will always result in extended entities.[21] We may contrast Locke's assertion, one that on the basis of his own views Augustine should have made:

> Every part of duration is duration too, and every part of extension is extension, both of them capable of addition or division *in infinitum*.[22]

---

[15] For the philosophical concept of flowing time in Aristotle and Iamblichus see Sorabji 33-51.

[16] transl. H. Cherniss, in *Plutarch's Moralia* 13/2 (Loeb Classical Library), Cambridge, Mass./London 1976, 839.

[17] See C.W.K. Mundle, art. Time, consciousness of, *Encyclopedia of Philosophy* 8 (1967) 138.

[18] Epicurus, *ad Herodotum* 72.

[19] Aristotle's time paradoxes are discussed by Sorabji 7-16.

[20] See Sorabji 33-7; the term 'token-reflexive' derives from H. Reichenbach, *Elements of Symbolic Logic*, New York 1948, §50f.

[21] Augustine's error was noted by Janich, especially 173f.

[22] J. Locke, *An Essay Concerning Human Understanding*, 2.15.9 (ed. J.W. Yolton, London 1961, 1. 165).

Augustine is less subtle than Aristotle, for whom 'now' is not a part of time but a mathematical limit marking a distinction of before and after in movement.[23] The Stoic Archedemus of Tarsus seems to have followed Aristotle in his assertion that 'now' is

> a kind of juncture and connexion of what is past and of what is coming on.[24]

The Stoics are generally more circumspect than Augustine in their talk of the present. Although, like him, they argue that 'only what is present exists (*huparkhein*)', they do so with reservations. Strictly speaking (*kat' apartismon*), one should not call any time present: one may talk 'loosely (*kata platos*)' of the present.[25] This is a recognition that what we mean by 'present' is a specious present which is, in fact, infinitely divisible into past and future. When the Stoics give an example of how the present may be said to exist they refer to the conditions under which a proposition about a contingent fact can be verified. For example, the temporally indefinite sentence 'I am walking' is true when, and only when, I *now* walk: by analogy, moment X exists when it *now* 'is'.[26] This example does not clarify the senses in which the present is real: the Stoics confound 'what is (now)' and 'what is true'.[27] Augustine inherits this Greek conceptual presupposition. He, too, as I have suggested, confounds 'what is (now)' and 'what is (the case)'.

(C) For Augustine, the past and the future do not exist (in the specialized sense of existing *now*), but past and future are present in memory and expectation respectively. One may have access to past or future events: they are objects of intellectual perception and therefore exist in some way:

> For where have they (sc. the prophets) seen the future events of which they sung, if these do not yet exist? For that which does not exist cannot be seen. And those who tell of past events would not at all be telling the truth (or: telling of true events), if they would not see them in the mind. If these *were* not, they could not be seen at all. So it follows that future and past events exist (§22).

Augustine goes on to explain the mode of such presence. Past events are present in the images derived from sense-perception (§23); the existence of future events is more difficult to account for, but we must assume that the presence of their 'signs' or 'causes' allows us to anticipate or predict them (§24). It follows from what Augustine says that he will criticize talk of three grammatical tenses.[28] We should, he argues, strictly speaking talk only of three *present* tenses, when we refer to past, present and future events (§26). To

---

[23] Aristotle, *Physics* 222a10-b27; see Conen (above n. 2) 62-116.

[24] Plutarch, *comm. not.* 1081E, transl. H. Cherniss (above n. 16) = *SVF* 3 p. 263.31-7.

[25] *SVF* 2.509 (p. 164.23-6). See further n. 40 below.

[26] For these points see *SVF* ib. ll. 22-30.

[27] See F.H. Sandbach, *The Stoics*, London 1975, 93. For a discussion of this phenomenon in Greek thought see J. Hintikka, *Time and Necessity. Studies in Aristotle's Theory of Modality*, Oxford 1973, 62-92.

[28] Augustine's criticism is influenced by the fact that *tempora* ambiguously means both 'times' and 'tenses': §22; 26.

talk of three tenses in the conventional way is to talk 'loosely (*non proprie*)'. This may remind us of the Stoic distinction in (B) above between what is in strict logic the case, and what language loosely suggests to be the case. But even more strikingly similar is the Stoic agreement that past and future are present in a special way: they 'subsist (*huphestêkenai*)', whereas only the present 'exists (*huparkhein*)'.[29] The Stoics, too, will criticize popular, untechnical ways of talking about tenses. Since 'a present sign is a sign of something present' past and future tenses of verbs refer to the present of whatever they signify, and so are, strictly speaking, present tenses. Thus it is technically correct to say that a wound is a sign that somebody '*is* having-been-wounded' (not 'has been wounded)', or that a heart wound is a sign that X '*is* about-to-die' (not 'will die').[30] Augustine's talk of a 'present of things past' and a 'present of things future' (§26) appears to make the same point.

It is a point whose subtlety should not be underestimated. All tenses *are* reducible to forms of the present tense. Augustine is aware of this, even if he is unaware of the inadequacy of discourse about the mode of existence of the present. We might say that his criticism of tenses is not extended to his understanding of the nature of events.

(D) For Augustine, time is measured in the mind (§36). The Stoics would appear to agree in so far as they include time among the incorporeals, thus considering it to be an object of thought rather than a material component of the external world.[31] Aristotle may also suggest that there would not be time if there were not soul.[32] To describe Augustine's theory of time as 'psychological' is, therefore, not necessarily to indicate its novelty in the ancient philosophical tradition. The notion that time is dependent on consciousness is found in Aristotle, for whom time, defined as the (potentially) numerable aspect of movement, appears to entail an enumerating mind.[33] The Stoic view of time as incorporeal is also 'psychological': 'Time like *lekta* has no independent existence but is rather something which rational beings make use of in order to explain the movements of bodies'.[34]

(E) Augustine says that we measure time when we measure duration (*spatium temporis, mora*, §27; 30). Duration may be the duration of change or movement, but Augustine takes great care to demonstrate that our ability to make temporal measurements is prior to, and independent of, any observed physical movement. In this context the argument in §30 deserves attention. It is a reply to the 'learned man'[35] of §29 who identifies time with the movement

---

[29] *SVF* 2, p. 164.26f.; p. 165.32-43. A convincing analysis of the terms *huparkhein* and *huphestêkenai* is given by A.A. Long, *Problems in Stoicism*, London 1971, 89-93; see also Goldschmidt (above n. 8) 247f.; Theiler (1982) 2.145.

[30] *SVF* 2.221 (p. 73.24-39).

[31] *SVF* 2, frs. 331; 335; 520f.

[32] Aristotle, *Physics* 223a21-9. See Conen (above n. 2) 156-69; Sorabji 89-97.

[33] Aristotle's definition 'expresses … the possibility of enumerating change' (Sambursky (above n. 8) 100).

[34] Long (1974) 138.

[35] The 'learned man's' identity is unknown: see Meijering *ad loc.* for a discussion.

of the heavenly bodies. A temporal term like 'day' does indeed refer to the
sun's orbit: Augustine therefore asks whether 'day' is to be defined as (a) the
movement of the sun itself, or (b) the duration of the movement, or (c) both
of these. Janich argues convincingly that (a) and (b) cannot be mutually
exclusive, but must be complementary: otherwise (c) would not be an
admissable alternative to (a) and (b).[36] If that is so, then Augustine's
argument would appear to be as follows. In (a) solar revolution qua
movement is regarded as defining 'day', whether that revolution takes one
hour or twenty-four hours. In (b) the normal twenty-four duration of solar
revolution is presupposed, and it is assumed that this gives us a standard unit
of time (like the marked unit on a clock). Now, if a solar revolution were to
last only one hour, 'day', by definition (b), would be still defined as
twenty-four hours, i.e. the time unit called day would be a quantified
duration derived from normal solar revolution but independent of any
changes, real or hypothetical, in the latter. In (c) the definition of 'day' is
made dependent on both solar revolution and its observable normal
duration.

What is Augustine's purpose in rehearsing these alternatives? It must be
more than a *reductio ad absurdum* of the views of the 'learned man': its
complexity suggests a further purpose. Now, immediately after this section,
Augustine abandons his investigation of the defining characteristics of 'day'.
He turns back to consideration of time in general, and away from the specific
time unit day. Time, he argues, is duration, but not necessarily the specific
duration of solar movement: when the sun is said in a Biblical passage
(Joshua 10:12f.) to have stood still, time qua duration still passed (§30).
Augustine is clearly not denying the relation of the temporal unit day to the
sun's revolution. What he asks is, what does this relation tell us about time?
In particular, what does it tell us about our ability to measure and compare
time periods? And his answer seems to be: it tells us *nothing* about all this. We
can hypothesize cessation of solar or celestial movement: we could still
measure other movement (e.g. the potter's wheel, §29) or change, or simple
duration. We seem to have a 'time sense' that can be applied to movement in
order to measure its duration, but is independent of movement. Augustine
cannot accept alternatives (a)-(c) because all three presuppose a necessary
astronomic clock, or a standard time unit derived from an astronomic clock,
in order to explain our consciousness of time. Time in §30 is shown to be
irreducible to conventional or observable time units. Whatever the precise
relation of the unit day to solar movement (and Augustine does not clearly
choose from alternatives (a)-(c)), the equation of time with movement by the
'learned man' fails to distinguish between time qua measurable duration or
change and time qua time unit.[37]

[36] Janich 178-84.
[37] Augustine himself explicitly makes this distinction in *civ.* 12.16, where he contrasts hours,
days, months and years as time units derived from the motion of the heavenly bodies with
motion or change independent of the existence of such bodies. Cf. *Gn. litt.* 2.14.28f., where it is
evident that Augustine develops his notion of time qua duration from reflections upon the fact
that Genesis 1:14-19 places the creation of the heavenly bodies in the fourth day: in what sense of

The Stoics, like Aristotle, will avoid a simple equation of time and motion: for them, time is the 'extension (*diastêma*)' of motion, it 'accompanies (*parakolouthoun*)' cosmic motion.[38] Thus, while they agree with Augustine that time and motion must be kept distinct, they will, like Plato,[39] regard cosmic motion as the standard clock, providing a universally common measure of time. Augustine, as we have seen, need not disagree with this, provided it is made clear that we are talking about time units and not about 'time sense'.

(F) Augustine considers time to be the measurement of a relation:

> If I observe (sc. a movement) for a long period, I can only report that it takes a long time, but I cannot say *how* long it is: for when we also say how long we do so by comparison (*conlatione*), as when (sc. we say) 'this is as long as that' or 'this is twice that' (§31).

We do not, however, measure time as it passes: Augustine seems to maintain that we do so at §21 and 23, but §34 refutes this view, for what 'is' passing time? It is temporally extended qua continuum but at any given 'present' moment it is extensionless. Nor can we give the length of any process while it is going on, but only after it has ceased, or we have arbitrarily ceased to observe it (§31). Thus Augustine is led to the hypothesis that it cannot be the processes themselves that we measure, but 'something in the memory' (§35), the 'impress (*affectio*)' which remains after perceptions (§36). Similarly, in the case of future processes, we can measure them by anticipation (*expectatio*) when we possess the necessary experience or knowledge to enable us to make advance calculations. Augustine's examples here in §36-8 are limited to anticipation of premeditated utterances or known songs: presumably, however, he would say that we can likewise calculate the time of other processes where anticipation is based on knowledge (for example, if similar processes have occurred in our past experience). In this respect, therefore, memory becomes as essential to calculations of future events as it is to the measurement of processes which have ceased.

We have no specific Stoic text to compare with these views of Augustine's. However, the idea that time is a relation dependent on the measurer's viewpoint finds an echo in the Stoic distinction between time as an infinite duration and partial (presumably 'present' in the 'loose' sense) time qua the least time that sense-perception can appropriate.[40] There are no Stoic views known to me on the question of whether we measure time as it passes.

(G) Augustine asks whether direct temporal comparisons with a standard unit of measurement are possible:

'day' are the first three 'days'? (cf. *Gn. litt. imp.* 3.7) Even if Augustine's interpretation of the six days of the creation account in Genesis is a non-temporal one, such considerations none the less lead him to posit a time that is independent of clocks. For the distinction see also Cicero, *nat. deor.* 1.21.

[38] *SVF* 2, p. 164.15-18 and 32-7; 2.510-16.

[39] Plato, *Tim.* 38b6-39e2.

[40] *SVF* 2, p. 164.18-22; Poseidonius, fr. 98.9-12 (Edelstein/Kidd) = F270 (Theiler), describes the present *sensu stricto* as 'point-like' and defines 'now' as 'the least perceptible time'.

I measure the movement of a body, using time. Do I not, then, measure time itself in like manner? (§33)

But he seems to deny that such a possibility exists.[41] He takes the example of a song which consists of sub-units of specific verses, feet and syllables: do we measure its parts in the same way that we can measure spatial magnitudes with a rule? What he concludes is that while we can speak of inner *relations* between a song and its parts, no unit of the song gives us a time unit in any absolute sense; for long and short syllables, verses, etc. can be so pronounced that they take a varying amount of time. Here Augustine's view seems to be substantially the same as, for example, Locke's:

> ... we cannot keep by us any standing, unvarying measure of duration, which consists in a constant, fleeting succession, as we can of certain lengths of extension, as inches, feet, yards, etc., marked out in permanent parcels of matter.[42]

(H) Augustine does not explain in the *Confessions* how memory (see (F) above) measures temporal magnitudes, but in *de musica* 6.21 he devotes some attention to this. Memory is essential to hearing even the shortest syllable, because the latter is temporally extended and so cannot be simultaneously perceived *in toto*. Just as in the case of sight rays emitted from our eyes enable us to see spatial magnitudes,[43] so memory ('the light, as it were, of periods of time') 'takes in' temporal magnitudes. Memory plays the same role in any observation of solids, which we can only perceive part by part in succession. Memory in this context seems to follow instantaneously upon perception: a passage in *de Genesi ad litteram* confirms this. The mind forms an image in itself of a perceived body, and

> as soon as it (sc. the light) has been seen by the eyes, its image is formed in the percipient's mind before an instant of time has elapsed (*Gn. litt.* 12.16.33).[44]

The example of hearing which follows in this last passage shows that Augustine is talking of memory.[45]

To conclude, we may say that while no explicit testimony proves his

---

[41] Lacey 222; 233 mistakes Augustine's question in §33 for an affirmative statement on the possibility of direct temporal comparisons.

[42] Locke, op. cit. (above n. 22) 2.14.18 (1.151).

[43] Cf. *quant. an.* 43.

[44] See pp. 87f.

[45] Augustine's views here may be interestingly contrasted with Aristotle's in his *de memoria*: 'nor does he (sc. the percipient) acquire memory from the start, for once the state or affection has been produced within a person, then there is memory. So memory is not produced within someone at the same time that the experience is produced within him ... remembering itself does not occur until time has elapsed. For a person remembers now what he saw or experienced earlier. He does not remember now what he experienced now' (Aristotle, *mem.* 451a23-5; 29-31, transl. R. Sorabji, *Aristotle on Memory*, London 1972, 53). As Sorabji points out, Aristotle seems to be arguing that since one can perceive a period as well as an instant, the present can be said to have duration and to include experiences which one has just had but which cannot yet be objects

dependence on Stoic views of time, Augustine considers traditional problems, and sometimes gives traditional answers, in his discussion in *Confessions* 11. He can make philosophical blunders, as when he assumes that infinite division will result in an extensionless, durationless present (B), but he can also display considerable acumen, especially in his analysis of the relationship between time sense, duration and movement (E). Augustine's greatest originality lies in his insistence on the indispensable function of memory in all time calculation (F,H).[46]

---

of memory (see *mem.* 449b13-15 and Sorabji, ib. 66; 91). Aristotle's views would seem to lead him to a different conclusion from that of Augustine: he might argue that one cannot estimate the absolute length of a short duration through memory (for it is only just past and so belongs to the present), but through a sensation which, as in William James's specious present, gives its apparent duration (Sorabji, ib. 18-21, discussing the implications of *mem.* 452b7-22. For the specious present in William James see his *The Principles of Psychology*, New York/London 1907, 1.605-42. I owe the reference to Sorabji, who cites the 1890 edition). For Augustine, however, the perception of the passage of time while it is passing involves such intellectual processes as image-forming and remembering: his logical scruples will lead him to deny that what is past can in any sense be present to perception, or that the concept of a specious (and so extended) present, accessible to sensation, is tenable.

[46] The most recent account of Augustine's views on time (and one which in many respects agrees with the foregoing) is by E.A. Schmidt, *Zeit und Geschichte bei Augustin*, Sitzungsberichte der Heidelberger Akademie der Wissenschaften, Philosophisch-historische Klasse, 3, 1985, especially 11-63. Schmidt criticizes my interpretation of *distentio* (see pp. 153f. above) on 23f. n. 36.

CHAPTER SEVEN

The Psychology of Human Knowledge

(i) The repudiation of scepticism

Disenchantment with Manichaeism made of Augustine in Rome in the year 383 a temporary sceptic:

> For the idea also occurred to me that the philosophers called Academics were wiser than the rest, because they had maintained that one should hold everything in doubt and had judged that no truth can be apprehended by humans (*conf.* 5.19).

> So in the manner of the Academics ... doubting about everything and hesitating over everything, I decided that I must leave the Manichees, believing in that time of doubt that I could not remain in that sect when I already preferred some philosophers to it (ib. 5.25; cf. *beata v.* 4).[1]

But confrontation with the Platonism of Ambrose's sermons at Milan from 384 onwards and contact with Milanese Christian Platonists at the same time, as well as the reading of the 'books of the Platonists' in 386,[2] soon (but not immediately[3]) laid the foundations of that dogmatic theory of epistemic certainty characteristic of his earliest writings (*contra Academicos, soliloquia, de immortalitate animae*) and developed in all its implications in *de trinitate*. It is none the less significant that Augustine devoted the first of his Cassiciacum dialogues – *contra Academicos* – to a critique of scepticism and a defence of the attainability of knowledge. By then he had come to believe that the scepticism of the New Academy was a device of Arcesilaus to protect genuine Platonic doctrine, in which the Academics continued to believe esoterically, against Stoic materialism (*c. Acad.* 3.37-9).[4] But even if the Academy could be absolved of radical scepticism, the latter's arguments had none the less to be met if the claims of rationally founded and unimpeachable truth were to be

---

[1] Although Augustine's scepticism was short-lived, he continued to employ sceptical critical method, especially in his anti-Manichaean polemic: see Alfaric 270-320. For the survival of some Academic positions in Augustine see ib. 321-58.

[2] See p. 9 nn. 19f.

[3] Cf. *conf.* 6.18.

[4] Cf. Cicero, *Acad. prior.* 60; Proclus, *theol. Plat.* 1.1 (5-7 Saffrey/Westerink). For a history of this view see J. Glucker, *Antiochus and the Late Academy* (Hypomnemata, 56), Göttingen 1978, 315-22. On the structure of *contra Academicos* in general see D.L. Mosher, 'The Argument of St. Augustine's *Contra Academicos*', *Augustinian Studies* 12 (1981) 89-113. The work is translated with notes by J.J. O'Meara, *St. Augustine: Against the Academics* (Ancient Christian Writers, 12), Westminster, Md. 1951.

maintained; and those claims must, Augustine believes, be maintained, if the foundations of morality are not to be shaken (*c. Acad.* 3.35f.) and the soul's liberation jeopardized:

> We are talking about our life, our character, and our mind, which believes that it will overcome the hostility of deceptions of every kind, and having once grasped the truth and, as it were, returning to the place of its origin, will triumph over desire and, espousing sobriety, will reign supreme, and so all the more serenely return to heaven (ib. 2.22).

The despair of ever attaining to the truth (*veri inveniendi desperatio*), which is inculcated by the arguments of the New Academy (*ep.* 1.3; *retr.* 1.1.1), must be removed if the soul is to find the rich nourishment that only philosophy can offer.[5] The sceptics represented for Augustine

> a most detestable chain by which I was held back from the fruitfulness of philosophy, through despair of (sc. attaining to) the truth, which is the food of the mind (*ench.* 20.7).

The refutation of scepticism[6] has implications beyond the immediate cognitive gain which intellectual certainty brings:

> It is not now a matter of fame (a trivial and childish subject!), but of life itself, and of a kind of hope for the soul's happiness, to the extent that we can discuss this among ourselves (*c. Acad.* 3.18).

Augustine nevertheless considers the possibility that the attainment of happiness – a universal human wish ('without doubt ... we wish to be happy,' *c. Acad.* 1.5)[7] – may be realized in the *quest* for truth, and need not depend upon acquiring the latter (ib. §5f.). One who has found the truth is indeed happy in the sense of being perfectly wise, but there may be degrees of happiness (§7). This is the position adopted by the Academics (ib. 2.11) and Cicero:

> Our Cicero was of the opinion that he who is inquiring into the truth is happy, even if he be not capable of attaining to its discovery (ib. 1.7).[8]

---

[5] For the emotional element in Augustine's scepticism – evoked by the phrase *veri inveniendi desperatio* and the language of the next quotation – see Alfaric 356-8. The metaphor of philosophy and truth as the soul's food is frequent, especially in the *Confessions* (e.g. 3.10; 6.17; 7.16).

[6] See Kälin 75-81; Gilson 48-55; Nash 13-20; Flasch 56-62.

[7] The universal will to happiness was a self-evident principle for Augustine since he had read Cicero's *Hortensius* at the age of 19 (*conf.* 3.7f.). For the impression which that reading left upon him see Brown 40-5; Testard 1.20-35; E. Feldmann, *Der Einfluss des Hortensius und des Manichäismus auf das Denken des jungen Augustins von 373*, 2 vols., Diss. Münster 1975. Beierwaltes (1981) discusses Augustine's views on happiness in relation to their background in the Greek philosophical tradition.

[8] The position is not found in Cicero's *Academici libri*, and was presumably an argument used in the *Hortensius*. See Sorabji 148.

If it is the case that living happily is living in accordance with that which is best in man, then to live happily is to live in accordance with reason (§5), and the quest for the truth can plausibly be described in such terms (§9). It may even be said to possess a perfection of its own:

> For if he is happy, as indeed he is, who lives in accordance with that part of the soul which appropriately governs the rest, and this part is called reason, does he not, I ask, live in accordance with reason who seeks after truth in an exemplary way? (ib.)

And, assuming the Academic position, the quest for truth as the activity appropriate to man (for he may be incapable by his very nature of actually finding the truth, ib.) may constitute, not merely human happiness, but also human wisdom:

> For in so far as he seeks he is wise, and in so far as he is wise, he is happy (§23).

Furthermore (and this is surely the reason for Augustine's tolerance of this line of argument), the position just described is not inconsistent with the Christian belief that perfect happiness and wisdom are, in the first place, divine (ib.), and, secondly, an eschatological hope for man:

> When he unwraps his mind as much as he can from all the coverings of the body ... when he does not allow himself to be lacerated by desires, but, ever serene, directs his attention to himself and to God, so that ... he may be found ready on the last day of his life to attain to what he desired, and may deservedly enjoy divine blessedness, having previously enjoyed human happiness (ib.).

Indeed, true philosophy, as understood here by Augustine,[9] deals in transcendental and eschatological categories that make assertions about the full attainability of truth in this life seem as implausible to him as they are to the Academic sceptic:

> For it (sc. philosophy) teaches, and teaches truthfully, that one should not at all cherish, but totally disdain, whatever is seen by mortal eyes and comes into contact with any of the senses. It holds out the promise that it will clearly reveal the most true and hidden God, and even now it sees fit to make him manifest, as if through bright clouds (ib. 1.3).

This theme is recurrent in *contra Academicos*:

[9] On the equation of true philosophy with true religion in the early Augustine see O'Connell (1968) 197-226; on the themes of the soul's flight from the body and 'return' to God, ib. *passim*, and especially 185-93. The themes are Neoplatonically inspired: O'Connell exaggerates Augustine's specific debt to Plotinus (see G. Madec's extensive review: 'Une lecture de *Confessions* VII, ix, 13-xxi, 27 (Notes critiques à propos d'une thèse de R.J. O'Connell)', *REAug* 16 (1970) 79-137). For the metaphorical use of the Platonic language of the soul's pre-existence, forgetfulness, recollection, and return in the early Augustine see pp. 199-201 below.

> Will this virtue not, then, break out one day ... and having expressed on earth indications, as it were, of the future, cast all its bodily burden aside and hurry back again to heaven? (ib. 2.2)

Proteus is a metaphor for the elusiveness of truth in our present condition (ib. 3.13). There seems, therefore, to be some affinity between the Academic and the Christian positions. Significantly, Augustine allows the thesis that wisdom may be the quest for truth to stand unrefuted alongside its rival – that only the attainment of truth may be described as wisdom – in the first book of *contra Academicos* (1.25). When he turns to the rebuttal of the Academic arguments in books two and three he will adopt a different approach through a series of arguments designed to expose inconsistencies and inadequacies in the Academic position; but he never repudiates the notion that the unremitting search for truth may be in itself a worthy human activity, that wisdom may be the path that leads to truth (ib. 1.13f.) and not merely the goal of truth discovered.

One inconsistency highlighted by Augustine is the notion of the 'persuasive' or 'trustworthy' (*pithanon*) in Carneades' theory of knowledge.[10] Even if no empirical judgement can be assented to as true or false, there is a criterion whereby the relative trustworthiness of such judgements may be established. Those judgements which are 'persuasive' are contingently and not necessarily so, yet we can, and do, act upon them. Suspension of judgement regarding the certainty of propositions need not, therefore, as critics of the Academic theory maintain, lead to inactivity or to a paralysis of human behaviour (*c. Acad.* 2.12; Cicero, *Acad. prior.* 23-6; 62). Thus far the Carneadean position. Augustine, who adopts Cicero's term *probabile* ('probable') as a translation of *pithanon*, implicitly agrees that a probability theory need not hinder human action, though he observes that error in practical matters may be no less – and on occasion even greater – if one wrongly follows the probable rather than chancing upon what is correct by an assent which the sceptic would consider rash (*c. Acad.* 3.34). But Augustine has a more fundamental objection to the probability theory. He criticizes its tenability on the basis of the Ciceronian synonym for *probabile*, viz. *veri simile* ('truth-like'; *c. Acad.* 2.12; 16; cf. Cicero, *Acad. prior.* 32, etc.). This criticism is already found in Cicero himself (*Acad. prior.* 33-5). Knowledge of what is 'like the truth' presupposes knowledge of the truth. We cannot assert that X is like Y (e.g. 'you resemble your father') if we do not already know Y (*c. Acad.* 2.16-20).

> The very facts cry out ... that those Academics of yours are laughable: they claim to follow the likeness of truth in their lives, although they do not know what truth itself is (ib. 2.19).

The criterion of what is apparently true can only be the true itself.

Augustine's argument is of limited value. To quibble over the term

---

[10] See Long (1974) 96-9; G. Striker, 'Sceptical Strategies', in *Doubt and Dogmatism. Studies in Hellenistic Epistemology* (ed. M. Schofield/M. Burnyeat/J. Barnes), Oxford 1980, 54-83.

'truth-like' does not meet Carneades' point, for Carneades' term – *pithanon* – does not contain any reference to 'true'. Furthermore, Carneades would accept that there can be true sense-impressions: what he denies is the possibility that we can recognize them as self-evidently true in an infallible sense. Hence his theory of probability is not without reference to a concept of truth, even if it is not based on knowledge of truth.[11]

A further Academic inconsistency for Augustine is the claim that there can be an Academic sage. Carneades agreed with the Stoics that a criterion of truth must satisfy the conditions formulated in Zeno's definition of the *phantasia kataléptikê*: correct reporting of the facts in a sense-impression, and recognition by the percipient of their correctness (*c. Acad.* 2.11; 3.18; 21). But Carneades argued that these conditions can never, in fact, be satisfied, a conclusion with which Augustine would agree (*c. Acad.* 3.39). Yet Augustine feels that even if Carneades' critique is justified, his demolition of the Stoic position does not entitle the Academic to lay claim to be wise, for wisdom is inconsistent with the denial of possible knowledge of truth (ib. 3.19). For to be wise one must know wisdom, i.e. one must have recognized it and assented to it for what it is. Yet it is precisely such assent that the Academic sceptic withholds (ib. 3.30-2). The claim to be wise can only be a claim to possess certainty and not mere opinion:[12]

> I consider, therefore, that the sage has certain wisdom, that is, that the sage has apprehended wisdom, and that for this reason he does not adopt an opinion when he assents to wisdom. For he assents to that thing without apprehension of which he would not be wise. Nor do these (sc. the Academics) assert that one should only assent to what cannot be apprehended. But wisdom is not nothing. Since, then, he knows wisdom and assents to wisdom, the sage neither knows nothing nor assents to nothing (ib. 3.32).

In fact, since happiness consists in possessing what one wants, and the sceptic evidently wants to possess the truth for which he is constantly seeking, the sceptic can never be happy. But happiness is a condition of wisdom, and so the sceptic cannot be wise (*beata v.* 14).

Augustine's argument is unsatisfactory, for it does not meet the Academic point. Being wise (*sophos*) for Arcesilaus and Carneades clearly meant, not possessing knowledge of any kind regarding a concept of wisdom, but rather so acting that one does not assent to what is not the case, to that for which there is insufficient evidence (Cicero, *Acad. prior.* 66f).[13] Academic 'wisdom' is the strategy of the sceptic and no more. Augustine's critique starts from the incompatible proposition that to be wise necessarily entails knowing wisdom (*c. Acad.* 3.9f.). But that proposition is not self-evidently the case, and so cannot be used to attack the Academics' quite different usage of 'wise'. Curiously, Augustine's critique is proffered without any reference to the

---

[11] Long (1974) 95.

[12] That the sceptic may opine and still be wise appears to have been Carneades' view (Cicero, *Acad. prior.* 67; 78) but not that of Arcesilaus (ib. 67).

[13] Cf. Cicero, *fin.* 3.31; see Holte 44; Striker (above n. 10) 74; 77.

thesis of book one of *contra Academicos* that wisdom may be the quest for truth. It is, as will be seen, based rather on the Platonic assumption, here unspoken, that 'wise' can only be predicated of X if X participates in the Idea or Form of Wisdom, and that such participation can only be a kind of cognition.[14]

Augustine further argues that disjunctive statements of the form 'p or q' are true and, in virtue of their truth, refute scepticism.[15] In such statements one of the two constituent elements (p or q) is true. Augustine's examples are: Zeno's definition of truth is either true or false (*c. Acad.* 3.21); there is either one world or many and, if many, either a finite or an infinite number, and so on (ib. §23). Similarly true are conjunctions of the type 'not p and q': for example, the same soul cannot be both mortal and immortal (§29).[16] The same applies to implications, that is, conditional statements of the form 'if p, then not q', such as: if there is one sun, there are not two (ib.).[17] Augustine is undeniably right to assert the truth of such statements, and his employment of them to refute the maintenance of radical doubt cannot be faulted. It should, however, be noted that among sceptics Carneades at any rate would have accepted the logical necessity, and hence truth, of certain propositions, while denying that such propositions tell us anything about states of affairs or events.[18] Indeed, Augustine himself will later distinguish between the truth-content of propositions (*veritas sententiarum*) and the validity of inferences (*veritas conexionum*). Valid inferences may be made from false premises. Yet the validity of inferences is objectively 'true'; it is part of the divinely instituted rational order and is not a construction of human minds (*doctr. chr.* 2.49-53).[19]

Some of the above statements exemplify logical principles whose self-evident and necessary truth Augustine thereby asserts: the law of contradiction (e.g. the same soul can not be both mortal and immortal) and the law of excluded middle (e.g. we are now either awake or asleep, §29) are two such cases. Mathematical propositions are likewise necessarily true (§25). Such examples build up the case against universal doubt.

So far we have considered specific arguments of Augustine's against apparent inconsistencies in the sceptical position or alleged logical inadequacies of that position. Augustine feels that these arguments are sufficient to refute the sceptic, if not to glut his own desire for total victory (*c. Acad.* 3.22). He must, therefore, devote his attention to showing that our sense-perceptions, as well as our consciousness of our mental states and processes, provide us with knowledge. The attack must be carried to the heart of the Academic defences.

The nature of Augustine's arguments concerning the reliability of the

---

[14] See pp. 184f.

[15] The terms and types of statement in this and the following examples are Stoic (disjunctive statement = Stoic *diazeugmenon*: cf. Cicero, *Acad. prior.* 97f.). See Darrell Jackson 34f.; B. Mates, *Stoic Logic*, 2nd edn., Berkeley/Los Angeles 1961, 42-57; Pépin (1976) 174-87.

[16] Conjunction = Stoic *sumpeplegmenon*.

[17] Implication = Stoic *sunémmenon*.

[18] See Long (1974) 102f.

[19] Pépin (1976) 175-80.

senses and the kind of knowledge they convey has been discussed in Chapter 3, where *c. Acad.* 3.22-26 and other texts are analysed.[20] The problems of dream-perceptions and hallucinations are also briefly considered by Augustine: they formed part of the standard sceptical attack on the reliability of sense-perception. Their treatment in *contra Academicos, soliloquia* and *de immortalitate animae* is not fully satisfactory, but it is not without philosophical interest.[21]

As in waking perceptive acts, so also in dreams and hallucinations something 'appears to be', with the difference that the appearance is always only apparently and never objectively the case. The illusions of the insane and the contents of dreams are, therefore, *falsa*, false, that is, from the common-sense viewpoints of the sane or those who are awake, who can judge the appearances to be, or have been, unreal. But the problem with dream images is that they are as persuasive to the dreamer as perceptions of the real world are to those awake. Augustine attempts to defend the senses by suggesting that it is not they who cause the *falsa* of dreamers or the insane, but for the totally inadequate reason that the same senses give true reports under 'normal' conditions. The senses are infallible, always only reporting what 'appears to be': error is a form of misjudgement about appearances. Yet, whereas in normal waking perceptive acts, the conditions under which judgement can be made are present, in dreams they are signally absent; and Augustine's point, that it is precisely sense-impressions that are *falsa* in dreams, whereas mathematical and logical principles are no less true when dreamt than in waking states, fails to take account of our normal waking ability to judge some sense-impressions to be true. He reveals the inadequacy of his argument by remarking that the sensation of taste is no less acute in dreams than when we are awake (*c. Acad.* 3.25f.).

In *soliloquia* Augustine implicitly corrects some aspects of these puzzles about dream images. The 'falsity (*falsitas*)' of dreams and hallucinations is a psychological condition, consisting in the internal working of the mind upon the material furnished it by the senses (*sol.* 2.11). But 'falsity' can also be in objects or occurrences, such as mirror-images and literary fictions (ib.). Now dreams are also objectively false, but for the dreamer they resemble reality so much that determination of their falsity is impossible while they occur, unlike, for example, the case of mirror-images, where certain testing criteria can be applied, such as absence of tangibility or sound (*sol.* 2.13). Dreams may be categorized among the necessarily false objects, of which it can be said that, like optical illusions, 'they fail to be what they try to be'; but they remain impenetrable to the scrutiny of the dreamer (*sol.* 2.17).

In *de immortalitate animae* Augustine emphasizes that soul's characteristic activities of sensation and thinking continue unimpaired in sleep. Dream-perception is somehow like sense-perception. But this observation cannot account for soul's exceptional fallibility in dreams, when it is a question of sense-perception. Our reasoning may be as valid in dreams as

---

[20] pp. 92ff.
[21] For the following see further O'Daly (1981,2).

when we are awake (cf. *c. Acad.* 3.25), but Augustine can provide no answer to the sceptical argument that dreaming sense appearances, and being convinced that they are real, casts serious doubts upon the trustworthiness of the judgements we make about perceptions (*imm. an.* 23).[22]

Augustine none the less feels that one argument is proof against sceptical objections, namely, that our consciousness of our own mental states and processes gives us indubitable knowledge of our existence. This fact even seems to answer the sceptical argument 'I may be dreaming', as applied to all perceptions and judgements:

> The knowledge by which we know that we are alive is the inmost knowledge, where the Academic cannot even say, 'Perhaps you are asleep and are unaware of it, and you see things in your sleep.' For who does not know that what dreamers see in their sleep is quite like what those awake see? But he who is certain about his knowledge concerning his own life does not, while alive, say, 'I know I am awake,' but 'I know I am alive.' Therefore, whether he be asleep or awake, he is alive. And he cannot be deceived in that knowledge through dreams, since both sleep and seeing in sleep are characteristic of the living man ... So let a thousand kinds of deceptive percepts be presented to him who says, 'I know I am alive': he will fear none of these, for even he who is deceived is alive (*trin.* 15.21).

This argument from a work of the mature Augustine is anticipated in the early writings:

> 'Do you at least ... know that you are alive?'
> 'I do.'
> 'Do you know, further, that you have a body?'
> He agreed that he did (*beata v.* 7).

In *sol.* 2.1 we read the following exchange between Reason and Augustine:

> Reason: You, who wish to know yourself, do you know that you exist?
> Augustine: I do.
> R: How do you get this knowledge?
> A: I don't know.
> R: Do you suppose that you are a simple or a manifold being?
> A: I don't know.
> R: Do you know if you are (sc. externally) moved?
> A: No.
> R: Do you know that you think?
> A: Yes, I do.
> R: Therefore it is true that you think?
> A: It is true.

We are indubitably conscious of our existence as thinking subjects. We can

---

[22] Augustine's interpretation of dreams as imaginative processes which may or may not be of prophetic value, and so may or may not be 'true' in a special sense, is discussed on pp. 114ff.

not be aware of our own existence unless we are alive, and these insights depend in turn upon the fact that we can think:

> Therefore, to begin with what is most evident, I first ask you if you yourself exist. Are you perhaps afraid that you may be deceived by this interrogation? But if you did not exist, you could not possibly be deceived ... Therefore, since it is clear that you exist, and this could not be clear to you unless you were alive, it is also clear that you are alive. Do you understand that these two facts are absolutely true? ... Then this third point is also evident, that is, that you understand (*lib. arb.* 2.7).

Even insight into the fact that we doubt is a form of knowledge of that doubt, itself entailing certainty and a concept of truth:

> Everyone who understands that he doubts, understands something true, and is certain of that which he understands. Therefore he is certain of something true. So everyone who doubts whether the truth exists has within himself something true, which should put an end to his doubt: and whatever is true is so only in virtue of truth (*vera. rel.* 73).

Just as dreams entail indubitable consciousness of our own existence, so does the fact of doubting. Despite our ignorance, and differences of opinion concerning the substance of which mind is formed,

> ... who is there who doubts that he is alive, and remembers, and understands, and wills, and thinks, and knows, and judges? (*trin.*10.14)

In other words, even so-called universal doubt presupposes life, memory, insight, will, thought, knowledge and judgement:

> Since, indeed, even if one doubts, he is alive; if he doubts, he remembers why he doubts; if he doubts, he understands that he doubts; if he doubts, he wishes to be certain; if he doubts, he thinks; if he doubts, he knows that he does not know; if he doubts, he judges that he ought not to assent thoughtlessly (ib.).

We are certain that we exist, and that we know that we exist, and these certainties are proof against Academic objections of the 'What if you should be mistaken?' kind, for being mistaken, like dreaming and doubting, entails conscious existence:

> For if I am mistaken, I exist (*si enim fallor, sum*). For he who does not exist cannot possibly be mistaken; and so I exist, if I am mistaken. So, since I, who am mistaken, exist, how can I be deceived as to my own existence, since it is certain that I exist if I am mistaken? Therefore, since even if I were mistaken I should have to exist to be mistaken, there can be no doubt that I am not mistaken in knowing that I exist. But it follows that I am not mistaken either in

knowing that I know. For just as I know that I exist, so, too, I know this: that I know (*civ.* 11.26).[23]

Augustine insists upon the impossibility of thinking of any kind without existing. From the fact of thinking he infers the certainty of our existence. Despite obvious similarities between this line of argument and Descartes's *cogito*, similarities which some of Descartes's first readers, among them Mersenne and Arnauld, observed, the Augustinian and Cartesian enterprises are different in aim. Descartes himself was aware of this, distinguishing between Augustine's purpose and his own, which was not so much concerned with proving that we indubitably exist, as with showing that the thinking subject is an immaterial substance.[24] The interpretation of Descartes's *cogito* remains controversial,[25] but Augustine's modest intention seems clear: the activity of thinking undermines the sceptical denial of all certainty.

(ii) Signs, communication and knowledge

The early dialogue *de magistro* is Augustine's fullest account of language and meaning. In particular, it explores the connection between the communication system of language, other forms of communication, teaching and learning. It is thus of primary importance as an account of Augustine's understanding of the way in which we acquire knowledge.[26]

Augustine's view of language in *de magistro* is functional. Language is a practical instrument with which we teach or inform, and call facts to mind or remind others: it expresses the speaker's will. Even when it is not articulated in speech, as when we conceive words mentally, it fulfils its function of calling to mind, in so far as it reminds us of the things or facts (*res*) of which the words are signs (*signa; mag.* 1f.).[27] For all words signify something. The sign-object correspondence seems obvious in a word like 'city'; it is less obvious in words like 'if' or 'nothing' (§3). Augustine suggests that the latter signify states of the mind, 'if' indicating doubt, and 'nothing' a perception

---

[23] See G.B. Matthews, '*Si fallor, sum*', in Markus (1972) 154-67; Bubacz (1981) 39-60 (substantially repeating his article in *Augustinian Studies* 9 (1978) 35-44); M.J. Coughlan, '"*Si fallor, Sum*" Revisited', *Augustinian Studies* 13 (1982) 145-9. Bubacz's work has serious general defects: see my review in *Religious Studies* 20 (1984) 312-5.

[24] R. Descartes, *Philosophical Letters*, transl. and ed. A. Kenny, Oxford 1970, 83f. But see *trin.* 10.16 and the other Augustinian texts quoted on p. 208 below. Cf. Sorabji 289; J.A. Mourant, 'The *Cogitos*: Augustinian and Cartesian', *Augustinian Studies* 10 (1979) 27-42.

[25] See J. Hintikka, '*Cogito, Ergo Sum*: Inference or Performance?' in *Descartes. A Collection of Critical Essays* (ed. W. Doney), London/New York 1967, 108-39; A. Kenny, *Descartes. A Study of his Philosophy*, New York 1968, 40-62; B. Williams, *Descartes. The Project of Pure Enquiry*, Harmondsworth 1978, 72-101.

[26] See Alfaric 494-9; Gilson 88-103; Markus (1957) = Markus (1972) 61-91; Nash 84-92; Duchrow; Mayer; Flasch 121-6; Watson. On *de magistro* see further the introduction and notes of G. Madec, *BA* 6 (1976); id., 'Analyse du *De magistro*', *REAug* 21 (1975) 63-71; E. Schädel (ed.), *De magistro*, Diss. Würzburg 1974.

[27] Augustinian definitions of word (*verbum*), sign (*signum*), and thing/fact (*res*) are found in *dial.* 5.1ff. The Stoic influence is discussed by Darrell Jackson; Ruef; Pépin (1976).

that there is no object or real thing there (ib.), that a sought thing apparently does not exist (§19).

We regularly explain words by means of other words, that is, we use signs to signify other signs. Such signifying also occurs when, for example, we point to visible objects (or perceptible qualities of such objects, e.g. colour) that are present: the pointing is itself no less a sign than a word would be, for the word 'wall' is signified by the gesture, and 'wall' and gesture mean one and the same thing. The same applies to other mimic gestures signifying not merely visible objects, but qualities (sounds, tastes, etc.), processes, and conditions. In all cases a sign makes a thing known. There seems to be only one exception to this rule. We can make certain forms of action, e.g. 'walking', clear by performing them, if we are asked to explain them while not actually performing them. In such cases the thing itself is shown without a sign. Moreover, 'speaking' can similarly be shown, even if we are asked to explain it while actually speaking (§4-6). Augustine does not consider the possible objection that performance of such actions as a form of explanation of the meaning of the appropriate term has in itself the function of a sign, though doubt is subsequently cast on the reliability of making something known through performance (§29).

Signs make things known: in conjunction, as propositions, they express sentences which may refer to real states of affairs and can be said to be true or false; or they take the form of conditional propositions which are necessarily true (§16). The relations of signs to one another – their semantic interaction – while important for Augustine's theories of language in general and meaning in particular, are not, however, of immediate consequence for his epistemology, which is primarily concerned with the sign-object correspondence, in which the object, the *significabile*, is not itself a further sign (§22). For the epistemological question is: what, if anything, do our signs, linguistic and otherwise, contribute to our knowledge of objects? Discussion of the ways in which signs indicate other signs (*mag.* 7-18) may, therefore, be omitted here, and we may turn to the association of sign and reality in §22ff.

It is natural that when we hear (or otherwise perceive) signs our attention is directed towards that which they signify (§24). This phenomenon is also usually an indicator of value: we move from the instrument (sign) which is inferior to, because functionally dependent on, the thing signified. Even where such inferiority is questionable (e.g. is the word 'filth' inferior to filth itself?) we can nevertheless assert another value indication. For the cognition of a thing is always superior to its sign:

> For this cognition has been given preference to the sign ... for no other reason than that it is incontestably demonstrated that the sign exists on account of the cognition, and not the cognition on account of the sign (§26).

Words are functional semantic means in the processes of teaching and acquiring knowledge (ib.). But what is the status of our cognition of the words themselves? Why is cognition of filth superior to cognition of 'filth', especially as it was observed that in such cases the sign is conceivably superior to the thing (§27)? What makes cognition of things in general superior to cognition of signs? Augustine indicates a preference for the principle that not just the sign, but also its cognition, are inferior, because both are means to cognition of the thing signified. But he does not prove this principle, and he leaves the question of value open (§28).

In §29ff. an important correction of the thesis hitherto defended – that, with some exceptions, things are made known through signs – is put forward. First it is suggested that there may be no exceptions, i.e. that nothing is taught without signs, not even in performance, as with walking, talking and teaching, for all seem upon analysis to require signifiers (§29f.). Then some examples are given which, once again, suggest that there are exceptions: observation of a fowler at work will teach the observer the art of snaring birds in all its complexity, if, that is, the observer is sufficiently bright; and this learning is by direct observation of performance, without the intermediary of signs (§32). Other phenomena, too, such as theatrical spectacles and the wonders of nature, are exhibited in themselves without signs (ib.). The conclusion now suggested seems to be, not that these are exceptions, but that if we consider the matter more profoundly, they may be the rule:

> Perhaps you will find that there is nothing that is learned by means of its signs (§33).

For if we do not know of what thing a given sign is a sign, the sign can teach us nothing; and if we do know, what does the sign teach us? The word for an exotic head-covering (*saraballae*) is a mere sound: it cannot in itself indicate what the object is that it signifies. We do not perceive things through words:

> Indeed, when these two syllables of the word *caput* (head) first struck against my ears, I knew as little what they meant as when I first read or heard '*saraballae*'. But when '*caput*' was often repeated and I took note and observed when it was said, I found it to be the word for a thing which was already quite familiar to me by sight (§33).

It is the perception of the object (head) which teaches us the meaning of the sign ('head'), its *significatio*: we learn nothing through words (ib.). Even the example of §5 – pointing to a thing as a sign of the thing pointed to – is now modified: the pointing is rather a sign of the demonstration of the thing than a sign of the thing demonstrated. In other words, it is the gesture corresponding to the word 'look!' (*ecce*, ib.). Augustine grants provisionally that a gesture or drawing might teach us what an unknown object is: but, even if that be the case, words could not achieve what the gesture might accomplish. The most words can do is draw our attention to what our eyes alone can show us (§35). In order to recognize the word as sign we must know what it signifies.

This development was anticipated in a brief exchange at the end of §2, in the excursus on prayer.[28] It had been argued that prayer cannot be communication of our wishes to an omniscient God and need not, therefore, be articulated in speech. When prayers are spoken, it is in order to remind, and obtain the prayerful consent of, those who hear them, as in the liturgy. But did not Christ, the 'supreme teacher',[29] teach us how to speak in prayer? Was it not precisely the words that he taught? Augustine's answer to this objection suggests that the words apparently taught by Christ were so transparent that he was, in effect, teaching things through them:

> For he did not teach them words, but the very things themselves through words, so that they might remind themselves who should pray and what the contents should be, when they pray in the inner sanctuaries of the mind (§2).

Words have the function of recalling to the memory the things of which they are signs. Now the ostensible meaning of this answer fits the trend of §2ff. For it suggests that words function as a means of teaching things; and this corresponds to the overall argument that signs generally make things known (or show them, or make them clear: the verbs used are *ostendere, monstrare* and *demonstrare*). But it is typical of this dialogue that apparent conclusions are repeatedly questioned, corrected or refined, that questions are answered and subsequently shown to be still open. This does not necessitate total abandonment of positions already established, but these may be newly formulated in a more precise manner. Thus, in the light of §33-5, it becomes clear that 'making known' or 'showing' things is not to be equated with 'teaching' them, that having something 'made clear' to me is not the same as 'learning' it. But the earlier conclusions (signs make things known, and its attendant theses) can stand, provided it is understood that they are not epistemological assertions: what Christ taught was the reality behind the words/signs, but he also communicated the signs, partly because they are the essential medium of his teaching, but chiefly in order that they may serve the function of reminding or recalling (*commonefacere*). Words have an instrumental function, and no more.

Thus §29ff. develop the implications of the earlier conclusions. The passage is also remarkable in that it deliberately limits the signs hitherto under consideration to verbal signs. Words are distinguished from gestures in §35, and only of words is it asserted that they can never teach. Speech was the chief semantic medium considered in §2ff., but other signs were considered there as well. The concentration on the theme of teaching/ learning leads naturally to a concentration on verbal signs, but the narrowing of focus in the latter part of the dialogue is not always noticed. It anticipates the verbal preoccupations of Augustine's subsequent semantic work:[30]

---

[28] Philosophical problems connected with prayer to an omniscient and eternally existent deity are interestingly discussed by E. Stump, 'Petitionary prayer', *American Philosophical Quarterly* 16 (1979) 81-91.

[29] On Christ as *summus magister* see also *mag.* 46.

[30] See in particular Duchrow 101-213.

For indeed it is words that have come to gain pre-eminence among men for signifying whatever the mind thinks, if anybody wants to express it (*doctr. chr.* 2.4).

Cognition of words follows upon cognition of things (§36). Even when we seem to learn a story, understanding it presupposes knowledge of the individual things signified, the elements of which the story is composed. Augustine clearly does not regard the combination of such known elements in a new and significant narrative as any addition to our knowledge (§37). Nor are words always adequate even to the modest tasks of drawing attention, reminding and prompting. There is no intrinsic connection between words and the speaker's intention: an Epicurean may expound the arguments on the soul's immortality, in which he does not believe, and a listener may judge these arguments to be true. Surely the Epicurean cannot be held to teach what he does not know to be the case, and, in fact, believes not to be the case (§41). Words do not always express the speaker's mind. We may be singing a memorized hymn but our thoughts may be elsewhere, or we may make a slip of the tongue (§42). Nor is there universal agreement on the meanings of words: *virtus* is ambiguous, for example, meaning 'bodily strength' to one and 'virtue' to another (§43). And even where there is agreement on meaning misunderstanding can occur through failure to hear clearly, so that words can be mistaken for one another (§44). Because of its limitations, language is discredited as a means of attaining to knowledge. The claim to know, to have access to the truth about things, cannot be made dependent on the communicative value of words. Verbal signs are a consequence of the fall of man (*Gn. c. Man.* 2.5), just as the confusing diversity of languages reflects his sinful pride and will to dominate (*doctr. chr.* 2.5).[31]

Thus far in *de magistro* the discussion has dealt with things (*res*) which are material, i.e. which we perceive through the senses (*sensibilia, carnalia*: §39). Augustine now turns his attention to things grasped by the mind (*intellegibilia, spiritalia*, ib.). He argues for direct acquaintance with the latter similar to that shown to be the case with the former, except that things grasped by the mind are not external to the percipient, but rather somehow within us, in (as Augustine, using a phrase from Ephesians 3:16, calls it) the 'inner man' (*interior homo*: §38):[32]

But when things are spoken of which we perceive through the mind, that is, through intellect and reason, we are talking about things which, being present, we see in that inner light, by which he himself who is called the inner man is illuminated, and in which he delights (§40).

---

[31] See U. Duchrow, '"*Signum*" und "*superbia*" beim jungen Augustin (386-90)', *REAug* 7 (1961) 369-72. For the Babel motif in Augustine see *civ.* 19.7.

[32] See G.B. Matthews, 'The Inner Man', *American Philosophical Quarterly* 4 (1967) 166-72 = Markus (1972) 176ff.; Bubacz (1981) 8-38 (repeating what was said in *The Modern Schoolman* 54 (1976/7) 245-57).

How such inner seeing occurs, and why it can occur, remain to be discussed: it will be noted that the passage just quoted refers to the theory of illumination.[33] The 'inner light' is one with the 'inner truth' of §38:

> But regarding everything which we understand, we consult, not the speaker who talks aloud from without (*foris*), but the truth which commands the mind within (*intus*).

This truth is the unchangeable divine excellence and wisdom, Christ (ib.), the one heavenly teacher of all (§46).

We 'learn', therefore, because the divine teacher, the principle of truth, 'teaches' us, i.e. because we, through introspection, are enabled to grasp intelligible truths 'in' our minds. But we are no passive recipients of these truths. We also teach ourselves. Cognition is an active process. Even those insights which are clarified by means of dialogue in which a questioner seems gradually to elicit knowledge in one who is questioned (Augustine, without referring to it explicitly, is thinking of the questioning of the slave in Plato's *Meno*[34]), are a form of self-instruction, in which one proceeds from knowledge of the parts to that of the whole:

> ... if he is guided there by the words of the questioner, not by words conveying instruction, but probing in such a way that he who is being questioned is capable of learning within himself (§40).

An example of such dialogue has been given in the progress of Augustine's son, the pupil Adeodatus,[35] in *de magistro* (§40;46). It is not the questioner's or the teacher's thoughts that the student learns, despite the popular assumption that this is so (§45): the normal temporal near coincidence between verbal instruction and cognition should not deceive us into believing that the instructor actually teaches us. We teach ourselves according to our several abilities (ib.) and dispositions:

> But to each is revealed as much as he can take in through his own good or bad will (§38).

In the ordinary language sense of the term we never 'learn' (§40).

The tendency of the argument in *de magistro* is to devalue the importance of signs in the process of learning. The function of both verbal and other signs in the acquisition of knowledge appears to be auxiliary. Direct acquaintance is the only way in which both *sensibilia* and *intellegibilia* may be apprehended. Yet among things apprehended we must include signs themselves, and the mechanism of signifying has implications for sense-perception as well as cognition. An account of some of these implications is found in two further

[33] See pp. 204-7.
[34] See the explicit reference to *Meno* in *trin.* 12.24.
[35] On Adeodatus and his unnamed mother see *conf.* 4.2; 6.25; 9.14. Cf. A. Solignac, *BA* 13, 677-9; *PAC* 32-4.

writings of Augustine, the *de dialectica* (§5) and *de doctrina christiana* (2.1-5). A brief look at these texts is essential to complete the present discussion of the relations of signs to knowledge.[36]

There are two stages in the signifying mechanism:

> A sign is something that both shows itself to a sense and shows something apart from itself to the mind (*dial.* 5.9f.).[37]

> For a sign is a thing which, apart from the form which it impresses on the senses, causes something else from itself to come into our thought (*doctr. chr.* 2.1).

The sign points beyond itself to the thing signified. The apprehension of this connection is thought (*cogitatio*). One example (a particularly frequent one in our everyday lives) of the content of *cogitatio* in this sense is the so-called *dicibile*:

> But whatever is perceived of a word, not by the ears, but by the mind, and is held fast within the mind itself, is called a 'meaning' (*dicibile*) ... what I have called the 'meaning' is a word, yet it does not indicate a word, but rather what is understood in a word and retained in the mind (*dial.* 5.50-2; 60-2).[38]

And it is precisely the meaning which is communicated from sign-giver to sign-recipient:

> Nor do we have any other reason for signifying, that is, giving signs, except to bring out and transfer to another mind what he who gives the sign has in his own mind (*doctr. chr.* 2.3).

What is in the sign-giver's mind is thought (*cogitatio*: ib. 1.12): a corresponding thought arises in the recipient's mind when the meaning of a sign is apprehended (cf. *trin.* 10.2). A more extended discussion of the *dicibile* (such as could have been given in the full version of the incomplete *de dialectica*) might have further clarified these cryptic remarks about the role of meaning in communication. One thing, however, does seem clear. The apprehension of the *dicibile* through *cogitatio* is an instance of becoming acquainted with an intelligible, as opposed to sensible, reality. Meaning is expressed by a sign: the sense-impression is, therefore, a necessary concomitant of this form of mental grasping. That marks it off from other kinds of apprehension which occur independently of signs. But in other respects it is like intellectual cognition. It is not communicated from an active sign-giver to a passive sign-recipient. The latter must conceive it in his own mind. Something is indeed 'transferred', but it would be more accurate to say that what one mind has apprehended is, in consequence of the expression of

---

[36] A full discussion is provided by Darrell Jackson = Markus (1972) 92-147.
[37] For references to *dial.* see p. 141 n. 22.
[38] The text is discussed on pp. 141ff.

the sign, apprehended by another mind. Such apprehension within the mind is by definition a form of direct acquaintance with the object of thought.

(iii) Reason and truth

A further early work of Augustine's, the second book of *de libero arbitrio*, written (or at any rate completed) at Hippo while he was a priest, i.e. between 391 and 394-5,[39] gives a revealing account of the arguments whereby Augustine develops his concepts of reason, cognition and the acquisition of knowledge or truth. The context is a demonstration of God's existence, which, although believed by faith and upon scriptural authority (*lib. arb.* 2.5), should also be understood by reason:

> that which we believe we also want to know and understand (ib.).[40]

The hierarchy existence-life-intelligence (*esse-vivere-intellegere*) is postulated as a self-evident ascending series: inanimate objects, as well as animals and men, exist; animals and men are living beings; man has intelligence (ib. §7). Both animals and men can perceive with their senses, and both possess internal sense, which co-ordinates, judges, and is aware of the activity, or non-activity of the senses.[41] But only when that which the senses perceive passes beyond the internal sense can there be knowledge (ib. §9). Knowledge is by definition rational:

> For whatever we know, we grasp and hold fast by reason (ib.).

Reason is a capacity for discernment, an ability to make distinctions over and above that of the internal sense: animals may be aware of their sense-activities, and even aware of the activity of their own internal sense in a reflexive manner (ib. §10), but they are not, for example, conscious of the fact that certain objects can only be perceived by certain senses, that light cannot be heard any more than sound can be seen, for only reason can possess such awareness (§9). Reason delimits, defines, distinguishing, for example, between (a) perceived colour, (b) the sense of sight that perceives, (c) the internal sense, and (d) itself, the distinguishing agent (ib.). Activity (d) is possible, because reason is self-intuitive:

> That same reason which distinguishes between its own servants and what they bring, and likewise recognizes the difference between these things and itself, and confirms that it is more powerful than they – does it apprehend itself by anything other than itself, that is, reason? Would you know that you possessed reason other than by perceiving this through reason? (ib.)

---

[39] *retr.* 1.9.1.

[40] See O'Meara (above n. 4) 191-8; Holte, chs. 7-9; O'Connell (1968) 227-57; T. Kondoleon, 'Augustine's Argument for God's Existence. *De libero arbitrio*, Book II', *Augustinian Studies* 14 (1983) 105-15.

[41] The concept of inner sense is treated on pp. 88-92; 102-5.

Its mere activity of understanding does not make it superior to other powers, for it is not the case that 'every intelligence is better than what is understood by it', as will be shown in the case of man's understanding of wisdom (§12). Rather it is its ability to form judgements about the senses and internal sense that makes it superior to them (§13), even if its often strenuous efforts to arrive at the truth, and occasional failures, show it to be mutable (§14).

Augustine stresses the principle that understanding need not be superior to that which is understood, as well as the mutability of reason, because he wishes to demonstrate that divine eternal immutability is both superior to human reason and yet can be known by it, or, to follow the argument of book two of *de libero arbitrio*, that something higher than our reason necessarily exists, i.e. that God exists. For it is sufficient to demonstrate the necessary existence of something superior to our reason to prove that God exists, whether God's existence be on a level immediately higher than that of our minds, or on a yet higher level still (§14). We need not work out the implications of this argument for Augustine's concept of God here,[42] except in so far as they affect his definition of truth, but it will become apparent that the extension of the hierarchy existence-life-intelligence by the addition of wisdom and God has decisive consequences for that definition.

The discussion of the relation of sense-perceptions to their objects in *lib. arb.* 2.15ff. establishes a principle that will be important in Augustine's analysis of knowledge's relation to *its* objects. The senses of taste and smell absorb what they perceive, and that part of the objects which they perceive is different for each percipient. The other three senses do not absorb or transform the objects of perception, but, whereas touching the same part of the object at the same time is impossible for different percipients, the latter can see or hear the same objects simultaneously, without effecting any change in these objects.[43] The objects of touch, sight and hearing can be called 'common (*communia*)', because they do not affect the substance of our senses by individual absorption, unlike the objects of taste and smell, each of which can be called 'personal (*proprium*)'. To sum up, it is established that some objects of sense-perception can be universally perceived without being thereby transformed:

> That should be understood to be ... common and, as it were, public, which is perceived by all who perceive it without undergoing any corruption or change (§19).

Augustine now argues by analogy that objects of reason can be identified which stand in similar relation to our minds as the objects of perception defined as common stand to our senses. The first example given is the truth of numerical concepts and computations (*ratio et veritas numeri*, §20). As the subsequent instances show, Augustine is thinking both of mathematical

[42] See TeSelle 81ff.; 219ff.; 320ff.
[43] See p. 83.

propositions such as '7+3=10' and of concepts such as the idea of absolute unity (§21f.), but also of systems of addition and division (§21). Our knowledge of these cannot be derived from sense-perception (i.e. they are not like the images formed in perception), but must somehow be impressed upon our minds because of something inherent in the nature of number itself. Augustine adheres from the start to the first alternative of the following question:

> If someone were to say that these numbers are impressed upon our mind as images, so to speak, of every visible thing, not in consequence of their own nature, but through those objects with which we come into contact via the bodily senses, what reply would you give? (§21)

Now it is in the nature of mathematical propositions that they are necessarily and universally true. That is to say, their truth does not depend upon contingent temporal factors, as is the case with the objects of sense-perception, which are as they are at the moment of perception, but not necessarily before or after that moment. The same holds good for mathematical ratios:

> 1:2 or 2:4 is a proportion (*ratio*) that is absolutely 'correct (*vera*)', and that proportion was not more correct yesterday than today, nor will it be more so tomorrow or after a year; and, not even if all this universe were to perish, could that proportion cease to be. For it is always as it is ... immortal (*ord.* 2.50).

Augustine contrasts changeable physical objects with 'incorruptible', sempiternally identical number. There can be no source in sense-perception for the latter concept, for it does not have the essential characteristic of physical objects, their mutability (ib.). Similarly, the number one is an intrinsic part of every number, because $n \times 1 = n$, but 'one' cannot be perceived by the senses, for all bodies are infinitely divisible and, therefore, complex (§22). It follows that not merely our concept of 'one' but also that of any number is acquired independently of sense experience, for we must possess a concept of 'one' in order to be able to count and compute. When we talk of halves or thirds of a unity, we are not talking of parts of the number one but rather of parts of a material complex considered as a unity (whereas it is, in fact, necessarily a plurality, ib.). Furthermore, in numerical series or progressions a constantly repeated pattern, of absolute regularity, may be observed. For example, the double of any number is as many positions in the series of numbers after that number as the number is from the beginning of the series. This may be observed in the sequence 1, 2 (=1+1), 3 (=2+1), 4 (=2+2), 5 (=3+2), 6 (=3+3), 7 (=4+3), 8 (=4+4). Two is the second number in the series: the double of two, four, is two positions after two. The double of three, six, is three positions after three, and so on. We can infer that this relation holds for an infinite series of numbers. Both this knowledge, and the knowledge that the relation is constant, indicate that here we are dealing with a fact that cannot be derived from the finite and changeable world of sense experience (§23).[44]

Augustine thus establishes the validity of mathematical truths independent of experience. The example of numbers is, for him, a prime instance of common intelligible entities, in the sense of 'common' established in §19. We may compare the discussion of 'unity' as a principle of structure and form in things in *mus.* 6.56 and 58, and the analysis of the rational nature of ideal numbers, and of 'being one', as both a structural principle and a willed (or instinctively desired) goal of conscious beings, in *ord.* 2.43-9. In *de libero arbitrio* he turns his attention next to ethical principles. In the case of wisdom we appear to be dealing with something that is quite different from number, for men's opinions as to what is wise seem to be subjective, varying from case to case as one gives preference to the active or contemplative lives, or to different forms of activity. Augustine argues that the reason for the diversity of what is found 'wise' is to be found in diverse opinions as to what is 'good'. All men strive for what seems to them 'good', just as all naturally desire to be happy. But the positing of something as 'good' neither makes it good nor ensures that attainment of it will bring about the agent's happiness (§25f.). Augustine offers a definition of wisdom which appears implicitly to distinguish between apparent subjective 'goods' and a real 'good', understood teleologically:

> Do you think that wisdom is anything other than the truth in which the highest good is perceived and held fast?(§26)

But it soon becomes apparent that he does not regard the 'highest good' here as necessarily a unity, i.e. that he cannot, or will not, argue for its teleological nature in an objective, universal sense. For he goes on to accept (for the sake of the argument) that there may be a diversity of 'highest' goods, that is, that individuals may legitimately regard this or that as 'their' highest good or goal (§27). But such a diversity of goods (Augustine is clearly now thinking, not of purely subjective fantasies about what is good, but of plausibly demonstrable goods) need not entail a corresponding plurality of wisdoms, for wisdom need be none other than the insight[45] into the diverse nature of the good. To that extent, wisdom may be one, and so common to all men. At least it does not follow that it need be plural, or peculiar to individual minds in the way that our thoughts (which are not discernible to others) are (ib.; cf. §28).

Because there is no good reason to doubt that wisdom, the insight into the true nature of the good, is singular (something in which we participate, inasmuch as we are wise, §25), Augustine now assumes that this is, in fact, the case, and turns his attention to the contents of that insight, or its realization, i.e. that which is true (§28). A single instance of truth (*unum verum*) perceived by two individuals can be said to be common to both. An example would be the assertion that 'wisdom should be sought after', taken

[44] See Nash 78-81. For the Platonic and Pythagorean background to such number theory see W. Burkert, *Lore and Science in Ancient Pythagoreanism*, Cambridge, Mass. 1972, 15-96; 401-82.

[45] Augustine employs the light metaphor ('the very light of wisdom') in §27. See Beierwaltes (1961).

to be a self-evident and unimpeachable truth. Apprehension of this assertion or principle is in each case the act of an individual mind, is a private act, as private as the individual's thoughts: but what is apprehended is one and the same (§28), it has the objectivity of what is commonly apprehended. The same applies to moral norms (that the worse should be subject to the better; that each person should be given his due, etc.) and to what may be called ontological principles (the eternal is better than the temporal; the incorruptible is better than the corruptible, etc.), as well as to such principles of evaluation of behaviour as that the incorrupt should be loved and striven after, or that an unshakeable moral resolve is preferable to an easily destabilized one (ib.). There seem to be several commonly accessible principles or 'rules' (*regulae*) of this kind:

> It (sc. the truth) is one and common to all to the extent that it is true (§28).

Insight into the rules qua truths is none other than wisdom, i.e. perceiving, choosing and acting wisely (§29). It would appear that such truths are no less objective and constant than the rules of number:

> Therefore, as true and unchangeable as the rules of number are, whose law and truth, you have said, are present in unchangeable manner and common to all who perceive them – equally true and unchangeable are the rules of wisdom. When you were questioned just now about a few of these individually, you replied that they were true and evident, and commonly available to be seen by all who are capable of seeing them (ib.).

Wisdom and number share the characteristics of objectivity and immutability, but what is their precise relationship to one another? Are they species of the same genus, or is the one included in, or dependent upon, the other? Wisdom does not appear to be dependent upon number, for (as Evodius amusingly remarks) accountants seem to be far thicker on the ground than wise men (§30). The answer to this problem depends upon another answer, to the question, 'Where are numbers and wisdom?' Augustine uses metaphor here in bold rhetorical fashion, speaking of the 'room ... sanctuary ... territory ... dwelling-place ... seat' of number and wisdom.[46] But the problem is none the less acute and precise. The objectivity of the truths which have just been mentioned raises the question of their ontological status: as objective existents they must subsist in some way, be 'somewhere' or 'in' something (ib.). The difficulty is that such objects are a far cry from the physical bodies which are part of our everyday perceptions. Even if we can think about them, expressing such thoughts in words is well nigh impossible (ib.). One thing, however, seems certain: numbers and wisdom are of one and the same kind (*una quaedam eademque res est*), even if numbers are commonly regarded as of less value than wisdom because

---

[46] Augustine's metaphorical and symbolical use of language in his preaching is masterfully analysed by S. Poque, *Le langage symbolique dans la prédication de saint Augustin*, 2 vols., Paris 1984 – a study that throws much light on his use of metaphor elsewhere.

number is found in all (even the lowest bodily) objects. So, if numbers can be said to transcend our minds (§31), the same can be said of wisdom. This is not altered by the fact that

men can count more easily than be wise (§32).

We may not be able to answer the question of their relationship with final certainty, for their immutable truth and transcendence do not proclaim their identity. Augustine offers an analogy to suggest how, while being one of a kind, wisdom and number may have different functions. The heat and brightness of fire, which are inseparable from one another, yet have different effects, heat warming what is in the vicinity of the fire, brightness illuminating what is further away, stand in a relationship similar to that of wisdom (the 'warmth' of rational souls) and number (the 'light' of bodily objects), ib.

Wisdom and number are not part of the nature of our minds, any more than the objects of sight and hearing are part of the nature of our eyes and ears. That in itself does not establish their superiority to our minds, for (to explore further the analogy with sense-perception) it is not necessarily the case that objects of sight or hearing are of more value than the senses which perceive them. What establishes the value of wisdom and number as aspects of truth is the fact that we apply them as 'rules of truth' in our judgements of e.g. corporeal objects or souls, whereas we do not, and cannot, make judgements about the rules themselves. We do not say that $7+3$ *ought to be* 10, or that the eternal *ought to be* more powerful than the temporal, in the way that we say that a corporeal object is less bright than it ought to be, or that somebody's disposition is less gentle than it should be. Augustine here evokes the principle referred to in §13, that the ability to form judgements about X is a sign of superiority to, or (at least) equality with, X. But the equality of truth and the mind is excluded by another consideration: if truth were equal in status to our minds it would, like them, be mutable. Yet it has been shown that truth, whether it be the truth of mathematical propositions or that of moral norms, cannot be mutable. Truth must, therefore, be more excellent than our minds (§33f.), and freedom (i.e. from error) is, paradoxically, submission to the transcendent truth (§37). Truth is accessible to all. Its appropriation depends upon our will to possess it, and it cannot be taken away from us against our will, unlike physical objects (ib.). Nor does it share the unstable qualities of the latter, for, whereas sights and sounds can only be perceived in their spatio-temporal extension, incomplete part by incomplete part in succession, the perception of truth is a form of contact with eternal being. If the will to know it is there, it is always totally present:

It is near to all, it is eternal for all; it is in no place, it is never absent (§38).

In our temporal existence we know what is eternal when we have cognition of truth.

It should be noted that Augustine has now demonstrated that something superior to our minds exists, i.e. on the basis of the principle enunciated in

§14, that God exists, whether God be the truth or superior to the truth (§39). He does not choose between the latter alternatives, merely recalling that the name 'father of wisdom' is given to God, but that the son, the 'wisdom' born of the eternal father, is equal to the father. We may infer that in knowing wisdom we also 'know' God: but that is not Augustine's immediate concern here. He turns to another aspect of the mind's knowledge of wisdom: can we know the latter without being wise? One who is striving after wisdom and happiness without having attained the goal (and it may be supposed that in our temporal existence we do not attain that goal) is not, strictly speaking, wise:[47] Augustine invokes the principle of the excluded middle to argue that between wisdom and foolishness there can be no mean state (§40). Yet it has been shown that we can have certain knowledge of wisdom:

> The fool, therefore, knows wisdom. For, as has already been said, he would not be certain that he wanted to be wise and that he ought to be so, unless an idea of wisdom (*notio sapientiae*) inhered in his mind (ib.).

> For just as before we are happy an idea of happiness is none the less impressed (*inpressa ... notio beatitatis*) upon our minds – for on account of this idea we know, and confidently and unhesitatingly assert that we wish to be happy – so, likewise, before we are wise we have an idea of wisdom impressed upon our mind, on account of which each one of us, if asked whether or not he wishes to be wise, replies without any shadow of doubt that he does so wish (§26).

The terms 'impressed, inherent idea' (*notio inpressa, inherens*),[48] although they are reminiscent of such texts as Cicero, *nat. deor.* 1.43f., which speaks of the 'engrafted, inbred notions' (*cognitiones insitae, innatae*) that men have of the gods ('because nature itself had impressed an idea (*notionem inpressisset*) of them in the minds of all', ib.),[49] do not have much in common with the *emphutoi prolêpseis* of Stoicism, the 'inbred preconceptions' which are not innate, but rather inferences based on observations deriving from sense-experience.[50] The *notiones* in question in Augustine are, as has been shown, a priori, deduced without sense experience. They are 'impressed' upon our minds because our minds are such that they are intrinsically capable of apprehending them. To that extent they are no more innate than Stoic preconceptions (*prolêpseis*), although apprehension of them is an introspective process, and in the case of certain ideas, such as that of happiness, seems to be a natural motivating force present in all and not unlike the Stoic principle of *oikeiôsis* (cf. *vera rel.* 77).[51] The question of the

---

[47] Note the implicit critique of the view allowed to stand unrefuted in *c. Acad.* 1.5ff., for which see pp. 163-5.

[48] Cf. *trin.* 8.4.

[49] The context in *nat. deor.* is Epicurean, but the terminology, here and elsewhere, is Stoically influenced: see Pease *ad loc.* Cf. Cicero, *leg.* 1.30; *fin.* 5.59.

[50] For *emphutoi prolêpseis* see H Cherniss on Plutarch, *Stoic. repugn.* 1041E (*Plutarch's Moralia* 13/2, Loeb edn., 480f.). Cf. F.H. Sandbach, '*Ennoia* and *Prolêpsis* in the Stoic Theory of Knowledge', *Classical Quarterly* 24 (1930) 44-51 = *Problems in Stoicism* (ed. A.A. Long), London 1971, 22-37.

[51] See p. 103 n. 53.

relation of truth to the mind will be returned to when the principles of intellectual memory and illumination are discussed.[52]

There is a relation between number and the principle of form in corporeal objects:

> They possess form because they possess number (§42).

This applies not merely to natural objects but also to artefacts. It is not just a structural principle, it is also that whereby material objects may be perceived:

> You cannot grasp whatever changeable thing you look at, either with the bodily sense or with the mind's reflection, unless it is maintained by some numerical form (§44).[53]

This form is eternal, immutable, like truth itself. Apprehension of it is apprehension of truth (ib.). And what applies to corporeal objects applies also to soul: form is that in virtue of which all created things exist. It is their 'providence' (§45). To contemplate the latter is indeed to gain insight into wisdom, but it is the insight of one who, on the road to fullness of wisdom, grasps the splendour of that which is, as yet, a destination not fully attained:

> So he who regards and contemplates the whole of creation while on the road to wisdom perceives that wisdom joyfully reveals itself to him along the way, and confronts him in every instance of providence. And the more beautiful the road is towards that goal which he passionately desires to reach, the more eagerly does he yearn to complete this journey (ib.).

Thus ends the discussion of mind and truth in book two of *de libero arbitrio*. What is said there may be complemented by some further discussions, particularly in other early writings of Augustine. To begin with, some analysis of the concepts of truth (*veritas*) and 'the true' (*verum*) will be considered.[54]

Augustine distinguishes between *verum* as an attribute of things, a quality in them, and *veritas*, a substance, a real existent independent of instances of *verum*. This terminological distinction is not consistently made: *verum* can also denote truth in the substantial sense. But the distinction of fact remains, and it is also terminologically explicit in *sol.* 1.27:

> Reason: First, then, let us see whether, since there are two words, 'truth' and 'true', you think that two different things also are signified by these words, or just one.

---

[52] pp. 199-207.

[53] See p. 96.

[54] For the distinction between *veritas* and *verum* see Nash 20-3. The distinction in Stoicism, which is likely to have influenced Augustine, is discussed by A.A. Long, 'Language and Thought in Stoicism', in *Problems in Stoicism* (ed. A.A. Long), London 1971, 98-104.

Augustine: Two things, I believe ... if something is true, it is undoubtedly true because of truth.

The quality of *verum* in physical or mortal things is transient: if they cease to be *vera*, the continued existence of *veritas* is not jeopardized (§28). If *veritas* is imperishable, then, Augustine argues, the following conclusion holds:[55]

A. Whatever is, is necessarily somewhere.
B. (sc. Truth is somewhere.)
C. (sc. Truth) is not ... in mortal things.[56]
D. There are, therefore, immortal things.
E. There is nothing true, however, in which there is not truth.
F. It follows, therefore, that there are no true things that are not immortal.
G. Whatever is false does not exist.
H. But everything that is not true is false.
J. Nothing, therefore, is rightly said to exist, except immortal things (§29).

The argument of which this is the climax is unsatisfactory, for Augustine (as e.g. in *sol.* 2.6-8) uses *verum* in the sense of 'real' as well as 'true', and *esse* ('to be') in the limited sense of imperishable being (G, J). Thus the reference to a tree which is *vera* in §28 is clearly to a really existing tree, and Augustine can conclude that, in the case of the tree, 'something that is *verum* perishes', which contradicts F. In other words, F can only be the case if the 'in which' of E is equivalent to the 'in a subject' of e.g. *imm.an.* 7,[57] i.e. if truth is 'in X' such that it cannot exist separately from X, which is the 'somewhere' (A) of truth. In this sense *verum* denotes 'what is permanently existent/real', and the '*vera* tree' of §28, is, in this sense of *verum*, a 'false tree', not because it does not exist, but because the mode of its existence is not that of true being.

The further development of the *verum*/*falsum* discussion in the second book of *soliloquia* need not be pursued here.[58] It is sufficient to note that Augustine defines 'truth' as that which is 'in' being: in *sol.* 2.8 it is clear that 'in' denotes 'equivalent to':

The true I consider to be what is.[59]

Such passages anticipate Augustine's later explicit equation of truth and perfect being:

For in the substance of truth, since it alone truly is, there is nothing greater, except in so far as it more truly is. But intelligible and unchangeable things are not truer than one another, since they are all alike unchangeably eternal, and

[55] His argument is formalized here: stage B, which is a necessary implicit consequence of A and an antecedent of C and D, is added for the sake of completeness and clarity.

[56] This follows from the preceding argument regarding the transience of mortal things and truth's necessary permanence.

[57] See pp. 36f.

[58] See the discussion in O'Daly (1981,2) and pp. 93f. above.

[59] I have deliberately extrapolated this proposition from its context, which is about physical objects. As a proposition, however, it follows from the argument of *sol.* 1.29 just discussed.

what is called great in them is great for the sole reason that it truly is ... (sc. since) in the essence of truth to be true is the same as to be, and to be is the same as to be great, to be great is, therefore, the same as to be true (*trin.* 8.2).

There are no degrees of truth, any more than there are degrees of perfect being. Truth in this sense can be identified with God:

Since, then, this law of all sciences is absolutely immutable, but the human mind, to which it is granted to perceive such a law, can suffer the mutability of error, it is quite obvious that there is a law which is called truth above our mind (*vera rel.* 56).

It should no longer be doubted that the unchangeable nature which is above the rational soul, is God, and that the highest life and highest essence are where the highest wisdom is (ib. 57).

Augustine's exegesis of Exodus 3:14 ('I am who am') corroborates this tendency.[60]

In *de immortalitate animae* Augustine attempts a definition of the term *ratio*. *Ratio* can mean

(a) the mind's sight, by means of which it looks at the truth directly and not through the body;
(b) the actual contemplation of the truth, not through the body;
(c) the actual truth contemplated (*imm. an.* 10).

(a) is the faculty of rational thought; (b) the activity of such thought, or its result;[61] (c) the idea: this last aspect corresponds to the Greek *logos* qua concept, a usage which is frequent in Augustine's writings. (a) and (b) are unproblematic: (a) is, (b) entails, a thinking subject, a mind. It is (c) that concerns Augustine, especially in its relationship to mind. Can *ratio* in the sense of truth subsist without a mind? There must be at least some connection (*coniunctio*) between the mind and truth, if cognition is to occur and ideas are considered to be 'in' the mind which thinks them, even if they are not contained physically in any place (ib.). Augustine argues that this connection is necessarily one of inseparability, whether truth is in the mind as in a subject, or mind is in the truth as in a subject, or even if each is a separate substance. In the first case, as §5f. have shown, eternal *ratio* is inseparably in the immortal mind. In the second case, a similar relation, in

[60] Cf. e.g. *ser.* 7.7; *trin.* 5.3; *Gn. litt.* 5.16.34; *conf.* 7.16. See A. Solignac, *BA* 13, 689-93; W. Beierwaltes, *Platonismus und Idealismus* (Philosophische Abhandlungen, 40), Frankfurt 1972, 26-37. For Augustine's similar interpretation of the term *idipsum* (Psalms 4:9; 121:3) as 'being in itself' in e.g. *conf.* 9.11; *trin.* 3.8; *en. Ps.* 121.5 see Solignac, *BA* 14,550-2.

[61] This becomes clear in *quant. an.* 53, where Augustine distinguishes between *ratio* and *ratiocinatio*: 'Reason (*ratio*) ... a certain sight of mind, whereas reasoning (*ratiocinatio*) is the search for truth, that is ... the motion of that sight.' This is precisely the distinction between (a) and (b) in the *imm. an.* passage under discussion. *Ratiocinatio* (which can also be called *scientia* in e.g. *quant. an.* 53 and *sol.* 1.12f.) is defined thus in *imm. an.* 1: 'Right reasoning is thought advancing from certainties to the investigation of what is uncertain.'

converse, of inseparability must follow. The third possibility would be more complicated, for *ratio* could then in principle continue to exist while mind perishes. In practice, however, as long as mind is not separated from *ratio*, it continues to live (for an active mind is a condition of their connection). A supervenient separating force would, therefore, have to be identified: it cannot be corporeal, and there seems to be no good reason why it should be another rational or mental power. *Ratio* itself would, inasmuch as it is superior to mind, be capable of effecting such a severance, but it is implausible to suppose that it would do so, for in its superabundant being it tends naturally to communicate itself to that to which it is joined, rather than 'begrudge' such communication: it lacks 'envy (*invidentia*)', as Augustine says (ib.).[62] Nor, finally can mind be imagined to separate itself voluntarily from its object, if non-localized entities can indeed be said to be separable. Rather must one assume that *ratio*, in communicating itself to mind, 'forces it somehow to be': mind's being is owed to the presence of *ratio* in it (§11). This point is based upon the argument of §1ff. that the eternity of science and of self-evident truths entails the mind's immortality.[63] The discussion of §2, which posits that *ratio* is either in the mind or to be equated with it, anticipates that of §10f., but in the former the meaning of *ratio* is not as clearly defined. It appears to denote the faculty of reason at the beginning of §2, but then to mean 'truth', as when it is said that the *ratio* of '$2+2=4$' is unchangeable.

The discussion of *imm. an.* 11 is a discussion of a hypothesis which Augustine is disinclined to accept, viz. that mind and truth are separate substances. The hypothesis is adduced in order to demonstrate that even if such separation is conceivable it stands in contradiction to the nature of mind and truth. Yet the two *are* notionally separable. Mind is not identical with truth; mind appears often to lack knowledge of truth; it is mutable, whereas truth is unchangeable. There can be no plausibility in the thesis that truth is generated or created by mind:

> What we discover is discovered nowhere else but in our mind, and to discover is not the same as to make or produce: otherwise the mind would be producing eternal things through temporal discovery (*imm. an.* 6).

Yet the discovery of truth 'in' the mind suggests that if it is brought to the level of consciousness and does not come from 'outside', it is latent in the mind before we come to know it. Augustine assents to the proposition that

> There is something in the mind, which is not in our thought at that moment (ib.).

[62] For the idea (ultimately derived from what Plato says in *Tim.* 29e about the Demiurge's lack of envy (*phthonos*)) see Plotinus, *Enn.* 2.9.17.17.

[63] Cf. *sol.* 2.22 and 24. Plotinian (e.g. *Enn.* 6.3.5.8f.) or Porphyrian (see Dörrie (1959) 152-5) applications of Aristotle's distinction between 'subject' and 'in the subject' (*cat.* 2, 1a20ff.) are likely to have influenced Augustine here (see pp. 36f.): the necessarily unchangeable nature of certain kinds of knowledge entails the substantial identity of the mind, in which, as in a subject, such knowledge is present (see further pp. 11f.).

Moreover, the mind only perceives that it possesses something of which it has become conscious. So there can be something in the mind, which the mind itself does not perceive to be in it (ib.).[64]

The eliciting of such knowledge as e.g. the truth of geometrical propositions shows that

It is evident ... that all true principles are in its hidden recesses, although, whether through ignorance or through forgetting, it seems not to possess them, or to have lost them (ib.).

The mode of this presence, and the means whereby such latent knowledge may be actualized, require analysis: the following sections on the Forms and on memory and illumination will deal with these topics.

(iv) Augustine and the Platonic theory of Forms

The influence of Plato's theory of Forms upon Augustine is mediated through the school tradition, which reinterprets, systematizes, and to a certain extent falsifies the intention of the theory. Even when Augustine has access to Platonic dialogues in translation (for example, *Phaedo* and *Timaeus*)[65] he will inevitably read them against a background of commentaries and doxological schematization.[66] An uncontaminated reading is, for him, out of the question, and his knowledge of Plato is never sufficiently extensive for him to be in a position to correct distortions introduced by the school tradition.[67] That tradition is not, however, to be despised. It refined and developed certain Platonic concepts in the light of criticism (particularly the criticism emanating from Aristotle and his school) of these. It had, initially at any rate (in the Old Academy), access to Platonic teachings that were orally transmitted or developed out of the work of the Academy, and which undoubtedly contributed to the systematization process.[68] If it formalizes Plato's thought in a dogmatic mould, there may be loss of argument and analysis through sacrifice of the dialectical method of the dialogues, but that does not mean that genuine Platonic insights are irretrievably lost, or that the problems which Plato identified disappear. A case in point is the relation between Forms and their instances: is it a causal relation, and, if so, in what sense? Is it a causal relation and no more? Augustine is fully aware of the

---

[64] That consciousness elicits latent, unconciously held contents of the mind is an apparently original idea of Plotinus: see Schwyzer (1960) 364-74; E.W. Warren, 'Consciousness in Plotinus', *Phronesis* 9 (1964) 83-97. Plotinian influence, direct or indirect, upon Augustine may be assumed here.

[65] See p. 10 nn. 25f.

[66] See Solignac (1958).

[67] A comprehensive survey of the tradition from the Old Academy to the second century AD is provided by Dillon: for specific developments in the theory of Forms see his index *s.v.* 'Idea(s)'.

[68] See Dillon 1-11; K. Gaiser, *Platons ungeschriebene Lehre*, Stuttgart 1963; J. Wippern (ed.), *Das Problem der ungeschriebenen Lehre Platons*, Darmstadt 1972.

ramifications of this particular problem, but also of other aspects of the theory.

An adequate account of Plato's theory of Forms is beyond the scope of the present study.[69] In the following brief and partial survey particular attention is given to some salient features which have had an indirect influence (and occasionally a direct one) upon Augustine.

(1) In Plato's earliest writings we already find assertions that e.g. holiness is that by which holy things, or instances, behaviour, etc., of which 'holy' can be predicated, are holy; or that beauty is that by which beautiful objects, etc., are beautiful, and so on. The implication is that holiness, beauty, justice, wisdom 'are something'.[70] For only something that exists can effect a determination of another existing thing. Beauty, for example, is not merely a word or concept, for words or concepts do not make beautiful things beautiful. We may speak of an implicit attribution of causal power to holiness, beauty, etc.

(2) Plato's language is sometimes _explicitly_ causal, but more often than not he employs metaphorical expressions. Thus Forms are 'in/present to/added to' their instances; instances 'have/accept/get/have a share in' Forms, or they 'participate in/partake of' Forms. Or the relation between Form and instance is expressed syntactically, e.g. by the instrumental dative (beautiful things are beautiful 'by beauty'), or by prepositions, e.g. beauty is that 'by reason of which' (_di' ho_) beautiful things are beautiful. Or beauty 'makes' (_poiei_) beautiful things beautiful. This causal language is never formalized in the dialogues in the manner of e.g. Aristotle's theory of causes, but elements of the formal and efficient causes may none the less be recognized.[71]

(3) Plato suggests that the existence of the Form is a necessary condition of things having the quality characteristic of that Form, but that it is not a sufficient condition of its presence in its instances. Only the presence of Form F in X is a sufficient condition of X being f. In order that the rose may be beautiful it is not sufficient that the Form of beauty exist: common sense alone suggests that soil, climate and gardening skill are all essential to the rose's development. Only when beauty is 'in' the rose, i.e. is present, is the rose beautiful.

(4) The controversies regarding the interpretation of the cosmogonic myth of the _Timaeus_ cannot be entered into here. But it may be observed that the

[69] A useful account of the Forms in the _Republic_ is given by J. Annas, _An Introduction to Plato's Republic_, Oxford 1981, 217-41. See further e.g. H. Cherniss, 'The Philosophical Economy of the Theory of Ideas', _American Journal of Philology_ 57 (1936) 445-56 (often reprinted); A. Wedberg, _Plato's Philosophy of Mathematics_, Stockholm 1955, 26-44.

[70] Cf. e.g. _Hippias maior_ 287c-d; 294e; _Gorgias_ 497e; 498d; _Charmides_ 160d. See E.N. Ostenfeld, _Forms, Matter and Mind_ (Martinus Nijhoff Philosophy Library, 10) The Hague/Boston/London 1982, 11-21.

[71] Aristotle's views on Plato's theory of Forms (with much incidental discussion of their role in his own philosophy) are discussed exhaustively by H. Cherniss, _Aristotle's Criticism of Plato and the Academy_, Baltimore, Md. 1944 = New York 1962, 174-478. For Aristotle's own causal theory see e.g. L. Robin, 'La conception aristotélicienne de la causalité', _Archiv für Geschichte der Philosophie_ 23 (1910) 1-28; 184-210. Cf. P. Merlan, _From Platonism to Neoplatonism_, 2nd edn., The Hague 1960, 197-202.

role of the intelligible Living Being in that dialogue (30c ff.) is akin to that of the Forms as outlined above. The Demiurge forms the universe after this Being, which contains all the intelligible living beings that exist and is the model of the visible world: it could be described as a complex of Forms. For our purpose it will be sufficient to note the implications of this account. The Living Being is a paradigmatic, but also a formal cause. Things are what they are because it is what it is and is somehow 'present' in them. But things do not exist merely because of the Living Being. In the language of the *Timaeus* myth, the Demiurge's goodness, and his will to maintain the universe in existence, are necessary conditions of the subsistence of things.

(5) The post-Platonic tradition, while it harmonizes, streamlines and extrapolates, does not essentially falsify or abandon these notions. If for Xenocrates the Form is

the paradigmatic cause of regularly recurring natural phenomena (fr. 30 Heinze)

he is not necessarily attributing more (or less) to the causal function of Forms than did Plato.[72] In insisting on *natural* phenomena he is being dogmatic where Plato hesitates, for Plato asks whether artefacts, or individuals, or perversions of natural states, or relational concepts, have Forms.[73] Xenocrates' definition becomes the school norm: it is found in Middle Platonic sources (e.g. Albinus, *didasc.* 163.21). Furthermore, for Xenocrates the Forms are numbers. The mathematical speculation of the later Plato, as transmitted via the indirect tradition, had elaborated a theory of ideal numbers as a generative model for the universe. This Pythagorean element in Platonism will persist in the later tradition.[74]

(6) The *Timaeus* becomes the most important dialogue of Middle Platonism.[75] An acute problem for later Platonists is, therefore, the relation of the Demiurge to the intelligible Living Being. It is well known that later Platonists identify the former with a supreme deity and the latter with the Forms, and that the latter are further equated with that deity's thoughts. This last identification is already assumed and uncontroversial in Philo of Alexandria and Seneca. The Aristotelian critique of the transcendent, independent existence of the Forms has left its mark.[76]

(7) The Middle Platonic terminology of causality extends and formalizes tendencies that can already be observed in Plato. In particular, what has

---

[72] See Dillon 28; R. Heinze, *Xenokrates. Darstellung der Lehre und Sammlung der Fragmente*, Leipzig 1892, 50-6 = Hildesheim 1965.

[73] e.g. *Parmenides* 130c; *Tim.* 51b; *Sophist* 266b; *Theaetetus* 185.

[74] See Merlan 15-9; Burkert (above n. 44); Heinze (above n. 72) 46-50.

[75] See, for the dialogue's general influence, M. Baltes, *Die Weltentstehung des platonischen Timaios nach den antiken Interpreten*, 2 vols. (Philosophia Antiqua, 30 and 35), Leiden 1976 and 1978.

[76] See Theiler (1930) 15-20; Dillon 93-6; H.A. Wolfson, 'Extradeical and Intradeical Interpretations of Platonic Ideas', *Religious Philosophy*, Cambridge, Mass. 1961, 27-68; A.H. Armstrong, 'The Background of the Doctrine "That the Intelligibles are not Outside the Intellect"', *Les Sources de Plotin* (Entretiens Fondation Hardt, 5), Vandoeuvres/Geneva 1960, 391-425.

been called the 'metaphysics of prepositions' is developed, and in the process Peripatetic and Stoic causal concepts are amalgamated with aspects of the Platonic theory.[77] Thus in Seneca (*ep.* 65.8) the Platonic Form (*idea*) is a cause qua exemplar, and God is said to be full of such geometrical forms (*figurae, modi*). The *idea* is the 'towards which' (*ad quod*) of existents.[78] Middle Platonic scholastic texts, and hence authors influenced by them, distinguish between *idea* (transcendent Form) and *eidos* (immanent form).[79] The distinction, and the concept of immanent form, are read back into *Timaeus* 51a and other Platonic texts.

Traces of Middle Platonic influence in Philo, Justin and Tertullian, in Gregory of Nyssa, Athenagoras and Irenaeus, cannot be gone into here.[80] Nor is it necessary to follow the development of the theory of Forms in Neoplatonism,[81] for Augustine's understanding of, and references to, the theory are essentially Middle Platonic in character. A survey of the vocabulary and content of several Augustinian texts will make this clear.

Instrumental and prepositional formulas abound. Thus, correcting the impression of *ord.* 1.32 that the 'intelligible universe' is referred to in John 18:36 ('my kingdom is not of this world'), Augustine explains (*retr.* 1.3.2) what Plato meant by the *mundus intellegibilis.*[82] It is the eternal and unchangeable principle by which (qua) God made the universe. This principle (*ratio*) must be 'present to him' (*apud eum*).[83] We note in passing that it is not clear that *ratio* is here identified with the divine mind: the phrase 'present to him' suggests that this is not so. With 'principle by which' we may compare *ep.* 14.4:

... the form of things, through which (*per quam*) everything is made ...

Or *vera rel.* 113:

... the word, by which (*per quod*) everything that ... is made, is made ...[84]

[77] See Theiler (1930) 1ff.; Dillon 135-9; H. Dörrie, 'Präpositionen und Metaphysik. Wechselwirkung zweier Prinzipienreihen', *Museum Helveticum* 26 (1969) 217-28.

[78] Cf. ib. 'from which (*ex quo*)' = material cause; 'by which (*a quo*)' = agent, or efficient cause; 'in which (*in quo*)' = immanent form; 'on account of which (*propter quod*)' = final cause. See previous note, and cf. E. Bickel, 'Senecas Briefe 58 und 65. Das Antiochus-Poseidonius-Problem', *Rheinisches Museum* 103 (1960) 1-20.

[79] Cf. e.g. Seneca, *ep.* 58.20; Albinus, *didasc.* chs. 4 and 10.

[80] See H.A. Wolfson, *The Philosophy of the Church Fathers*, vol. 1, Cambridge, Mass. 1970, 257-86; id., 'Greek Philosophy in Philo and the Church Fathers', *Studies in the History of Philosophy and Religion*, vol. 1, Cambridge, Mass. 1973, 78-84; id., 'The Knowability and Describability of God in Plato and Aristotle', ib. 98-114.

[81] See, for Plotinus, Schwyzer (1951) 553-9; for Porphyry, Theiler (1933) 11ff. = Theiler (1966) 172ff.

[82] For the term see also *c. Acad.* 3.37; *ord.* 2.47 and 51. It is Plotinian (*kosmos noêtos*): e.g. *Enn.* 2.4.4.8; 3.4.3.22f.; 3.8.11.36; 4.1.1.3.

[83] The influence of John 1:1-3, interpreted Platonically, is obvious. Cf. *apud ipsum deum* in Tertullian, *de anima* 18.3. For Marius Victorinus and the interpretation of John see Hadot (1971) 235-41. Was Simplicianus the intermediary of such interpretations to Augustine? See *conf.* 8.3; *civ.* 10.29; and, for an extended interpretation, *conf.* 7.13ff. Cf. Courcelle (1968) 168-74.

[84] Cf. *per quid*, of the word, *civ.* 11.21.

Or *div. qu.* 23:

> ... the highest shape (*species*), by which (*qua*) everything is shaped, and form, by which (*qua*) everything is formed.

Speaking of the *ideae*, it is asserted in *div. qu.* 46 that

> ... after their pattern (*secundum eas*) everything that has a beginning and an end is said to be formed.[85]

As an instance of the instrumental formulation *div. qu.* 23 may be quoted:

> Every pure thing is pure through purity, and every eternal thing is eternal through eternity, and every beautiful thing (sc. is so) through beauty, and every good thing (sc. is so) through goodness. And so, too, every wise thing (sc. is so) through wisdom, and every similar thing (sc. is so) through similarity.

For Augustine, as for the Middle Platonists, the Forms are the thoughts of God:

> The *ideae* ... are primary forms (*principales formae*), or stable and immutable principles of things, which are not themselves formed, and for that reason eternal and always maintaining themselves in the same state; and they are contained in the divine understanding (*in divina intellegentia*) (*div. qu.* 46).

The Forms are 'in the creator's very mind' (ib.); otherwise he would have to look outside himself in order to create. It is important to note that in this text Augustine believes that it is Plato's teaching that he is reporting: what he offers is Middle Platonic *Timaeus* exegesis.[86] A similar alleged report of Plato's teaching is given in *civ.* 12.27:

> And ... God, as Plato constantly reminds us, held in his eternal understanding the forms, not only of the entire universe, but also of all animate beings.

Augustine frequently expresses this notion by saying that the Forms are in the son of God qua 'word':[87]

> ... that highest truth and wisdom and form of things, through which everything is made, whom our religion declares to be the only son of God (*ep.* 14.4).

> And this is the truth and the word in the beginning, and the word is God with God ... his light is the form of everything that is, and is that which most closely resembles the beginning (*vera rel.* 66).

---

[85] Cf. *ideas ... secundum eas*, *civ.* 7.28.

[86] See above all Baltes (above n. 75); Wolfson (above nn. 76 and 80); J.H. Waszink, art. Calcidius (Nachtrag zum *RAC*), *Jahrbuch für Antike und Christentum* 15 (1972) 239-44.

[87] See Schmaus 331-61 for a general account of *verbum* in Augustine's metaphysics and creation theory. Cf. Duchrow 149-84; D.W. Johnson, '"Verbum" in the Early Augustine (386-397)', *RechAug* 8 (1972) 25-53.

Religion should, therefore, bind (*religet*) us to the almighty God, because between our mind, whereby we apprehend that father, and the truth, that is, the inner light, through which we apprehend him, no created being is interposed. Let us, therefore, also venerate that same truth, which is in no way unlike him, in him and with him; it is the form of everything made by the One and striving after the One ... the word, through which everything is made ... (ib. 113).

God's creative activity operates

through the eternal and unchangeable and enduring principles of his word, which is coeternal with him (*Gn. litt.* 1.18.36).

The causal force of these principles is stressed:

... the primary causes in the word of God ... through which the world was made (*civ.* 9.22).[88]

The son qua word of God can also be called God's creative plan (*consilium, Io. ev. tr.* 1.9).

The Xenocratic definition of the Form is echoed in *vera rel.* 113:

... the word through which every *natural* created substance is made.

That instances of Forms participate in those Forms is asserted at *div. qu.* 23:

The soul ... is made eternal through participation in eternity ... this may be understood to be the case also with beauty and goodness.

With this text one may compare ib. 46:

... the *ideae* ... by participation in which it comes about that every existent is the way it is.

The Forms are laws:

... in the eternal and unchangeable laws of God, which live in his wisdom (*civ.* 9.22).[89]

They are principles of cosmic order:

... prime causes in the word of God ... by which ... all things are ordered (ib.).

They are the source of the numerical and aesthetic form (*numeri, convenientia*)

---

[88] Cf. *div. qu.* 23; *conf.* 11.8-10 (for which see Meijering 28-36). See further Lorenz (1955/6) 250; Holte 340; Schindler (1979) 669-72.
[89] Cf. *ver rel.* 57f.

of the universe, and human artists create in imitation of their perfection (*div. qu.* 78). This demiurgic metaphor is found elsewhere in Augustine:

> ... a certain skill (*ars*) of the almighty and wise God, full of all living, unchangeable principles (*trin.* 6.11).[90]

God's creative work imposes inherent, and not merely external, form on his creation. This fact, and also the fact that the created inherent form has itself causal force, distinguish his creation from the products of craftsmen:

> For there is one kind of form that is applied from without to every bodily substance, such as potters, smiths and other artisans of this sort produce. But there is another kind that has inherent efficient causes which derive from the secret and hidden will of a living and intelligent nature, which, without itself being made, makes not only the natural forms of bodies but also the actual souls of living beings. The former kind may be attributed to the various craftsmen, but the latter only to one craftsman, the creator and maker, God, who made ... the world itself (*civ.* 12.26).

The forms of all created things are in the divine word as an immutable (because eternal) and living force:

> Because, therefore, the word of God is one, through which everything was made, which is the unchangeable truth, everything is there together in a primary and unchangeable manner; not only that which is now in this whole creation, but also what was and what will be. There, however, it neither was nor will be, but only is; and all is life, and all is one, or, rather, it is one being and one life (*trin.* 4.3).[91]

The manner in which the Forms, or 'eternal principles', function in the creation and history of the universe, in particular their relation to the created 'seminal' or 'causal principles', which subsist as potentialities in the created order until the appropriate time for their development has come, is a subject beyond the scope of this book.[92] In so far as it is relevant to the creation of the human soul this theory has been discussed above.[93]

Neoplatonic theories of intellection and the forms did not influence the structure of Augustine's theory, except in one important respect. His adaptation of the concept of the hypostasis *Nous* (Mind) to his account of the status of the angelic order and its cognition, especially in its conversion to God qua truth, becomes the model for the conversion of the human mind towards truth.[94] This theme apart, some terminological features of no great

[90] Cf. Seneca, *ep.* 65.7f. The principles of Augustine's aesthetics are well set out by W. Beierwaltes, 'Aequalitas numerosa. Zu Augustins Begriff des Schönen', *Wissenschaft und Weisheit* 38 (1975) 140-57.

[91] Cf. *Gn. litt.* 2.6.12.

[92] See Agaësse/Solignac, *BA* 48, 653-68.

[93] pp. 15-20.

[94] See A.H. Armstrong, 'Spiritual or Intelligible Matter in Plotinus and St. Augustine', *Augustinus Magister* 1 (1954) 276-83.

significance may betray Neoplatonic influence. For example, the distinction 'intellectual-intelligible' is likely to have been influenced by Plotinus or Porphyry. At *trin.* 4.31 Augustine speaks of the

> ... rational or intellectual (for this is what some have chosen to name what the Greeks call *noeron*) ... spirit.

At *conf.* 12.9 he says of the 'heaven of heaven'[95] that it is

> a kind of intellectual creation.

But the most interesting of all such passages is *Gn. litt.* 12.10.21, where it is argued that *intellectus*, unlike *spiritus*, is not multivalent in meaning:

> Whether ... we say intellectual or intelligible we mean the same thing.

Augustine questions the distinction between mind ('intellectual') and its object ('intelligible'). Mind can only be cognitively apprehended (ib.). The question raised by this point, whether something that is not intelligent can be intelligible, is, however, left unanswered, indicating Augustine's lack of interest in such speculation.[96]

Two isolated passages in the early *de ordine* betray Neoplatonic, probably Plotinian, influence. True philosophy is said to teach

> what the origin without origin (*principium sine principio*) of everything is, and to what extent intellect remains in it (sc. the origin), and what has flowed thence, without any deterioration, for our preservation (*ord.* 2.16).

In the subsequent lines the analogy with the Christian Trinity is drawn. A little later in the same work we read, in a list of topics appropriate for intellectual investigation:

> ... what intellect (sc. is), in which all things inhere, or which is rather itself all things, and what, over and above all things, are the origins of all (ib. 2.26).

That here traces of Plotinus' views on the One transcending *Nous*, and *Nous* as the totality of being, can be identified, seems likely.[97] But the topic is not

---

[95] The phrase 'heaven of heaven (*caelum caeli*)' of Psalm 113:16 in the Neoplatonic sense attributed to it by Augustine has been studied by J. Pépin, 'Recherches sur le sens et les origines de l'expression "*caelum caeli*" dans les Confessions de saint Augustin', *Archivum Latinitatis Medii Aevi* (Bulletin du Cange) 23/3 (1953) 185-274 = Pépin (1977) 40-129; A. Solignac, *BA* 14,592-8; Armstrong (see previous note).

[96] On the 'intelligible-intellectual' distinction in *G. litt.* 12.10.21 see J. Pépin, 'Une curieuse déclaration idéaliste du "De Genesi ad litteram" (XII, 10,21) de saint Augustin et ses origines plotiniennes (Ennéade 5,3,1-9 et 5,5,1-2)', *Revue d'histoire et de philosophie religieuses* 34 (1954) 373-400 = Pépin (1977) 183-210; cf. Agaësse/Solignac, *BA* 49,566-8.

[97] See W. Theiler, 'Augustin und Origenes', *Untersuchungen zur antiken Literatur*, Berlin 1970, 552. It is surprising that O'Connell (1968), always so anxious to find explicit Plotinian traces in Augustine, has not exploited this obvious one.

further pursued and is indeed out of place in Augustine's developed theory of the divine mind.

In conclusion, we must consider Augustine's treatment of a special topic in the Platonic tradition. The question 'Of what entities are there Forms?' puzzled and perturbed ancient Platonists. The principle put forward in Plato's *Republic* (596a), that there is a Form for every group of things that have a common name, was more honoured in the breach than the observance, even by Plato himself. Concern about the types of thing of which there are Forms mostly focussed upon entities that were felt to be too unworthy or insignificant to qualify, upon artefacts or hybrids, or accidental bodily attributes. Thus among the doubtful cases were mud and dirt, beds and chariots, colours, and parts which are not also wholes, such as hands or heads. These examples are not exhaustive; even Plato can doubt whether there are forms of man or of the elements,[98] and Neoplatonic accounts from the Middle Platonist Albinus to Proclus contain differing lists of exclusions. The principle of *Republic* 596a was modified, explicitly or implicitly, to the extent that it could be said that there are indeed only Forms of things with a common name, but that this necessary condition of their being Forms is not a sufficient one.

Concern about Forms of individuals is part of this question, but, as it were, at the other end of the spectrum. The intrinsic value of certain individuals seems to necessitate, or at least make plausible, the positing of a corresponding Form. This is obviously the case with the two types of forms of individual admitted by Proclus. Both are divine: the godly souls of the *Timaeus* and the heavenly bodies (*in Parm.* 815ff.). But, as Albinus tells us (*didasc.* 163.24f.), even if the question of individual Forms of individual men was also raised in his day, Platonists were reluctant to adopt such a hypothesis in defiance of the traditional position.

Plotinus raises the question of Forms of individuals also, and never explicitly denies the hypothesis.[99] His concern, however, has less to do with the consideration of worth or value than with that of degrees of individuality and their implications. His question is: when does a distinction, whether physical or numerical or of some other kind, denote a real existential difference? Thus the problem applies equally to animals and to material bodies, even if Plotinus can only seriously entertain the hypothesis of Forms of individual men. And this last point is the one significant issue in the discussions of the question. Is there an ideal *paradeigma* or model of Socrates distinct from Socrates' eternally existent soul? Augustine also refers to the question, and appears to imply that there are forms of species only. There is a Form of Man and one of Horse; individuals are created in accordance with their specific Form:

[98] See p. 191 n. 73 above.
[99] See the controversy between J.M. Rist and H.J. Blumenthal: Rist, 'Forms of Individuals in Plotinus', *Classical Quarterly* 13 (1963) 223-31; Blumenthal, 'Did Plotinus believe in Ideas of Individuals?', *Phronesis* 11 (1966) 61-80; Blumenthal (1971) 112-33; Rist, 'Ideas of Individuals in Plotinus. A Reply to Dr. Blumenthal', *Revue Internationale de Philosophie* 24 (1970) 298-303. The following discussion adopts Rist's version of Plotinus' views.

Nor is man (sc. formed) by the same Form as a horse ... individual (sc. kinds) are created by their own particular Forms (*div. qu.* 46).

But Augustine is also aware of Platonic scholastic doubts on the matter, particularly regarding individual men. An early, brief, and condensed discussion of the problem is found in *ep.* 14.4. The little known passage is here translated in full:

> You also ask whether that highest truth and highest wisdom, the form of all things, through whom all things are made, whom our holy mysteries declare to be the only son of God, contains not merely the Form (*ratio*) of Man in a generic sense, but also the Form of each and every one of us. A difficult question! Still, my view is that, as far as the making of man is concerned, only the Form of Man is actually there, and not the Form of you or me; but as far as the revolution of time is concerned, I believe that different Forms of men live in that pure goodness. Now, since this is an extremely obscure matter, I am at a loss for an analogy that might elucidate it, unless one is to have recourse to those sciences which are in our minds. For in the science of measurement there is one Form of Angle, another of Square. And so, as often as I wish to describe an angle, the Form of Angle, and only that Form comes to my mind; but I could in no way describe a square if I could not contemplate the Form of four angles at one and the same time. Thus any individual man is made by the one Form whereby man is comprehended; but nevertheless it is not a Form of Man, but of Men, that brings it about that a people should be made, even though it, too, is *one* Form. If therefore Nebridius is a part of this universe, as indeed he is, and every whole consists of parts, God, the creator of the whole, could not lack a Form of the parts. And so the fact that there is a Form of a plurality of men there does not affect the individual man himself, although, on the other hand, all things are, in wondrous fashion, gathered into one.

What are the implications of this passage? At first sight, it is an explicit denial of the necessity of positing a Form of individual men in the traditionally received sense. But Augustine also points out that man's existence is historical, in the 'revolution of time', and that this existence is, moreover, social. Nebridius is a member of a *populus*, a human society. He is, in this respect, a part of a whole. But he is not a mere part: he is a whole in his own individual right. To recall the school example, he is not, in being a member of a society, like the head or hand of a body. Augustine's geometrical analogy is intended to stress this. I *can* describe an angle which is not part of a complete geometrical figure, but angles are, in fact, generally and appropriately parts of wholes, of triangles, squares, etc. Described squares participate in the Form of Square and thinking the Form of Square entails thinking the Form of a multiple, in this case, a quadrangular entity. Similarly, thinking the Form of people entails thinking of individual a, b, c, etc., that is, it entails thinking numerical distinction and plurality. For the individual this means that he both participates in the Form of Man and in the Form of People. That is no problem for a Platonist, as Augustine observes. But his insistence on the plurality inherent in the Form of People is intriguing, and provokes that cryptic phrase 'although all things are, in wondrous fashion, gathered into one' (*quamquam miris ... modis ad unum omnia redigantur*). It is not merely the fact of the historicity of man's existence that makes individuals members of groups, though that historical existence draws our initial attention to the implications of the term *populus*. Just as the geometrical figure enjoys its privileged ontological status as a kind of intelligible one-in-many, so also does the idea of the group. Man is naturally and (we may add) eschatologically social. Membership of a *populus* is not accidental; a *populus* is not a mere aggregate of individuals; individuality can be part of the multiple totality of a Form. 'All things are gathered into one' is at once a statement about the unity of the universe and about the terminus of history.

Ep. 14.4 may, therefore, be regarded as a remarkable, if isolated, development of an insight into the nature of the world of Forms and its relation to particulars. It arises out of reflection upon the traditional school problem regarding Forms of individuals. Individuality, in the form of plurality within a species, is introduced into the Forms, or to some among them. The discussion in *ep.* 14.4 seems to have had no repercussions, either in Augustine's other writings or elsewhere. It is yet another example of the speculative daring that Augustine can display under the stimulus of Nebridius' provocative questioning.

(v) Knowledge, memory and illumination

Augustine is familiar with the Platonic theory of recollection (*anamnêsis*) as an explanation of the presence in the mind of knowledge that is not derived from sense-experience. An essential feature of that theory is the belief in the soul's eternal existence, and hence its existence prior to embodiment. Recollection is nothing other than the recovery of knowledge possessed in an antenatal existence, and 'learning' can be equated with such recovery of knowledge.[100]

When he discusses the complex questions of the soul's origin and the mode of its embodiment (*lib. arb.* 1.24; 3.56-9)[101] Augustine considers pre-existence to be a possible hypothesis, but without opting for it. Nowhere in his early writings does he unequivocally assert the soul's pre-existence: it is never more than one possibility among others. For the Christian Augustine pre-existence does not entail the eternity of soul in a Platonic sense. Soul's immortality is not to be equated with God's eternal being,[102] and soul is created, with the consequence that its possible pre-existence is incompatible with eternity. Augustine *could*, of course, argue that even such creaturely pre-existence might account for the mind's possession of knowledge, but he does not do so, preferring to explain the latter in a manner that does not necessitate the pre-existence hypothesis.

On the other hand, Augustine utilizes the Platonic language of 'memory' and 'forgetting' to express active and latent states of the mind's possession of

[100] See above all the *Phaedo* and Gallop's nn.; cf. C.E. Huber, *Anamnesis bei Plato* (Pullacher Philosophische Forschungen, 6), Munich 1964.
[101] See pp. 15ff.
[102] See pp. 34f.; cf. *Gn. c. Man.* 2.11.

knowledge. 'Learning' for him is also, in a special sense, 'recollecting'. Such language is more explicit in the early writings, and led to misunderstandings in Augustine's lifetime.[103] He takes special care, therefore, over the correction of his terminology in the *retractationes*. For example, referring to *c. Acad.* 1.22, where, speaking of the mind's search for truth, he had said that, once found, it enables mind

> ... as it were, returning to the place of its origin, ... all the more serenely to return to heaven,

he comments (*retr.* 1.1.3) that, had he written 'go' rather than 'return', he would have avoided the implication that embodiment is a fall or punishment for sin. But he does not recant the word used (*rediturus*): he justifies his language by references to Ecclesiastes, Paul and Cyprian. His phrase in *c. Acad.* is, in any case, to be understood metaphorically. The qualifying 'as it were' which introduces it indicates as much, and its metaphorical nature is explicated in *retr.* 1.1.3:

> I said 'to heaven', as if I were saying, to God, who is its creator ... without doubt, therefore, God himself is a kind of place of origin of the soul's happiness.

A similar passage is *sol.* 2.35, where, speaking of those 'trained in the liberal disciplines', Augustine says that such persons

> by learning elicit and, in a certain sense, disinter the knowledge buried in forgetfulness in themselves.

One example given is the knowledge of the truth of geometrical propositions. This passage is at the end of a work in which Augustine has referred on more than one occasion (*sol.* 1.13; 15; 2.33) to his illumination theory. It must, therefore, be read in that context.[104] That means that the use of the term 'forgetfulness (*oblivio*)' cannot guarantee any belief in pre-existence. For, given the illumination theory, such Platonically influenced terms as 'forgetfulness' and 'recollection' could be no more than a convenient, symbolic ('in a certain sense') way of speaking of the mind's access to a priori truths and the fact that such truths have to be actualized by thought.[105]

---

[103] See *retr.* 1.8. For the following see O'Connell (1969) and the critique by O'Daly (1974), whose main points are repeated here. O'Connell has in turn criticized this and other articles of mine in 'Pre-existence in the early Augustine', *REAug* 26 (1980) 176-88, but without, in my opinion, adding anything of substance to his earlier views. See also G. Madec, *BA* 6, 578-83. For other early Christian views on the soul's pre-existence (e.g. Synesius and Numenius) see Wallis 103f.

[104] See pp. 204-7; cf. *ord.* 2.41.

[105] This is precisely the way in which Augustine speaks of the mind's 'memory' in *conf.* 10.17f. Cf. *retr.* 1.8.2. O'Connell (1969) 69 makes the valid point that, for Plotinus, there is no inconsistency in maintaining simultaneously an 'illumination' theory and a 'reminiscence/pre-existence' one. However, Plotinus does so explicitly and unequivocally (see Harder/Beutler/Theiler 6.135), whereas Augustine's illumination theory is an equally explicit and unequivocal alternative to pre-existence.

Furthermore, Augustine's mention of the passage in *retr.* 1.4.4 need refer to no more than the way in which he has expressed himself. All he says there is that the illumination theory would have 'more credibly' expressed what he believes.

A similar metaphorical use of the *oblivio* motif is found in *imm. an.* 6, which speaks of the 'so-called forgetfulness or ignorance' of the mind, in a context referring to the phenomenon of latent knowledge which can be actualized or 'found in the soul'. The interdependence of knowledge and the mind in §1 is not argued to show that the human soul has no beginning, merely to demonstrate that, once granted the existence of mind, its relation to knowlege is such that it cannot perish (cf. §11). Finally, nothing in *imm. an.*, which is in other respects influenced by Plotinus 4.7, indicates that the pre-existence doctrine found in that Plotinian treatise on soul's immortality influences Augustine.[106]

In *quant. an.* 34 Augustine speaks of the soul bringing knowledge with it at birth, and identifies learning with recollection. Although he postpones discussion of this thesis, it is none the less the most explicit, and, therefore, most puzzling of his references to the recollection theory. It is, however, to be observed that in the discussion of the acquisition of knowledge in §50ff. no further reference to the thesis is made. Rather, Augustine stresses there that 'knowledge is implanted in us' and is elicited by reasoning. Further, nothing said there or elsewhere in the dialogue departs in any way from the concept of knowledge developed in *sol.* and *imm. an.* Finally, Augustine's comment on the passage in *retr.* 1.8.2 clearly criticizes only the expression used.[107] I conclude that the language of recollection is as metaphorical in *quant. an.* 35 as elsewhere, but that the metaphor is confusingly assertive there.

I have shown in detail elsewhere[108] that the language of *ep.* 7 cannot be used to defend a pre-existence and recollection belief. Once again, the temporal language of the recollection theory is used figuratively. Thus references to a condition of the mind 'before' it became involved in sensory illusions (*ep.* 7.3) or when it was 'not yet' subjected to such illusions (§5) undoubtedly refer to a state of mind reached independently of sense-experience. But the terms 'before' or 'not yet' need mean no more than 'not influenced by' or 'not caused by', i.e. they need carry no literal connotation, and do not have to refer to a temporally prior condition of the soul. Other references in the letter to an antenatal state of the mind or soul are either hypothetical (§3; 6; 7) or merely report the Platonic theory (§2).

When we turn to Augustine's later writings, there can be no doubt that any literal acceptance of the recollection theory is excluded. To the latter, explicitly referred to in *trin.* 12.24, Augustine prefers the following view:

> But we should rather believe that the nature of the intellectual mind is so
> formed that, joined (*subiuncta*) by the creator's plan to intelligible objects in a

---

[106] Plotinus, *Enn.* 4.7.12.8-11; 4.7.13. See O'Connell (1968) 135-45 for the influence of *Enn.* 4.7 upon *imm. an.*

[107] See Gilson 95 n. 1.

[108] O'Daly (1974) 232-5.

natural arrangement (*naturali ordine*), it sees those objects in a kind of incorporeal light of a special kind (*sui generis*), just as the eye of the flesh sees objects in its immediate vicinity in this bodily light, for it has been created receptive to, and compatible with, it.[109]

The mind can apprehend truths

> because it is an intelligible nature and is joined (*connectitur*) not only to intelligible but also to immutable objects, and has been formed in an arrangement such that when it directs itself towards those objects with which it is linked, or towards itself, it gives a true report concerning these, to the extent that it sees them (*retr.* 1.8.2).

What this light is, and how mind and truth are 'joined', have yet to be explained. But beforehand there is more to be said about Augustine's concept of a 'memory' of certain intellectual truths that does not presuppose pre-existence.

Our principal evidence here is in the discussion of memory in book ten of the *Confessions*.[110] There, in addition to his treatment of empirical memory, such as that of objects perceived by the five senses, Augustine discusses a memory that does not deal in images of the things remembered. The contents of the sciences are a case in point:

> Here (sc. in the memory) is also all that we have apprehended of the liberal sciences and not yet forgotten ... and it is not their images, but the objects themselves that I have. For what grammar is, or the art of debate, how many kinds of questions there are – all that I know of these subjects is in my memory, not as if I kept the image and left the object outside (*conf.* 10.16).

Understanding that there are

> three kinds of questions: whether a thing is, what it is, of what kind it is,

is direct understanding of the questions themselves: it is not acquired by sense-perception.

> When I learned them, I was not believing in another person's intelligence, but recognized them in my own, and assented to their truth ... so they were there (sc. in my mind) even before I learned them, but they were not in my memory (ib. §17).

Or, Augustine asks, perhaps they were latent in the memory, and needing some external motivation to be actualized? And he inclines to this latter view. 'Learning' such things is not importing them from somewhere else into the memory, but rather eliciting them from memory itself by a process of mental

---

[109] For the translation 'of a special kind' of the phrase *sui generis* see Kälin 57; Gilson 114ff.

[110] See A. Solignac, *BA* 14, 557-67; Söhngen; Mourant. Cf. further Chapter 5 for a discussion of Augustine's treatment of empirical memory.

concentration and ordering (ib. §18).[111] The same faculty of memory seems to have both latent or unstructured (Augustine uses the terms 'scattered, in disarray, neglected' in §18) and conscious, ordered aspects. What applies to knowledge in the sciences also applies to the 'innumerable principles and laws of numbers and measurements'. These, too, are 'present', and

> He knows them who recognizes them within himself without any concept of a body of any sort (ib. §19).

Later in the discussion Augustine speaks of the quest for a happy or blessed life, which he identifies with a quest for God. It is, he believes, a universal desire. All men want to be happy.[112] Do we seek happiness through memory of something which has been lost, or through a wish to know what we have never known? Or despite the fact that our forgetting of it is unconscious? We *know* it in a certain sense, because it determines our behaviour (§29). On the basis of a criterion established in §23 it must, therefore, be in our memory, for (so the criterion), if I can recognize X or understand what the word 'x' refers to, then X must be in the memory. The desire for happiness is not, however, in the memory like the image of a corporeal object, for desire is not a corporeal condition. Nor can it be compared with our memory of numbers, for such knowledge is its own end and prompts no further quest: but that is not the case with happiness. Nor again is it like scientific knowledge, for although here, as with happiness, the further quest applies, we can, in the case of the sciences, perceive it through the senses, as when e.g. we observe another's eloquence. Even if our delight in this eloquence is none the less 'from an inner notion', we cannot say of happiness that, like eloquence, it is in any way sensually perceived in another. Augustine would clearly not be satisfied by the validity of the observation 'N appears to be happy' based on a sense-perception of N's happiness. We cannot see into N's inner self and identify the presence of happiness there in the same way that we can observe his eloquence. Memory of happiness is, rather, like recollected joy, for joy is also remembered when we are in the contrary state, and both joy and happiness are interior experiences rather than sensed ones (ib. §30).

But where and when have I experienced joy and happiness which I now recall and desire? For, as is the case with happiness, all men desire joy, even if their understanding of it differs from individual to individual (§31).[113] Similarly, all rejoice in the truth: indeed one may say that the happy life is none other than 'joy in truth', and that knowledge of truth and love of truth are knowledge of love and happiness. We have a concept (*notitia*) of happiness in our memory (§33).

The account in book ten of the *Confessions* ends indecisively. That knowledge of happiness is in the memory seems undeniable, but the mode of

[111] See p. 137, where the passage is quoted. For the following point about numerical principles see pp. 179ff.

[112] See p. 163 and n. 7.

[113] See Bourke (1979).

its coming to be (or being) there remains a puzzle. Even if Augustine's use of *'memoria'* in *conf.* 10 extends the connotations of the word beyond any normal usage, so that it becomes practically equivalent to the sum total of my conscious and unconscious awareness,[114] the puzzle does not go away. For the phenomenon of being aware that we desire happiness before we are verifiably happy raises a problem about that awareness qua knowledge.

The fundamental insight underlying Augustine's account of the presence of actualized knowledge to our minds is found as early as the Proteus simile of *c. Acad.* 3.11-13:

> Only a divine power ... can show man what the truth is.

> Divine help should be implored with utmost zeal and piety (ib. 2.1).

> We have a guide to lead us into the very secret places of truth, with God ... showing us the way (ib. 3.44).

More explicit, and introducing the light metaphor characteristic of the illumination theory, is *sol.* 1.15:

> So, whoever apprehends what is transmitted in the sciences, admits without any hesitation that this is absolutely true; and it must be believed that it could not be apprehended, if it were not illuminated by another sun, as it were, of its own. So, just as one can observe three things about this (sc. physical) sun – that it exists, that it shines, that it illuminates – there are likewise three things about that most hidden God whom you wish to apprehend: namely, that he is, that he can be apprehended, and that he causes everything else to be apprehended.[115]

Illumination of the mind is a metaphor based on an analogy with the mechanism of physical sight:

> For the mind has its own eyes, so to speak, the senses of the soul. And the several most certain truths of the sciences are like those objects which are lit up by the sun, so that they become visible – such as is the earth, and all earthly things. But it is God himself who illumines (sc. the former). I, reason, am in minds as sight is in the eyes (*sol.* 1.12).

---

[114] A similar extended usage of *memoria* is found e.g. in the case of memory qua self-knowledge in *trin.* 14.14, where 'to remember oneself' = 'to be present to oneself'. At *trin.* 10.15 the desire for self-knowledge is attributed to a 'hidden memory, which has not abandoned it (sc. mind), although it has advanced a long way, and believes that it cannot arrive at that same end (sc. of its own security and happiness) unless it knows itself'.

[115] Cf. ib. 1.23-5; *mag.* 40 (quoted p. 175). The literature on the illumination theory is vast. See especially Kälin 53-66 (the best concise account); Gilson 87-137; Nash 90-124; Bubacz (1981) 133-61; Markus (1967) 362-73; F. Körner, 'Deus in homine videt. Das Subjekt des menschlichen Erkennens nach der Lehre Augustins', *Philosophisches Jahrbuch* 64 (1956) 166-217 (Körner's and other interpretations are surveyed by C.E. Schuetzinger, *The German Controversy on Saint Augustine's Illumination Theory*, New York 1960); Lorenz (1964) – a masterly analysis; R.H. Nash, 'Some Philosophic Sources of Augustine's Illumination Theory', *Augustinian Studies* 2 (1971) 47-66; D. Chidester, 'The Symbolism of Learning in St. Augustine', *Harvard Theological Review* 76 (1983) 73-90.

Understanding is for the mind what seeing is for the sense (*ord.* 2.10). Just as light and the objects which it illuminates can be distinguished, so can God the illuminating force[116] be distinguished from the truths thus made visible, i.e. from the apprehension of these truths by the human mind:

> ... in that category of intellectual percepts there is a distinction between what is perceived in the soul itself, such as the virtues ... and the very light by which the soul is illuminated, that it may have a true perception of everything apprehended either in itself or in it (sc. the light). For the latter is God himself, the former a creature, although created rational and intellectual in his image. When it attempts to see that light it trembles in its feebleness and has not the necessary strength; yet whatever it is strong enough to grasp comes from there. But when it is transported thither, and withdrawn from the fleshly senses, it is more directly held out to that vision, not in any spatial dimension, but in some manner peculiar to itself, and it sees above itself that by whose help it also sees whatever it sees in itself through intellection (*Gn. litt.* 12.31.59).

What applies here to the apprehended virtues can be maintained regarding other forms and necessary truths: reason perceives these with

> as it were, some kind of face or inner and intelligible eye of its own (*div. qu.* 46).

God as light may be apprehended in the act of intellection along with the apprehended object:

> The light ... reveals itself as well as other things (*Io. ev. tr.* 47.3).[117]

The divine light illuminates not merely the truths apprehended, but also the apprehending mind:

> The rational soul ... is closest to God when it is pure; and the more it cleaves to him in love, the more does it see, suffused somehow with that light and illumined through his agency, (sc. seeing) not with the eyes of the body, but with those of its own primary faculty ... that is, its intelligence, those principles through whose vision it is made most happy (*div. qu.* 46).

> For we are not the light that 'enlightens every man', but we are enlightened by you, so that we who were 'once darkness' may be 'light' in you. O if only they could see the inner eternal (sc. light!) (*conf.* 9.10).[118]

The notion of illumination is often linked to that of participation, e.g.:

---

[116] In the prayer of *sol.* 1.2 God is invoked as 'father of intelligible light, father of our awakening and illumination'.
[117] Cf. *sol.* 1.15 (quoted p. 204); *Gn. litt.* 12.31.59 (quoted above).
[118] The pervasive influence of John 1 is obvious; cf. *vera rel.* 72.

For our illumination is participation in the word, namely, in that life which is the light of mankind (*trin.* 4.4).[119]

The light of truth is also the light in which we make judgements:

> Man alone among living beings has this powerful and remarkable urge (sc. to know); and even if some animals have a much keener sense of sight than we to look into this (sc. physical) light, they cannot attain to that incorporeal light by which our mind is somehow irradiated, so that we are able to judge all these matters rightly. For our capability to do the latter is in proportion to our absorption of that light (*civ.* 11.27).[120]

For the illuminated truth conveys to us the criterion whereby the truth of our particular judgements may be verified, whether these judgements be about intelligible phenomena or sense-perceptions:[121]

> For on account of this even the ungodly have a notion of eternity and rightly find fault with and praise much in human behaviour. And by what rules do they judge this, if not by those in which they see how everybody ought to live, even though they themselves do not so live? Where do they see them (sc. the rules)? For they do not see them in their own nature, since they are without any doubt seen by the mind, and it is certain that their minds are changeable, whereas he who sees them, at the same time perceives these rules to be unchangeable. Nor (sc. do they see them) in their own mental character, for these rules are rules of justice, whereas their minds are surely not just. Where are these rules written, where even the unjust man recognizes what justice is, where he discerns that one ought to have what he himself has not? Where, then, are they written, if not in the book of that light which is called truth? (*trin.* 14.21)[122]

The theory of illumination is not intended to deny to mind its proper cognitive activity. It is no supernatural invasion of the human mind. On the contrary, it is the means whereby man's true mental nature is realized (*trin.*

[119] Cf. *conf.* 4.25; *civ.* 10.2. Here and elsewhere the influence of Plotinus' illumination metaphors (e.g. *Enn.* 5.3.17.36; 5.5.7-8; 6.7.23.1) upon Augustine is likely: see Beierwaltes (1961); Nash, art. cit. (above n. 115).

[120] Cf. *trin.* 12.2; *ep.* 120.11.

[121] Cf. *trin.* 9.9-11.

[122] Gilson 116ff. was undoubtedly correct to stress the importance of this aspect of the illumination theory. But his attempt to confine illumination to a normative or formal role, i.e. to the function of enabling the mind to judge that certain ideas are necessarily true and to apply this judgement in practice, fails to do justice to the scope of Augustine's views, which have an inescapable ontological dimension. Illumination is an attempt to account for the mind's contents, i.e. for its access to concepts and ideas, and not merely an explanation of its ability to judge. See Nash 97-101; Chidester (above n. 115), who stresses the role of the creative divine word in the knowledge process. Most attempts to elucidate Augustine's theory have been either fundamentally misconceived (like the Thomist account of it in terms of an abstraction *more Aristotelico* of universals from the data of experience: see the criticism of Kälin 60-6 and Nash 94-7) or too confined (like Gilson's). The present account limits itself to setting out the main principles of Augustine's theory and its claims, without entering into the controversial history of its interpretations (for which see, besides Nash 94-124, the treatment of medieval views by J.

12.24).[123] It is natural, and its efficacy depends upon the natural capacity of the individual thinking mind (*Gn. litt.* 12.31.59),[124] which may be aided by skilful questioning to uncover its true contents (*retr.* 1.4.4).[125]

Angels may play an intermediary and preparatory role in making our minds ready to receive illumination:

> Thus God by himself, because he is the light, illumines pious minds, that they may understand what is divinely spoken or revealed. But if he uses an angel as a helper to this end, the angel can indeed effect something in man's mind, that he may receive the divine light, and through it may understand. But he (sc. the angel) is said to give understanding to man and, if I may use the expression, to, as it were, intellectualize (*intellectuare*) man, in the way that someone is said to give light to a house, or illumine a house, in which he makes a window. For he does not permeate and light it up with his own light, but merely opens up an entrance through which it may be permeated and lit up (*En. ps.* 118, *ser.* 18.4).

Once again, there is no suggestion that such an angelic role is anything other than the normal, natural process whereby knowledge is reached.[126]

Finally, illumination is first and foremost a means of apprehending intellectual truths, but its influence extends to all forms of knowledge, belief, and imagination:

> ... and the light itself, through which we discern all these things, in which it becomes sufficiently clear to us what we believe that is unknown (sc. to us), what knowledge we do possess, what bodily form we recollect, what we invent with our thought, with what the bodily sense comes into contact, what bodily likeness the mind imagines, what certain fact, totally distinct from all things bodily, the understanding contemplates – this light, then, when it makes all these judgements, shines invisibly and in indescribable fashion and yet intelligibly, and is ours with the same certainty that it imparts to all that we perceive in accordance with it (*ep.* 120.10).

(vi) Introspection and will

The mind in its search for intellectual knowledge engages in a type of inner perception: introspection and self-knowledge are prerequisites of all knowledge, which is in a sense a transcending by the mind of its own level of being:

> Do not go outside, return into yourself. Truth dwells in the inner man, and if you find your nature to be mutable, transcend yourself also. But remember that

---

Owens, 'Faith, Ideas, Illumination, and Experience', in *The Cambridge History of Later Medieval Philosophy* (edd. N. Kretzmann/A. Kenny/J. Pinborg), Cambridge 1982, 440-59).

[123] See pp. 201f., where the passage is quoted.

[124] See p. 205, for an extended quotation of this text.

[125] See p. 176.

[126] For Augustine's angelology see the literature referred to on p. 124 n. 36.

when you transcend yourself you are transcending a reasoning soul (*vera rel.* 72).[127]

The terminology of introspection is rich in Augustine. The mind is said 'to return into itself' (*redire in se(met) ipsum*),[128] 'to restore itself to itself' (*se sibi reddere*),[129] 'to collect itself in itself' (*se ipsum in se colligere*),[130] 'to be focussed on itself' (*in se intendi*),[131] 'to return' (*reverti*),[132] and above all, 'to turn towards/be turned towards' (*convertere/converti*)[133] God and the truth. The brief prayer of *sol.* 2.1,

> O God, who are always the same, grant that I may know myself, grant that I may know you!

does not merely express Augustine's twofold wish, but also situates the phases of that wish in the one possible order of their realization.[134]

Self-knowledge, if properly realized, is total, for the immaterial mind can only know itself as a totality:

> When ... it (sc. soul) knows itself in its searching, it knows itself as one whole subject, and so as one whole object; for not as one thing (sc. knows) another, but as a totality, does it know itself (*Gn. litt.* 7.21.28).[135]

It is also exempt from error:

> And we know ourselves more surely than the others, because our conscience and will are known to us (*nat. et or. an.* 4.30).

This knowledge is compatible with the mind's nature. It is by definition on one level with the mind:

> But when the mind knows itself, its knowledge does not surpass it, because it is itself the knower and the known. When, therefore, it knows itself as an entirety, and not as something else alongside itself, its knowledge is commensurate with itself, for its knowledge, when it knows itself, is not derived from another

---

[127] The Neoplatonic background of this motif is delineated by Theiler (1933) 44 = Theiler (1966) 214. Cf. *conf.* 7.16, on which see Henry (1934) 112; A. Solignac, *BA* 13, 687; E. Booth, 'St. Augustine's "notitia sui" related to Aristotle and the early Neo-Platonists', *Augustiniana* 27 (1977) 70-132; 364-401; ib. 29 (1979) 97-124.

[128] e.g. *c. Acad.* 2.4; 2.5; 2.8; 3.42; *conf.* 7.16.

[129] e.g. *c. Acad* 1.1; *ord.* 1.3; *quant. an.* 55.

[130] e.g. *c. Acad.* 1.23; *ord.* 1.3.

[131] e.g. *c. Acad.* 1.23.

[132] Also *recurrere, redire, regressus*: e.g. *c. Acad.* 2.2; *ord.* 2.31; *sol.* 1.3; *vera rel.* 113; *conf.* 3.7.

[133] e.g. *ord.* 1.22; *sol.* 1.3; *imm. an.* 19; *vera rel.* 79; *conf.* 13.2-4; 13.10; *Io. ev. tr.* 15.19; *Gn. litt.* 1.1.2; 1.4.9; 1.5.10; 3.20.31; 4.18.31; 8.10.23; 8.12.25; *trin.* 8.4; 12.10; 12.21; 14.21. Cf. Theiler (1933) 44ff. = Theiler (1966) 214ff.; O'Connell (1968) 65-86.

[134] See O'Daly (1973) 7-19; P. Courcelle, '*Connais-toi toi-même' de Socrate à saint Bernard*, 3 vols., Paris 1974/5; J. Pépin, *Idées grecques sur l'homme et sur dieu*, Paris 1971, 71ff.; cf. pp. 56f. above.

[135] Cf. *trin.* 10.6.

nature. And when it perceives itself, and nothing more, as an entirety, it is neither less nor greater (*trin.* 9.4).

Mind, knowing itself, knows its own immaterial substance: if it were one of the elements, then it should know itself as such, and differently from its awareness of the element in question (*trin.* 10.16). Furthermore, the desire for self-knowledge is a natural and universal human desire. The link between knowledge (*notitia*) and 'love' (*amor*), which is present in all knowledge, or, rather, in all striving after knowledge, is particularly obvious in introspection.[136] One cannot love, or long for, that of which one is totally ignorant. There can, of course, be 'love through hearsay': X's reputation for beauty may make X, though unknown, desirable. But in this case one knows the genus (e.g. physical beauty) prior to any knowledge of the instance. Similarly, one can desire to know a good man, but here again one already knows the virtues that constitute goodness and determine the desire. Even in the case of a desire for knowledge, e.g. scientific knowledge, we either know its results in others, by hearsay or experience, or we have 'at least a slight impression' of the knowledge involved in a particular discipline (*trin.* 10.1). When signs are completely unknown, as might be the case with, for example, a word for an alcoholic drink (*temetum*), one at least knows that it is not a mere non-linguistic sound: one knows that it has a meaning. But what does one love or desire in this instance? Not, surely, the significance or meaning of the word, for that is precisely the unknown, and so by definition unlovable, factor. What is loved is, rather, the very knowledge by which one perceives

in the principles of things how beautiful learning is, in which the knowledge of all signs is contained; and what benefit there is in that practical knowledge whereby human beings mutually communicate what they have apprehended (*trin.* 10.2).

There is a desire to realize the ideal of knowledge in oneself, especially when this latter is seen to be attainable:

... that they may also comprehend in practice what they know beforehand by reason (ib.).

What is here described as 'known beforehand' is the generic insight that knowledge is good; what is then 'comprehended in practice' is the individual piece of knowledge, e.g. the meaning of the obscure word. Even someone who simply wishes to know the unknown from inquisitiveness

does not love the unknown in itself, but loves knowledge itself (§3).

Even to assert 'I do not know' implies knowledge of what 'to know' means (ib.).

Now the desire of mind to know itself cannot be explained either by

[136] See O'Donovan 60-92.

hearsay or knowledge of other souls, or by some awareness that it is fine to know oneself, or by the promise of contentment and happiness, or even by the phenomenon of a wish for knowledge for its own sake (§5). Since mind can only know itself totally (§6),[137] we cannot say that one part of it seeks to know the others: it has, in any case, no 'parts'. Nor can its self-knowledge be limited to factual knowledge of its structure or awareness of, for example, its emotional states. The latter would, in fact, be a distraction from self-knowledge, a preoccupation with the obsessions and accretions which distract the mind from its true self (§7f.):

> When, therefore, it is commanded to know itself, it should not search for itself as if withdrawn from itself, but it should withdraw what it has added to itself (§11).[138]

The imperative element in the urge to self-knowledge has an ethical dimension:

> Why, therefore, is it commanded to know itself? I suppose, so that it may contemplate itself and live in conformity with its own nature, that is, strive to be regulated in conformity with its own nature, under him, to be sure, to whom it ought to be subject, and above that to which it is to be preferred ... which it ought to rule (§7).

It is a further characteristic of self-knowledge that the very phenomenon of 'seeking oneself' (*se quaerere*) entails self-awareness of a kind (§12; 15). Mind is never absent from itself:

> For what is so present to knowledge as that which is present to the mind, or what is so present to the mind as the mind itself? (§10)

> When it is said to the mind, 'Know yourself', it knows itself by that very thrust by which it understands the expression 'yourself'; and for no other reason than that it is present to itself (§12).

The desire of mind to know itself, then, appears to be self-evident. It is not to be accounted for in terms of any of the other desires for kinds of knowledge. But it has in common with them the pre-existence of knowledge as a means to further knowledge. Mind seeks itself because it knows itself: to seek is, for mind, already to know. It can never be totally self-ignorant, any more than it can lack consciousness and remain mind.

Self-knowledge is a model for other types of knowledge, for it is verifiable, certain knowledge, and it exemplifies, as has been seen, the role of 'love' (*amor*) in cognitive activity. Of the latter Augustine writes:

---

[137] See p. 208.

[138] See p. 150. That the impulse to self-knowledge is the means by which man can realize the (Stoically inspired) imperative to live in conformity with his nature (*secundum naturam suam*), and that this nature is a medial one between God and other creatures (for which see pp. 38ff.), is stressed in the following quotation.

The desire (*appetitus*) that there is in the seeking comes from him who seeks, and is somehow in suspense, and does not rest at that goal to which it is directed, unless what is sought is both found and joined to him who seeks. And this desire, that is, inquiry, although it does not appear to be love by which that which is known is loved ... is, nevertheless, something of the same kind. For it can be called will, inasmuch as everyone who seeks wishes to find ... if he wishes it passionately and urgently, he is said to be zealous ... therefore, a kind of desire precedes the mind's giving birth ... knowledge itself is born as its offspring, and for this reason that desire, by which knowledge is conceived and given birth to, cannot rightly be called birth and offspring. And the same desire ... becomes the love of what is known ... it unites knowledge to its begetter (*trin.* 9.18).

Self-knowledge is the realization of self-love:[139]

... the mind's self-knowledge is commensurate with its being ... its self-love is commensurate with its self-knowledge and its being (ib.).

Every quest for knowledge is a willed orientation of the mind towards the desired object: Augustine speaks, as we have seen, of *appetitus* and *amor*, and he also talks in this connection of the *voluntas* and *intentio* of the mind. A key passage is *sol.* 1.13:

But even this sight cannot direct (*convertere*) its eyes, although they are already healthy, towards the light, unless those three (sc. faith, hope and love) endure ... there follows upon the seeing the actual vision of God, which is the end (*finis*) of the seeing, not because the latter ceases to be, but because it has nothing further to strain after (*quo se intendat*).

Human knowledge is formed by the purpose (*per intentionem*) of thought (*trin.* 15.43): intention is the essential motor that enables the mind to initiate the process leading to cognition (*trin.* 10.11).

(vii) Knowledge of God

The demonstration that God necessarily exists, because something superior to our minds exists, was discussed in section (iii) above,[140] in the analysis of the second book of *de libero arbitrio*. In *conf.* 10.35 it is stressed that God is in the memory, but his presence there is not like that of any of the other objects identified as also being in the memory (§36). Yet

where ... I found truth, there I found God (§35).

[139] For the notion that the will to find the truth, whether about oneself or other objects, is moved by love (*delectatio*) of the proposed objects see further *beata v.* 33; 35; *ord.* 2.35; *mus.* 6.23f.; 6.29; *lib. arb.* 2.36; *quant. an.* 15.
[140] pp. 178ff.

What, then, is the sense in which we have a 'memory' of God?[141]

> Where, then, did I find you, so that I could learn of you? For you were not in my memory before I learned of you. So where did I find you, so that I could learn of you, except in yourself, above myself? (§37)

Unlike the Forms, which are said to be in the memory before they are apprehended by deliberate thought, God appears to be in the memory only from the time in which he is consciously apprehended:

> You thought fit to live in my memory from the time I learned about you (§36).

The 'where' of God before he is known remains mysterious:

> And there is no place; and (sc. though) we withdraw and draw near, still there is no place (§37).

Augustine suggests that, while we can be certain of the fact of God's existence, he is *known* above all through his actions, that is, externally. Thus it is normal and natural for men to understand that God is the maker or creator of the universe:

> For such is the power of true divinity that it cannot remain absolutely and completely hidden from a created rational being which actually uses its reason. For apart from a few, whose nature is too corrupted, the entire human race acknowledges that God is the creator of this world. Therefore, inasmuch as he made this world with sky and earth for all to see ... God is known to all peoples (*Io. ev. tr.* 106.4).

Yet a comprehension, not merely of God's existence and activities, but of the nature of that existence, is not normally available to man. Men

> find by trial that the highest good in that which is perceived by the most purified minds, and that it cannot, therefore, be discerned or understood by them, because the eye of the human mind is weak and is not directed upon such a surpassing light, unless it is nourished and invigorated by the rectitude of faith (*trin.* 1.4).

The last phrase suggests that only the Christian may hope to know God directly, but Augustine emphasizes elsewhere that some philosophers (he is undoubtedly thinking of the Platonists) have gained partial understanding of the divine:

> For some of them have been able to penetrate with their mind's eye beyond all

---

[141] See the articles of L. Cilleruelo: 'La "memoria Dei" según san Agustín', *Augustinus Magister* 1 (1954) 499-509; 'Porqué "memoria Dei"?', *REAug* 10 (1964) 289-94; 'Pro "memoria Dei"', *REAug* 12 (1966) 65-84; cf. G. Madec, 'Pour et contre la "memoria Dei"', *REAug* 11 (1965) 89-92.

created things, and touch, to however small a degree, the light of unchangeable truth (*trin.* 4.20).[142]

It has been shown above that in texts which expound the illumination theory it is stressed that not merely is the apprehended object known, but that God the illuminator may also be apprehended (*Io. ev. tr.* 47.3; *Gn. litt.* 12.31.59).[143] Because God is the light of truth he is, ultimately, somehow knowable to man (*sol.* 1.15).[144] Yet Augustine none the less insists on the paradox that God is at once

… nearer to us … the creator, than any created thing …

and

an ineffable substance (*Gn. litt.* 5.16.34).

The Forms can be more difficult to reach than God, even if, like our minds, they are incorporeal. It is, therefore, not merely more desirable, it is also easier for a pious disposition to 'sense (*sentire*)' God than to understand the nature and structure of the intelligible universe (ib.) Yet, although it can be said of God's nature that

We so contemplated it, that it was not far from us, and was above us, not spatially but through its own venerable and extraordinary pre-eminence, so that it seemed to be with us by the presence of its light (*trin.* 15.10),

it none the less remains the case that

that ineffable light repelled our gaze, and it was made somehow obvious that our mind in its weakness could not as yet be made compliant with it (ib.).[145]

In one sense, therefore, God is 'unknowable':

We are speaking of God, so what is surprising about your not understanding? For if you understand, that is not God … to touch God to some small degree with the mind is great felicity: but to understand him is absolutely impossible (*ser.* 117.5).

Just as in normal vision total perception of a seen object is not at any moment possible, for we see only those parts directly accessible to us, so can God only be 'touched' by the mind in a way that falls short of total comprehension:

---

[142] Cf. Augustine's assessment of Platonism elsewhere, e.g. *conf.* 7.27; *civ.* 8.4-13.

[143] pp. 205f.

[144] This text is quoted above, p. 204.

[145] Cf. the similar experiences described in *conf.* 7.16; 7.23; 7.26, for which see Henry (1934) 111-19; P. Courcelle, 'La première expérience augustinienne de l'extase', *Augustinus Magister* 1 (1954) 53-7; Courcelle (1968) 157-67; Solignac, *BA* 13, 698-703.

What ... eye of the mind understands God? It is sufficient that, if the eye is pure, it touch him. And if it touches, it touches with some sort of incorporeal and spiritual touch, but it does not understand (ib.).[146]

Yet in other senses God is knowable, for he is truth (*trin.* 8.3), the Good (ib. §4), of which we have an 'impressed concept' (ib.):[147]

If you can, putting aside those things which are good through participation of the good, discern the good itself, by participation in which they are good (for, when you hear of this or that good, you cognize at the same time the good itself as well); if, then, you can remove those things and see the good in itself, you will see God (§5).

We can know of God that, given his unchangeable perfection, whatever is predicated of him, i.e. that he is great, wise, true, just, is not accidentally but substantially predicated:

For the human ... mind, to be is not the same as to be strong or sensible or just or temperate. For a mind can exist, and possess none of these virtues. But for God to be is to be the same as to be powerful or just or wise, or whatever is said of his simple multiplicity or manifold simplicity, in order to intimate his substance (*trin.* 6.6).[148]

For the divine nature is a simple substance:

God is indeed multifariously called great, good, wise ... but his greatness is the same as his wisdom ... and his goodness is the same as his wisdom and greatness (*trin.* 6.8).

The programme pithily asserted in *sol.* 1.7 –

What, then, do you wish to know?
... I desire to know God and the soul.
Nothing more?
Nothing whatsoever.

– is, therefore, not straightforwardly implemented. The discussion there of what 'knowing God' implies, anticipates the insights and problems of Augustine's later treatments of the topic. If, asks Augustine, one does not yet know God, how can one know when one has acquired sufficient knowledge of

---

[146] God is known by 'not knowing' (*ord.* 2.44 and 47); knowledge of him is 'learned ignorance' (*docta ignorantia, ep.* 130.28). See V. Lossky, 'Les éléments de "Théologie négative" dans la pensée de saint Augustin', *Augustinus Magister* 1 (1954) 575-81; Sorabji 171 n. 112; 437. On the theme of 'touching God' see *conf.* 9.24 (quoted p. 216) and *trin.* 15.2: cf. B. Aland, 'Cogitare Deum in den Confessiones Augustins', *Pietas. Festschrift für Bernhard Kötting* (edd. E. Dassmann/K. Suso Frank) = *Jahrbuch für Antike und Christentum*, Ergänzungsband 8, 1980, 93-104.

[147] See pp. 184f.

[148] Cf. *trin.* 7.1-3. For the philosophical background of this concept of God's attributes see C. Stead, *Divine Substance*, Oxford 1977, 162-6.

him? If one does not know him, can one know that one knows 'something like God'? Is knowledge of God the same as, or similar to, knowledge of persons? It is certainly more like the latter than, for example, foreknowledge of the moon's next phase, for such foreknowledge is a knowledge of sense-objects, so that what will happen cannot be predicted with absolute certainty, for the behaviour of the objects is liable to change, even if this is unlikely in the case of the moon. Knowing, or desiring to know, another person as a friend, for example, is, however, a kind of intellectual knowledge, whether possessed or aimed at:

> That ... part whereby he is my friend, that is, his very soul, I desire to reach with the mind (*sol.* 1.8).[149]

Yet even such knowledge is an unsatisfactory analogy: Augustine argues that a closer parallel is found in our knowledge of geometrical figures – a stable knowledge of something immutable. But if this is knowledge of 'something like God' it is so only as far as the kind of intelligence exhibited in both cases is concerned: there is a discrepancy in the objects known. We may compare it with sight: the same eyes can look upon the earth or the more desirable sky (§9-11).

The intelligence of one who would see God must, however, be trained, not just intellectually like the geometer's, but also, and above all, morally:

> 'Healthy sight' is a mind free of all bodily taint, that is, detached and purged of desire for things mortal (§12).

Belief in its attainability is a prerequisite of reaching this state, as are hope and desire for it as a goal. So, if reason is the 'sight of the mind', then 'right/perfect sight' is the mind's goodness, and vision of God is none other than the perfection in turn of that goodness, that is, the 'end of sight' in which happiness is found (§13). God is indeed knowable (*intellegibilis*, §15) to the morally purified disposition:

> ... when it (sc. soul) has brought harmony and order into itself, and made itself well-formed and beautiful, then it will venture to see God, and the very spring from which all truth flows, and the father of truth himself (*ord.* 2.51).

But the 'venture' will perforce remain incomplete in man's temporal condition. Augustine proffers an *interpretatio christiana* of the Neoplatonic vision of the One or supreme principle. The divine wisdom may be momentarily 'touched' in rare instants of our lives:

---

[149] Augustine's views on friendship in relation to the philosophical tradition of the theme are discussed by M.A. MacNamara, *Friends and Friendship for St. Augustine*, Staten Island, N.Y. 1964; see also Testard 2.135; Brown 200-2.

We just touched it (sc. wisdom) briefly with a full blow of the heart ... we strained forward and in an instant of thought we touched the eternal wisdom that abides over all (*conf.* 9.24f.).

But such moments of understanding pass, for they are a mere foreshadowing of the paradisal state which the Christian anticipates (ib.).[150]

---

[150] See P. Henry, *La vision d'Ostie. Sa place dans la vie et l'oeuvre de saint Augustin*, Paris 1938 (Eng. tr. *The Path to Transcendence*, Pittsburgh, Pa. 1981); A. Mandouze, 'L'extase d'Ostie', *Augustinus Magister* 1 (1954) 67-84; A. Louth, *The Origins of the Christian Mystical Tradition. From Plato to Denys*, Oxford 1981, 132-58.

Augustine's Works
Abbreviations, Titles, Editions

The following list includes those works of Augustine cited in the book. The titles given are those in general use: in several cases they do not reflect the earliest evidence, viz. Augustine's *retractationes* and the *indiculum* (ed. A. Wilmart, *MA* 2.149-233) of his associate and first biographer Possidius. It seemed prudent, however, not to introduce novel titles and abbreviations into the present book. A full synopsis of the variant titles of Augustine's works is provided in *Augustinus-Lexikon* 1, 1/2 (1986) xxvi-xli.

Dates, or approximate dates, of composition have been given, but it should be noted that in many cases the chronology of Augustine's works is uncertain. The dates given here are, in general, those of Perler/Maier, but La Bonnardière and Zarb have also been consulted. The reader is referred to these studies for full discussions of chronological problems.

In the citation of texts of Augustine in the book, references are given, where appropriate, to book (or letter, or sermon, etc.) and paragraph. Chapter numbers are also given for some works where the *CSEL* edition does not provide paragraph references (*Gn. litt.*, *Gn. litt. imp.*, *c. ep. fund.*), or where the paragraph numbers are subdivisions of chapters (*c. Adim.*, *div. qu. Simpl.*, *retr.*). In references to *retr.* the traditional enumeration of *PL* is adopted.

c. Acad.	*contra Academicos* (386) *PL* 32 *CSEL* 63 *CCL* 29
c. Adim.	*contra Adimantum* (393/4) *PL* 42 *CSEL* 25,1
adn. Iob	*adnotationes in Iob* (399) *PL* 34 *CSEL* 28,2
agon.	*de agone christiano* (396) *PL* 40 *CSEL* 41
beata v.	*de beata vita* (386) *PL* 32 *CCL* 29
cat. rud.	*de catechizandis rudibus* (399) *PL* 40 *CCL* 46
civ.	*de civitate dei* (412-426/7) *PL* 41 *CSEL* 40 *CCL* 47-48
conf.	*confessiones* (397-401) *PL* 32 *CSEL* 33 *CCL* 27; ed. M. Skutella
cons. ev.	*de consensu evangelistarum* (399/400-?) *PL* 34 *CSEL* 43
cont.	*de continentia* (395?) *PL* 40 *CSEL* 41
corrept.	*de correptione et gratia* (426/7) *PL* 44
cura mort.	*de cura pro mortuis gerenda ad Paulinum* (422?) *PL* 40 *CSEL* 41
dial.	*de dialectica* (387-9) *PL* 32; ed. J. Pinborg
div. qu.	*de diversis quaestionibus octoginta tribus* (388-395/6) *PL* 40 *CCL* 44A
div. qu. Simpl.	*ad Simplicianum de diversis quaestionibus* (395-6) *PL* 40 *CCL* 44
divin. daem.	*de divinatione daemonum* (408) *PL* 40 *CSEL* 41

doctr. chr.	de doctrina christiana (397-426/7) *PL* 34 *CSEL* 80 *CCL* 32
duab. an.	de duabus animabus (391/2) *PL* 42 *CSEL* 25,1
en. Ps.	enarrationes in Psalmos (from 392?) *PL* 36-37 *CCL* 38-40
ench.	enchiridion ad Laurentium de fide et spe et caritate (422?) *PL* 40 *CCL* 46
ep.	epistulae (from 386-7) *PL* 33 *CSEL* 34; 44; 57; 88
c. ep. fund.	contra epistulam quam vocant fundamenti (396) *PL* 42 *CSEL* 25,1
c. ep. Pel.	contra duas epistulas Pelagianorum (420-1) *PL* 44 *CSEL* 60
c. Faust.	contra Faustum (397-398/9) *PL* 42 *CSEL* 25,1
c. Fel.	contra Felicem (404) *PL* 42 *CSEL* 25,2
Gn. litt.	de Genesi ad litteram (401-14) *PL* 34 *CSEL* 28,1
Gn. litt. imp.	de Genesi ad litteram imperfectus liber (393/4-426/7) *PL* 34 *CSEL* 28,1
Gn. c. Man.	de Genesi contra Manichaeos (388/90) *PL* 34
imm. an.	de immortalitate animae (387) *PL* 32 *CSEL* 89
Io. ev. tr.	in Iohannis evangelium tractatus CXXIV (1-16: 406-7) *PL* 35 *CCL* 36
c. Iul.	contra Iulianum (421-2) *PL* 44
c. Iul. imp.	contra Iulianum opus imperfectum (428-30) *PL* 45 *CSEL* 85,1
lib. arb.	de libero arbitrio (388-94/5) *PL* 32 *CSEL* 74 *CCL* 29
loc. hept.	locutiones in heptateuchum (419-?) *PL* 34 *CSEL* 28,1 *CCL* 33
mag.	de magistro (388/90) *PL* 32 *CSEL* 77 *CCL* 29
mend.	de mendacio (394/5) *PL* 40 *CSEL* 41
c. mend.	ad Consentium contra mendacium (420) *PL* 40 *CSEL* 41
mor.	de moribus ecclesiae catholicae et de moribus Manichaeorum (387/8-399) *PL* 32
mus.	de musica (388/90) *PL* 32
nat. et or. an.	de natura et origine animae (419-20) *PL* 44 *CSEL* 60
nupt. et conc.	de nuptiis et concupiscentia ad Valerium comitem (418/9-420/1) *PL* 44 *CSEL* 42
ord.	de ordine (386) *PL* 32 *CSEL* 63 *CCL* 29
pecc. mer.	de peccatorum meritis et remissione et de baptismo parvulorum ad Marcellinum (411-2) *PL* 44 *CSEL* 60
c. Prisc. et Orig.	ad Orosium presbyterum contra Priscillianistas et Origenistas (415) *PL* 42 *CCL* 49
qu. hept.	quaestiones in heptateuchum (419-?) *PL* 34 *CSEL* 28,2 *CCL* 33
quant. an.	de quantitate animae (387/8) *PL* 32 *CSEL* 89
retr.	retractationes (426/7) *PL* 32 *CSEL* 36 *CCL* 57
c. Sec.	contra Secundinum (398) *PL* 42 *CSEL* 25,2
ser.	sermones (from 391) *PL* 38-39 *CCL* 41 *SMP* 1 *RB* 51 (1939) –
ser. Denis	sermones a M. Denis editi *PL* 46 *MA* 1
ser. dom. m.	de sermone domini in monte (393/4) *PL* 34 *CCL* 35
sol.	soliloquia (386-7) *PL* 32 *CSEL* 89
spir. et litt.	de spiritu et littera (412) *PL* 44 *CSEL* 60
trin.	de trinitate (399-422/6) *PL* 42 *CCL* 50-50A
vera rel.	de vera religione (390) *PL* 34 *CSEL* 77 *CCL* 32

Bibliography

Agaësse, P./Solignac, A. *Oeuvres de Saint Augustin: De Genesi ad Litteram*, 2 vols., *BA* 48-9, Paris 1972.

Alfaric, P. *L'Evolution intellectuelle de Saint Augustin. 1: Du Manichéisme au Néoplatonisme*, Paris 1918.

Amat, J. *Songes et visions. L'au-delà dans la littérature latine tardive.* Paris 1985.

Baltes, M. 'Die Zuordnung der Elemente zu den Sinnen bei Poscidonios und ihre Herkunft aus der alten Akademie', *Philologus* 122 (1978) 183-96.

Bardy, G. 'Saint Augustin et les médecins', *L'Année Théologique Augustinienne* 13 (1953) 327-46.

Barwick, K. *Probleme der stoischen Sprachlehre und Rhetorik*, Abhandlungen der sächsischen Akademie der Wissenschaften zu Leipzig, Philologisch-historische Klasse, 49/3, Berlin 1957.

Beare, J.I. *Greek Theories of Elementary Cognition from Alcmaeon to Aristotle*, Oxford 1906.

Beierwaltes, W. (1961) 'Plotins Metaphysik des Lichtes', *Zeitschrift für Philosophische Forschung* 15 (1961) 334-62, reprinted in: *Die Philosophie des Neuplatonismus* (ed. C. Zintzen) = *Wege der Forschung* 436, Darmstadt 1977, 75-115, with *Nachwort* 116-7.

——. (1967) (ed.) *Plotin über Ewigkeit und Zeit*, (Enneade III 7) Frankfurt 1967 (3rd edn., 1981).

——. (1981) *Regio Beatitudinis. Zu Augustins Begriff des glücklichen Lebens*, Sitzungsberichte der Heidelberger Akademie der Wissenschaften, Philosophisch-historische Klasse, 6, 1981.

Bidez, J. *Vie de Porphyre le philosophe Néo-Platonicien*, Gand/Leipzig 1913 = Hildesheim 1964.

Blumenthal, H.J. (1971) *Plotinus' Psychology. His Doctrines of the Embodied Soul*, The Hague 1971.

——. (1981) 'Some Platonist Readings of Aristotle', *Proceedings of the Cambridge Philological Society* n.s. 27 (1981) 1-16

——. (1982) 'Proclus on Perception', *Bulletin of the Institute of Classical Studies* 29 (1982) 1-11.

Bonner, G.I. '*Libido* and *Concupiscentia* in St. Augustine', *Studia Patristica* 6 = *TU* 81 (1962) 303-14.

Bourke, V.J. (1954) 'St. Augustine and the Cosmic Soul', *Giornale di Metafisica* 9 (1954) 431-440.

——. (1979) *Joy in Augustine's Ethics* (The Saint Augustine Lecture Series), Villanova, Pa. 1979.

Brown, P. *Augustine of Hippo. A Biography*, London 1967.

Bubacz, B. (1975) 'Augustine's Account of Factual Memory', *Augustinian Studies* 6 (1975) 181-92.

———. (1981) *St. Augustine's Theory of Knowledge. A Contemporary Analysis* (Texts and Studies in Religion, 11), New York/Toronto 1981.

Buckenmeyer, R.E. 'Augustine and the Life of Man's Body in the Early Dialogues', *Augustinian Studies* 2 (1971) 197-211.

Cardauns, B. *M. Terentius Varro, Antiquitates Rerum Divinarum* (Abhandlungen der Geistes- und Sozialwissenschaftlichen Klasse, Akademie der Wissenschaften und der Literatur, Mainz), 2 vols., Wiesbaden 1976.

Colonna, M.E. *Enea di Gaza: Teofrasto*, Naples 1958.

Cornford, F.M. *Plato's Cosmology. The Timaeus of Plato translated with a running commentary*, London 1937.

Courcelle, P. (1948) *Les lettres grecques en Occident de Macrobe à Cassiodore* (Bibliothèque des Ecoles Françaises d'Athènes et de Rome, 159), 2nd edn., Paris 1948 (Eng. tr. *Late Latin Writers and their Greek Sources*, Cambridge, Mass. 1969).

———. (1957) 'Interprétations néo-platonisantes du livre VI de l'*Enéide*', *Recherches sur la Tradition Platonicienne* (Entretiens Fondation Hardt, 3), Vandoeuvres/Geneva 1957, 95-136.

———. (1965) 'L'Ame en Cage', *Parusia. Studien zur Philosophie Platons und zur Problemgeschichte des Platonismus. Festgabe für Johannes Hirschberger* (ed. K. Flasch), Frankfurt 1965, 103-16.

———. (1968) *Recherches sur les Confessions de Saint Augustin*, 2nd edn., Paris 1968.

Darrell Jackson, B. 'The Theory of Signs in St. Augustine's *De Doctrina Christiana*', *REAug* 15 (1969) 9-49 = Markus (1972) 92-147.

Decret, F. *L'Afrique Manichéenne (IVᵉ-Vᵉ siècles). Étude historique et doctrinale*, 2 vols., Paris 1978.

Del Corno, D. *Graecorum de re onirocritica scriptorum reliquiae* (Testi e Documenti per lo Studio dell'Antichità, 26), Milan/Varese 1969.

Deuse, W. *Untersuchungen zur mittelplatonischen und neuplatonischen Seelenlehre* (Akademie der Wissenschaften und der Literatur, Mainz. Abhandlungen der Geistes- und Sozialwissenschaftlichen Klasse. Einzelveröffentlichung 3), Wiesbaden 1983.

Dihle, A. (1982) *The Theory of Will in Classical Antiquity* (Sather Classical Lectures, 48), Berkeley/Los Angeles/London 1982.

———. (1983) 'Vom sonnenhaften Auge', *Platonismus und Christentum. Festschrift für Heinrich Dörrie* (ed. H.-D. Blume/F. Mann) = *Jahrbuch für Antike und Christentum*, Ergänzungsband 10, 1983, 85-91.

Dillon, J. *The Middle Platonists* (Classical Life and Letters), London 1977.

Dinkler, E. *Die Anthropologie Augustins* (Forschungen zur Kirchen- und Geistesgeschichte, 4), Stuttgart 1934.

Dodds, E.R. (1963) *Proclus. The Elements of Theology. A Revised Text, with Translation, Introduction and Commentary*, 2nd edn., Oxford 1963.

———. (1973) 'Supernormal Phenomena in Classical Antiquity', *The Ancient Concept of Progress and other Essays on Greek Literature and Belief*, Oxford 1973, 156-210.

Dörrie, H. (1957) 'Kontroversen um die Seelenwanderung im

kaiserzeitlichen Platonismus', *Hermes* 85 (1957) 414-35 = Dörrie (1976) 420-40.

——. (1959) *Porphyrios' 'Symmikta Zetemata'. Ihre Stellung in System und Geschichte des Neuplatonismus nebst einem Kommentar zu den Fragmenten* (Zetemata, 20), Munich 1959.

——. (1976) *Platonica Minora* (Studia et Testimonia Antiqua, 8), Munich 1976.

Duchrow, U. *Sprachverständnis und biblisches Hören bei Augustin*, Tübingen 1965.

Dulaey, M. *Le rêve dans la vie et la pensée de Saint Augustin*, Paris 1973.

Du Roy, O. *L'intelligence de la foi en la Trinité selon Saint Augustin. Genèse de sa théologie trinitaire jusqu'en 391*, Paris 1966.

Evans, G.R. *Augustine on Evil*, Cambridge 1982.

Ferraz, M. *De la psychologie de Saint Augustin*, Paris 1862.

Festugière, A.-J. *La Révélation d'Hermès Trismégiste*, vol. 3: *Les Doctrines de l'Ame*, Paris 1953.

Flamant, J. *Macrobe et le néo-Platonisme latin, à la fin du IVe siècle* (Etudes préliminaires aux religions orientales dans l'empire romain, 58), Leiden 1977.

Flasch, K. *Augustin. Einführung in sein Denken*, Stuttgart 1980.

Fortin, E.L. 'Saint Augustin et la doctrine néoplatonicienne de l'âme (*Ep.* 137,11)', *Augustinus Magister* 3 (1954) 371-80.

Gannon, M.A.I. 'The Active Theory of Sensation in St. Augustine', *The New Scholasticism* 30 (1956) 154-80.

Gilson, E. *Introduction à l'étude de Saint Augustin* (Etudes de philosophie médiévale, 11), 3rd edn., Paris 1949 (Eng. tr. *The Christian Philosophy of Saint Augustine*, London 1961).

Goldbrunner, J. *Das Leib-Seele Problem bei Augustinus*, Kallmünz 1934.

Guitton, J. *Le temps et l'éternité chez Plotin et Saint Augustin*, Paris 1933.

Hackforth, R. *Plato's Phaedrus. Translated with Introduction and Commentary*, Cambridge 1952.

Hadot, P. (1962) 'L'image de la Trinité dans l'âme chez Victorinus et chez saint Augustin', *Studia Patristica* 6 = *TU* 81 (1962) 409-42.

——. (1968) *Porphyre et Victorinus*, 2 vols., Paris 1968.

——. (1971) *Marius Victorinus. Recherches sur sa vie et ses oeuvres*, Paris 1971.

——. (1981) 'Ouranos, Kronos and Zeus in Plotinus' Treatise against the Gnostics', *Neoplatonism and Early Christian Thought. Essays in Honour of A.H. Armstrong* (ed. H.J. Blumenthal/R.A. Markus), London 1981, 124-37.

Hagendahl, H. *Augustine and the Latin Classics* (Studia Graeca et Latina Gothoburgensia, 20. 1/2), 2 vols., Göteborg 1967.

Harder, R./Beutler, R./Theiler, W. *Plotins Schriften*, 6 vols., Hamburg 1960/71.

Henry, P. (1934) *Plotin et l'Occident. Firmicus Maternus, Marius Victorinus, Saint Augustin et Macrobe* (Spicilegium Sacrum Lovaniense, 15), Louvain 1934.

——. (1960) *Saint Augustine on Personality* (The Saint Augustine Lecture Series), New York 1960.

Hicks, R.D. (ed.) *Aristotle, De Anima*, London 1907 = Amsterdam 1965.

Holte, R. *Béatitude et Sagesse. Saint Augustin et le problème de la fin de l'homme dans la philosophie ancienne*, Paris/Worcester, Mass. 1962.

Ingenkamp, H.G. 'Zur stoischen Lehre vom Sehen', *Rheinisches Museum* 114 (1971) 240-6.

Janich, P. 'Augustins Zeitparadox und seine Frage nach einem Standard der Zeitmessung', *Archiv für Geschichte der Philosophie* 54 (1972) 168-86.

Kälin, B. *Die Erkenntnislehre des hl. Augustinus*, Sarnen 1920.

La Bonnardière, A.-M. *Recherches de chronologie augustinienne*, Paris 1965.

Lacey, H.M. 'Empiricism and Augustine's problems about time', *Review of Metaphysics* 22 (1968) 219-45.

Lechner, O. 'Zu Augustins Metaphysik der Engel', *Studia Patristica* 9 = *TU* 94 (1966) 422-30.

Lloyd, A.C. 'On Augustine's Concept of a Person', Markus (1972) 191-205.

Lohse, B. 'Zu Augustins Engellehre', *Zeitschrift für Kirchengeschichte* 70 (1959) 278-91.

Long, A.A. (1974) *Hellenistic Philosophy* (Classical Life and Letters), London 1974.

——. (1982) 'Soul and Body in Stoicism', *Phronesis* 27 (1982) 34-57.

Lorenz, R. (1950/1) 'Fruitio dei bei Augustin', *Zeitschrift für Kirchengeschichte* 63 (1950/1) 75-132.

——. (1952/3) 'Die Herkunft des augustinischen frui deo', *Zeitschrift für Kirchengeschichte* 64 (1952/3) 34-60; 359f.

——. (1955/6) 'Die Wissenschaftslehre Augustins', *Zeitschrift für Kirchengeschichte* 67 (1955/6) 29-60; 213-51.

——. (1964) 'Gnade und Erkenntnis bei Augustinus', *Zeitschrift für Kirchengeschichte* 75 (1964) 21-78.

Lütcke, K.-H. *Augustinus. Philosophische Spätdialoge: Die Grösse der Seele. Der Lehrer* (with G. Weigel), Zürich/Munich 1973.

Madec, G. *Oeuvres de Saint Augustin: De Magistro, De Libero Arbitrio, BA* 6, 3rd edn., Paris 1976.

Madvig, J.N. (ed.) *M. Tullii Ciceronis de finibus bonorum et malorum libri quinque*, 3rd edn., Copenhagen 1876 = Hildesheim 1965.

Mannebach, E. *Aristippi et Cyrenaicorum Fragmenta*, Leiden/Cologne 1961.

Markus, R.A. (1957) 'St. Augustine on Signs', *Phronesis* 2 (1957) 60-83 = Markus (1972) 61-91.

——. (1967) 'Marius Victorinus and Augustine', *The Cambridge History of Later Greek and Early Medieval Philosophy*, ed. A.H. Armstrong, Cambridge 1967, 329-419.

——. (1972) (ed.) *Augustine. A Collection of Critical Essays* (Modern Studies in Philosophy), New York 1972.

——. (1981) 'The Eclipse of a Neoplatonic Theme. Augustine and Gregory the Great on Visions and Prophecies', *Neoplatonism and Early Christian Thought. Essays in Honour of A.H. Armstrong* (ed. H.J. Blumenthal/R.A. Markus), London 1981, 204-11.

Marrou, H.-I. *Saint Augustin et la fin de la culture antique* (Bibliothèque des Ecoles Françaises d'Athènes et de Rome, 145), Paris 1938 and '*Retractatio*' (ib. 145 *bis*), Paris 1949.

Martin, J. *Saint Augustin*, Paris 1901.

Matthews, G.B. 'Augustine on Speaking from Memory', *American Philosophical Quarterly* 2/2 (1965) 1-4 = Markus (1972) 168-75.

Mayer, C.P. *Die Zeichen in der geistigen Entwicklung und in der Theologie Augustins*, 2 vols., Würzburg 1969, 1974.

Meijering, E.P. *Augustin über Schöpfung, Ewigkeit und Zeit. Das Elfte Buch der Bekenntnisse* (Philosophia Patrum, 4), Leiden 1979.

Merlan, P. 'Greek Philosophy from Plato to Plotinus', *The Cambridge History of Later Greek and Early Medieval Philosophy*, ed. A.H. Armstrong, Cambridge 1967, 13-132.

Miles, M.R. *Augustine on the Body* (American Academy of Religion Dissertation Series, 31), Missoula, Montana 1979.

Mondolfo, R. 'La teoria agostiniana del senso interno ed i suoi antecedenti greci', *Momenti del pensiero greco e cristiano*, Naples 1964, 59-84.

Moreau, J. *L'âme du monde de Platon aux Stoïciens*, Paris 1939 = Hildesheim 1971.

Mourant, J.A. *Saint Augustine on Memory* (The Saint Augustine Lecture Series), Villanova, Pa. 1980.

Nash, R.H. *The Light of the Mind. St. Augustine's Theory of Knowledge*, Lexington, Kentucky 1969.

Nörregaard, J. *Augustins Bekehrung*, Tübingen 1923.

Nourrisson, J.F. *La philosophie de Saint Augustin*, 2 vols., Paris 1866 = Frankfurt 1968.

Nuchelmans, G. *Theories of the Proposition. Ancient and Medieval Concepts of the Bearers of Truth and Falsity* (North-Holland Linguistic Series, 8), Amsterdam/London 1973.

O'Connell, R.J. (1968) *Saint Augustine's Early Theory of Man, A.D. 386-391*, Cambridge, Mass. 1968.

——. (1969) 'Pre-existence in Augustine's Seventh Letter', *REAug* 15 (1969) 67-73.

O'Daly, G.J.P. (1973) *Plotinus' Philosophy of the Self*, Shannon 1973.

——. (1974) 'Did St. Augustine ever believe in the Soul's Pre-existence?', *Augustinian Studies* 5 (1974) 227-35.

——. (1976) 'Memory in Plotinus and two early texts of St. Augustine', *Studia Patristica* 14 = *TU* 117 (1976) 461-9.

——. (1977) 'Time as *distentio* and St. Augustine's Exegesis of *Philippians* 3,12-14', *REAug* 23 (1977) 265-71.

——. (1981,1) 'Augustine on the Measurement of Time: Some Comparisons with Aristotelian and Stoic Texts', *Neoplatonism and Early Christian Thought. Essays in Honour of A.H. Armstrong* (ed. H.J. Blumenthal/R.A. Markus), London 1981, 171-9.

——. (1981,2) 'Anima, error y falsum en los primeros escritos de san Agustín', *Augustinus* 26 (1981) 187*-194*.

——. (1983) 'Augustine on the Origin of Souls', *Platonismus und Christentum. Festschrift für Heinrich Dörrie* (ed. H.-D. Blume/F. Mann) = *Jahrbuch für Antike und Christentum*, Ergänzungsband 10, 1983, 184-91.

——. (1985,1) art. Augustins Theologie, *Evangelisches Kirchenlexikon* 1/1 (1985) 326-32.

———. (1985,2) '*Sensus interior* in St. Augustine, *De libero arbitrio* 2.3.25-6.51' *Studia Patristica* 16 = *TU* 129 (1985) 528-32.

O'Donovan, O. *The Problem of Self-Love in St. Augustine*, New Haven/London 1980.

O'Meara, J.J. (1951) 'The Historicity of the Early Dialogues of Saint Augustine', *Vigiliae Christianae* 5 (1951) 150-78.

———. (1954) *The Young Augustine. The Growth of St. Augustine's Mind up to his Conversion*, London 1954.

Pease, A.S. (ed.) *M. Tulli Ciceronis de divinatione libri duo*, Urbana, Ill. 1920 and 1923 = Darmstadt 1977.

Pelland, G. *Cinq études d'Augustin sur le début de la Genèse* (Recherches, 8), Tournai/Montreal 1972.

Pelz, K. *Die Engellehre des heiligen Augustinus. Ein Beitrag zur Dogmengeschichte. 1: Augustinus über die Natur der Engel* (Diss. Breslau), Münster 1912.

Pembroke, S.G. '*Oikeiôsis*', *Problems in Stoicism* (ed. A.A. Long), London 1971, 114-49.

Pépin, J. (1964) 'Une nouvelle source de saint Augustin: le *Zêtêmata* de Porphyre "Sur l'union de l'âme et du corps" ', *Revue des Etudes Anciennes* 66 (1964) 53-107 = Pépin (1977) 213-67.

———. (1965) 'Influences païennes sur l'angelologie et la démonologie de saint Augustin', Entretiens de Cerisy-la-Salle sur l'Homme et le Diable, Paris/The Hague 1965, 51-9 = Pépin (1977) 29-37.

———. (1976) *Saint Augustin et la dialectique* (The Saint Augustine Lecture Series), Villanova, Pa. 1976.

———. (1977) *Ex Platonicorum Persona. Etudes sur les lectures philosophiques de Saint Augustin*, Amsterdam 1977.

Perler, O./Maier, J.L. *Les voyages de saint Augustin*, Paris 1969.

Pohlenz, M. *Die Stoa. Geschichte einer geistigen Bewegung*, 2 vols., 5th edn., Göttingen 1978, 1980.

Reid, J.S. *M. Tulli Ciceronis Academica*, London 1885 = Hildesheim 1966.

Rief, J. *Der Ordobegriff des jungen Augustinus* (Abhandlungen zur Moraltheologie, 2), Paderborn 1962.

Rist, J.M. *Plotinus. The Road to Reality*, Cambridge 1967.

Robert, L. *Une vision de Perpétue martyre à Carthage en 203*, Académie des Inscriptions et Belles-Lettres, Comptes Rendus 1982, 228-76.

Robinson, T.M. *Plato's Psychology* (Phoenix Supplementary Volume, 8), Toronto 1970.

Ruef, H. *Augustin über Semiotik und Sprache. Sprachtheoretische Analysen zu Augustins Schrift 'De Dialectica' mit einer deutschen Übersetzung*, Berne 1981.

Schindler, A. (1965) *Wort und Analogie in Augustins Trinitätslehre*, Tübingen 1965.

———. (1979) art. Augustin/Augustinismus 1. Augustin, *TRE* 4 (1979) 645-98.

Schmaus, M. *Die psychologische Trinitätslehre des hl. Augustinus* (Münsterische Beiträge zur Theologie, 11), Münster 1927.

Schneider, R. *Seele und Sein. Ontologie bei Augustin und Aristoteles*, Stuttgart 1957.

Schumacher, W.A. *Spiritus and Spiritualis: A Study in the Sermons of Saint*

Augustine (Pontificia Facultas Theologica Seminarii Sanctae Mariae ad Lacum. Dissertationes ad Lauream, 28), Mundelein, Ill. 1957.

Schwarz, R. 'Die leib-seelische Existenz bei Aurelius Augustinus', *Philosophisches Jahrbuch* 63 (1955) 323-60.

Schwyzer, H.-R. (1951) art. Plotinos, *RE* 21/1 (1951) 471-592; ib. Suppl. 15 (1978) 311-28.

——. (1960) ' "Bewusst" und "Unbewusst" bei Plotin', *Les sources de Plotin* (Entretiens Fondation Hardt, 5), Vandoeuvres/Geneva 1960, 343-90.

——. (1974) 'Plotinisches und Unplotinisches in den APHORMAI des Porphyrios', *Plotino e il Neoplatonismo in Oriente e in Occidente* (Accademia Nazionale dei Lincei, Problemi Attuali di Scienza e di Cultura, Quaderno N. 198), Rome 1974, 221-52.

——. (1983) *Ammonios Sakkas, der Lehrer Plotins*, Rheinisch-Westfälische Akademie der Wissenschaften, Vorträge G 260, Opladen 1983.

Smith, A. *Porphyry's Place in the Neoplatonic Tradition. A Study in Post Plotinian Neoplatonism*, The Hague 1974.

Söhngen, G. 'Der Aufbau der augustinischen Gedächtnislehre. Conf. X c. 6-27', *Aurelius Augustinus, Festschrift der Görres-Gesellschaft zum 1500. Todestage des Heiligen Augustinus* (ed. M. Grabmann/J. Mausbach), Cologne 1930, 367-94 = *Die Einheit in der Theologie*, Munich 1952, 63-100.

Solignac, A. (1954) 'Analyse et sources de la Question "De Ideis",' *Augustinus Magister* 1 (1954) 307-15.

——. (1958) 'Doxographies et manuels dans la formation philosophique de s. Augustin', *RechAug* 1 (1958) 113-48.

——. (1962) *Oeuvres de Saint Augustin: Confessions*, 2 vols., *BA* 13-4, Paris 1962.

Solmsen, F. 'Greek Philosophy and the Discovery of the Nerves', *Museum Helveticum* 18 (1961) 150-67; 169-97 = *Kleine Schriften*, vol. 1, Hildesheim 1968, 536-82.

Sorabji, R. *Time, Creation and the Continuum. Theories in Antiquity and the Early Middle Ages*, London 1983.

TeSelle, E. *Augustine the Theologian*, London 1970.

Teske, R.J. 'The World-Soul and Time in St Augustine', *Augustinian Studies* 14 (1983) 75-92.

Testard, M. *Saint Augustin et Cicéron*, 2 vols., Paris 1958.

Theiler, W. (1930) *Die Vorbereitung des Neuplatonismus* (Problemata, 1), Berlin 1930 = Berlin/Zürich 1964.

——. (1933) *Porphyrios und Augustin*, Schriften der Königsberger Gelehrten Gesellschaft, Geisteswissenschaftliche Klasse 10, 1933 = Theiler (1966) 160-251.

——. (1966) *Forschungen zum Neuplatonismus* (Quellen und Studien zur Geschichte der Philosophie, 10) Berlin 1966.

——. (1970) 'Die Seele als Mitte bei Augustin und Origenes', *Untersuchungen zur antiken Literatur*, Berlin 1970, 554-63.

——. (1982) *Poseidonios. Die Fragmente* (Texte und Kommentare, 10 1/2), 2 vols., Berlin/New York 1982.

Thonnard, F.-J. (1952) 'Les fonctions sensibles de l'âme humaine selon Saint Augustin', *L'Année Théologique Augustinienne* 12 (1952) 335-45.

——. (1953) 'La vie affective de l'âme selon Saint Augustin', *L'Année Théologique Augustinienne* 13 (1953) 33-55.

——. (1958) 'La "cognitio per sensus corporis" chez saint Augustin', *Augustinus* 3 (1958) 193-203.

Verbeke, G. *L'évolution de la doctrine du pneuma du Stoicisme à S. Augustin*, Paris/Louvain 1945.

Voss, B.R. *Der Dialog in der frühchristlichen Literatur* (Studia et Testimonia Antiqua, 9), Munich 1970.

Wallis, R.T. *Neoplatonism* (Classical Life and Letters) London 1972.

Warren, E.W. 'Consciousness in Plotinus', *Phronesis* 9 (1964) 83-97.

Waszink, J.H. (ed.) *Q.S.F. Tertulliani de anima*, Amsterdam 1947.

Watson, G. 'St. Augustine's Theory of Language', *Maynooth Review* 6 (1982) 4-20.

Wieland, W. *Offenbarung bei Augustinus* (Tübinger Theologische Studien, 12), Mainz 1978.

Wolfson, H.A. 'The Internal Senses in Latin, Arabic and Hebrew Philosophic Texts', *Harvard Theological Review* 28 (1935) 69-133 = *Studies in the History of Philosophy and Religion*, vol. 1, Cambridge, Mass. 1973. 250-314.

Zarb, S.M. *Chronologia Operum S. Augustini secundum ordinem Retractationum digesta*, Rome 1934.

Index locorum

References to the pages of this book appear in **bold** type.

General index